High Life

Matthew Gordon Lasner

High Life

Condo Living in the Suburban Century

YALE UNIVERSITY PRESS / NEW HAVEN AND LONDON

Published with assistance from the Graham Foundation for Advanced Studies in the Fine Arts.

yalebooks.com/art

On the cover: (*front*) Villa San Pasqual, Pasadena, 1954, prospectus (fig. 99, detail); (*spine*) United Nations Plaza, New York, 1963–66 (fig. 119, detail).
Title page: Amalgamated Cooperative Apartments, Bronx, 1926–27 (fig. 39, detail).
Page vi: 860–880 North Lake Shore Drive, Chicago, 1948–51 (fig. 116, detail).
Page viii: Advertisement for Gimbels (fig. 66, detail).

Designed and set in Century Expanded by Laura Lindgren

The Library of Congress has cataloged the hardcover edition as follows:
Lasner, Matthew Gordon.
  High life : condo living in the suburban century / Matthew Gordon Lasner.
     pages cm
  Includes bibliographical references and index.
  ISBN 978-0-300-16408-4 (cloth : alk. paper) 1. Condominiums—United States.
2. Apartment houses, Cooperative—United States. I. Title.
  HD7287.67.U5L37 2012
  307.740973—dc23   2012002911

ISBN 978-0-300-26919-2 (pbk.)
eISBN 978-0-300-26934-5

A catalogue record for this book is available from the British Library.

For Dan Goldstein, and in memory of Fagie Mandel Gordon

Contents

6-ROOM

garden apartment with fully equipped kitchen and bath, 3 bedrooms, a huge 14' 9" x 19' living room . . . down payment and carrying charge start at as little as **$1775** down   monthly **$120**

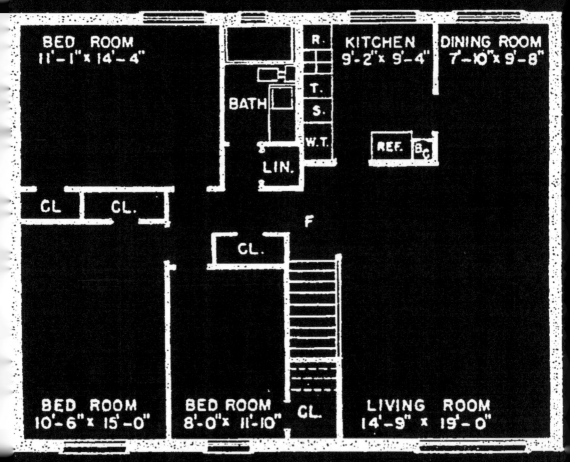

Acknowledgments

Many people have helped me to produce *High Life*. As the project first took shape, I enjoyed much support from Harvard University for travel, research, and writing, including from the John F. Kennedy School of Government's A. Alfred Taubman Center for the Study of State and Local Government and the Graduate School of Design's Real Estate Academic Initiative at Harvard University. Staff at the Loeb Design Library were also tremendously helpful, especially Mary Daniels, Alix Reiskind, and Barbara Mitchell. My colleagues at the GSD and across Cambridge Street in the History of Art and Architecture created a rich atmosphere for new thinking: Erik Ghenoiu, Robin Schuldenfrei, Seng Kuan, Brendan Moran, Timothy Hyde, Bill Rankin, Diana Ramirez Jasso, Erica Allen-Kim, Kenny Cupers, Jennifer Mack, Mariana Mogilovich, Cammie McAtee, Krista Sykes, Charissa Terranova, Cole Roskam, Ana Miljacki, Amanda Reeser Lawrence, John Spelman, and at MIT, Kath Phelan von Wyss. This diverse and engaged community helped make the process of research and writing rewarding, stimulating, and often fun.

Jennifer Hock was a special comrade in arms who always understood my ideas—and their limitations—and offered invaluable insight at important crossroads. She and Rosita Choy also proved great sources of illuminating condo ephemera, from *Condominium* the novel to *Condo* the sitcom, and engaged in serious dialogue about their personal experiences living in, and owning, condos. Meredith Martin was a constant friend and coach, commenting on writing, no matter the hour, and asking clarifying questions. The Warren Center fellows of 2004–5 offered advice and support, especially Alice Friedman, Paula Lupkin, Eric Avila, and Paul Groth (who persuaded me to research California). Most of all from Harvard I am grateful to Margaret Crawford for helping me find my voice as a scholar. She recognized the potential value of the condo project and my approach, and pushed me to make my research more meaningful. Deepest thanks also go to Eve Blau, Danny Abramsom at Tufts, and Bob Breugmann at the University of Illinois at Chicago. Danny grasped the significance of my subject long before I did. Bob helped me wrestle with countless research problems and steered me through much of the writing.

For his encouraging words, excellent scholarship, and help navigating the process of turning my research into this book, I thank Brad Hunt at Roosevelt University. In this regard I am also grateful to Michelle Komie at Yale University

Press, who was tremendously accommodating, and who did a terrific job at finding superior anonymous reviewers for the manuscript. I am fortunate to have had reviewers so committed to my topic and am appreciative of the lengths to which all three went to help me make this book into one that I hope readers will find useful and authoritative. Thanks, too, to friends and colleagues who read all or part of the manuscript: Meredith Martin and Nikhil Rao at Wellesley College and, especially, Suleiman Osman, at George Washington University.

For their help in shaping specific portions of the project I acknowledge David Brownlee, editor of the *Journal of the Society of Architectural Historians,* and the anonymous reader who reviewed an article there; and Hilary Ballon, co-editor of *Robert Moses and the Modern City,* and Sally Weiner at Columbia University, who edited my writing for that volume with astonishing precision. Thanks, too, to Marta Gutman at City College for bringing my work to Hilary's attention. I am also grateful to the Urban History Association, Society of Architectural Historians, Vernacular Architecture Forum, Society for American City and Regional Planning History, the Business History Conference, and the Chicago Urban History Seminar for allowing me to present research in progress at their meetings.

Robert Fogelson at MIT, Robert Natelson at University of Montana, Joseph Bigott at Purdue University, Robert Charles Lesser, Micah Mayell, Bettina N. Kornbluh (kindly introduced to me by Andrea Tuttle Kornbluh), David Parry in San Francisco, Mitch Novack in Miami Beach, Mary Ruiz, and Amanda Elioff and Candice Hemming at Villa San Pasqual in Pasadena all graciously shared research, materials, or reminiscences. I reserve extra special thanks in this regard for Robert M. Swedroe, who allowed me into his office for several weeks and gave me access to his archives, including from his years with Morris Lapidus, as well as space to work and permission to copy and scan. Thanks go to Bobby Klein for facilitating these many visits. Thanks, too, to George Berlin at Turnberry Associates for speaking with me at considerable length on two occasions, and for access to archival materials. For general financial support for research I thank the Department of History at Georgia State University. For support for production I thank the Graham Foundation for Advanced Studies in the Fine Arts.

While traveling for research I could never have navigated Puerto Rico without Dalina and Hilda Sumner, and Enrique Vivoni Farage at the Escuela de Arquitectura at the University of Puerto Rico, Rio Piedras. Likewise, Miami would have been impossible without John Stuart at Florida International University; Robin Bachin, Allan T. Shulman, and Greg Castillo at University of Miami; and local experts Jeff Donnelly, Arva Moore Parks, and Howard Kleinberg. I am especially grateful to Kathy and Larry Hurwitz, who generously allowed me to stay in their

Bay Harbor Island condo. In Southern California, Cecilia Cabello and Kelly Kagan guided me on site visits, as did Sharon and Irving Picard in Westchester. Kelly also met me in Florida and took extraordinary photographs of Aventura, some of which appear in this book. My grand condo tour of Florida would also have been incomplete without Dalina Sumner, Bekah Burgess, and Daniel Cole. For hosting me on several research trips to New York and ferrying me to Long Island City and Sunset Park, I thank Amanda Cox.

In Atlanta I am grateful to Georgia State University colleagues Joe Perry, Kate Wilson, Richard Laub, Lauren Ristvet, Jeffrey and Carrie Glover, and Kim Reiman, as well as Nihad Farooq at Georgia Tech. I also thank my graduate students in the American Built Environment and the American Suburb, especially Chelsea Arkin and Grace Lynis Dubinson, who made fine ambassadors to the Sunbelt city. Chelsea was also an enthusiastic research companion on my condo tours of metropolitan Atlanta. I should also acknowledge my fellow co-owners at Palmer & Phelan for allowing me serve on the board and to learn first-hand about the challenges and rewards of condo governance.

For help with research, thanks go to the staff at the Historical Museum of South Florida; the Special Collections room at Florida International University's Steven and Dorothea Green Library; the Special Collections Division at University of Miami's Otto G. Richter Library (as well as Jessica Martin, a fellow researcher at Richter who kept her eyes peeled for material of interest); the Environmental Design Library and Environmental Design Archives at University of California, Berkeley, especially Waverly Lowell, who unearthed wonderful documents before I had the chance to ask; the Community Associations Institute; the Library of Congress, in particular the Law Library; and Claudia Funke at Avery Architectural and Fine Arts Library at Columbia, who brought critical material to my attention that I would otherwise have overlooked.

For assistance with images I thank Robbi Siegel at the Museum of the City of New York, David Laspina at Esto, Michele Hitzik at the Rockefeller Archive Center, Allan Raney at the New York State Library, Mike Sherbon at the Pennsylvania State Archives, Merrideth Miller at the *New Yorker*, Bill and Marlys Ray, Barb Morley at the Kheel Center for Labor-Management Documentation at Cornell, and Miranda Schwartz and Nicole Contaxis at the New-York Historical Society. I also thank Christopher Gray at the Office for Metropolitan History for help finding some elusive photographs.

Last but not least I thank my family, which has grown in the most wonderful ways since I started working on the condo, and now includes all the Goldsteins, Brods, and Pearces. Edie and Dick Lasner made great research aides in Washington and helped in innumerable other ways, large and small. Emily Brod and Sandra and Ron Goldstein have offered never-ending support. Matt Goldstein, Miranda Pearce, and Suzy Pearce hosted me at various points in Cambridge. Jacob Oliver Goldstein kept me out and about, and our late-night walks around Buena Vista Park became a crucial space for clear thinking. Finally, biggest thanks go to Dan Goldstein, who inspires and sustains me with his brilliance, clarity, and calm.

Collective Homeownership

In 1969, twenty years after Bell Park Gardens in Bayside, Queens, first opened, tensions at the garden-apartment complex were running high (fig. 1). The full-time manager spent many hours each week trying to resolve disputes among the homeowners. One resident had recently phoned him and after a "long harangue" invited him to "come down and watch me kill my neighbor!"[1] At a communitywide meeting of the homeowners' association emotions were equally raw. Owners attacked the elected board of directors with "vitriolic vituperation." The specific issues were soon forgotten: people could have been upset about bulk-purchase of air-conditioning units, plans to update wiring, or problems with snow removal. Disagreement was endemic.[2]

Some quarrels were related to age and duration of tenure: new homeowners against old. Most of the members of the community's governing board of directors were original owners. They had bought their apartments as young veterans and reared their families there. They had cared for the place for two decades. Now their

Fig. 1: Bell Park Gardens, Springfield and Bell Boulevards, Sixty-seventh to Seventy-third Avenues, Bayside, New York, 1948–50. United Veterans Mutual Housing, developer; William M. Dowling, architect. General view.

Fig. 2: Bell Park Gardens homeowners and Herman T. Stichman. New York State, Division of Housing, *Annual Report of the Commissioner of Housing to the Governor and the Legislature*, 1949.

children were leaving home. Many of the opposition, by contrast, were younger newcomers who felt that the board was out of touch—despite having been recently reelected (electoral inertia meant that leadership rarely changed).[3] Board members, meanwhile, resented the discontent and regarded their new neighbors as poorly behaved, with insufficient community spirit, and, according to one grumpy elder, overly permissive methods of parenting. (Noise from children playing was a frequent complaint.)[4]

More generally, conflict stemmed from routine difficulties of self-governance—especially enmity between volunteer leaders and the ungrateful rank-and-file. "The bitterness shown in our last assemblies," wrote Charles H. Lavigne, editor of the monthly *Bell Park News*, "indicates a lack of mutual understanding and co-operative spirit." In an editorial on the financial ruin of owner-occupied apartment complexes during the Great Depression, Lavigne argued that apart from specific deficiencies like poor management and excessive debt, the chief undermining characteristic was "Bitter Personal Strife" between owners and boards. In particular he warned against the "jealousy, personal spite, differing philosophies, personal prestige and other human factors" that had "forced capable volunteers to resign in disgust." At Bell Park, he continued, hundreds of homeowners "who never lifted a finger to help this housing corporation" were behaving like "tenants" when they "attack[ed] hard working leadership." Shape up, he suggested, or ship out.[5]

Yet while occasionally disruptive, this friction was of little overall consequence. It did not negate the strong sense of community that had characterized Bell Park since the late 1940s (fig. 2). To the contrary, community life not only carried on but thrived amid the latest struggles. Homeowners continued to organize an annual blood drive and to maintain a choral group, a credit union, a Boy Scout troop, a dieting club, a literary club, and a group on veterans affairs. Additionally, they supported a regular program of cultural outings to places such as the Metropolitan Museum of Art in Manhattan, and social events, like weekends away at the Homowack Lodge in the Catskill Mountains and dinner dances at the San Su San nightclub in Mineola, Long Island, which attracted as many as four hundred homeowners.[6]

Conflict, in fact, seemed to strengthen Bell Park. It had the positive effect, for example, of teaching the community's children about democratic self-governance. Armed with a list of their own frustrations, in December 1969 seventeen teenagers blocked entrances to the offices of the Community Council, a volunteer organization which ran Bell Park's social activities. Prepared for a long fight with hot thermoses and snacks, the teens marched with picket signs. Their demands centered on access to power. They wanted to serve on Community Council committees, and they wanted the homeowners' association to establish a teen advisory committee. They also demanded that *Bell Park News* hire teens to write, and that teens be permitted to serve, in uniform, on the community's auxiliary police patrol. Big-city social ills like vandalism, graffiti, and drug use were beginning to impinge upon Bell Park's domestic tranquility and they were as eager as their parents to keep vice at bay.[7]

Bell Park Gardens was far from utopian. Neighborhood dynamics often meant discord. By most measures, however, the community was a success. Twenty years after opening, the garden-apartment complex had seven hundred names on its waiting list—nearly one for every home—and the list moved slowly. Only two dozen families left each year and, as of 1970, no one had given up a three-bedroom unit since 1956.[8] More importantly, Bell Park residents had a strong sense of common purpose. Instead of the transience and idleness that writers like William H. Whyte and Betty Friedan had found in suburbia, Bell Park families were, according to Lavigne, "working together, to make life better for themselves and others" by providing shelter "at cost"—that is, as owners rather than rent-payers—and participating, in one way or another, in governance. They were "committed to working together for a better tomorrow ... to help carry out this pledge. A better life in the '70s."[9]

Locating the Condo

The American built environment is perhaps most distinguished for its high concentration of detached, single-family houses. During what others have framed as a long "suburban century"—which began as early as the 1830s and continued through the real-estate bubble of the early twenty-first century—the American city rose, fell, and (to some extent) rose again. Throughout, single-family suburbia grew. Tens of millions of people from around the heartland and around the globe moved to U.S. cities. But just as quickly, the majority left to pursue the "American dream" of owning a house with a yard. By the 1920s, and certainly the 1950s, the United States had become as well known for its bungalows as its skyscrapers, and for its crabgrass as its factories. If downtown was where Americans worked, suburbia was where we reared our children, relaxed, and reconnected to nature, away from the baleful influences of the modern, workaday world. By the early twenty-first century, two-thirds of U.S. households owned their own dwellings, and around eighty percent of these were freestanding houses. More than a quarter of U.S. renters also lived in single-family houses.[10]

Suburbia, however, was never universal. The condo emerged as a hybrid between suburban and urban impulses. Throughout the suburban century, millions of Americans who could afford the suburban lifestyle—the middle class, broadly defined—chose otherwise. Some, like the families at Bell Park, embraced suburban locales but not the burdens of owning a whole house. Others rejected the metropolitan fringe in favor of the convenience and variety of the center, buying urban row houses. Yet others rejected both suburbia and the house, opting for carefree, well-located dwelling types like hotels, boarding houses, and, increasingly, apartments.

The owner-occupied apartment—the antecedent of what most Americans today call "condominium"—emerged on this spectrum of alternatives. Physically, condos and earlier forms like cooperatives, or co-ops, were one-family dwelling units in multiple-family complexes. In this sense they were like rentals and were arranged either as conventional apartments, with units above and below each other, or as "townhouse" complexes, with units side by side (fig. 3). Unlike most apartments, however, condos were owned rather than rented, with shared elements held and governed jointly.

Although still less common than other kinds of housing, co-owned multifamily housing is today ubiquitous. In many places it predominates. By the turn of the twenty-first century, roughly one in ten U.S. homes, and one in eight owner-occupied homes, was in a multifamily complex. In metropolitan areas the share of homeowners in multifamily housing rose higher: to as many as three or four of every ten homeowners in metropolitan Boston, Miami, New York, and L.A., including Orange County. These homes included nearly ten million condos and co-ops, and as many as seven million additional units in common-interest townhouse complexes. Three-quarters of these homes—perhaps twelve million in all—were owner-occupied (the rest were second homes or rented out). Without them, the growth in homeownership of the previous fifty years—since the end of the post–World War II suburban boom—all but disappeared. The share of households in owner-occupied, single-family houses in 2007 was precisely the same as it had been in 1960 (forty-nine percent) despite the fact that rates of homeownership had risen from sixty-two to sixty-eight percent.[11]

High Life explores this third, hybrid dwelling type in historical perspective, from the earliest experiments with co-ops, in the mid-nineteenth century in

Fig. 3: Howell Mill Plantation, 3081 Howell Mill Road NW, Atlanta, ca. 1981.

Manhattan, until about 1980, by which time condos had become a mainstream
housing type nationwide. Contrary to conventional wisdom, the United States
can and does support modes of middle-class settlement other than single-family
suburbia. In fact, as homeownership became more accessible over the course of the
suburban century, proportionately fewer Americans came to live in houses. In this
book I examine how and why condo living emerged as a countertrend, who built
condos, what condos looked like, what kinds of people were drawn to them, how
homeowners governed them, who supported and challenged this housing alternative,
and why. Along the way I explore the many ways in which people employed what I
variously refer to as collective homeownership, multifamily homeownership, and co-
ownership to meet new housing problems.[12]

That co-ownership emerged as a typical dwelling practice in the United
States is surprising in certain respects. At the dawn of the Space Age, "condo"
and "condominium" were unknown terms in the U.S. Few were familiar with the
concept of individual ownership of apartments, even where co-ops had been around
for decades. More importantly, although the heyday of suburbia was in the 1950s,
there was no shortage of suburban sprawl in the decades that followed. The full
impact of freeways, shopping malls, and white flight was not felt until the 1960s
and 1970s; the U.S. did not become majority-suburban until about 1980; and big-box
stores, soccer moms, and McMansions did not appear until the 1990s. Groups once
firmly associated with the city center, including African Americans, gay men, new

immigrants, and the poor, also began suburbanizing. By the millennium even the
Mafia and drug dealing were suburban, at least on television. Despite high gasoline
prices and the home-foreclosure crisis that began in 2007, suburbia remained
more entrenched than ever in the 2010s as a way of life and as a way of organizing
metropolitan space.

Nonetheless, over the course of the suburban century co-ownership expanded
from a handful of expensive East Side buildings in Manhattan to a highly democratic
and diverse phenomenon. Today, condos offer a wide range of building types and
living experiences—from lower middle-class townhouses at the urban periphery
with barbecues and Boy Scout troops, to the extreme luxury enclaves of New
York's TriBeCa and L.A.'s Wilshire Corridor. During the real-estate bubble of the
first decade of the twenty-first century the nonprofit group Habitat for Humanity,
after decades of building owner-occupied houses for low-income families, started
developing co-ops and condos in Brooklyn, Washington, D.C., and the San Francisco
Bay Area. Romantic movie comedies like *The Break-Up*, about young professionals
in Chicago, and television sitcoms like *The Game*, about a National Football League
team in San Diego, were set in condos. Downtowns, from Boston to Chattanooga
to Portland, Oregon, saw glittering new condominium towers, the suburban fringe
filled with New Urbanism townhouse complexes, and urban planners measured
a statistical rise in the rate of downtown homeownership for the first time in
U.S. history.[13]

In this age of housing excess, some of the most expensive new homes were
apartments. Fifteen Central Park West on Manhattan's Upper West Side, completed
in 2008, was the most lavish. Developed by the Zeckendorf family and designed by
Robert A. M. Stern, it included a Gilded Age penthouse of eleven thousand square
feet with eight bedrooms, ten baths, and fourteen-foot ceilings; it sold for $45 million.
Stern designed comparable projects in other cities, including sprawling Atlanta
and Los Angeles. In L.A., buyers included Candy Spelling, one of Hollywood's
richest women. That Spelling, who had built one of the largest, most expensive
houses in L.A. in the 1980s, planned to spend $47 million to buy a Century City
apartment made it onto the front page of the *New York Times* (and, in 2012, was
the subject of a primetime television special on HGTV).[14] Several of Stern's "white"
and "gray" compatriots of the 1970s architectural avant-garde—including Frank
Gehry, Richard Meier, Michael Graves, and Charles Gwathmey—similarly capped
their careers with condos. Condos also became a rite of passage for the next
generation of "starchitects": Rem Koolhaas, Bernard Tschumi, Santiago Calatrava,
Daniel Libeskind, Herzog & de Meuron, Jean Nouvel, and Shigeru Ban, as well as
rising talents like Annabelle Selldorf, Enrique Norten, and SHoP (fig. 4). Philip

Johnson, never one to miss a design turn, posthumously realized Urban Glass House, a Manhattan condominium named after his own suburban Glass House of 1949. The conversion of iconic hotels, such as New York's Plaza, to very expensive apartments further cemented the condo trend.

As a mortgage-based financial crisis eviscerated demand for owned housing beginning in 2007, the condo attracted even more attention, in this case negative. Many projects, including several with highly innovative designs, were left unbuilt. Some that got built begged for buyers, even at everything-must-go auctions. One thirty-two-story building in Fort Myers, Florida, made national news for having just a single owner in residence. The story offered some comic relief but the perils of such situations were real. In countless complexes developers and residents found they could not afford to keep up common elements, leading to empty swimming pools and premature disrepair. High rates of foreclosure in markets where sales prices had been most out of line with new realities further jeopardized condos' physical and financial health. Throughout the downturn, however, no one questioned the basic premise of co-ownership. By the twenty-first century the condo had become permanently woven into the fabric of American housing.

Fig. 4: 100 Eleventh Avenue, New York, 2008–10. Cape Advisors, developer; Ateliers Jean Nouvel, architect.

Condominium Demand

A central question of *High Life* is why in the suburban century, in the world's most suburban nation, people who could afford homeownership chose apartments. There is a large and substantial existing literature on American housing, from a range of fields. Virtually none, however, has touched on this issue. One reason for this gap is that debates about residential patterns have generally overlooked the physical form and tenure of housing in favor of broad neighborhood characteristics (the "city" versus the "suburb"), leaving important issues unexamined. These include how different dwelling types cater to different kinds of families and facilitate (or complicate) social reproduction, the advantages and difficulties of specific physical forms and population densities, and the transformative—but far from straightforward—role of tenure (ownership and tenancy) in shaping how people experience, consume, and care for their housing. I believe that all of these questions are central to understanding urban change.[15]

High Life emphasizes demand as a factor in the ascendance of the condo. A primary argument is that the condo emerged because it appealed to different, in some ways paradoxical, aspects of the human experience, fulfilling both individual, often mercenary, interests as well as collective desires. When scholars first engaged in serious debate about middle-class alternatives to suburbia, they wrestled over whether the shift to city living was caused by large-scale social or economic changes. Especially contentious was the weight of demand and supply-side factors. There was vigorous debate but little consensus; attention soon shifted to new problems. But the question of what causes spatial change as dramatic as mass suburbanization or gentrification remains relevant. I revisit it because to understand the condo it is critical to ask not only what caused these dramatic shifts but also what underlying forces led people to different kinds of housing.[16]

One of the leading reasons for the condo countertrend was changing demographics. Different kinds of dwellings appeal to different kinds of households at different stages of life. Condos tend to suit older households and younger (fig. 5). Most larger families, by contrast, especially two-parent families with school-age children, prefer to live in single-family houses. Such families remain as likely as ever to live (or at least aspire to live) this way. But they became much less common. In 1950, nearly four in five U.S. homes included a married couple, and nearly half had a married couple with children. By 2010 fewer than half of American households were married, and just one in five included a married couple with children. At the same time, the number of very small households grew. As people had fewer children, married later, divorced more frequently, and lived longer, average household size fell from 4.8 people in 1880 to 2.6 in 2010. By the early twenty-first century, one in four U.S. homes included a single person living alone. The number of people in the U.S. grew eightfold in the suburban century, and the number of homes grew by a factor of fifteen.[17]

Smaller families have always been at the forefront of co-ownership in the U.S. Not only do they tend to require less space, but as a group they prefer more highly serviced kinds of housing, often because they are unable to devote time to maintenance or cannot afford their own handymen and lawn care. Co-ownership

At The Pines you get more than just a luxury apartment. You get a life style.

The Pines offers a unique concept in apartment living...the idea that staying home can be more fun than going out.

So naturally we attract a younger, more carefree crowd. Airline stewardesses, teachers, nurses, salesmen, young marrieds.

The kind of people who just don't settle into a place, but actually change it to suit their needs.

For example, we have things like a large heated pool that stays open all night long.

Our billiard room is open late, so you'll have plenty of time to make like Minneapolis Fats. Of course, if you're built like Minneapolis Fats, the sauna and gym are also open late.

There's a recreation room for playing cards, barbecue pits for playing with fire and a few other nice things, like a fountain and a running brook to make The Pines even more enjoyable.

We have beautiful draped and carpeted, fully insulated and soundproofed apartments. With anywhere from 4 to 7 rooms. Each apartment has its own den (or gameroom, library or anything you want to make it.) The master bedroom suites have walk-in closets. The kitchens have plenty of cabinet space. Also serving bars, tile sinks, dishwashers and built-in electric ranges. And each apartment has sliding glass doors leading to its own private patio or balcony.

How many apartments do you know that have their own built-in night life?

The Pines.
6000 Canterbury Drive in beautiful Fox Hills.
(213) 641-3337

When you come to the Pines this week end, you will receive a free Pine tree. You will also see Scuba Films and demonstrations by Pacific Divers Supply, Inc., of Los Angeles

Fig. 5: The Pines, Los Angeles. Advertisement, *Los Angeles Times*, January 23, 1972.

helps makes the "high life"—or at least independence from extended families and institutions like women's hotels and old-age homes—affordable by collectivizing the cost of staff among multiple households. For decades developers have marketed co-ops and condos as having no lawn to mow, and co-owners frequently cite freedom from physical maintenance as a major appeal of this kind of housing (fig. 6). This effect is especially pronounced for older households and those headed by women:

Fig. 6: Tanglewood Townhouse, Norwalk, California. Advertisement, *Los Angeles Times*, January 16, 1966.

among unmarried buyers of multifamily homes, for example, women have always far outnumbered men, and in many studies women show a stronger preference for better located, more highly serviced kinds of housing, with fewer labor demands and less travel time to work and to errands like household shopping.[18]

Although I prioritize demand in this book, many who study urban change have emphasized other forces. Puzzling through the impact of the sexual revolution—and young urban professional—on housing patterns in the 1970s and 1980s, the pathbreaking geographer Neil Smith acknowledged that demand-side changes were important. Yet as isolated historical events, he concluded, they could hardly be causal. "Why did not the 'proto-yuppies' of six or eight decades ago [the 1920s or 1900s]," he asked, "initiate the gentrification process instead of spearheading the rush to the suburbs?"

Similarly, he wondered if "women were in the official work force before World War 2, albeit in smaller numbers, and some of these were in relatively well-paying professional positions," why was it that "no gentrification process seems to have blunted the suburban flight of the time"? Instead, he argued that structural economic changes mattered most. Gentrification occurred when capital could not help but flow to cities after decades of anti-urban policy had artificially depressed property values.[19] *High Life*, paralleling other recent scholarship exploring the metropolis from the sidewalk up (and parking lot in), finds these lost women and proto-yuppies.[20]

Demand was shaped by more than raw demographics. Living outside of the nuclear family was not new, but only in the suburban century did there emerge appreciable numbers of such people, including younger people, older people, and single people who were able to afford to maintain households of their own (fig. 7). In

Fig. 7: Advertisement for Goldrich-Kest-Kayne and Regis Development, detail, *Los Angeles Times*, August 1, 1965.

previous eras they would have lived with extended families, in hotels, or in lodging houses. Public policy and innovations in home financing dramatically democratized ownership beginning in the 1920s and 1930s. Perhaps more importantly, greater overall prosperity allowed for the formation of more, smaller households; for the consumption of more, better housing; and for greater rates of homeownership. For both financial and emotional reasons few people prefer to rent; across time and space, the higher one's income the more likely one has been to own one's own home.[21] This shift is especially apparent in the case of women, who achieved major gains in the paid workforce, and seniors, thanks to private pensions and Social Security (introduced in 1935). Unmarried women and seniors, who counted among the most vulnerable of city dwellers, always have been the most frequent kinds of co-owners. In 2006, for example, more than forty percent of apartment buyers were single women. Although data are scarce, my research suggests this share was also typical in earlier eras, going back to the co-op's debut in the nineteenth century.[22]

Yet another demand-side reason for the growth in co-ownership was change in the social geography of American metro areas, which brought more middle-class families to high-demand locations where competition for space made houses impractical. As early as the 1920s young professionals and bohemians began transforming well-located city neighborhoods into fashionable enclaves by rehabilitating down-at-the-heels houses. Although statistically insignificant and limited to a handful of especially charming, central neighborhoods, such as Greenwich Village, Georgetown, Russian Hill, and Beacon Hill, by the 1970s this type of transformation had a name—"gentrification"—and had spread nationwide. Deindustrialization, exodus of the working class from city centers to suburbia and the Sunbelt, and changing tastes refashioned the city's identity for the middle class from a place of difference and fear to one of authenticity.[23] Simultaneously, multifamily housing became common in many suburbs as early as the 1920s. By the 1960s at least half of all new multifamily housing was built in suburbia. Whether at the city center or the urban edge, condos allowed broader ownership in popular locations.

Structural Shifts

On the structural side, the twentieth century saw a change in America's "reigning property culture," to borrow a concept from historian Daniel Rodgers. One part of this was a decline in landlords' ability of to make appealing profits, combined, perhaps oddly, with an increased willingness on the part of individuals to invest in ownership of a multifamily home. Rising costs of operating buildings, long-term downward pressure on rents, higher standards for housing, and the difficult task of building management, along with tenant-directed policies like rent control, made being a landlord less lucrative as the suburban century unfolded. At the same time, rising demand for well-equipped, well-located multifamily dwellings, even amid the urban crisis of the 1960s and 1970s, coupled with the availability of new financing, helped transform the individual unit into a potentially profitable commodity. Many people came to value their apartments as much for their exchange value as their use value. For many, expectations of ever-rising resale values became a major incentive to own what they otherwise might have rented.[24]

This reading of the condo as a product of neoliberal market-driven impulses is underscored by its cultural associations with greedy social types, by the fact that condos seem to be more frequently owned as investment properties (for renting out) than are houses, and by the fact that in most of the U.S. the condo market contracts more rapidly than that for houses during periods of economic turmoil: few Americans want to buy a house when prices are flat or falling, but even fewer want to buy an apartment. In part, however, these trends simply speak to condo demographics. Americans own apartments for less time, on average, than single-family houses. In stalled real-estate markets, then, it makes little financial sense for people in transition to buy.

Another important supply-side force was the mortgage-banking industry's effort to promote the condominium format over older, related kinds of homeownership, such as the co-op. Unlike other types of collective homeownership, the condo system generates individual deeds and titles for each dwelling unit. The condo served in practice, if not in explicit intent, as a way to stimulate business when demand for single-family houses was flattening.

A third structural force that helped stimulate condo living was government. Although the relationship between government and suburbanization has been long explored, the history of collective homeownership suggests that the impact of government on middle-class housing has been ambiguous. Suburbia was not the only possible outcome for mass homeownership. Indeed, Washington was among the most ardent advocates—and, for decades, the leading source of funding—for middle-class multifamily housing, both rented and owned, in cities and in suburbs. Meanwhile, urban planners, city and state governments, and suburban counties cultivated co-ownership. It has long been an article of faith that ownership promotes good behavior, including physical maintenance of housing and neighborhoods, and reduces some of the pathologies associated with poverty. Not everyone in government devoted the same energy to multifamily housing as to single-family, and most Americans preferred houses when given a choice. But public bodies, including the Federal Housing Administration (FHA), not only promoted co-ownership in the suburban century, they were central to its proliferation.[25]

Creating Community

Tenure in housing—whether we rent or own—matters. For the writer bell hooks, owning an apartment transformed New York City from a place of loneliness to one of joy. "Unlike the small towns that have claimed my heart," she found the city a "harsh place. . . . a wilderness—a place where . . . the familiar must be tenderly cultivated." To do so, she bought and renovated. "I wanted French doors to close off the living room and dining room. New closets were added to the bedroom. A doorway leading from the living room to the bedroom was closed off and a wall . . . was added to create a tiny workroom off the bedroom. . . . These changes created more private spaces and made the flat . . . a space of light and warmth." Simply by "purchasing a flat," she recalls, "I feel that I am making a commitment to life in New York City. . . . Outside on city streets, I am less a stranger for I am always coming home to a place where love is—a peaceful sanctuary."[26]

During the foreclosure crisis of the early twenty-first century, there was much public discussion of when it might be appropriate to abandon an "underwater" home, where the amount of the outstanding mortgages was higher than the resale value. Some economists suggested that abandonment was the only sensible course but that most homeowners refused to walk away because they felt a moral obligation to stay. Rarely mentioned was the emotional connection people had to their homes and communities. Whether because they added French doors or flowerbeds, became involved with the local school, or made friends with neighbors, for many walking away was never a simple financial calculation. More importantly, as suggested by scholars as diverse as anthropologist Constance Perin and, more recently, historian Matthew Lassiter in his work on the politics of race in the postwar South, "homeowner"—and homeownership—serves as a critical element of people's identities.[27]

Another major argument of *High Life* is that apart from demographic and supply-side changes, collective homeownership emerged because in a society characterized by fear of change and of others, ethnic and cultural pluralism, and, especially, high geographic mobility, ownership helped to create community. It did this in part by forcing owners to deal with one another in ways they might not have if they had a landlord, and by familiarizing the unfamiliar—transforming strangers into neighbors: a crucial comfort to many in a world continually made unknowable by frequent change. This is neither to suggest that community automatically formed in condos (and that it could not exist in rentals), nor that community could not sometimes be acrimonious, as at Bell Park Gardens. But finding community was an important by-product of, and often an impetus to, co-ownership.[28] Co-ownership helped to domesticate the alien by regulating behavior and structuring conflict and interaction among neighbors through by-laws; by eliminating some of the anonymity of multifamily housing by mandating social interaction; by facilitating physical customization of interiors while ensuring that no one expressed his personal taste at the exterior; by engendering a sense of rootedness and minimizing transience by setting high emotional and financial thresholds for entry; and by establishing a bounded social space symbolically apart (if not physically protected) from the city or the suburban sprawl outside.

The condo was not for everyone. The U.S. was the first nation in history to make "fee-simple," or outright, property ownership widely available to ordinary citizens. In Europe, all land was assumed to have been once owned by the state. Even in the twenty-first century much remains under the control of a small elite, whether through direct ownership by the church and aristocratic families or through strong, centralized land-use planning. In the U.S., by contrast, a belief in a decentralized system of land ownership and control has dominated.[29]

The detached house remains a normative model. Condos, by contrast, enjoyed an ambiguous position as neither full-status detached houses nor marginal-status rental apartments. Like other hybrid types, including other kinds of collectively owned, common-interest residential communities such as gated single-family subdivisions, they do not fit comfortably into the categories we use to make sense of the city and suburb. Many people interpret their self-governance and emphasis on common rather than individual rights in property as a departure from America's long tradition of homesteading and fee-simple, single-family homeownership. At least one writer has complained of the "dictatorship of the condo proletariat" prohibiting the expression of owners' "human individuality." As the *New Yorker* put it in the 1980s, the condo offers only the "illusion" of ownership (fig. 8).[30]

In every community there exists a tension between private and communal rights in property. When introducing the concept to law students, legal scholars describe property rights as a "bundle of sticks." The bundle of rights an owner or tenant has in a particular property changes over time. Some, like minimum construction standards, have for centuries remained firmly in the realm of the communal. Others, such as the right to select residents on the basis of race, were once understood as private but today have been eliminated entirely. One's particular bundle is shaped by law and custom. It is also determined by leases and contracts among groups of

Fig. 8: "Welcome to Condoville and the Illusion of Owning Your Own Property," Jack Ziegler, *New Yorker*, September 3, 1984.

owners, usually in the form of binding covenants in each owner's deed. Restrictions may specify what kind of building an owner may erect and what color she may paint it, and require her to contribute money for the maintenance of areas owned in common. In the extreme, they may require owners to spend time working in a community garden, kitchen, or day care center, as in co-housing complexes.[31]

The condo offers the most private rights in property of all alternatives to the detached house—certainly more than renting. Rights in property inherent to most forms of co-ownership concern occupancy—including security of tenure, the ability to transfer tenure to heirs, and the freedom to accrue personal equity over the course of one's tenure—and control—including the liberty to remodel one's unit. At the same time, condos allow homeowners a limited but crucial number of collective rights, including varying degrees of control over resales.

Property-rights advocates have long insisted that unfettered ownership is one of the most important buttresses of individual rights. They have fought efforts to curb individual rights, whether introduced by urban redevelopment authorities, housing reformers, or environmentalists. But the condo shows that urbanization in the U.S. has been accompanied by a voluntary jettisoning of conventional rights in property for conditional ones, suggesting that many Americans believe that more communal rights in property—and fewer private ones—make for better metropolitan living. At the everyday level this idea is reflected in the fact that sense of community and a lively social atmosphere are two of the aspects of co-ownership that people seem to like most. We also see evidence of this in the contemporaneous rise of the "common-interest," "homeowners' association," and gated community. Although these are often single-family developments, like condos they are self-governed and broadly circumscribe owners' individual rights for the collective.[32]

Measuring the promise of community relative to that of profit or other factors like location and ease of maintenance is difficult. Studies of housing choice have proved unreliable and imprecise. We know that women choose shorter commutes; nearly everyone has a strong preference for big, new homes; and that 9/11 did not stimulate demand for compact or traditional neighborhoods. Much, however, remains a mystery. People identify closely, personally, and intensely with their homes, and choosing one can be as highly personal, complex, and arbitrary as finding a mate. Unlike other commodities, every dwelling is unique if only by virtue of its location, even in the case of identical apartments on different floors. Even insiders like real-estate developers and sales agents cannot reliably predict the preferences of different kinds of clients.[33] As Marjorie Garber argues in *Sex and Real Estate*, the home serves "as love, mother, body or self, fantasy, trophy, history, and escape." To the extent that we can decipher the record of condo living, however, my research suggests that engendering a sense of community and establishing rules of engagement have been critical to its spread.[34]

Kinds of Collective Homeownership

One of the most fascinating attributes of co-owned housing is its great flexibility. Americans have employed several different plans of collective homeownership over the past 150 years, each in response to new and specific social, demographic, and large-scale economic and political conditions. I have spoken so far primarily of condos. Today the condo is so common that many use the term to refer to whole physical forms (usually townhouses and well-equipped high rises), even when these are rentals. This book, however, all but concludes with the emergence of the condominium plan of co-ownership in the 1960s and 1970s. Most of *High Life* concerns the earlier evolution of this dwelling practice and the great variety of experiments with plans of ownership—as well as different physical forms, urban and suburban—that led us to the types of communities we now view as "condominium."

Other systems of collective homeownership have included the stock cooperative, or co-op, which was the dominant system of co-ownership in most of the U.S. until the 1960s and which remains common in several markets, especially New York; the limited-equity stock cooperative, which was developed in the 1910s to maintain low sales prices over long periods of time in self-help and philanthropic worker housing; the own-your-own, which was native to Southern California and used there, along with the co-op, from the 1920s until the 1960s; and the common-interest development, which became widespread in the 1960s in townhouse complexes. Other, more minor systems that I touch upon only briefly include the trustee co-op in Chicago and group ownership and TIC (tenancy-in-common) in San Francisco.

Although scholars have shown increasing interest in co-owned housing since the 1990s, the general lack of attention has meant that knowledge is fragmented. This has had some damaging consequences that I hope this book will correct. The biggest one is that despite fundamental similarities between the various systems of ownership, the law treats them unequally because we erroneously perceive each plan as fundamentally unique. *High Life* offers the first comprehensive look at this genre of dwelling across time and space.[35] It shows that to classify different kinds of co-ownership as substantively separate denies the historical fact that although each plan establishes co-ownership through a different kind of private contract, and each offers a slightly different balance of private and common rights, all emerged to achieve the same primary purpose: ownership of a one-family unit in a multiple-family complex.

The most egregious examples of unequal treatment are found in San Francisco and New York. In San Francisco, a municipal ordinance was passed in the 1980s to restrict the conversion of rental apartments to condo. A quirk of the condo format is that it requires city or county recorders to recognize each unit as a separate parcel. Inadvertently, this gave them the power to restrict formation of condos by withholding recognition. When San Francisco began using this power to preserve low-cost rentals, developers and prospective homeowners devised an ad-hoc work-around that went by the letters TIC. TIC, which was based on the common law of tenancy-in-common, makes multiple parties owners of the same property, with each party agreeing by contract to occupy a separate portion. In effect, it is a condo stripped of standard, time-tested, condominium-type by-laws, which are essential to facilitating self-governance, engendering felicitous relations among co-owners, and ensuring physical upkeep. Without these safeguards, lenders have looked upon TIC as inferior. As a result, financing is difficult, expensive, and short term (five- to seven-year mortgages typically). Despite the handicaps, demand for co-ownership remained robust. By the millennium TIC accounted for as many as one in four apartment sales in San Francisco.[36]

New York also developed a two-tiered system of co-ownership and confers an array of legal and financial privileges to co-ops that it withholds from condos and common-interest townhouses. Justification rests on three myths: that co-ops are unique, that co-ops were intended to be different from other forms of collective homeownership, and that co-ops are not primarily a form of housing (this despite the fact that co-ops argue precisely the opposite to maintain homeowners' tax deductions). Special rights given to co-ops include effective virtual immunity from local, state, and federal anti-bias housing ordinances; exemption from municipal mortgage-recording taxes; favorable property-tax valuations; and unlimited power by boards of directors to reject new buyers for arbitrary undisclosed reasons. This special status has not gone without challenge, but the city's large numbers of co-op owners make change politically difficult.[37]

Just as co-ownership may take many legal forms, it also exhibits great physical diversity. It is impossible to speak of a specific architecture of co-ownership. As a legal mechanism rather than a building typology co-ownership is a shape-shifting container that has been adapted in any number of ways for different communities and in a variety of metropolitan locations, urban and suburban. Some co-owned complexes have had unique or cutting-edge designs by virtue of an atypical or avant-garde clientele. Most, however, are physically indistinguishable from rentals. Historically this meant that, like rentals, most were urban apartment houses or, beginning in the 1920s, suburban garden apartments. Since the 1960s, as co-ownership has grown in popularity, there has been more physical diversity—especially in the direction of townhouse complexes.

The condo's flexibility of form and its fluid geographies underscore the importance of thinking about housing not just as an object but as a social and economic container. To aid in this task I rely, in part, on prices. We often tell ourselves that we live one way or another because we cannot afford to do otherwise. Mapping home prices over the course of the suburban century reveals a much greater degree of choice. It forces us to focus on the cultural meaning of different housing and neighborhood types. Even in expensive markets like New York, for example, families able to buy a suburban house were nearly always also able to afford a city apartment albeit with fewer square feet; likewise, those choosing suburban apartments could often afford a house although perhaps in a more modest neighborhood.

To make historic prices more useful I convert them to 2010 dollars using the unskilled-wage index. Of the indices commonly used for conversion of historic prices it is the most helpful because the cost of housing, unlike many other commodities, remains tied to wages with remarkable consistency (despite periodic bubbles). The more common consumer price index, which compares the cost of a typical bundle of household items, assumes that goods and services are fixed in their relative prices to one another. It cannot account for innovations that have dramatically lowered the cost of some things, like radios and frozen blueberries, but not others. CPI, for example, converts $20,000 in 1883 and $70,000 in 1928—each the cost of a middle-class, family-size apartment in Manhattan—to $450,000 and $900,000 in 2010, respectively. Not only are the 2010 figures quite different from each other, they give the misleading impression that apartment prices rose dramatically between 1883 and 1928, and again between 1928 and 2010, when such apartments cost $2 to $3 million. The wage index, by contrast, translates the 1883 and 1928 prices to $2.6 million and $2.8 million.[38]

Inspiration for the Book

Part of my interest in the condo stems from the fact that I have encountered it often in my everyday life but have found little writing that accounts for its history or apparent popularity.[39] Indeed, despite the growing importance of the condo in the U.S., we rarely notice it. One reason is that the condo is a difficult-to-detect phenomenon (fig. 9). Historians and social scientists have long equated homeownership with the single-family suburban house. At the same time, they have tended to read social and cultural change through innovations in physical form, taking note mainly of new kinds of suburbs, malls, and high-rise public housing

Fig. 9: "I Am Not a Condo" sales sign, 300 West Eighteenth Street, New York.

projects.[40] The condo, however, is aspatial. Another problem is that a good deal of condo construction has been in outlying sections and in Sunbelt cities, out of view of urban and architectural critics. Also, despite many high-style examples, the condo landscape is largely generic.[41] A second reason we have overlooked the condo is that it challenges popular narratives about the American city and the American home. Conventional formulas, reinforced by images from popular culture, suggest that for most of the suburban century government and big business offered middle-class families few alternatives to owning a suburban detached house. The growth of alternative models like the condo belies this idea.[42]

I began investigating the condo ten years ago with a study of Aventura, a massive high-rise condo city-within-a-city in North Miami Beach, Florida, which I discuss in chapter five. Larger than Levittown—although not done all at once by a single developer—Aventura was begun by a shopping-mall builder in the 1960s (today it is best known for its mall) and completed over the course of the 1970s, 1980s, and 1990s. My grandparents retired there in 1982. They bought an apartment in Ensenada II, a mid-rise elevator building designed by Morris Lapidus, built in 1971 (fig. 10).

As a modernistic, tower-in-the-park development conceived of just as low-cost examples like Pruitt-Igoe were failing, Aventura fascinated me. I began exploring it through site visits, the *Miami Herald*, and plans and sales ephemera, as well. I also interviewed members of the development team, the project architect, and residents. I was struck by how ordinary and inevitable the place seemed to those involved. I was also struck by the question of ownership. Although it was conceived at the dawn of the condo era, no one seemed to have noticed that there was anything unusual about it being co-owned. No one could recall why it was a condo or what distinguished a condo from any other project in terms of design or financing. The appeal of co-ownership to both the producers (developer, lenders, mortgage bankers) and the consumers (homeowners) was taken by all to be self-evident. The main explanation offered was circular: Aventura was condominium because the state had recently made condo ownership "legal." Indeed, in the early 1960s Florida lawmakers had passed a law making it simpler to create condos. But it did so, I

Fig. 10: Ensenada, 3401–75 North Country Club Drive, Aventura, Florida, 1970–72. Donald Soffer and Arlen Properties, developer; Morris Lapidus, architect. Ensenada II and recreation building.

soon discovered, in response to an established boom in co-ownership in the form of co-ops.

The co-op, in turn, brought me to New York, Chicago, Washington, D.C., and, eventually, Los Angeles. My investigation revealed a long history of innovative, modern, and varied housing. Co-ops had appealed to smaller, often older, often artistic families. They appealed to many women, including single, professional women, as well as socialites and widows. They appeared in the city center, but also in suburbia and in resort areas. They appealed to many rich families, but also to many workers, especially those with an ideological commitment to the commonweal rather than the privatism often associated with the house. I also found that many common qualms about the condo were foreshadowed by concerns about co-ops. Writers in the 1920s, for example, described co-ops as creatures of the modern metropolis and as satisfying the needs of "modern man."[43] The *New Yorker* magazine, from its start in the 1920s, regularly catalogued these anxieties. Even the language Americans devised to refer to these homes ("co-op" rather than "apartment") suggested the novelty of the arrangement. (In Europe, where ownership of apartments has been common for centuries, these specific terms do not exist, reflecting the much longer roots of the practice.)[44]

Methodology

Ideologically, this project is rooted in two strands of mid-twentieth-century thought. One is the work of French theorists led by Henri Lefebvre and Michel de Certeau, who first articulated an interest in the "everyday." Although Lefebvre saw homeownership—which he understood primarily as ownership of a suburban house—as corroding the "urban consciousness," both he and de Certeau were intensely interested in "reading" ordinary behaviors and spaces for evidence of individual agency in a world they saw as increasingly controlled by large-scale impersonal forces. The second strand is the work of iconoclastic American writers like critic J. B. Jackson, sociologist Herbert Gans, and architect Denise Scott Brown. They rejected the kinds of critiques made by designers and allied critics of environments produced for speculative profit (generally designed by nonprofessionals). Instead, they studied places like the postwar automobile strip, Levittown, and the casinos of Las Vegas, finding meaning in the logic of their production, and their reception and use by ordinary people.[45]

The uniformity of these places is, for many, unforgivable. Each type is a niche setting intended to cater to a particular group of consumers, following ever more standard formulas. They are exemplary of what urban theorist Margaret Crawford describes as the "increasingly specialized yet generic spaces that parcel daily

Fig. 11: Highrise of Homes, SITE, 1981. Courtesy of S-I-T-E Sculpture in the Environment.

experience into separate domains."[46] A further problem, especially with the condo, is the difficulty of personalization. While producing undifferentiated spaces, the market also encourages us to assert our individuality through consumption of mass-produced products. As a form of housing that defies customization, at least at the exterior, the condo strikes many as a hateful, alienating symbol of the mass-built postwar landscape, along with the mall and McMansion. Some designers, like James Wines's SITE (Sculpture in the Environment), have imagined alternatives that accommodate difference, but these were rarely practical (fig. 11).

Rather than dwell on formulas that deny difference, we can also, following de Certeau, see generic spaces as blank slates that allow us to evade conformity. By exploring the condo's creation at close range we can also discover more of a dialectical relationship between producer and consumer than their homogenous physical appearance might betray. As a relatively new type of housing, which until the 1950s and 1960s all but lacked standard formulas, the condo affords a privileged perspective for observing this dynamic. It allows us to continue the task of placing developer-built housing into an "everyday" framework.[47]

Methodologically, my work draws from cultural landscape studies, and from work by historians of the built environment influenced by it. In his "axioms" for reading the landscape, geographer Peirce Lewis dictates that all "items" reflect culture in some way and none is more important than any other. As Edward Relph, another geographer, suggests, modern landscapes are "for the great majority of us . . . the context of daily life." Because their production "has required substantial investments of money, time and effort . . . it is safe to assume that their appearance is neither accidental nor incidental." Looking at the built environment in its entirety requires that we take a non-normative stance toward design. As architectural historian Dell Upton writes, normative prescriptions about design run counter to "the weight of twentieth-century understanding of psychology, class, and culture."[48]

Ordinary, especially speculative, housing is not often associated with social or physical innovation, yet there is an important story to be told about the creativity and variety of homebuilding between the mid-nineteenth and late twentieth centuries. The suburban century saw the gradual emergence of regional and national "merchant builders," and, after World War II, mass-built, large-scale, visually homogenous suburban subdivisions. Advancements were often limited to the efficiencies of speed and cost. Nevertheless, local developers were able to try out other varieties of housing. This experimentation was facilitated by improvements in financing mechanisms for homebuilding (both government-aided and "conventional") that ensured housing remained an open field, with low barriers to entry.[49] Larger companies could build and sell homes for somewhat less than local builders because of greater economies of scale, but these savings were not so great that new, smaller firms could not compete. Small firms in particular were open to testing new kinds of housing, including owner-occupied multifamily housing.

Organization and Sources

The history of collective homeownership in America unfolded in three overlapping waves. The first, which I discuss in chapters one and two, "The Browne Decades" and "Town & Country," began just before the Civil War (1861–65) and ended with the Great Depression in the early 1930s. It was in the early part of this period that the co-op was first devised, serving as an experimental form of housing mainly for a small number of well-to-do families in Manhattan. Then, after World War I (1917–18), co-ownership evolved into a mainstream speculative real-estate practice, with co-ops and own-your-owns becoming a broadly accessible alternative to tenancy for middle-class and well-to-do families in several larger cities, including Chicago and Washington, D.C. The co-op also expanded to the suburbs in this period.

The second wave, which began in the 1910s and extended through the 1960s, concerned the limited-equity co-op: a form of low-cost worker housing that emerged, in part, as a critique of the mainstream housing market. I examine the development of this kind of housing and its influence on New Deal housing policy in chapter three,

"Cooperative Commonwealth." In chapter four, "Vertical Subdivisions," I focus on efforts to make the limited-equity co-op a national housing priority after World War II.

The third wave of co-ownership, which corresponds with the era of mass-suburbanization, brought a revival in market-rate co-ops and condos, beginning in the late 1940s and 1950s. By the 1970s production had reached an all-time high, unmatched before or since. I explore this phase in chapters five through seven. Chapter five, "Leisure Worlds," documents the rise of co-ownership as a form of retirement housing, primarily in resort areas like Miami. It also explores the introduction of the condo format, by way of Puerto Rico, as a way to better cater to this burgeoning market. Chapter six, "California Townhouses," looks at the growth of the suburban row-house complex. The focus here is on Southern California. This chapter also explores the emergence of fee-simple common-interest ownership as an alternative to the co-op. Chapter seven, "Back to the City," returns to New York and other large centers to show how new generations of city dwellers used co-ownership to solve postwar housing problems. It focuses primarily on conversion of rented housing to co-ownership in the 1960s and 1970s.

Following cultural geography's lead, my main source of information is not the printed word (or, as in many architectural histories, the plan), but metropolitan America's condoscape: our millions of co-ops, condos, own-your-owns, and common-interest townhouse complexes. The ordinary built environment around us reveals a great deal about who we are, including many things that we might otherwise not notice. To help make sense of this raw material I employ a variety of primary and secondary printed sources, including government reports, congressional hearings, urban-planning studies, newspaper articles, national trade publications, housing exposés, housing surveys, and other material that directly or, more often, indirectly addresses the question or status or experience of co-owned housing. I also make use of doctoral research done in the 1970s on certain aspects of condo living, and more recent work by planners, political scientists, anthropologists, and historians on some of the wider implications of the type of self-governance inherent in multifamily homeownership.[50]

To get at the buildings themselves I rely chiefly on a less respectable set of materials: local real-estate news and real-estate marketing. These sources are inherently problematic, not least because they were often one and the same. The main job of U.S. real-estate editors, at least until the 1970s, was to sell advertising space. Developers' marketing agents ran beautifully illustrated display advertisements (many examples of which are reproduced in *High Life*) that, as Dolores Hayden has emphasized, straddle "the line between life and entertainment, reality and fantasy."[51] In return, homebuilders expected stories promoting their projects. Many articles appear to have been supplied directly by developers' sales agents. For an important outfit, this arrangement could result in weekly articles for months, sometimes years, charting construction and sales progress, and touting project amenities. Most articles also included drawings, plans, and/or photos of model homes, also supplied by the builder.

As housing attorney and critic Charles Abrams noted in the 1940s—a critique that applies just as well to the 1970s and, all too often, the 2010s—the real-estate business "is interpreted only by self-serving real estate brokers, quoted as oracles in the Sunday supplements." While newspapers all had "competent writers on financial matters," he continued, "few well-informed, impartial real estate analysts are in evidence. News and comment are based on everlasting optimistic [press] releases by real estate brokers and developers with a financial stake in optimism."[52] Nevertheless, real-estate news and advertising documents what got built, what it looked like, and how much it cost—that is, what kind of housing was available at a given moment in a given market. In aggregate, over very long periods, this material enables us to map the shifting contours of housing production and sheds light on how and when new kinds of housing emerged and became successful.

To supplement this material, I have visited most of the projects I write about to take photographs and, if possible, chat with residents. This is not to suggest that I have done oral history or ethnography. Although I incorporate the voices of ordinary co-op and condo owners whenever they have made it into the published record, such evidence is sporadic. I have instead relied on the buildings themselves to create a history of this generic yet quintessentially American housing type. It is my hope that *High Life* encourages future scholars and students to take this research in alternative and uncharted directions.[53]

CHAPTER 1

The Browne Decades

In 1869, Junius Henri Browne advised readers of his latest collection of essays, *The Great Metropolis: A Mirror of New York,* to avoid multiple-family living. This dwelling practice was becoming increasingly common, with a majority of people in cities like New York already housing themselves in communal buildings, from the roughest East Side tenements to the city's finest palace hotels on Broadway.[1] The thirty-six-year-old Manhattan-based journalist was wary. Although "public houses"—which he contrasted with the "private" single-family house—might be comfortable, they were "never more than endurable, and rarely that." Furthermore, they were suitable only for single men ("masculine celibates"). Repeating a common critique of the day, he warned that multifamily arrangements offered social opportunities that would be of greater appeal to women than their domestic duties: because women were easily prone to loneliness and "need of society," and forever in want of leisure and "interesting companions," he "is unwise who takes his wife and family there for a permanent home."[2]

A little over ten years later, Browne (1833–1902), who had first become well known for his reporting on the Civil War, found himself not just living in a multifamily building but owning his own apartment—and not just for himself, but for his wife and young family. This arrangement was not perfect, he protested. It was no substitute for a house. How could it be, he wondered, with "no cellar, no nursery, no storeroom, no closets worthy of the name"? But an apartment such as theirs, he conceded, could reasonably "furnish a very small family with a wholly separate habitation and a certain kind of independence."[3]

Two advancements in multifamily living helped change Browne's mind. One was the advent of a new physical typology: the apartment house. In 1869, Browne had been writing about boarding houses and hotels. At that time, these were the primary alternatives to the house, at least for higher-class families in New York.

Fig. 12: The Rembrandt, 152 West Fifty-seventh Street, New York, 1880–81, detail. Philip G. Hubert, Jared B. Flagg, developers; Hubert, Pirsson, architect. Photograph by Brown Brothers.

(The working-class tenement was a fourth type.) For decades middle-class and well-to-do families had been drifting to hotels and boarding houses on a permanent or semi-permanent basis, drawn by their luxury and convenience. To meet the needs of a broader range of families, people also began to experiment with apartment houses. Unlike a hotel suite, an apartment was a self-contained dwelling unit, more physically and socially private, usually with its own kitchen and space for live-in domestic servants. Adapted from hotels catering to families ("family hotels") and from European, especially Parisian, prototypes, the first American apartment buildings appeared in the 1850s and 1860s in Boston and New York, and in other cities in the 1870s and 1880s. Reflecting these dual origins, in Boston these new buildings continued to be called "hotels," while in New York they were, at first, called French flats.[4]

The second innovation that led Browne to a "public house" was individual ownership of apartments. Collective homeownership further distinguished the apartment house from older types of congregant housing and helped cement perceptions of the new apartment-house typology as respectable, in part by promising to better shield residents, socially if not physically, from the lures of propinquity which concerned Browne. On the basis of this promise—along with appealing design and the good reputation of the developer and of the other buyers, with whom Browne seems to have been socially acquainted—Browne bought an apartment in New York's first owner-occupied building (fig. 12). The family remained in residence for more than twenty years; Junius died in the apartment in 1902.[5]

The story of Browne's building and those that followed over the next thirty years reveals the creative capacity of the American homebuilding system, the flexibility of property law and tenure, and the degree to which family status, gender, and class inform housing choice and design. The struggle to live well in very large, fast-growing cities like New York generated many experiments in housing between the Civil War and World War I; co-ownership was one. Interest in co-op living was fueled by multiple, often contradictory, strands of progressive and conservative thought, including frustration with speculatively built housing, calculated desire to own rapidly appreciating real estate, and social snobbery. The number of buildings was quite small: just two dozen by 1885, and another five dozen by World War I; several others failed to get built. As a group, however, they suggest how aspects of homeownership, including control of one's environment, could be as powerful as design in shaping a community's long-term success.

Rapid Urbanization and New Dwelling Types

That Browne changed his mind about multifamily living over the course of a dozen years, and that new housing types like the apartment house and the owner-occupied apartment could appear in the same short span, reflected the rapid pace of development and innovation in nineteenth-century U.S. cities. New modes of production, new social classes, and new ways of organizing urban space meant that between the 1820s and 1880s American cities saw their first banking halls, shopping arcades, department stores, office buildings, public parks, train stations, and skyscrapers, as well as their first "downtowns," "uptowns," and suburbs. By World War I the U.S. had all but transformed from an agricultural society into an urban industrial one, with cities increasingly characterized, as historian Daniel Rodgers writes, by extremes of wealth and deprivation, impersonal relations governed by markets and wages, and above all else, the ceaseless motion of populations and property.[6]

The basic how and where of American housing shifted in this era. The poor become concentrated in central but leftover neighborhoods, either in leftover houses, carved up to accommodate many families, or, after the 1850s, in higher-density, developer-built tenements. Better-off families, who, as architectural historian Dell Upton writes, increasingly felt "socially and physically claustrophobic," moved to new neighborhoods, leaving older, more central areas for conversion to downtown business uses or to working-class housing.[7]

A range of choices opened up for people of means. Attached row houses, which became common after 1800, grew larger, taller, and more elaborate. Rich families built palaces, sometimes attached, sometimes freestanding. In a quest to nurture the family's physical and moral health, many people moved to nearby "country" towns or new parklike suburbs, which began appearing in the 1850s and became popular nationally by the 1880s and 1890s. Whether in the city or the country, new genres of housing reflected the shifting role of the home for middle-class families from a productive space, in which all the household participated, to a refuge from a new world of industrial production that increasingly excluded wives and children. Of special concern in this age of the cult of domesticity was isolating the family. For middle-class women and children this meant separation from concentrated poverty and sites of paid work; for men, diversion from the dullness of sedentary white-collar work and the routine of the clock.[8]

These new conditions led many middle-class families to buy or rent self-contained houses, with more and more specialized rooms, and perhaps with a yard. Others, however, chose multifamily arrangements, which offered highly serviced accommodation without requiring large staffs of domestic workers, freeing people to devote their increasing amounts of leisure time—the weekend, for example, was new to this era—to pursue pleasure. As early as the 1810s American families began living in hotels. By the 1820s new hotels were being designed to accommodate permanent residents. By mid-century as many as three-quarters of the well-to-do in New York were living this way.[9]

The apartment emerged to cater to people like Browne who were attracted to multifamily arrangements yet frowned on the communal elements of hotel and boarding-house life. Critiques of hotel living could be moralizing and overblown, but they were grounded in widespread anxieties. As a result, the French flat caught on quickly. By the mid-1870s New York had more than twenty first-class apartment houses. Within a decade the apartment had joined the hotel as a fact of Manhattan life.[10]

Palace Home

The idea of individual ownership of apartments surfaced alongside early discussions about the new building typology, suggesting something of the fundamental appeal of co-ownership. While in the 1850s New York advocates of the Parisian apartment—including the reform-minded architect Calvert Vaux, who was a vocal enemy of the boarding house—were lamenting slow adoption on the part of builders, a group of enterprising men, about whom little is known, attempted to take matters directly to the public. Operating as the Central Home Association, with a George H. Pollock as president, the group proposed to undertake a building "built and owned by the occupants, and . . . conducted for them under their supervision, and on their account." Called the Palace Home, and projected for a site on the Upper West Side "about three minutes' walk from the Ramble in the Central Park on one side, and the North [Hudson] river on the other side," the idea was to "avoid the many inconveniences and evils now connected with the mode of living in our great city" and "to secure that degree of comfort and elegance in living which modern improvements have rendered necessary."[11]

The project, which was to have been built on plans by George H. Johnson, was ambitious. Johnson was head architect at Daniel D. Badger's Architectural Iron Works company and had designed several of the city's early cast-iron buildings. His plans for the Palace Home called for five hundred "houses for families and individuals"—far more than under any other one roof in the U.S.—in apartments ranging from single rooms of just 100 to 225 square feet, to suites with four or more bedrooms, a parlor, and library. All rooms were to have outside windows for receiving daylight and fresh air. Heating, gaslight, kitchens, and laundries were to be central, modern, and efficient. Conviviality and luxury, "equaling in splendor our finest residences and largest hotels," would be assured with management comparable to that of the "best hotels in the country." Common facilities were to include parlors, reading rooms, and public and private dining rooms. At the same time, privacy—at least acoustical—was assured. Each apartment was to be separated from the next by brick walls. "The inmates will thus live as isolatedly as in separate houses," promised an 1860 sales prospectus.[12]

One reason given for organizing Palace Home on an owned rather than rented basis was to lower the cost of well-equipped multifamily housing. Chief among the "inconveniences and evils" of New York cited in the prospectus were the "exorbitant rates of rent." The promoters promised a bargain, with single rooms at the new building priced from $300, four-bedroom apartments $1,500 to $1,800 (depending on the floor), and the largest suites topping out at $3,000 ($50,000, $250,000–$300,000, and $500,000, respectively, in 2010 dollars). All prices were to be payable over five years in monthly installments.

Money mattered for a second reason: financing. Capital for large-scale real-estate development was scarce in the nineteenth century and developers faced burdensome upfront expenses. Typically there was a real-estate "operator," an individual, perhaps with the financial support of partners, or firm that served as the developer. The operator chose a site, put an "option" (refundable down payment) on it, and then had to find investors and secure short-term construction loans. The operator had to secure forty percent—sometimes as much as seventy percent—of a project's total cost in cash. Depending on his interests and skills, the developer might then erect the building himself or hire a building contractor—a firm specializing, perhaps among other activities, in construction. The developer could then either market the building directly or, again, hire a more specialized firm, typically a rental agency. Likewise, upon completion of the project the developer could retain and manage the building (directly or through an agent) or sell the entire building to another real-estate operator. For virtually all multifamily housing, the entire process was speculative. This meant that the operator undertook the project not for a fee from a specific client but in hope of future profits to be generated either through immediate sale or through ongoing operation.

With few developers or lenders willing to risk their capital on a new type like the French flat—much less one large enough to achieve significant economies of scale for the residents—the idea behind Palace Home seems to have been to distribute the cost of production (and the financial risks) among all the tenants by making them homeowners. Because the market for high-class apartments was too limited; because the idea of individual ownership too foreign, suspect, or unappealing; or perhaps because of anxiety about the coming Civil War, Palace Home was never built. The only element completed appears to have been the prospectus.

Concerns About Rented Apartments

As the high-class apartment at last took hold in New York in the 1870s, debates about multifamily living multiplied. Collective ownership resurfaced as a response. Critiques of the city's rental buildings focused on the evils of what many people saw as small size, high rent, and poor design. No sooner had the Stuyvesant—which many regarded as Manhattan's first proper apartment house—opened in 1870, for example, than the *New York Times* declared disappointment at its rents because the suites were "exceedingly" small.[13] Ten years later the same complaints continued to appear about new buildings. As one writer mused in 1881, "Even those [apartments] designed for the best class of tenants, are, with few exceptions, badly planned, badly ventilated, badly lighted, and deficient in room."[14]

Such frustrations seem to have escalated with rents. Like all first-class housing in Manhattan, the first apartments were extremely expensive. Many of those that followed were even more so. The Stuyvesant, for example, charged $1,200 to $1,500 a year for its six-room suites, depending on the floor, at a time when a successful upper-middle-class household earned only $3,000 and $5,000 a year, and an ordinary middle-class family less than half that. Price-conversion indices suggest that these rents equaled $11,500 to $14,500 per month in 2010 dollars. At other buildings of the 1870s rates were $150 to $250 a month ($20,000 to $33,000). Such rents could have commanded an entire single-family row house in all but the most competitive Manhattan neighborhoods.[15]

A secondary set of critiques of the apartment concerned the landlord-tenant relationship. Tenants had few rights: rental arrangements did not protect them from fluctuating housing costs (rising rents) and did not offer security of tenure—

one could be evicted at the landlord's whim at the end of one's lease. Furthermore, tenants had little recourse in the event of disputes. Nineteenth-century law was far more sympathetic to landlords than to renters.[16]

A related concern was the apparent willingness of some landlords to permit buildings to fall apart in order to maximize profits. Anonymous remarks published in the *Times* around the time that the Stuyvesant opened suggest this idea: "The tendency of all community-houses whether 'apartment' or 'tenement' is, for various reasons to deteriorate." This got worse as more modest buildings came on the market. As a more recent critic has pointed out, tensions inevitably arise between landlord and tenant, because the transaction requires the customer to continually pay for something she already has: access to a dwelling that cannot help but get older, and presumably worse, with each passing month.[17]

A third set of issues concerned the question of how to live so near to others. This was an old problem, but it took on new importance as expectations for space and privacy rose. Many people, especially those still living in houses, found sharing a structure to be challenging, both conceptually and in actuality. Multifamily living was commonly associated with transience and social promiscuity, not to mention nuisances such as noise and cooking odors. There was also the question of good neighbors. As in hotels and boarding houses, apartment landlords screened their residents, sometimes requiring letters of reference. The Stuyvesant, for example, resembled a private club, with tenants drawn from the builder's own elite social circle, including Calvert Vaux, the early advocate of Parisian living in New York. Even so, one could end up in close quarters with unpleasant people.[18]

The Frenchman's Flats

The first owner-occupied project completed in the U.S. opened in 1881. The project was marketed by its developer and architect, Philip Gengembre Hubert, Sr., as a solution to many of these concerns about multifamily living. French by birth, Hubert emigrated to the U.S. as a teenager. As a young man he worked as a college professor, playwright, and inventor. During the Civil War he sold a self-fastening button to the U.S. Army for $120,000 (approximately $15 million in 2010 dollars), achieving financial independence. After the war he visited Paris, moved to New York, and, following his father, became an architect, forming a partnership with James W. Pirsson. Like many reform-minded New York designers of his era, Hubert (1830–1911) was concerned by the lack of high-quality housing for middle-class families in Manhattan and enamored of the Parisian way of apartment living.[19]

Hubert outlined his ideas for co-ownership in a series of writings in which he contrasts the problems of New York with what he suggests are more ideal conditions in Paris. One of his critiques of the New York apartment was that builders spent too much on superficial elements that appealed to prospective tenants but that contributed little to quality of life. By encouraging longer-term tenancy and discouraging turnover, co-ownership, he argued, could empower builders to shift resources from entrances, lobby décor, and other frivolities to utilitarian features, like soundproof and fireproof construction. Describing the Paris apartment, he marvels at the high quality of construction (thick floors and walls) and the absence of costly modern conveniences: the single rough-hewn stairway rather than separate accommodations for masters and servants, the absence of lobby and elevators, and the simple appointments within apartments, including "dry" kitchens and bathrooms (with no running water).[20]

Another of Hubert's critiques concerned management. In Europe, Hubert suggested, the more permanent nature of tenancy resulted in fewer abuses by management. (In the nineteenth century Americans of all social classes changed homes more frequently than did families in Europe.) He contrasts the noblesse oblige of Monsieur, the benevolent and presumably aristocratic landlord, with the New York landlord, who was always raising rents to maximize his return on investment. This practice, suggested Hubert, prompted tenants to relocate even more frequently than they otherwise might have, taking an unnecessary physical toll on buildings. By placing management in the hands of the residents, co-ownership could minimize this problem.

A third critique was that New York buildings quickly deteriorated, both physically and socially. He recounts the experience of middle-class "friends" who move to a new walk-up building. Immediately they suffer from poor soundproofing and a lack of privacy, air, and sunlight. Within two years the building "lost its freshness." The wood and plaster settled and shrank, leaks stained the ceilings, and the "showy but somewhat cheap carpeting on the landings and stairs was much worn." Worse yet, because "most of the tenants were too genteel to spend their summers in town, and too weak financially to pay rent for apartments they did not occupy," turnover was high. Because of the physical decay, the building became occupied with "lower grade" families "with a painful disregard as to their toilet." After three years the family left. Buildings in Paris, he maintained, suffered no such problems.[21]

Hubert made two other arguments in favor of collective homeownership. One was economic. Co-ownership provided an opportunity to save money. It transferred potential for profit through appreciation from the landlord to residents. It also reduced ongoing expenses. As in all multifamily homes, each household cost less to run than a standalone house because of economies of scale. Co-ownership as

proposed by Hubert promised another economic incentive: income from extra
apartments which the homeowners would own in common and rent out to defray
operating costs. For all these reasons, Hubert wrote, co-ownership could help
"people of very modest means . . . to occupy apartments which, as regards light, air
and privacy, would be accessible only to our wealthier classes."[22]

Hubert's other argument was that owning your own apartment was more
socially appealing than renting. Rather than rely on the landlord's discretion, co-
owners could, like members of a club, exercise control over resales and rentals,
"insuring the owners against the intrusion of objectionable parties."[23] Owners
could also amend house rules, redecorate the lobby, replace the doorman, and evict
problem neighbors as they saw fit. Ownership, in short, promised to eliminate many
of the social and financial uncertainties associated with apartment living. In doing
so, it would transform the "public" apartment house into something more like a
"private" home. To this end, Hubert marketed his buildings as "home clubs."

The Rembrandt

In spite of the many potential benefits of co-ownership, it took some time for
Hubert's idea to find an audience. The architect circulated a prospectus in 1879 and
filed plans that year for a building, but like the Palace Home it seems to have not
been built. Another developer, Lord Portman, who was rumored to have successfully
developed owner-occupied apartments in London, also failed to get a project off
the ground around this time, despite a feature in *Scribner's Monthly* magazine
illustrated with a floor plan and elevation, and several weeks of advertising in the
New York Times. Because the co-ownership idea was untested—and because it was
already difficult to find construction financing for apartment buildings—there was
no thought, at first, of constructing these buildings in advance of sales.[24]

The first owner-occupied project completed was the Rembrandt, on West
Fifty-seventh Street, in the heart of one of Manhattan's higher-class residential
districts (see fig. 12). The Rembrandt attracted buyers not through advertisements
or magazine articles, however, but through the enthusiastic salesmanship of Jared
Bradley Flagg, a one-time minister and artist who had become convinced of the
merits of co-ownership. Connected socially to many rich people, he sold seven
friends on the idea, including Junius Henri Browne. The group of eight was enough
for Hubert to organize the small building, whose name reflected the group's artistic
pretensions. It opened in 1881 (it was demolished around 1970).[25]

Hubert's design suggested the twin goals of economy and privacy. The
building stood on a modest lot, fifty feet wide and one hundred feet deep, and
employed a stripped-down Second Empire visual vocabulary, with a mansard roof

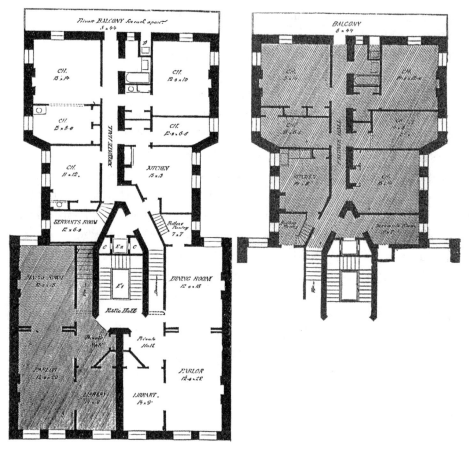

Fig. 13: The Hubert duplex plan, Hubert, Pirsson. *Scribner's Monthly,* April 1881.

enclosing the sixth floor. In this respect it suggested the French origins not just
of apartment living but of Hubert—and perhaps the idea of co-ownership, since
collective homeownership had been common in some French cities for centuries. The
minimally ornamented façade and oversized windows also recalled Richard Morris
Hunt's Néo-Grec Tenth Street Studios of 1857–58, a well-known prototype for the
apartment house, itself based on French precedents. True to Hubert's word, the
Rembrandt was far less ornate than other apartment houses of its social caliber.

Common areas were also modest. As others have pointed out, lobbies helped
make multifamily residences such as hotels respectable by offering middle-class
women a place that was both public and private. Yet as Betsy Blackmar and
Elizabeth Cromley note, the image of common hotel space as the "special territory
of women also made it a favored object of ridicule." By excluding the lobby Hubert
not only promised to protect the family from unwanted contact but he addresses
specific gendered concerns of men like Browne. No lobby meant no stage for women

to perform the play of public life while at home. The Rembrandt, more so than many buildings, promised to allow the "private family" to flourish in the modern city.[26]

In contrast to the Rembrandt's common elements, its individual apartments were generous. The building featured a unique plan that accommodated ten single-story (simplex) apartments as well as eight two-story (duplex) "studio" apartments (fig. 13). The duplexes, each of which had eleven rooms, were sold individually, while simplexes, with eight and nine rooms, were owned in common and rented out by the group to defray their own expenses. Both types of units had their own bathrooms, and every room had an outside window for light and air. This was essential before electric lighting and forced air, yet typically neglected in meaner buildings. The duplex type—based on the artist's studio, which rose two stories to admit more sunlight—was popular and became a home-club hallmark. Though developers of rental buildings sometimes borrowed this plan, it remained distinctly associated with collective ownership until well after World War I.[27]

Choosing Control

People appear to have bought—and remained in—home-club apartments for many of the reasons that Hubert anticipated they would. Chief among them was control through self-governance: the idea that co-ownership transformed a shared building into a private realm. Browne, for example, wrote that Hubert's assurances of congenial neighbors and harmonious community was the "primary condition which had been the inducement to enter into the enterprise." Similarly, Browne boasted publicly that in the home club, no one could sell or rent out his apartment "without the concurrence of his associates."[28]

This sort of social exclusion was not limited to Hubert home clubs. As America and American wealth grew more ethnically diverse in the second half of the nineteenth century, drawing and policing new social boundaries in public accommodations became a major sport. The managers of resort hotels were the most withering referees; Jews were perhaps the most frequent victims—not least because Black people and other ethnic minorities were so thoroughly segregated that it was often unnecessary to formally exclude them in such settings. Commercial landlords also excluded. As architectural historian Daniel Bluestone has written, first-class office buildings worked to screen "objectionable occupations and persons." To tenants "unsettled by 'intrusions' upon their residential and religious precincts," he writes, landlords "offered reassurance . . . [that their] skyscraper might present a more stable restricted enclave than many other urban settings." Racial and ethnic restrictions were also endemic in rental apartments. Managers of better buildings attempted to apply standards as ruthless as the hotels'. Co-ownership, with its clublike system of self-enforcement, proved especially effective in assuaging the ethnocentric concerns of people like Browne.[29]

Restrictions in co-owned apartment houses were sometimes contested. But in a deeply prejudiced age when, as historian Robert H. Wiebe writes, for many Americans "strange people constituted an omnipresent threat to the community," the state invariably agreed that screening of new occupants was necessary to keep co-ownership viable, whatever harm it did to those whose options were circumscribed. In 1886, for example, a person renting an apartment from an individual homeowner attempted to sublet the place to a third party. House rules required homeowners to secure permission from the building's elected board of directors to rent out their units but there was no specific language regulating what renters could do. Feeling that this renter had violated the spirit of the building's by-laws, the board of directors sued. The court sided with the building not because the sublet violated policy but because it believed that the social atmosphere, resale value, and financial viability of the building would be compromised if unrestricted leasing were permitted.[30]

While in this respect co-ownership appealed for its ability to exclude, it also appealed for whom homeowners could *include*. According to Browne, whose first child was born just a year after moving to the Rembrandt, "there has never been a city whose situation and construction are more unfavorable, not to say inimical, to progeny. They seem to be regarded here as interlopers. . . . In leasing houses, apartments, or rooms, the landlord or agent invariably asks the applicant, 'Have you any children?' very much in the tone and manner that he would ask 'Have you committed murder?' . . . . [If yes,] he insults you with a glance of hatred or contempt, and if he fails to reject you altogether, accepts you with an air of protest, but only at an advanced rate. . . . New York may be an Elysium for bachelors, but for a husband and a father with an ordinary income it is next door to Hades." Landlords regarded children as noisy, disruptive, and destructive—in short, a drain on their income. Even family hotels, while "admirably kept," were "not desirable for children." The Rembrandt, by contrast, offered the Brownes a multifamily home, free of the landlord's surveillance, where their children were welcome. They reared three sons in the building.[31]

Financial Advantages

Another major appeal of the home club was financial. Collective homeownership, for various reasons, tended to be less expensive on a month-to-month basis than renting. Like other kinds of city real estate, owned apartments could also quickly appreciate in value. Browne's co-owners at the Rembrandt included a variety of people "of less income than culture" but who were nonetheless willing to risk investing, and living in, a kind of dwelling yet untested in the U.S. In practice this seems to have meant successful creative types and people of moderate independent wealth, half of who were women. They included the well-known landscape painter Robert Swain Gifford, the journalist and publisher John Elderkin V, an unmarried daughter of a New York Central Railroad executive, and three other women, perhaps unmarried, perhaps widowed, about whom little is known.[32] Until the home club, wrote Browne, it was "extremely difficult" for a man with a family living on a "typical income" of $1,500 a year ($200,000 in 2010 dollars) to stay in Manhattan. Renting a house cost $2,500 or more a year. Apartments, meanwhile, "capable of accommodating a small family, with an elevator, and pleasant, well-ventilated rooms," could not be rented for under $1,500. Some went for less, "but they usually have dark chambers, they are ill arranged, and are seldom really wholesome. As a generalization, it may be said that reasonable apartments are not good, and that good apartments are not reasonable." The home club changed this equation.[33]

Co-owned apartments were far from inexpensive. Units at the Rembrandt cost approximately $16,250 ($2.4 million), of which $8,750 had to be paid down in cash ($1.25 million). Each owner initially contributed $5,000 ($725,000) and a building-wide mortgage for $60,000 was secured ($7,500 per owner [$1.1 million]). As construction costs rose from an estimated $100,000 to the actual $130,000, however, everyone paid in an additional $3,750. No financing appears to have been made available for these cash contributions, although it is possible that buyers might have secured short-term personal loans from outside lenders.[34]

From the vantage point of two years later, Browne justified the cost on grounds that his share of ongoing expenses for maintenance, utilities, staff, property taxes, and debt service for the buildingwide, or "blanket," construction loan was less than sixty percent of the rental value of his apartment. After deducting the income from the extra jointly owned rental units, Browne and his neighbors each expected to spend only $500 a year to maintain their homes ($5,700 a month in 2010 dollars). If Browne chose to rent it out, he felt assured of a generous annual return on his initial investment. More critically, perhaps, was that resale values had already risen "easily" to $25,000 ($3.4 million): a potential profit of more than $2 million in 2010 dollars after just two years.[35]

Before the home club, Browne believed that apartments were merely "abodes where persons stay until they can find an opportunity or the means to go somewhere else." But as a result of the new housing arrangement, he, like many of his neighbors, remained for decades. John Elderkin, for example, lived at the Rembrandt until his death, in 1926. And as another Hubert home club was being razed, in the 1930s, the *Times* noted that it was "famous as having a larger number of tenants [homeowners] for many years than any other apartment structure in the city."

Among them were well-known artists, museum curators, and lawyers, including one whose grandfather had been an original owner.[36] This sort of continuity was highly unusual in nineteenth-century American cities. Most renters—which is to say the great majority of city dwellers—moved annually. Moving Day for everyone was May 1 or October 1, depending on the city. In an essay bemoaning this ritual, Browne expressed envy for those in the "privileged class . . . which owns its houses." Co-ownership helped extend this "comfortable dream" to the French flat.[37]

The Cooperative Apartment

The system of co-ownership used by Hubert and others in the nineteenth-century U.S. quickly came to be known as "cooperative," or co-op. Under this plan, the developer established a limited-liability joint-stock company—that is, an ordinary corporation—to buy (or, occasionally, lease) the land and undertake construction. Upon completion of the building the corporation retained legal ownership of (and title to) the land and building. Each homeowner received shares in the company in the form of a stock certificate. In most buildings the number of shares allotted to each owner was proportionate to the size of her apartment. Each owner also received a long-term "proprietary" lease that conferred ownership by entitling her to exclusive permanent occupancy of her apartment. This lease typically cost a nominal $1 a year. In an alternative arrangement, employed somewhat later in Chicago (where until after World War I state law limited corporate ownership of real estate), co-ops were set up as trusts and buyers received trust certificates.[38]

In addition to conveying ownership the proprietary lease served as a bill of rights and responsibilities that spelled out how the homeowners were to get along with one another and maintain the building physically and socially. Leases required compliance with corporate by-laws. They also typically prohibited a range of more specific behaviors that might decrease the appeal of a building and, in turn, the resale value of apartments. Typical of proscribed activities were things that were commonly associated with working-class tenement living, such as hanging laundry out of windows.[39]

Chief among the obligations was the requirement that shareholders pay association dues, or "further rent," to cover their share of the building's expenses. These included physical maintenance, wages for service employees such as superintendents, property taxes, debt service on any construction loans (which where usually converted to permanent blanket mortgages upon completion of the building), and a reserve fund to be held for larger periodic expenses such as major repairs, or retirement of loans. Mortgages in the nineteenth century were not self-amortizing and had to be paid off at expiration with a lump-sum "balloon" payment.

Association dues, typically called "maintenance charges," were calculated according to the number of shares a homeowner had. By-laws empowered the co-op to evict any owner who did not keep up with her maintenance charges. As in any business corporation, they also established specific procedures for governance through a board of directors. Typically, boards comprised three, five, or seven shareholder-owners who were elected annually at a general meeting of the whole building. The board was responsible for everything from hiring and supervising building staff to purchasing supplies (such as coal) to keeping account books to paying property taxes to approving all resales and rentals. Under the Chicago trust system, governance was overseen by an appointed board of trustees.

Because many recognized in co-ownership a degree of mutual aid, the generic term for it from the start was "cooperative." Even though Hubert used the term "home club"—and that term continued to surface from time to time into the 1900s—real-estate reporters nearly always referred to his buildings as "cooperative." At the time, Americans used "cooperative" in a variety of ways. One was for rented multifamily buildings, especially ones offering common, or cooperative, housekeeping services, such as central kitchens and dining rooms.[40] Another was for mutual-aid housing societies. Mortgages in the late nineteenth century were difficult to get and short in duration. To acquire houses, groups of workers in England in the late eighteenth century had begun to form investment clubs. After establishing a company, each member contributed to a common fund. When the pot was sufficient the company built a house and auctioned the right of first occupancy. Each family, in turn, would come to own a house. By the 1860s these early savings-and-loan societies appeared in the U.S. Many perceived multifamily homeownership as an extension of this mutual-aid arrangement.[41]

Origins of the Co-op

The actual co-op plan was rooted as much in the history of housing as in that of other social and business institutions. In Europe, multifamily homeownership dated back to the twelfth century when burghers in the walled towns of some Germanic kingdoms began taking ownership of individual floors of houses. According to legal historians, neighboring areas of what became France, Switzerland, and Italy also adopted the system, and by the fifteenth century the practice was accepted in Brussels, Paris, Grenoble, Orleans, and Milan, and by the sixteenth century in Glasgow and Edinburgh.[42]

The system of ownership employed in these places was different from the American co-op. The European plan—today known in the U.S. as "condominium"—rested on the principle of individual titles. It worked by dividing a single property, or "fee," into multiple fees, each with a unique deed that conveyed "fee-simple," or outright, ownership of a cube of air. Each deed also provided for an indivisible share, though tenancy-in-common, of the land; of structural elements such as walls, roofs, and plumbing; and of common areas such as lobbies, stairways, and corridors. Restrictions in deeds spelled out how the owners managed the common elements.[43] To ensure smooth operation, the system had been supported by the state for centuries, at first through erroneous interpretations of Roman law, and, when it later became clear that Roman law had not actually supported co-ownership, through specific new statutes. It became all but standard when Napoleon included it in the Civil Code.[44]

In New York, co-ownership was re-created from scratch. English common law, upon which American law is based, contained no provisions for collective homeownership. Although owned apartments were common in Scotland, in England they were unknown until 1803, with the opening of a complex in London called Albany. Still in operation next door to the Royal Academy in Piccadilly two centuries later, Albany converted a foreclosed mansion into seventy-one "independent Freehold [fee-simple] Apartments" for well-to-do bachelors (women were prohibited for many years). Early residents included dilettantes, writers, and politicians, including Lord Byron and a young William Gladstone, whose father bought him an apartment upon graduation from college, and in which he lived until he married.[45]

Stateside, a new plan was devised—perhaps because there was no local legal precedent, or perhaps because New York developers felt they lacked the expertise required to craft adequate deed restrictions. The American system was the corporate-title "cooperative." Rather than focus on complicated deeds, it followed two simpler, more familiar models: the business corporation and the private social club. The corporation enjoyed a rapid rise in the U.S. in the nineteenth century and the legal basis for corporate ownership of property was well established in most places. Meanwhile, a similar legal framework appears to have already been in use for private social clubs, country clubs, and single-family communities where land, at least in part, was held in common. At planned suburban developments like Llewellyn Park, New Jersey, for example, the roads and the Ramble were owned jointly, with title to the park placed in the hands of three self-perpetuating trustees. Upkeep was the responsibility of an elected board of directors.[46]

No one can claim credit for inventing this system of co-ownership. Application of its model to an apartment building was novel, but many saw it as logical—so much so that several developers seem to have come up with the idea independently in the nineteenth century. Even developers who were likely aware of the individual-title European plan, such as French-born Hubert, rejected that model for the new corporate-title plan. (Although permitted in France, co-ownership was rare in Paris in the nineteenth century so it remains unclear how much Hubert knew about it.)[47] Hubert was the first to complete a co-op, but others, beginning with the Palace Home twenty years earlier, proposed essentially the same. As the *Times* put it: "There is and can be no legal obstacle in the way of these co-operative buildings" because they are organized as ordinary business corporations.[48]

Not Communitarian

Some have regarded Hubert's program as utopian.[49] Beginning in the 1820s, Americans reluctant to embrace modernization and the market began to experiment with utopian communities that offered economic alternatives to capitalism, and social alternatives to the nuclear family. Hubert was surely familiar with Fourierism, the largest of these experiments in communitarian socialism. Charles Fourier rejected big business (and monogamy) and proposed organizing community life and work around self-contained complexes called *phalanstères*. When Hubert was a toddler, his father designed one of these complexes in France. At least one Hubert design for an unbuilt Manhattan home club seemed to recall the idea.[50]

Despite the shared name, however, the co-op was not cooperative in the sense of mutual-aid or collective housekeeping. In his writings, Hubert often faulted the speculative housing market for producing overpriced, poorly designed housing. He argued that the competitive housing situation in Manhattan was the result of a "combination of adverse circumstances *which cannot be overcome without a radical change in the division of land,* our mode of building, and a study of yet unsolved and most intricate social questions." But for all its novelty, Hubert's home club, in practice, was a conservative endeavor. For Hubert, the co-op was not so much a critique of capitalism and capitalist social relations as a more focused argument against typical real-estate practices in New York.[51]

Hubert explicitly rejected the idea that the home club was informed by communitarian sentiment. Indeed, once he had successfully developed the Rembrandt and was able to secure better financing for owned apartments, he began developing speculatively. Furthermore, in his writings he insisted that the co-op was purely pragmatic and that relations among owners were strictly business. Hubert justified social exclusion on the grounds that it would "greatly increase the value of the property." Elsewhere he highlighted the "facility with which members desiring to sell have disposed of their interests . . . at a large premium." He also emphasized that the co-op arrangement "satisfies the shrewd business sense of the wealthiest and most intelligent classes of our community" and that a member's "connection with

GRAND INTERIOR COURT AND ARCADES,
CENTRAL PARK APARTMENTS.

Fig. 14: Central Park Apartments, 150–80 West Fifty-ninth Street and 145–75 West Fifty-eighth Street, New York, 1883–85. Philip G. Hubert, José Francisco de Navarro, developers; Hubert, Pirsson, architect. View of courtyard. Hubert, Pirsson & Company, *Where and How to Build,* prospectus, ca. 1892.

his neighbors must be of a business—but need never be of a social—nature."[52]

Early co-op designs, like the Rembrandt's, reflected this position, generally emphasizing privacy over community. Hubert specified that common corridors be wide enough for residents to pass each other "without objectionable contact." Additionally, he worked to ensure that "floors and partitions . . . be deafened, the gas and water arrangements entirely independent, and all things avoided that might bring families or their servants in contact while engaged in the performance of household duties."[53] Unlike hotels and many early rental apartment buildings, co-ops also eschewed "cooperative" housekeeping facilities, apart from the occasional fine-dining restaurant, such as that operated by Louis Sherry of Delmonico's, the city's leading restaurateur, on the eighth floor of the ultra-smart Gramercy, completed in 1883.[54]

Even visual representations of co-ops emphasized privacy. In the prospectus for Hubert's largest project, a complex of eight buildings called the Central Park Apartments, a rendering of the interior courtyard shows at least five figures, or small groups of figures, and two carriages, but all quite apart from one another (fig. 14). At the right stands a well-dressed woman with a parasol holding a child's hand. At center is a couple with their child, and at left a small figure with a dog (signaling that the family pet would also be welcome in the "private" home club, unlike in many rental buildings); in the distance, behind the fountain, two lone figures are strolling. Not only does the image convey the spacious (if exaggerated) dimensions of the courtyard but the idea that physical contact between neighbors would be minimized and that, despite the family-size apartments, children would never become a nuisance.

Boom and Bust

The Hubert home club did not ignite an immediate revolution in New York housing. By the mid-1880s it extended to only nineteen buildings plus several developed by others. But following the Rembrandt, collective homeownership briefly became a preferred mode of multiple-family living in Manhattan among those who could afford it. Between 1882 and 1885, nearly two dozen co-ops got under way, many far larger, taller, more modern, and more expensive than the original. This volume of building was far smaller than that of rental apartments, of which there were at least a thousand by the mid-1880s. But most rental buildings by then were middle-class, and many differed little from lower-class tenements except in location. High-class rentals also proliferated, but the thrust of development after 1881 was toward co-ops, and many of the "best" new buildings were in co-ownership.

After Jared Flagg helped put together the Rembrandt his brother organized a second home club, and Jared's son, the architect Ernest Flagg, a third. According to the *Real Estate Record* all three men "made a great deal of money" through these projects, presumably by selling their own apartments at a profit once they had been completed.[55] Several additional buildings were put together by others, both with and without Hubert's help. For a time, the home club idea seemed to sell itself. Among the products of this boom were the Gramercy, today the nation's oldest surviving co-op; 121 Madison Avenue, which, in a break from hotel tradition, pioneered the practice of not taking a name; and the Chelsea (later transformed into the Chelsea Hotel; fig. 15). When the first *Social Register* was compiled in the 1880s three of the five most represented buildings were Hubert home clubs: the Knickerbocker, 80 Madison Avenue (fig. 16), and 121 Madison Avenue. Nearly twenty years

Fig. 15: The Chelsea, 222 West Twenty-third Street, New York, 1883–85. Philip G. Hubert, developer; Hubert, Pirsson, architect.

later the Knickerbocker still ranked high, with twenty *Register* families.[56]

For all the talk of permanence and security, however, just as quickly as the co-op came into favor, the market crashed. Building, buying, and selling subsided by 1885, and construction remained dormant for more than a decade. In part the hiatus was caused by new building laws, which limited the height of residential buildings, and by new rapid transit lines, which made peripheral areas more accessible and thrust the city out rather than up. But in larger part it was that the quick downturn left homebuyers and builders wary, underscoring the importance of profit motive as a condition for co-ownership.

This collapse of the co-op market was precipitated by the financial failure of the city's largest and most opulent apartment complex: the Central Park Apartments (fig. 17). The group was developed and designed by Hubert with the aid of a Spanish socialite and entrepreneur named José Francisco de Navarro. Conceived around 1881 and built beginning in 1883, the complex comprised eight, ten-story buildings on Central Park South. The buildings, which were grouped around three courtyards, each contained twelve or thirteen apartments of five to eight thousand square feet. As in most duplex-plan buildings, lower ceilings in back rooms, which contained some of the family bedrooms and all the servants' rooms, meant that there were half again as many stories at the rear (see fig. 14).

The circumstances surrounding the project's failure remain obscure. It appears that the complex was fully sold and tenanted but that initial maintenance estimates could not meet expenses, which included servicing blanket mortgages. (One third of the $240,000 [$32 million] cost of each building had been financed.) The only solution

No. 80 MADISON AVENUE, CORNER OF TWENTY-EIGHTH STREET.
OFFICES OF HUBERT, PIRSSON & CO., 19 EAST TWENTY-EIGHTH STREET

Fig. 16: 80 Madison Avenue, New York. Philip G. Hubert, William Flagg, developers; Philip G. Hubert, architect. Hubert, Pirsson & Company, *Where and How to Build,* prospectus, ca. 1892.

Fig. 17: Central Park Apartments. View to the southeast. Photograph, 1889.

was for the owners to raise their monthly maintenance charges. They refused. The lenders sued the eight cooperative corporations and Navarro; they foreclosed in 1888. As part of the arrangement, owners' proprietary leases were voided and their equity lost, leaving them as tenants in a building they no longer owned.[57]

This failure was not the only reason for disillusionment with co-ownership, however. Interest in the co-op had already begun to wane due to general overbuilding of apartments and because maintenance often made co-ops more expensive to live in than developers initially promised. In 1884, the *Times* reported a "growing feeling among the public at large against so-called home club associations and co-operative apartment-houses. A number of persons . . . found them so expensive that they deemed it prudent to sell." Similar problems plagued contemporaneous experiments in the U.K. An additional problem was that some owners found the burdens of self-governance not worth the bother. As the *Times* continued, "There is a well-founded apprehension that these co-operative buildings will ultimately lead to a good deal of litigation between the various parties in interest."[58] Elsewhere, a real-estate reporter further cautioned that a successful co-op needs a "first-class architect, a first-class builder, and last, but not least, a first-class lawyer."[59]

The Central Park Apartments proved to skeptics that collective homeownership was inherently flawed. One trade paper took the occasion to declare co-ownership culturally anathema and "that the principle of home clubs on which these speculations are based is scarcely consistent with American ideas of house ownership." It continued: "A noble mansion affords the owner a gratification. . . . When grouped together, as in these monstrous apartment houses, these homes of taste and luxury are merged in a building of, it may be, fine architectural effect, but the individual is lost. . . . Such a system of living, however successful in Paris, is entirely foreign to American ideas. The necessity for economy may force people of moderate means into flats and apartments, but wealth should give the world the benefit of that cultivation which luxurious and tasteful dwellings afford."[60] The *Times* reached a similar conclusion, suggesting that "whereas a clubman can abandon his club whenever his surroundings there become unpleasant," in the arena of housing "a prudent man will hesitate before committing himself and his money to circumstances," such as a co-op, "that he can neither foresee nor control."[61]

The Painters of Modern Life

Although the Central Park Apartments invited schadenfreude and many homeowners were hurt financially, co-ownership retained its fundamental appeal and a new generation of co-ops appeared with the next cycle of residential construction, just after the turn of the century. As in the 1880s, the first examples responded to a perceived gap in the speculative housing market. In this case an artist named Henry Ward Ranger found himself in want of an unusual type of home: an apartment with a well-lighted studio. Previous generations of New York artists had faced similar difficulties and undertaken to construct special facilities. One was Richard Morris Hunt's Studios building of 1857, which had been financed by a rich patron. In 1880, the popular landscape painter Frederic Edwin Church persuaded another benefactor to erect a new building. Ranger, also a well-known landscape painter, now sought another.[62]

Without a developer-patron of his own, Ranger (1858–1916) recruited several friends in 1901 to form a cooperative. They bought and developed a project on an inexpensive block of Sixty-seventh Street on the unfashionable West Side. Among the group were some of the nation's most successful artists (if not always critically, than at least financially, through regular work at magazines). They included Childe Hassam, Frank DuMond, Robert Vonnoh, Bessie Potter Vonnoh, and Walter Russell. Hassam, the most well known of them, may have been particularly enthusiastic: he had once lived in the Rembrandt.[63]

The new building, with an austere design by Sturgis & Simonson, was called the Sixty-seventh Street Studios (or, by some accounts, the Co-operative Studio Building) (fig. 18). It opened in 1903. Russell was familiar with the European plan of individual-title ownership. In 1905, he described co-ownership to the American Institute of Architects in 1905 as "very similar to the custom in Venice of different floors in a building belonging to different owners." The building, however, was organized as a standard joint-stock cooperative.[64]

The project was successful physically, socially, and financially: so much that several of the homeowners went into business together developing additional co-ops. Like Hubert's home clubs, the Sixty-seventh Street Studios included several smaller rental apartments in addition to large duplexes for owners. The rentals leased so well that the income covered all of the owners' expenses. One year it was rumored that the homeowners were paid a cash dividend. Realizing the immense appeal of this situation, several among them, including Ranger, Vonnoh, and Russell, began helping other artists organize buildings. By 1905 at least three were under way, all on the same block of West Sixty-seventh Street.[65] Within a few years Ranger, Vonnoh, and their contractor, William J. Taylor, who had first suggested the idea of a co-op to Ranger, were developing for profit and had established the nation's first

Fig. 18: Sixty-seventh Street Studios, 27 West Sixty-seventh Street, New York, 1901–3. Henry Ward Ranger, developer; Sturgis & Simonson, architect. Photograph by Wurts Bros., 1905.

company dedicated to the speculative production of owner-occupied apartments, the Co-operative Building Construction Company. Walter Russell (1871–1963) incorporated a firm of his own for the same purpose, the Stuyvesant Co-operative Buildings Corporation. Between 1907 and U.S. entry into World War I, in 1917, around four dozen co-ops were built in Manhattan. These two companies developed at least eighteen of them.[66]

The Private World of the Co-op

In the late 1900s and early 1910s co-ops grew larger and more elaborate, and the clientele became more mainstream. Several projects on the West Side continued to attract creative types. Increasingly, however, co-ops were built on the East Side and the buyers were bankers, businessmen, and lawyers, who, as William Taylor suggested, came to see co-ops as "something better than ordinary apartments." As the *Times* mused in 1909, with more than a hint of exaggeration, "Spare a tear for

Fig. 19: Sixty-sixth Street Studios, 131–35 East Sixty-sixth Street, New York, 1905–6. Co-operative Building Construction Company, developer; Charles A. Platt, architect. View of interior staircase, apartment C. *Architectural Record*, July 1908.

the sons and daughters of the rich who married just before the co-operative [that] . . . bridges the chasm between the bride's father's $1,000,000 place . . . [and the] $2,000,000 establishment [$100 million and $200 million] that her husband will have in a few years if the hunting continues good. . . . A single apartment may consist of fifteen rooms on three floors . . . with the result that a large percentage of the population of New York co-operative apartment buildings is composed of those who were reared in fine houses on fashionable thoroughfares." Taylor supported these claims, stating that his primary clientele had become rich households who could no longer afford houses in Manhattan.[67]

Many of the East Side buildings abandoned Ranger's original studio plan for a new, better-selling duplex that shifted space from double-height rooms designed to capture the northern light needed by artists, to rooms for servants. This plan also better reproduced the atmosphere of a house (fig. 19).[68] As one writer remarked at the time, the modified spatial arrangement "though expensive, seems to solve the problem of home living, better than any other kind of apartment."[69] At the façade, this change was reflected in substitution of window walls for Beaux-Arts Neoclassicism (fig. 20).

Fig. 20: Sixty-sixth Street Studios. General view.

In this era, advertisements for co-ops began running regularly in the "apartments to let" section of the *Times* ("apartments for sale" did not appear until 1920). Most posed the question to readers, common in ads for single-family houses, "Why Pay Rent?" Frequent themes included the potential for profit through resale, the freedom to customize, and the lower monthly cost of owning relative to other housing options. One, for example, claimed to solve the problem of "How to Live Cheaply in NEW YORK IN AN UP-TO-DATE ELEVATOR BUILDING," while another claimed that in the co-op "THE OTHER FELLOW PAYS YOUR RENT."[70] This was an exaggeration. Cash returns such as those reported at Sixty-seventh Street Studios were highly atypical. Nevertheless, maintenance was often lower than rent. Perhaps more importantly, resale values were once again rising. Early owners at the Rembrandt were rumored to have resold their apartments after twenty years for double the initial prices, and William Taylor claimed that apartments in his buildings doubled in price after just a few years.[71]

For increasing numbers of upper middle-class New York families, the "private" co-owned apartment also appealed, more than ever, as a means to exclude. In an especially candid article, in 1911, *Architectural Record* reminded readers that the only way to ensure good neighbors in an apartment house was to choose a co-op—good neighbors being ones who were neither Irish nor Jewish. "Unless all the coöperators unite to constitute themselves a vigilance committee," it warned, "some day there will elude the vigilance of the . . . real estate agent a 'peroxide Juno' . . . or a hook-nosed tenant, of the kind of hook nose you know and apprehend." ("Peroxide Juno" referred to the Irish in a recent O. Henry story.) "When one of these intrudes," it continued, "you have to own that the coöperativeness of the coöperative apartment house, the privacy of the apartment house, is destroyed and the value of the investment grievously impaired."[72]

Restrictions cost virtually nothing to include and appealed to buyers' sense of self-importance. They also promised a modicum of control over large-scale social change. The U.S., especially its large cities, had always been ethnically diverse. But the share of foreigners had risen steadily since the Civil War. Fewer were from Britain and other Northern European countries; more were Catholic or Jewish. As Irish, Jewish, and other "ethnic" families sought modern, well-equipped housing, policing racial and ethnic boundaries emerged as a major concern. In politics, many older-stock Americans fought for restrictions against immigration, and in higher-class suburbs developers began experimenting with racial restrictions. In genteel co-ops, the custom of exclusion served a similar purpose.[73]

A Future for the Co-op

By the start of World War I the co-op had become, with roughly seventy-five buildings, a standard, even generic, housing type in parts of Manhattan. That said, the overwhelming majority of New Yorkers remained tenants, while many of the rich continued to own row houses. Even among first-class apartment houses, co-ops were outnumbered by rentals and no co-op matched the size or grandeur of rentals like the Ansonia (1903) or the Belnord (1909). One reason for this was money: for most New York families, as one writer concluded in a 1907 essay on the question of "Choosing a Home," co-ops "are too costly." No financing was available, so purchase was possible only for those with significant sums of cash. Lingering doubts about the desirability and financial security of co-ownership also limited its expansion.[74]

Another moderating factor was the growing appeal, and falling cost, of the suburban house. Among the rich, as the *Times* noted in 1905, "society is gradually abandoning private residences in Manhattan more for country homes than for apartment houses or hotels."[75] Middle- and working-class families were also leaving the city center. Between the Civil War and World War I, Manhattan's population grew from 810,000 to 2.3 million but that of the rest of metropolitan New York, including the suburban counties, grew from 820,000 to 6 million.

For those who could afford it, the home club could address anxieties about money, privacy, and status just as effectively as the bungalow. Many co-op owners did not need whole houses. Others, like Junius Henri Browne, did but could not stand to leave the cosmopolitan center, writing that he would "rather be crowded into rear fourth-story rooms here [in Manhattan] than own a handsome home beyond the smell of the sea" or in "the rear of Brooklyn, along the lines of the New Jersey railroads, among the sand knolls of Long Island, or amid the pastures of Westchester." Unlike new skyscraper office buildings which responded to the corporation's need for centralized management and armies of white-collar staff, the co-op proved that in the domestic sphere any number of physical forms could fulfill similar social and economic functions.[76]

For this reason and, in particular, because it shifted power and responsibility from landlords to tenants, as early 1910 some began to recognize in co-ownership a great possibility for improving city life for ordinary households. At the time, most architects, housing reformers, and others associated with the nascent field of city planning were focused on encouraging wage earners to decentralize—to move from congested tenement districts, widely seen as unhealthful, to better-equipped apartments and small houses in peripheral sections of the metropolis.

In a rare discussion of co-ownership, however, the City of New York's Tenement House Department wrote of the co-op favorably. Echoing Philip Hubert, its annual report for 1910–11 explained that the "erection of such buildings is of general interest because of the fact that in them the speculative element is practically eliminated, and with it much that is undesirable and even bad." Ownership of the apartment, it assumed optimistically, "renders it imperative upon the builder to attain as near perfection as possible in construction and design." More to the point, it imagined that co-op owners cared more about the quality of their homes and neighborhoods than renters did. "Not the least desirable result of this" ownership, it continued, "is the added interest which the occupant takes in the erection and maintenance of the building. The lack of interest in the home and its surroundings in this city has long been attributed to the fact that the majority of householders in New York City are merely rent payers." Whether the "co-op movement" could spread enough to "overcome this feeling" was unknown. But, foreshadowing later arguments in favor of homeownership, the Tenement House Department clearly speculated that a city of more co-ops might be a better city.[77]

Such assumptions ignored the fact that the evidently "better" behavior of apartment owners was surely as much a result of their higher social status as their role as property owners. But they did suggest how the city apartment was not as different from the suburban house as their physical forms and divergent geographies might suggest.

CHAPTER 2

Town & Country

Collective homeownership stood trial before the U.S. Senate in the spring of 1921. Occasional disputes among co-owners had been heard by New York courts since the 1880s but now some of the nation's leading lawmakers were asked to evaluate the entire premise. The official topic was extension of Washington, D.C.'s, Ball Rent Act, an emergency measure introduced to limit rent increases during a severe housing shortage after World War I. Congress, which oversaw governance of the District, was trying to determine how acute the crisis remained. A leading question was whether co-ownership was a legitimate practice. Washington had only two co-ops before the war but recent pressures had generated a significant demand for multifamily homeownership. In 1920 alone an estimated twenty-five co-ops went on sale in the city, arousing suspicion. As one city commissioner saw it, "cooperative sale of apartments is absolutely a fake," employed to put apartments in the hands of individuals better positioned to evade rent laws than larger-scale landlords. Supporters countered that it was both legitimate—nine out of ten owners were living in their apartments—and desirable.[1]

Among the witnesses who testified was Isaac Gates. Gates, an attorney with the federal government, owned and lived in an apartment at the Parkwood, an eight-story building on K Street, downtown (now demolished). The real-estate developer Allan E. Walker and Company had put the building up for sale a little more than a year before. Its twenty-eight, seven-room apartments sold out within a few months (fig. 21).[2] Gates, who had moved to the city right after the war, decided to buy after seeing an advertisement. Although previously unfamiliar with co-ownership, he was taken by the idea that it made more financial sense than renting. "I sought out Allan E. Walker myself," he reported, "and got information from them which confirmed the opinion I had previously formed, and purchased an apartment."[3]

Fig. 21: Advertisement for Allan E. Walker and Company, *Washington Post*, November 20, 1920.

Although Gates liked owning his apartment, he realized that many were skeptical. "We have a good deal of sympathy extended to us, and a good many people think we are very unfortunate," he explained. "We thank them very much for their sympathy but so far we have no complaint." Apart from the financial satisfaction of ownership, he preferred it to renting because the "service is just exactly what the owners of the apartment make it." And Gates made the most of it: he ran for the building's board of directors and was serving as its first president. He felt confident that the building would continue to operate well. "If the board of directors run this apartment house on business principles, as we try to do . . . there is no reason why it should not be a success." Others at the hearings expressed similar feelings. M. O. Eldridge, a homeowner from another Walker building, proclaimed that he and his fellow co-owners were "delighted" with their situation.[4]

Apart from individual financial benefits, many also told the Committee on the District of Columbia, which convened the hearings, that multifamily homeownership was good for their neighborhoods, the city, and the nation. Developers in particular embraced this position. A Walker executive suggested that buying an apartment not only had the "effect of first making a home owner, a taxpayer, and good citizen" but that owners often enhanced their buildings and neighborhoods by making physical improvements. Another developer recited a similar story: "One man who is a distinguished lawyer in Washington, who has lived here for the past 60 years, when he bought his apartment he scraped and painted and repapered his apartment, because he wanted it done in a certain way. He has put [wall]paper on that cost four times as much as in any apartment I ever saw. He was making a real home for himself." Co-op ownership, this developer concluded, "is not only fair from the point of view of the people who have been living in apartments and want real homes, but it is an absolutely fair proposition from any point of view." Individual homeowners agreed with the homebuilders. Eldridge, for example, noted that in his opinion multifamily homeownership was "doing more to curtail the activities of the rent profiteer and to encourage people to own their own homes in cities than anything else which has happened in a generation."[5]

Grievances against the co-op were detailed as well, but they tended toward rumor and lacked the presence of the developers, with their reassurances, and the real-life homeowners. The committee found them less convincing than the arguments in support of co-ownership. At the end of the hearings Senator Gooding, a Republican from Idaho, declared that he was "very much in favor of the cooperative plan" and would "be glad to encourage . . . people owning their own homes." Reflecting on his own experience as a "pioneer in homesteading," he added: "You feel better from the fact that you have your own home. . . . And more independent." Sufficiently persuaded that co-ownership could be of genuine benefit to the community, the Committee—as part of its approval of the Rent Act extension—recommended the city's Rent Commission release co-ops from regulation and recognize buyers as "bona fide owner[s]" of real estate.[6]

When thinking about metropolitan housing in the 1920s, historians have focused on the twin poles of town and country. There are studies, for example, devoted to the grand apartment-house districts of New York, Chicago, and Washington. Others have examined efforts by developers, builders, and bankers—along with catalogue retailers, like Sears—to make up-to-date houses available to ordinary families. The expansion of co-ownership to Washington and other cities represents a third turn. As before the war, it was driven, in part, by the rich and avant-garde. It also came to appeal to new kinds of co-op clientele, including working women and young professionals like Isaac Gates, as new economic realities and improvements to the co-op mechanism transformed apartment ownership into a mainstream, increasingly middle-class dwelling practice.

The Apartment Decade

The 1920s saw an unprecedented surge in housing construction in the U.S., with more new housing (relative to the existing stock) than in any decade before or since. Prosperity, advancements in home construction and financing, new and more restrictive building and zoning codes, more and faster roads and rapid-transit lines, and changes in the family helped ignite this boom. Much development was concentrated in suburban, single-family houses, as celebrated in Sinclair Lewis's novel *Babbitt*.[7] But much of it was also in apartment houses. Co-ownership flourished in this context, spreading beyond Manhattan (and the one or two early examples in

Chicago, Washington, and San Francisco) to a variety of metropolitan locations. If at the start of World War I multifamily homeownership was a novelty everywhere but New York City, by Black Monday it had become a common alternative to tenancy.

The growth in collective homeownership was part of a larger shift to apartment living. More than a million apartments were built in the U.S. in the 1920s. In 1880, only seven million Americans lived in cities or towns with a population over 50,000 (one million of them in New York). Ninety percent of "non-farm" dwelling structures were single-family houses (or at least houses originally built for a single family). By World War I, much had already changed. The nation's population, which doubled between 1880 and 1916, was increasingly concentrated in cities. The share of single-family houses among new dwellings had fallen to sixty-eight percent by the early 1900s, and then to sixty-two percent in the 1910s. These trends accelerated in the 1920s. By 1928 more than half of new dwellings built in the nation's 225 principal housing markets were multifamily. In the densely settled Midatlantic states, the share of apartments reached seventy percent; in New York and Chicago, eighty. Even in suburban districts and in small towns the apartment gained traction; in suburbs nationally the share of apartments was fifty-eight percent in 1928, and in small towns, twenty. In Westchester County, New York, only half of all homes were single-family by 1934.[8]

In the age of metropolitanism, the apartment, whether rented or owned, became for many the convenient and modern way to live. New wealth, rising expectations for quality in housing, and widespread car ownership (three-quarters of families by the late 1920s) led millions of Americans to suburban houses. For others, however, these changes enhanced the appeal of apartment living. New apartment-house districts flourished both for the working class—making its way out of tenement districts— but also for the more affluent. According to land-use economist Coleman Woodbury, writing in 1931, this growth reflected a "changed attitude toward the desirableness and acceptableness of apartment-house living."[9] As one particularly exasperated suburban resident wrote to *Colliers'* magazine: "I am tired of fretful looking fellow-beings toting rakes, lawn mowers, evergreen shrubs, snow shovels, spades, bulbs, paint, wire netting, young chicks, radio parts, and garden trucks." An apartment obviated these kinds of concerns.[10]

Structural economic forces also help account for the upturn in apartment-house construction. Increasing wealth permitted people to consume more and better housing. At the same time, home financing remained difficult to obtain. The rate of homeownership in the 1920s grew from forty to forty-six percent but the path to ownership remained arduous, especially for those without steady, secure wages. For many, renting a modern apartment was the best available housing option. Meanwhile, the 1920s saw new lenders enter the field of housing finance, with savings-and-loan banks joined by commercial banks and life-insurance companies. These institutions preferred to work with large-scale builders on large-scale projects, which typically meant apartments. Home production followed the money.[11]

Within the greatly expanded apartment field several additional factors stimulated co-ownership, and around one in twenty-five new apartments nationally in the 1920s was owned. In rich areas, the share was much higher. Along Park and Fifth Avenues in New York and the lakefront on Chicago's Gold Coast, about half of all buildings were co-op. Nearly every larger city, from Boston to Baltimore to Birmingham, had at least one high-class co-op building.[12] Data are scarce, but the number of projects reported in newspapers and trade journals suggest that by 1930 there were thirty thousand co-op units in metropolitan New York, five thousand in greater Chicago, three thousand in Washington, D.C., two thousand in California (half each in Southern California and in San Francisco), and another two thousand in other cities, combined.

One reason for this turn was an increase in the number of kinds of households that could afford homeownership but who preferred apartments, like those in which women worked outside the home. Another was improvements in the way co-ops were organized, managed, and sold, including the introduction of installment financing. A third was marketing. Co-op developers waged long and often highly visible sales campaigns in the 1920s, and like Isaac Gates, many Americans first learned about co-ownership through ads. Additionally, housing reformers and better-homes groups advocated for ownership of apartments in exhibitions that were widely covered. As with radio sets and automobiles, this publicity helped turn apartments into glamorous, if not quite mass-market, consumer objects.

Financial incentives to homeowners also stimulated co-ownership. Steep rent increases during and after World War I led many tenants to pursue homeownership, giving owner-occupied housing significant momentum, which was sustained after the return to normalcy by a buoyant economy. Rising resale prices, in turn, continually validated co-ownership, making it an appealing investment well into the second half of the decade (although at least one Cassandra warned at the peak of the market, in 1927, that the "real outcome of the first stages of the development [of co-ownership] will not be known until the country has gone through a reaction in real estate values.")[13] Many remained skeptical of buying what they could otherwise rent, and cost remained an issue for all but the rich. For tens of thousands of Americans, however, multifamily homeownership became an appealing way to live.

On the supply side, co-ownership proved an attractive alternative to rentals for speculative developers. Selling units rather than renting them out gave builders a chance at quick return on their capital investment in a project, allowing them to free their money for the next apartments. In practice, slow sales and high advertising costs often foiled this plan. For these and other reasons—including, presumably, wariness of a still unproven investment model—many of the largest-scale, longest-standing apartment developers continued to focus on rentals. Many younger, newer firms, however, found great financial success with for-sale buildings.

Wartime Housing Crisis

Demand for co-ownership had always fluctuated with larger economic cycles, and much of the growth in the 1920s was generated as a response to high inflation during and after World War I. Inflation meant rising rents and declining service. Both made the predictability of ownership more appealing. By 1920, average rents across the U.S. were thirty-five percent higher than they had been in 1914, with most of the increase since Armistice, in late 1918. These rises were far more pronounced in centers of war administration and production. In New York, for example, vacancy rates fell from nearly six percent in 1916 to one-third of one percent in 1920. Decrepit, long-empty tenements filled up again. In every city, landlords cut back on services, sometimes eliminating heat and hot water. Problems were compounded as rising rents encouraged speculation. Full rent-rolls inflated the value of buildings, prompting landlords to sell. New owners, with more cash invested, expected larger returns. Each Moving Day brought increases of anywhere from fifteen to a hundred percent, sometimes more.[14]

There were a variety of responses to the crisis. One was rent strikes, which the Socialist Party helped tenants organize beginning in 1917 and which became widespread in 1920. Organized tenants demanded and won temporary rent controls like the Ball Rent Act in more than a dozen cities and states. The housing crisis also prompted a number of more private responses. Landlords divided apartments into smaller ones, although city leaders, at least in New York, frowned upon this practice. Many families removed themselves from the rental market entirely by buying. As one advertisement announced in 1919: "Owing to the increased cost of labor and materials and the consequent lack of production, rent will increase this Fall and for years to come. By the ownership of one these apartments you pay no rent, merely your share of the actual running expenses." Unlike in rentals, it further advised, in a co-op you "have absolute control."[15]

As early as 1918 developers began working to create new co-ops. With material and labor in short supply, however, building from scratch was difficult. Instead, they produced co-ops by "converting" existing rental buildings to owner occupancy. The first conversions were undertaken by developers with experience in the field. New York's Walter Russell, one of the owners at the Sixty-seventh Street Studios who had begun speculatively developing co-ops in the decade before the war, appears to

have been the first. That year, he and another artist bought a rental building on West
Sixty-seventh Street, emptied it of tenants, renovated it, and sold the apartments.
They did the same at another nearby building a few months later.[16]

In Washington and Chicago, firms that were new to the co-op, such as Allan E.
Walker and Company, followed Russell's lead. Walker, under the advisement of an
enthusiastic sales agent named Edmund J. Flynn, began buying up-to-date buildings
(none was more than ten years old) in desirable neighborhoods in 1919. At the time
Washington had only two co-ops: one from 1891 and one from 1909, both developed
by small groups of friends for their own use. Flynn, however, was familiar with New
York co-ops and low-rent, mutual-aid housing in the U.K. When he learned that
Walker, a longtime developer of houses, was considering for-sale apartments, he
joined the firm specifically to develop and market them.

Washington's large numbers of professionals made it especially suited to co-
ownership. According to Flynn (1889–1983), the city had a "reservoir of Government
workers who were on the economic level of industrial workers but the comparison
ended there. Most of them were cultivated people. Cooperative apartments would
provide them with nice homes at a price they could afford." The first group of
buildings Flynn converted for Walker included Isaac Gates' Parkwood, the Hoyt
near Meridian Hill Park, as well as buildings in Georgetown and Lanier Heights,
near Rock Creek Park (see fig. 21). Flynn bought an apartment for himself at the
Hoyt, served on its board, and lived there until he moved to a new co-op that he
helped develop in the late 1920s.[17]

Mass Conversion

Conversion's low barriers to entry allowed ordinary groups of tenants to also initiate
the process. As rents spiraled up dozens of groups of tenants banded together
beginning in early 1920 to buy their homes from the landlord. In some buildings
tenants had already drawn together to protest rent increases. The leap toward
discussion of conversion would not have been great. So long as tenant groups offered
fair prices, many landlords appear to have been happy to sell, especially once
rent controls were imposed in New York and Washington (Chicago never adopted
such laws).[18]

Little is known about these tenant-led conversions. Many happened in expensive
buildings, like 1550 North State Parkway in Chicago, where tenants paid between
$52,500 and $72,500 ($1.9 to $2.6 million in 2010 dollars) for their apartments. Most,
however, happened in ordinary buildings in middle-class neighborhoods—Morningside
Heights, Harlem, and Washington Heights in Northern Manhattan; Fort Greene in
Brooklyn; and Evanston, just north of Chicago—signaling the emergence of a new

clientele for multifamily homeownership during the crisis. In New York's bohemian Greenwich Village at least one group of fifty writers and artists bought five old ten-family tenements and modernized them. The cost to each, including renovation, was $5,000. Developers, too, began to branch out to middle-class areas. The best-selling buildings during the crisis were, in fact, the cheaper ones. The Hoyt, for example, which was the least expensive Walker building, with units ranging from $4,000 to $5,900 ($145,000 to $210,000), sold out in one weekend. At the Parkwood, where apartments cost $11,000 to $13,000 ($395,000 to $465,000), sales took several months.[19]

Most people seem to have championed tenant-led conversions as victories for ordinary families because it offered a way to escape a challenging rental market. Typical newspaper headlines in the *Brooklyn Eagle* and the *New York Times* proclaimed "Tenants Buy Fine Apartment House to Avoid Gouging" and "Buying by Tenants Found Practical." The real-estate industry was even more vocal in articulating this position, presumably in part because conversion helped temper support for rent control and because in the absence of new construction, conversion generated work for brokers and lenders. According to one real-estate operator: "Instead of these co-operative plans being a menace to the public, we consider them for the public's greatest good." Another added that unless "co-operative house buying" were encouraged, "the breach between the profiteering landlord and tenant will become greater rather than less."[20] As one Walker ad put it, "In the light of existing conditions . . . the most economical way of living is to own your own habitation." This, it continued, puts one "beyond the influences of, and competitive disturbances in, rent and occupancy."[21]

Creating a co-op, with its many by-laws, was not simple; tenant-led groups appear to have had help. None of the developers known to have been active builders of co-ops seem to have been involved. Certain names appeared in connection with multiple conversion projects, but it remains unclear exactly who they were, how they became involved, what they did for tenants, and how they were paid. They may have been real-estate lawyers, brokers, or investors. While they surely profited, there is nothing in reports to suggest that they were unscrupulous or sought to exploit tenants.[22]

Many outside of real estate also agreed that the co-op could be of benefit. Echoing the Senate Committee on the District of Columbia, the *New York Times* argued that it would be "absurd" to condemn co-ops as a rule. So, too, did the courts. In one early lawsuit on the matter a Queens Municipal Court ruled that the new owners of converted buildings had no obligation to renew the leases of tenants who did not buy. The court based its decision on the logic that to extend this right to tenants would discourage conversion, which it saw as a public good.[23]

In New York, as many as one thousand buildings converted in the early 1920s.[24] In the immediate wake of the war, when conversion was most frenzied, rumors about nefarious practices and rent profiteering abounded. Especially in the spring of 1920, reports circulated of landlords who converted but made immediate family the sole owners of apartments, which they then rented out at rates in excess of those permitted under rent control. Others alleged that landlords, in violation of rent laws, forced tenants to buy or be evicted. Word of such abuses was so widespread that city leaders issued a public advisory and at least one alderman suggested that the city regulate or restrict conversions.[25] Investigation by the city's Tenement House Commission, however, failed to substantiate most of these claims.

To the contrary, New York leaders encouraged conversion, whether led by tenants or landlords. Commissioner Frank Mann endorsed the co-op, drafting guidelines for their conversion and operation. "There is nothing inherently wrong in selling multi-family houses on the co-operative plan," he wrote. "There are no more dangers in the pathway of co-operative ownership than in individual ownership of one and two family houses." In an interview with the *Times* he further clarified: "Under the tenant-ownership plan the tenant is protected against increase of rents and is assured a permanent home and is afforded a safe and profitable investment. There is no better asset to a community than for its citizens to be interested in home ownership."[26]

The Park Avenue Type

Despite this surge in middle-class co-ownership, rich families continued to dominate the market for co-op living in the 1920s. As shortages of materials and labor eased in the early 1920s the impetus to, and pace of, conversion diminished markedly. But interest in co-ownership remained higher than ever among the well-to-do, and developers began to construct new housing, much of it in the mold of the East Side projects of artist-developers like Henry Ward Ranger from before the war. Alongside myriad new suburban subdivisions and rental apartments, the 1920s saw around one thousand new co-op buildings nationally, with twenty thousand homes. At least a third of these were in city-center palace-type buildings. In New York the greatest concentration of these co-ops appeared on Park Avenue, which was in the process of being redeveloped after electrification of railroad tracks which

Fig. 22: Park Avenue, New York. Postcard, ca. 1930.

ran beneath it (fig. 22). Developers came to call this the Park Avenue type co-op: a modern, well-equipped building with large, expensive apartments in a first-class urban location, catering to rich cosmopolitans forgoing town houses. Many Park Avenue type co-ops were also built on other uptown East Side avenues, in the West Fifty-seventh Street corridor south of Central Park, and beyond. In Washington, several were built in Lanier Heights and on Connecticut and Massachusetts Avenues, in San Francisco on Russian Hill, in Chicago along the lakefront, and in Los Angeles in the MacArthur Park and mid-Wilshire districts west of downtown (fig. 23).

Fig. 23: The Gaylord, 3355 Wilshire Boulevard, Los Angeles, 1924. J. B. Lilly and P. B. Fletcher, developer; Walker & Eisen, architect. Advertisement, *Los Angeles Times*, February 28, 1924.

In New York and Chicago and to a lesser degree elsewhere, the Park Avenue type co-op tended to take the form an overscaled palazzo, rising ten, twelve, even twenty stories, set flush to the street and to adjacent buildings. If surrounded by lower-rise structures the building might appear as a skyscraping tower, although residential buildings were rarely as tall as the era's first-class office buildings. Buildings were clad in a mixture of expensive materials like limestone and more ordinary ones like terra-cotta and Colonial Revival red brick. Windows were large and plentiful, typically with double-hung sashes and small panes of glass set in painted muntins to engender feelings of hominess.

"Faintly forbidding though these habitations be on the outside," one observer noted, "within they have individuality and warmth."[27] Owners and guests entered through understated, staffed lobbies, decorated like the foyer of a home (fig. 24). The rest of the first floor usually housed commonly owned suites for doctors and other professional tenants, or extra maids' rooms that homeowners could buy. Professional suites often had separate outside entrances; domestic workers and trades people also had a separate entrance leading to a service elevator. Attended elevators carried residents and guests to small landings with doors to one or two apartments,

These pictures show parts of the lobby in Alden Park Manor, Brookline, Massachusetts.
The lobby in Alden Park Manor, Philadelphia, will be equally as good.

Fig. 24: Alden Park Manor Brookline (today Longwood Towers), 20 Chapel Street, Boston, 1924–25. C. C. Mitchell and Lawrence E. Jones, developers; Harold F. Kellogg, architect. View of lobby. *Alden Park Manor Philadelphia*, prospectus.

and sometimes directly into the apartment itself. Units were typically one to a floor or two to a floor but spread over two stories, employing a modified, nonstudio duplex plan.[28]

Among the well-to-do such buildings became a standard housing type in the 1920s, rivaling the town house in price and status. As economist Coleman Woodbury noted, the "social prestige once associated with the ownership of a big house seems to have waned in favor of a 'grand apartment' in some 'Manor' or 'Arms.'" More than 125 new co-ops were built on the East Side of Manhattan alone. If promotional materials for some of these co-ops are to be believed, there was hardly anyone in the *Social Register* by the end of the decade who did not own an apartment. As writer Will Irwin mused in 1927: "Only the newly rich, I thought to myself; the seasoned families will never live on apartment-house terms, like larvae in a honey-comb. And yet—every month some member of the 'exclusive set' was giving up his mansion . . . and 'buying a duplex' in a Park Avenue apartment-house."[29]

In Chicago, co-ownership made comparable gains. In 1920, the city had just two co-op buildings, including the "millionaires' flat" at 1130 Lake Shore Drive, built in 1911. After the war, however, a majority of new first-class apartment buildings were owner-occupied. North Lake Shore Drive between Walton Place and Lincoln

Park, one of the most exclusive districts in the city, had six apartment buildings in 1916, of which only one was a co-op; by 1929, it had sixteen buildings, of which ten were owned.[30]

Designed by leading architects—including Warren & Wetmore, Walker & Gillette, Rouse & Goldstone, and James Gamble Rogers in New York, and Holabird & Roche, Robert S. De Golyer, Benjamin Marshall, and Fugard & Knapp in Chicago—as well as specialists in the field of apartment design like New York's Rosario Candela and J. E. R. Carpenter, Park Avenue type apartments typically cost $30,000 for seven or eight rooms ($1.3 million in 2010), $60,000 for eleven rooms ($2.5 million), and $100,000 for a fifteen-room duplex ($4.2 million) in New York, and in Chicago somewhat less. (By way of comparison, prices in both cities were similar to those fetched for neighboring town houses, and about half again higher than comparable houses in expensive suburbs.) The very largest suites fetched several times these amounts. One forty-one-room duplex on Fifth Avenue, for example, sold for $375,000 ($15 million); a slightly smaller penthouse nearby sold for $425,000 ($17.5 million). Buyers often spent just as much customizing interiors—in one extreme case, $1.1 million, bringing the total cost to $1.5 million ($60 million in 2010). Monthly maintenance for this unit was about $5,800 ($240,000).[31]

In other cities, high-class co-ops tended to be more modest. In Washington's 1661 Crescent Place, for example, which was perhaps the city's best-equipped co-op in the 1920s (and the first apartment house included in the *Washington Post*'s Home Beautiful exhibition, in 1928) the developers included apartments of four rooms to ten rooms, with the largest duplexes selling for around $35,000 ($1.5 million).[32] A handful of similarly well-equipped co-ops were also built as seasonal housing at resort areas in the 1920s, most notably at Long Beach, California, but also at Long Beach, New York, on Long Island, and in Miami, St. Petersburg, and Jacksonville, Florida. To some this made little sense. "With all the loose land in Florida," asked one writer, "who wants to buy an apartment when he might have a purple stucco bungalow, is somewhat of a mystery." The appeal, at least in part, was that co-ownership allowed one to buy in popular locations, like the oceanfront, "where otherwise only the rich, and few of them, could find foot room."[33]

Jackson Heights

Alongside the Park Avenue type co-op, another more novel kind of co-owned complex emerged in the 1920s, called the "garden apartment." The garden apartment had little precedent before World War I. It was devised to serve a new kind of client: people with steady, middling incomes—often affluent professionals, but also workers—who, following the postwar crisis, preferred ownership but wished to

live in a modern apartment rather than a
suburban house. Many such families opted
for second-tier buildings in neighborhoods
like Chicago's South Shore and Hyde Park
districts. But following the suburban trend
that distinguished so much of American
life in the 1920s, others chose new co-op
colonies built in leafy peripheral sections
like the Fens in Boston, Fairmount Park
in Philadelphia, Van Cortlandt Park in the
Bronx, Cleveland Park in Washington,
and Indian Boundary Park in Chicago.
Although many rentals were also built
in this mode in the 1920s, the pioneering
examples were co-ops.

Fig. 25: The Chateau, Eightieth and Eighty-first
Streets, Thirty-fourth Avenue, Jackson Heights,
New York, 1922. Queensboro Corporation, developer;
Andrew J. Thomas, architect. Advertisement, *New
York Times*, January 23, 1923.

The prototype for the co-op garden-
apartment community, and the largest of
all nationally with some fifteen hundred
apartments, was Jackson Heights, Queens
(fig. 25). In agricultural use until subways and commuter rail reached the area in
the early 1910s, Jackson Heights took shape when developer Edward Archibald
MacDougall traveled to Berlin just before the war. He had already built a few dozen
row houses and half a dozen small rental apartments at the site, and he planned to
develop most of the rest of his 350 acres with bungalows. In the Charlottenburg
section of Berlin, however, he saw a new possibility: high-quality, low-density groups
of apartments built around common recreational spaces in a suburban setting.[34]

In this type of design, which recalled college dormitories more than typical
apartment houses, MacDougall (1874–1944) immediately saw the potential appeal to
middle-class New York families. Upon his return, he began the Garden Apartments,
a complex of fourteen buildings designed by George H. Wells that included rear
gardens and, in a break from urban profit-making norms, sat back from the street
several feet (fig. 26). MacDougall added community amenities, including a clubhouse
fashioned out of an old farmhouse on the site, and the first of thirty eventual tennis
courts. After the war was over MacDougall further developed this recreational
program, adding a riding "academy" and a twelve-hole golf course (fig. 27).

Working with a new architect, Andrew Jackson Thomas, he also more fully
realized the garden-apartment idea. Thomas (1875–1965) was a self-trained designer
dedicated to improving housing for ordinary wage-earning families. According

to housing activist Louis Pink, Thomas was a "genius and enthusiast, excitable, talkative, always making speeches in favor of better housing and often commanding newspaper space on the first page. Housing is his religion." Thomas had grown up in tenements in New York and, when orphaned at thirteen, collected rents for slum landlords to support himself. He was frustrated by his first apartment-house commissions, before the war, which offered him little creative freedom. In MacDougall he found an ideal client.[35]

Thomas worked out his vision for the American garden apartment at his first project for MacDougall: Linden Court. The buildings themselves were generic: red brick "modern colonial" walk-ups whose economy was relieved only by round-arch front doors, thin bands of Spanish roof tile peeking above the cornices, and other vaguely Mediterranean touches (fig. 28).[36] The site plan, by contrast, was innovative. Unlike Wells's complex, Thomas conceived of Linden Court as an entire perimeter-block unit, with ten shallow buildings enclosing a spacious interior quadrangle (fig. 29). Each structure housed twelve to sixteen apartments of four to six rooms, with garages on the garden side for three to six cars.[37] The design served as the basis for all future complexes at Jackson Heights, although over time parking was moved to allow for more complete use of the courtyards as green space (fig. 30) and the buildings grew to six stories, acquired elevators, and assumed more whimsical, richer looking façades.

Linden Court also broke new ground for being a co-op. It is not known whether MacDougall conceived of the project, which opened in 1919, as owner-occupied. The Garden Apartments of 1917 had been rentals (although MacDougall would convert them to co-op, in 1925, changing their name to the Greystone Apartments). Given the rapidly escalating costs, rent strikes, and rent controls of the postwar years, becoming a landlord would hardly have appealed to any developer at the time Linden Court got under way. MacDougall's lender for the project, the Title Guarantee and Trust Company, agreed and awarded him a half-million-dollar mortgage for what was the largest group of individually owned apartments to be built since Philip Hubert's Central Park Apartments. Unlike that earlier example, Linden Court was a financial success.[38]

Despite the volatile rental conditions, when sales began in the summer of 1919 Linden Court did not immediately attract the upper-middle-class buyers MacDougall had intended it for. To convince 144 people to invest in a new kind of community in a new, fairly remote part of town, he orchestrated a great marketing campaign. It emphasized the economic value of ownership ("Do you Wish to Reduce Your Present High Cost of Living?") and Thomas's innovative physical form ("Sunshine in Every Room," "Ample Garage Accommodations"), as well as unique

Fig. 26: The Garden Apartments (today the Greystone Apartments), Eightieth Street between Thirty-fifth and Thirty-seventh Avenues, Jackson Heights, New York, 1916–17. Queensboro Corporation, developer; George W. Wells, architect. Photograph by Wurts Bros., ca. 1917.

Fig. 27: Jackson Heights golf course. View showing Hawthorne Court (Seventy-sixth Street between Thirty-fifth and Thirty-seventh Avenues, Jackson Heights, New York. Queensboro Corporation, developer; George H. Wells, architect, 1922). *Architectural Forum*, November 1922.

Fig. 28: Linden Court, Eighty-fourth and Eighty-fifth Streets between Roosevelt and Thirty-seventh Avenues, Jackson Heights, New York, 1919–21. Queensboro Corporation, developer; Andrew J. Thomas, architect. General view.

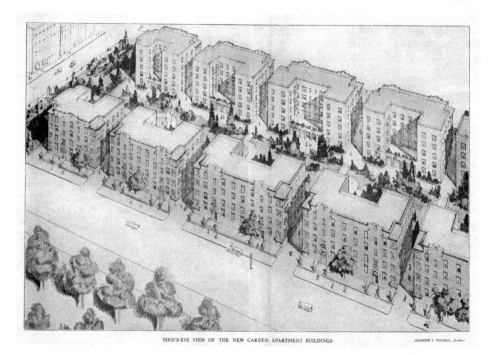

BIRD'S-EYE VIEW OF THE NEW GARDEN APARTMENT BUILDINGS

Fig. 29: Linden Court, bird's-eye view. *Jackson Heights News: The New Garden Apartments, Co-operative Ownership Plan*, prospectus.

Fig. 30: Cambridge Court, Eighty-fifth and Eighty-sixth Streets between Roosevelt and Thirty-seventh Avenues, Jackson Heights, New York, 1922–23. Queensboro Corporation, developer; George W. Wells, architect. Photograph by Wurts Bros., 1925.

shared elements ("Have You Golf Links, Tennis Courts, Garden, Playgrounds at your front door?"). Ads also sold an idea of community. A central message was the promise of a "Real Home Community" (fig. 31). Unlike your current rental, they suggested, Jackson Heights felt like a permanent home. This notion hinged on collegiality through leisure—"home," ads implied, included quick access to tennis and golf. It also hinged on clearly denoting who was invited and who was not.[39]

The promises of happiness, personal fulfillment, and high social status—transformation through purchase of a real-estate commodity—put MacDougall at the vanguard of American real-estate marketing. The media he used were similarly advanced. Most ads for housing in 1919 (and before) resembled overscaled classified listings: dull blocks of dense text, with only the occasional elevation, plan, or blurry half-tone photograph. MacDougall, a pacesetter in the emerging "science" of real-estate marketing, greatly increased the size of ads, and the size and visual sophistication of the images they contained. Following his sales message, he also emphasized people. The illustrations in many ads left the buildings in

JACKSON HEIGHTS is a Real Home Community

Where the carefully selected tenants and resident owners enjoy tennis, golf, have playgrounds for children, and all forms of recreational and social activities.

4, 5 and 6 Room Garden Apartments
(Now under construction)

On Our Collective Ownership Plan

The only real protection against rent increases—a method of helping apartment house tenants to reduce their rent to the actual cost of operation. $2,500 to $3,750 to be invested.
References Required

For further details call or write

The Queensboro Corporation

Manhattan Office   Jackson Heights Office
50 E. 42d St., Cor. Madison Ave.   Opposite 25th St. Subway Station
Telephone Murray Hill 7057   Telephone Newtown 2361

To visit Jackson Heights by most convenient route take Subway to Grand Central, transfer to Queensboro Subway (Corona Line) to 25th St. Sta.
22 MINUTES FROM 42D ST.

Fig. 31: Linden Court. Advertisement, *New York Times*, August 30, 1919.

the background, focusing instead on children and young couples at play. Some eliminated the buildings entirely in favor of vaguely rendered interiors with occupants on their way outside for community activities.[40] MacDougall was also quick to exploit radio. The first radio networks, which were created after the war, were supported, commercial-free, by manufacturers as a way to sell receivers. In 1922, however, AT&T began testing a new model, creating a new station in New York that would sell airtime, allowing people to broadcast whatever they liked for pay. The very first program was a ten-minute spot for Jackson Heights co-ops. MacDougall also did cross-promotions with department stores, sponsoring, for example, a "golf school" at Gimbels.[41]

The relentless merchandising—along with the unique physical form and community facilities—helped MacDougall sell fifteen hundred apartments by 1925. Jackson Heights became known worldwide for its high-quality design and unique blend of co-ownership and suburban facilities.[42]

Suburban Garden Apartments

Although Jackson Heights eventually proved a poor match for conventional suburbs—even MacDougall returned to building houses in the late 1920s—sales proved that the garden-apartment co-op had a place in New York's metropolitan housing landscape. Other homebuilders emulated it. In Northern Manhattan, Charles V. Paterno developed Hudson View Gardens on the site of his old country house (fig. 32). The new complex, which took advantage of the sloping site to offer sweeping views of the Hudson River, contained a mixture of four- and six-story buildings designed by George Fred Pelham. Although it lacked an interior quadrangle, it clearly drew inspiration from Thomas's Jackson Heights plan.[43] Other developers made more modest efforts to incorporate garden-apartment elements in Manhattan. Several "garden plan" co-ops designed by the reform-minded architect Arthur C. Holden, for example, reserved up to half their East Side lots for rear yards.[44]

Garden-apartment co-ops also appeared beyond New York City. Suburban homeowners often resisted multifamily development and, according to sociologist George Lundberg, "denounced apartment dwellers as 'social tramps' whose ambition it was to have 'a room or two, steam-heated, near a delicatessen, a couple of golf sticks [clubs], and a car.'"[45] Nevertheless, the greatest concentration of garden apartments outside of Jackson Heights appeared in Westchester County, in the highly restricted town of Bronxville. At least one each was also built in half a dozen other towns in Westchester, northern New Jersey, and Long Island. In Washington, complexes such as Tilden Gardens, Hampshire Gardens, and the Cleveland Park Apartments all sold well. In Chicago, Gubbins, McDonnell & Blietz developed several complexes fronting Indian Boundary Park, while others appeared in Oak Park, Wilmette, and Evanston.

As in New York, these buildings seemed to appeal to middle-class families too busy or small to want whole houses, yet who were not interested in high-rise city-center living. As one Chicago woman wrote: "We should like comfortable, modern apartments but are not the least interested in the fancy appurtenances featured in the ultra smart coöps. . . . We are not looking for a cubby in a 27 story skyscraper, but should be satisfied to live in a 'walk-up' building."[46]

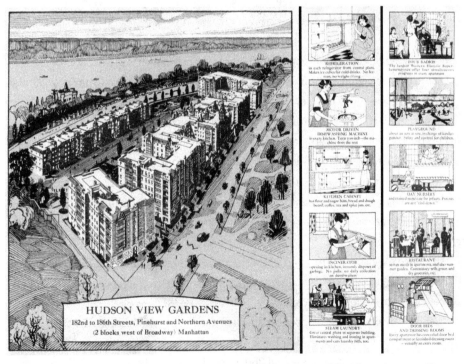

Fig. 32: Hudson View Gardens, 182nd to 186th Streets, Pinehurst and Northern Avenues, New York, 1923–25. Charles V. Paterno, developer; George Fred Pelham, architect. Collage of details from *Hudson View Gardens*, prospectus.

Fig. 33: Cleveland Park Apartments, 3018–28 Porter Street NW, Washington, D.C., 1924. Edmund J. Flynn, sales agent; Monroe and Robert Bates Warren, developers; James E. Cooper, architect. Detail of Advertisement, *Washington Post,* September 7, 1924.

Suburban sites allowed developers to be more generous with dimensions, shared elements, and open space while keeping costs competitive. At one Westchester project, for example, four-room apartments included seven closets and master bedrooms of sixteen by thirty feet. Even many small-scale suburban projects included restaurants, "hotel" rooms for owners' guests, formal gardens, covered parking, and, occasionally, tennis courts and swimming pools. The lower cost of land in suburbia also allowed developers to loosen Thomas's perimeter-block physical form. In Washington, for example, projects like Hampshire Gardens reduced the scale of buildings to three stories, while at the Cleveland Park Apartments the apartment-house model was rejected altogether for multiple freestanding buildings that looked like large single-family houses but in fact contained six apartments each (fig. 33). Chicago's Park Gables (and Park Manor, Crest, and Castles), which also rose just three stories, opened directly to Indian Boundary Park (fig. 34). As in Thomas's arrangement, units in all of these projects had at least two exposures—often three or four. More exposures improved illumination and the flow of air. They also made apartments feel more like houses. A number of developers emphasized this aspect, marketing their co-ops as "bungalow type" apartments.[47]

Developers also experimented with taller garden-style buildings. In 1922, for example, work began on Alden Park Manor in Detroit, a rental complex that housed around 350 apartments—and 350 cars—in four, eight-story buildings. Two years later, its developers built Alden Park Manor, a co-op in Brookline, Massachusetts, just outside of Boston. It was followed by Alden Park Philadelphia,

designed by Edwin Rorke, a co-op next to Fairmount Park in Germantown (fig. 35).
Although the Pennsylvania site was far larger, the developers built up rather than
out. The surrounding grounds housed swimming pools, tennis courts, putting
greens, gardens, and woods. An initial phase comprised three, nine-story towers
of cruciform plan, a model previously tested at Brookline. The towers in the park
proved popular and later phases rose taller, with four, fourteen-story Y-plan
towers (two freestanding, two attached). The Y-plan was also employed at some

beach resort high-rises in the 1920s (see
fig. 96). It had the further advantage
over the X-plan of offering every window
unobstructed views.[48]

Some saw this migration of the tall
apartment house to suburbia as odd. In
one *New Yorker* cartoon a real-estate
agent directs a young couple toward
an image of a skyscraper and asks,
"Something in the suburbs? Say about
the thirty-sixth floor?" Another shows a
woman in a ninth-floor apartment next to
a window that looks out onto another tall
building. "You and Stanley simply *must*
come out here for real Thanksgiving Day
in the country," she says into the phone.
"We're in apartment C9."[49] Yet however
improbable suburban apartments might
have seemed, as the advertising manager

Fig. 34: Park Gables, 2438–60 West Estes Avenue,
Chicago. Gubbins, McDonnell & Blietz, developer.
Chicago Tribune, March 25, 1928.

Fig. 35: Alden Park, Wissahickon Avenue and School House Lane, Philadelphia, 1925–26.
C. C. Mitchell and Lawrence E. Jones, developers; Edwin [Edwyn] Rorke, architect. Photograph
by Aero Services Corporation, 1933.

for one developer of Westchester co-ops observed, many people wished to maintain
their homes "with the minimum amount of effort" but also desired more "fresh air,
sunshine and scenery" than Manhattan congestion permitted. For them, suburban
co-ops made perfect sense.[50]

100% Co-ops and Paid Management
The co-op's great flexibility not only permitted new shapes, sizes, and geographies
in the 1920s but new ways of organizing and managing buildings. Efforts to improve
collective homeownership in these directions were part of a trend toward increased
efficiency in home-building and -management: single- and multi-family, rented and
owned. Real estate could never be as streamlined as Henry Ford's assembly lines
but as the market for new, well-equipped housing expanded and the proliferation
of new subdivisions and apartment complexes generated opportunities for new

economies of scale in production and operation, best practices were codified to improve profits. Developers in particular worked to adopt uniform proprietary leases (or, as they were sometimes called "certificates of ownership") and, for houses, deeds. Across the board, the real-estate field worked to adopt "scientific" management practices. These many innovations emerged incrementally, but were broadcast widely through new national channels such as conferences and publications of the National Association of Real Estate Boards (NAREB).[51]

Efforts to improve ownership and management of co-owned apartments was also necessitated by the fact that the "private" co-op necessarily became less cloistered in the 1920s. In its earlier phases co-op living had, in practice, been by invitation only. Projects were small and many were developed by groups of friends. And although disagreements among owners occasionally went to the courts, the clublike atmosphere helped minimize disharmony.

This model continued in the 1920s at projects like Forty-nine East Seventy-ninth Street, developed in 1925 by a group of friends led by the etiquette writer Emily Price Post. According to Post in her 1930 book *Personality of a House:* "If you can pay a somewhat startling price, nothing is easier than finding apartments with good-sized front rooms, adequate closets, and first-class plumbing; but finding one with a light kitchen and servants' dining-room and four or even three bedrooms for them goes only with a front part of enormous size and a rental that is . . . enormouser." Her solution was to round up a group of women (who, like her, owned country houses at Tuxedo Park, New York), hire architect Kenneth M. Murchison, buy a lot, and develop themselves. The result was a fourteen-story palazzo with custom-designed apartments for each owner. Some had as many as eight servants' bedrooms and four servants' bathrooms.[52]

Post's co-op was atypical. Increasingly, co-ops were being built speculatively by large-scale developers, where co-owners were strangers. It thus became critical that co-ops be set up to accommodate, and withstand, conflict. One strategy was adoption of full owner-occupancy: the "100% co-op." Through World War I, most co-ops in New York were organized on Hubert's old home-club model, with up to half of units owned in common and rented out to defray the homeowners' monthly maintenance. This plan reflected the financial anxieties of many early co-op owners who, as artists and writers, presumably had a lot of equity but irregular income. Some, like Walter Russell, continued to defend this model in the 1920s, but it rapidly fell out of favor.[53]

Excising rentals relieved new co-owners of the burdens of being a landlord. Furthermore, while often effective in lowering owners' maintenance costs, "semi-cooperatives" allowed little security in the event of a poor rental market. There was also a perceived social problem. Because apartments for owners were

typically larger and better equipped than those for renters the system could result
in a mixture of social types within buildings. This was at odds with conventional
marketing wisdom of the 1920s which privileged homogeneity over difference. Many
in the field of real estate, especially sales and managing agents, claimed including
rental units could destabilize a building's social appeal and undercut resale values.[54]

Perhaps most importantly, the hundred-percent plan saved buyers money
since they did not have to acquire an ownership share of the rental units. New
institutional lenders and the salaried men and women who became the predominant
buyers of apartments in the 1920s clearly seemed to prefer this model. By 1930 four
out of five co-ops on Manhattan's East Side were hundred-percent, as well as nearly
all of those in the suburbs, in Chicago, and in Washington, D.C.[55]

Although eliminating income-producing rentals left owners responsible
for meeting all of their buildings' maintenance obligations, the ongoing cost of
ownership (exclusive of any financing) was still cheaper than renting because it
cut out vacancies and other turnover expenses, which equalled ten to fifteen
percent of units' monthly value. For example, in apartments with an annual rental
of $1,000, landlords lost an average of $100 to $150 each year between tenants
and repainting, repairs, and advertising. Owner-occupied buildings incurred no
such overhead.[56]

Another innovation of the 1920s was full-time "professional" management.
Before the war, co-owners had to be quite active in building affairs. Paid
management, which in residential buildings was undertaken mainly by large-scale
rental and sales agencies, relieved this burden. The managing agent called the first
meeting of new owners once all the apartments had been sold and helped them elect
a board of directors. As in rental buildings—where paid management had become
common just before World War I—these firms also assumed most day-to-day duties,
including managing accounts, hiring and supervising staff, and buying supplies.
When minor conflicts among owners arose or there were questions about house
rules, the manager could be trusted to resolve problems without having to burden
the board of directors or turn to the courts.[57]

Like the hundred-percent co-op, paid management appealed to lenders, in this
case because it promised to make buildings run more smoothly and, presumably,
better retain their value. As one writer noted, bankers "realize that coöperative
enterprises based upon mutual effort . . . have never worked in America. The
individualistic American is disinclined to personal effort for the common good. He
feels no especial need of the support of the group to which he may not be attached
six months hence. He will coöperate with his dollars, but that is usually about his
coöperative limit. He will not give time or thought to the details of any business out

of which he is not getting his major income and interest in life. Failure to recognize this American characteristic has wrecked many well-meant coöperative enterprises of various sorts." Indeed, he continued, some "early efforts at coöperative home owning nearly went on the rocks because they were based on the plan of every tenant-owner and his wife having a finger in the pie." Without the manager's "almost arbitrary authority in matters over which groups and committees are prone to quarrel or which they are reasonably sure to neglect," he concluded, the co-op could never have become so common.[58]

While expensive—a typical annual fee at an East Side building was $6,000 ($250,000 in 2010)—paid management also offered co-owners savings through bulk purchase of coal and other materials across multiple properties. Such savings could be substantial because the largest firms managed fifty, sometimes a hundred, buildings. An additional financial advantage was that, at least once postwar inflation had subsided, some firms guaranteed their fees. By the mid-1920s most co-ops employed such firms, leaving the board responsible only for evaluating managers' work and screening resales and subleases. As one Park Avenue co-op owner noted casually when asked what he and his fellow board members really had to do: "The only important matter which I can recall now was to decide whether the door men should wear long trousers or knee breeches. We had quite a spirited debate."[59]

References Required

As in earlier eras, a major appeal of collective homeownership in the 1920s was that it promised to make the "public" apartment house "private." Exclusion was an important part of this process. Some justification for screening was that co-ownership required financial vetting. One did not, it was argued, wish to own a building with people unable to meet their obligations (although when apartments required thousands or tens of thousands of dollars in cash to buy, it is questionable how much additional proof of fiscal fitness was necessary). The primary concern, however, was social vetting, especially as buildings became larger and more anonymous.

In the xenophobic and status-conscious 1920s, developers found that selling an aura of clublike snobbery paid well, while costing them nothing. Virtually every co-op builder exploited the promise of social transformation through exclusion as a sales tactic, insisting that a happy home was a restricted one. As an inducement to preconstruction sales, some agents even awarded first buyers the right to approve of subsequent ones. To promote this arrangement at Chicago's 1120 North Lake Shore Drive, an eighteen-story midpriced co-op (five rooms from $12,800) designed by Robert S. De Golyer, the sales agent boasted to the *Tribune*, in 1924, "It's going to be about as hard for the first five [buyers] to prove their right to residence as it would be for a Chinaman to get into the K.K.K. Ability to pay the purchase money will be only a minor consideration in the searching scrutiny into the applicants' claims to entrance."[60]

The emergence of formal processes for exclusion in co-ops reflected a more general emphasis in real estate in the 1920s on creating stable, predictable environments that, unlike so much of the American metropolis, would maintain their physical quality, social character, and, in turn, resale value. After decades of experimentation with zoning and deed restrictions—concerning occupancy and ethnicity but also physical upkeep—both kinds of restrictions became widespread in the 1920s, and were promoted heavily by groups like NAREB.[61]

Sales agents in the 1920s made much of their ability to select people who would make good co-owners and neighbors, and seemed to believe that a track record in this regard was essential to attracting business from developers and home-seekers. In a presentation to the Cooperative Apartment Division of the National Association of Real Estate Boards, Robert Bates Warren distilled conventional wisdom on the matter. Warren had developed several high-class co-ops in Washington, including the Cleveland Park Apartments (see fig. 33). In his talk he emphasized that it was the sales agent's responsibility to "sort out" families and ensure they were placed in buildings only with others in "their particular strata of society." He warned that to grab quick sales commissions by doing otherwise was to work against human nature and risk "snares" and a building full of unhappy owners. "Although we live in a free democratic country," he explained, "the old saying of 'Birds of a feather flock together' still holds true. It is human nature and . . . the Realtor must know the feathers of the birds and thereby determine to which flock they belong. . . . In our country according to the tenets of our forefathers, all of us are created free and equal and should be able to enjoy life, liberty and the pursuit of happiness to our liking. But down through the ages there has been a distinction between classes . . . [that] still exists today in spite of the high sounding phrases of our respected forefathers." He urged his fellow developers and agents to develop the ability to "size up" applicants quickly and accurately while maintaining a diplomatic tone that would not alienate buyers who could be steered elsewhere.[62]

Stories about co-ops in popular magazines supported these egregious retrograde fantasies. *Saturday Evening Post* offered for entertainment the spectacle of an "infuriated multimillionaire" who was refused entry by a sales agent to an $80,000 co-op ($3.4 million), despite making the "almost pathetic" gesture of offering an additional $50,000 ($2.1 million). The reason for the rejection was that among earlier buyers were several "acquaintances or associates" who for "reasons satisfactory to themselves . . . had [n]ever had any social relations with him" and who believed that the man's "wife's public manners . . . would depreciate the value of the property." The rebuke was thus framed as being better for everyone rather than as an example of snobbery or, presumably, anti-Semitism. "This man and his family would not have been happy in the enforced neighborliness" of a co-op, claimed the writer, in which the "standard of manners and an outlook on life" was so different from the other owners'. Furthermore, he claimed that New York had so many co-ops that "almost any family" could find one "within its means and with the assurance of congenial neighbors." If not, "it is a perfectly simple procedure . . . for the seeker to find enough like-minded associates to buy an apartment house or have one built for their own use." Very few families, of course, had the time, let alone money, for this task.[63]

Although rarely mentioned directly, exclusion primarily concerned ethnicity. Black prospects were generally regarded by whites as so beyond the social pale in this era that it was not even necessary to exclude them formally; those few Black families with enough money to buy a co-op in a white building rarely tried because they understood they had no chance of gaining entry. Elite institutions from co-ops to colleges to resorts did, however, delight in prohibiting Jews, Catholics, and everyone else not of Protestant Anglo-American stock. This was true even in housing developed by Jewish and Italian operators.

Among those prohibited from buying homes were the Seals. In 1923, Dr. J. Coleman Seal, a dentist at New York's Beth Israel Hospital, and his wife started looking to buy an East Side Manhattan apartment. Three major sales agents, according to the *Chicago Tribune*, told Mrs. Seal "that she, being a Jew, would not be taken in." Two of the brokers "freely admitted" to her that "restrictions against Jews are common." In its investigation of the matter, the *Tribune* found that restrictions were in fact becoming more severe. "The invasion of many families from more humble quarters of the city, with fortunes made during the war, is represented as partly responsible." In its own defense, an executive of one of the agencies, Pease and Elliman, said, "We advise owners, our clients, against such restrictions because we have found that Jews are just as good tenants as gentiles of the same class. . . . But many still insist on excluding them." The Seal family eventually did find a suitable home on Park Avenue, but only in a rental.[64]

Co-ops far from Park Avenue also excluded. Many did so very publicly, as though restrictions might impart some Gold Coast sheen. No developer waged a longer, louder, and more thorough war against social heterogeneity in the effort to sell apartments than Jackson Heights' Edward MacDougall. Ads for his first co-op initially focused on the economy of ownership over renting. When the apartments did not immediately sell, however, MacDougall tried a new tactic: "References

Required." Later ads were yet more aggressive. One bluntly asked: "Who are your neighbors?" Another stated that the development, "socially, is strictly 'American.'"[65] Ads further underscored this message by depicting residents engaged in the community's self-consciously genteel recreational activities (see figs. 25, 31). Lists of buyers that he published to prove the development's social pedigree—a common sales tactic in the 1920s—confirmed that MacDougall sold almost exclusively to people of English or Scottish descent, or those passing as such. As one longtime resident later recalled, there were "no Catholics, Jews, or dogs in those days."[66]

The architecture at Jackson Heights underscored this message. Linden Court, the first co-op, was extremely simple (see fig. 28). Later complexes, however, employed a pastiche of historicist styles that conveyed genteel privilege (see fig. 25). This eclecticism spoke to homeowners of permanence, "home," and "community."[67] Norman and Tudor motifs appeared everywhere in residential architecture in the U.S. in this era, including in neighborhoods built for non-Anglo ethnic groups. But when looking at Jackson Heights complexes like the Elm, Hawthorne, and Cambridge Courts (see figs. 27, 30), which George H. Wells modeled explicitly on Harvard's Old Yard residence halls, it is difficult not to see deep cultural anxieties of a Northern European nation awash with immigrants from Southern and Eastern Europe. As architectural historian Gwendolyn Wright has argued, the "quaint stylistic diversity of American suburban architecture belied hostilities against ethnic minorities." Such hostilities were in wide evidence not just in design but in the postwar red scare directed against Italians and Jews, and in the campaign to pass 1924's Immigration Act, which all but closed U.S. doors to them.[68]

The harm done by restrictions did not go unnoticed. Brave prospects like the Seals occasionally volunteered their humiliation in protest. Other times—in an ironic break from the promise of community through exclusion—progressive homeowners turned against their more conservative neighbors. In 1927, for example, a co-op owner in New York's Washington Square filed suit against her board of directors when it refused to allow her to rent her place to a Jewish family. The prospect, she claimed, was "a member of a prominent [law] firm, married, of unimpeachable moral character, a quiet and satisfactory neighbor, of excellent financial standing and director of a trust company." Given his enviable credentials, she charged that her neighbors' refusal to admit him, even as a renter, was "arbitrary and unreasonable." The court, however, disagreed.[69] Meanwhile, most mainstream media, including Jewish-owned newspapers like the *New York Times*, all but ignored the problem while running ads for houses and apartments that its publishers could not buy. Ethnic papers like the *Forward*, by contrast, openly criticized MacDougall and others who profited by exploiting people's hunger for unearned social status.[70]

Financing Ownership

Among the many efforts to improve co-ownership in the 1920s, the most crucial was the introduction of financing. As a rule, housing cost far more than most people could afford. In the 1920s, the absolute cheapest apartments in older, converted buildings sold for $4,000 or $5,000, and most buildings asked two or three times that. As late as 1926, only 27,000 (of approximately 700,000) men in Manhattan earned more than $10,000 a year ($410,000 in 2010 dollars). Although one study showed the average income on Park Avenue was $75,000, a typical middle-class family earned $1,800 to $3,000 ($75,000 to $125,000). Outside of New York earnings were lower; nationally, average wages were about $1,200 in 1921 and $1,450 by 1928.[71] These rates were incompatible with ownership of a co-op. Financing plans, which permitted one to put down as little as twenty or thirty percent in cash and to pay the rest in equal monthly installments over anywhere from three to twenty years, broadened access to ownership.

To pay for his apartment at the Parkwood in Washington, for example, Isaac Gates took advantage of a plan offered by Walker that allowed him to finance up to two-thirds of the cost, payable in equal monthly installments over eleven years, seven months. "I might have made a financial arrangement by which I could have paid cash altogether," he explained to Congress, "but I deemed it inadvisable from a business standpoint to put eight or twelve thousand dollars into a project which had not been sufficiently investigated by me to know whether it would be successful or not. So I bought on the installment plan, paying one-third cash, and the balance is paid in monthly installments of $126 [$4,600]. At the end of 139 months I will stop paying on the apartment and will own it." This seemed more reasonable to him than spending $125 or $150 a month to rent a comparable apartment.[72]

Buying "on terms" through installments had a long informal history by the 1920s but remained a marginal practice. It had been stigmatized by the middle class and, in particular, middle-class men for its associations with the poor and with women, neither of whom, it was supposed, could resist credit's temptations. The automobile industry, however, did much to legitimize installment buying between 1915 and 1930, making it a mainstream way to handle expensive purchases, including apartments.[73]

Jackson Heights succeeded in part because the Queensboro Corporation offered extraordinarily liberal terms. Thanks to project financing from the Title Guarantee and Trust Company and, later, the Metropolitan Life Company, one could put down as little as ten percent with the balance paid over as many as twenty years.[74] Under this plan a typical five-room apartment in an elevator building, which included a front bedroom, a rear bedroom (with en suite bath and dressing room), dining room, living room, and kitchen, along with a maid's room in the basement, cost $10,400

($490,000). One could, however, put down $2,000 ($94,000) and finance the rest over thirteen and a half years with payments of $73; extra payments shortened the loan period. Buying on these terms was not inexpensive. With monthly maintenance charges of $77, the total cost to the homeowner was $150 ($7,000). But it appealed to white-collar families with secure, high salaries. Most buyers, indeed, were in the professions or business, with a typical income of perhaps $5,500 ($260,000).[75]

Even among the rich, financing helped popularize co-ownership. Co-ops catering to the well-to-do almost never offered terms, especially in New York and Chicago. Nevertheless, buyers could still get financing in the form of personal bank loans. By the mid-1920s, according to one source, "few" buyers on the East Side still paid all cash. These kinds of loans were offered on much shorter terms than those extended by developers like Walker and MacDougall. They typically ran just two to four years. They were also generally limited to well-known, high-quality buildings. With highly encumbered shares of stock as collateral, bankers were not inclined to lend in marginal buildings or for longer terms. But in co-ops that they approved of buyers could borrow up to eighty percent of the cost of shares. To encourage these kinds of loans Manhattan co-op owners from the field of banking established a lending institution specifically for this purpose in 1924. A similar group was established in Chicago in 1928.[76]

Working Women

An important new clientele for co-ownership in the 1920s was working women. Apartments, both rented and owned, appealed to many women because they were easier to care for than houses yet offered more privacy and freedom than other common options, such as residential hotels. Women's residences offered companionship and, perhaps, housekeeping services like meals, but they compromised privacy and freedom. The apartment, by contrast, was much less restrictive. Even in expensive buildings with full-time doormen and attended elevators these male figures functioned primarily as silent guardians, without the moral imperative of a matron.

In an apartment building a woman could come and go as, when, and with whom she pleased. One such figure was Elizabeth Jordan, a successful young editor at *Harper's*, who also wrote popular (and, ironically, moralizing) stories for women's magazines. According to an acquaintance, Jordan shared an "impressive co-operative apartment twelve stories up above the lovely old houses on Gramercy Park" with two friends. The threesome lived "more like contented bachelors than resigned spinsters."[77]

Along with creative types (like artists and writers), older, younger, and smaller families, including single women, had always counted among the most frequent buyers of apartments. With the rise of the "New Woman" in the 1920s, women became a larger force in the urban real-estate market. Despite earning far less than men, middle-class women were more independent, more educated, and more employed than ever before. Perhaps with the help of rent-paying roommates, who might include sisters, mothers, and friends, women bought half or even a majority of some buildings' units; even at family-friendly, suburban Jackson Heights one in four buyers was a woman. In many co-ops women served on the board; in one Morningside Heights building all the directors but one were women.[78]

Women formed a particularly active market in Washington thanks to their high participation in the federal workforce, with its good, steady wages. At nearly every building in the capital city between a quarter and half of owners were women. Immediately after the war some developers had concerns that "girls living alone" was "off color." Once it became clear how crucial women were to the success of co-ops, however, developers and sales agents actively courted them. At one 1927 building ads even featured "A Business Woman's Testimonial": "Co-operative ownership of an apartment home is just the thing for the business woman of today. Relieved of care and surrounded by the comforts and luxuries of a splendid environment she can devote herself to her work and be able to entertain her friends." The ad also reprinted a letter from buyer Miss Edyth B. Holland thanking the developer for her new home.[79]

Like the artists and writers who were first drawn to co-ops, many women lacked secure, steady income; co-ownership, with its steep initial but lower ongoing costs could be well suited to their more precarious finances. As one anonymous but apparently well-known businesswoman (with a salary that "never . . . touched the five-thousand-dollar mark," despite rumors) explained in the *Atlantic Monthly*, she had bought her apartment when she was flush, before the war, precisely so that she could be assured of a good home for her, her sister, and their mother in leaner times.[80]

Also presumably of interest was the security that the co-op's "private" social environment promised to women. In Wanda Fraiken Neff's 1928 novel *We Sing Diana*, Helen Spring—free-spirited, bohemian, and just a year out of one of the Seven Sisters colleges—lives in a co-op in Greenwich Village that had the warmth of a private club. Her apartment, which looked out upon a little garden, was "very charming with . . . long, low proportions and a wood-burning fireplace." It was in an "old-fashioned four-story house" that "some enterprising women" had converted to co-ownership, selling each unit "to members of their sex engaged in some unusual but approved employment." According to Helen, it was a "fascinating" place to be with the "most interesting people."[81]

Co-ops (like rented apartments) also seem to have appealed to married couples in which women worked outside the home. As one business editor assured his male audience in the 1920s, this arrangement was "no longer looked upon as queer."[82] More importantly, as *Architectural Record* also noted, it was becoming common. Thirty-eight percent of women were working outside the home, the magazine advised, and nearly half of them were married. These women, it continued, were just as responsible for looking after their homes as full-time housewives were. Their dual roles, however, did not generate interest in co-operative housekeeping—working women, like most Americans, generally preferred modern appliances to communal facilities. But it did make the apartment more practical.[83] A separate study showed that half of all families living in apartments said they would, hypothetically, prefer a "modern" house in a "suburban garden community at the same cost." But in families in which the woman worked, this share fell to just one third. The reasons such families offered for wanting to stay in multifamily dwellings "had to do with convenience, less housework and responsibility, and more leisure."[84]

Recognizing that women played an increasingly important role in decisions about housing, major marketing campaigns, even for family-friendly complexes like Hudson View Gardens, appealed directly to women ("Super Apartments Are Necessary if Woman Is to Keep Pace With Modern Life").[85] As the *Times* reported: "According to brokers, the majority of apartments are rented and sold today to women. Before the war it was the man who made the search and signed the contracts."[86] In part, Hudson View Gardens targeted women through a partnership with the John Wanamaker department store. Wanamaker furnished three model sales units in the "Colonial" style from its Budget Home Shop and promoted the development in its ads. Unlike most real-estate ads, Wanamaker's appeared in the front of the newspaper alongside promotions for baked beans, aspirin, and other household products.[87] Appeals to women also appeared in Hudson View Gardens' own marketing materials (see fig. 32), which emphasized the community's many labor-saving amenities, from refrigerators ("No Iceman, no weight-lifting") and dishwashers to a day nursery ("parents are not 'tied down'") and restaurant so that "when Bridge or Mah Jong interfere with cooking, you can keep father cheerful."[88]

The End of an Era

By the end of the 1920s co-ownership occupied an important place in the metropolitan U.S. housing landscape, with a variety of housing types and clienteles—including ones who would come to play an important role in the expansion of co-ownership after World War II. That said, as the post–World War I real-estate boom cycled down in the late 1920s, so too did the appetite for co-ops. Rapid suburban development and widespread car ownership made "country" living easier. Overproduction of apartment buildings, new rapid-transit lines, and restrictions on immigration relieved significant pressure on city rents, eliminating much of the earlier financial incentive toward co-ownership. Meanwhile, developers began offering the burgeoning urban middle classes new housing choices that competed with the owned apartment. In neighborhoods such as Washington Square, Sutton Place, and Turtle Bay, for example, operators transformed old tenements and rooming houses into expensive row houses and rental apartments with modern conveniences but Early American charm. The Village, in particular, was flooded with "pseudo-bohemian" young professionals in search of an artistic atmosphere.[89]

As early as 1924 and 1925 the most savvy developers of co-ops, like Edward MacDougall, shifted production to houses. (His ongoing interest at Jackson Heights, which included management contracts for its co-ops, perhaps encouraged him to cultivate a robust resale market rather than produce new buildings that would compete with the old ones.) By 1927 and 1928 the pace of construction in co-ops slowed everywhere and new buildings went begging. Some took in renters to cover costs. The Real Estate Board of New York, desperate to stimulate sales, sponsored a state bill in 1929 to allow co-op owners to deduct from state income taxes the portion of maintenance charges spent on taxes and interest on first mortgages (it passed in 1931). In 1930, the first-ever installment plan was offered on Park Avenue.[90]

Anticipating this downturn, other developers turned to rentals. Among new buildings slated for completion after 1929 such as the Westchester and the Kennedy-Warren in Washington, the preponderance were of this type. By 1931, only one co-op, on Fifth Avenue, appears to have been completed in the entire country. Still, as late as 1930 the Chicago Real Estate Board boasted that not a single hundred-percent co-op building had defaulted on a mortgage. Rich buyers, meanwhile, continued to customize units they had bought in the late 1920s (a million-dollar renovation of a thirty-room apartment on the upper stories of a Manhattan tower could take years).[91]

By 1931 and 1932 the market for apartments froze and many cooperative corporations found themselves in financial straits. When owners could not keep up with monthly maintenance, they looked to sell—or to rent their places out. But as the Great Depression deepened, both became impossible. Some buildings tried to subdivide apartments but this was difficult and costly. When buildings came up short, lenders foreclosed. Buildings converted to operation as bank-owned rentals, and all the homeowners, even ones current with their maintenance, lost whatever equity they had put in. Very few well-financed projects met this fate: the Allan E. Walker co-ops in Washington and the Jackson Heights complexes, for example, all survived. At least one in ten East Side buildings failed, however, and a much larger share in Chicago. By the most pessimistic estimates (proffered by critics of co-ownership), half of all co-ops met this fate.[92]

That one's neighbors could no longer meet their obligations—or that one's own sudden poverty could put innocent neighbors at financial risk—was a traumatic experience for apartment owners. People had spent tens and hundreds of thousands of dollars on apartments with every assurance that they were perfectly safe investments. Now everyone was in financial danger, if not because their own wealth had vanished then because their neighbors' had.

John P. Marquand conveys some of the tension in his 1949 novel *Point of No Return*. In it, Charles visits his friends, the Whitakers, in an apartment they own on the fifteenth floor of a Park Avenue building, originally bought from the developer in 1926 for $200,000 ($8.2 million). As Charles slips under the handsome awning through the travertine doorway, into the travertine lobby, he recalls how during the Depression resale values had "dropped from nothing to a minus quantity" and that owners "frantically endeavored to avoid their upkeep and mortgage charges by giving away their equities and even paying prospective tenants handsome bonuses for taking them off their hands. That was the period when people used to say the purchase of a co-operative apartment was like buying the hole in a doughnut." Although the building managed to survive, it flirted with ruin. In 1933, its "lawyers, agents, and even its uniformed attendants had worn the worried and courteous expressions that he had observed on the faces of all persons dealing with white elephants."[93]

Although from the depths of the Depression co-ownership seemed like so much fair-weather wishful thinking, with additional hindsight it is evident that the fundamental principle of people owning apartments remained sound. With the Depression, the American city entered a period of long, deep decline, one that often seemed inexorable and irreversible. But in the ashes of the 1920s lay the seeds of a bright, if distant, recovery. Very long-term shifts, such as movement of middle-class women into the paid workforce, increasing availability of mortgage money, concentration of white-collar work in city centers, rising productivity, falling costs of production, and growth in the number of smaller households all meant that there was already a considerable latent market for future co-ownership. In these respects, the 1920s were as much the end of an era as the start of a new one.

CHAPTER 3

Cooperative Commonwealth

In the fall of 1926 the first homeowners began moving into a large new garden-apartment complex in the Bronx, a section of New York that had not seen many co-ops. Like Hudson View Gardens in Northern Manhattan, this new development, called the Coops, had an innovative physical form that drew upon the work of Andrew Thomas. The design, by Springsteen & Goldhammer, featured a large, elaborately landscaped courtyard surrounded by four, six-story Tudor Revival buildings (fig. 36). The buildings were divided into small sections, each with a separate entrance. This plan required many stairwells but eliminated interior corridors, saving space and money. The apartments were up to date but modest: three, four, and five rooms, along with a smaller number of one-room units for single people and couples without children. The project had many community amenities. The first floors of each building were set aside for common facilities, including an assembly hall, dining hall, library, gymnasium, electric laundries, and rooms for a kindergarten and nursery. Space was also reserved for professional suites so that the new neighborhood could have a doctor and dentist.[1]

Although similar to other New York garden-apartment co-ops, the Coops (rhymes with "hoops") differed radically from earlier examples in terms of cost, in the type of developer, and in the social characteristics of the homeowners. Most co-ops in the 1920s, especially larger-scale complexes, were developed by speculative real-estate operators like Edward MacDougall at Jackson Heights. The cost of apartments had to cover not just land, materials, and labor but compensation for the developer's time and a competitive return on the capital invested. It also had to cover the expense of marketing the apartments, which in some cases ran as high as $1,000 per unit ($40,000 in 2010 dollars). Some smaller projects avoided these expenses because they were undertaken directly by prospective homeowners, but this option was too expensive and impractical for most families.[2]

Fig. 36: The Coops, Bronx Park East, Allerton Avenue, Britton Street, Barker Avenue, Bronx, 1927. United Workers, developer; Springsteen & Goldhammer, architect.

The Coops was built by a different kind of organization: a mutual-aid group called the United Workers. United Workers was established in 1913 by a group of young, mainly single Zionists, communists, and other left-leaning wage earners on the Lower East Side of Manhattan, in part to acquire housing and manage it on an at-cost basis for members. Most of the group's members were Jewish garment workers, although there were several Italians, Greeks, and African Americans. One of the group's first endeavors was to lease a tenement with rooms for members and a community kitchen. The group also hosted readings, lectures, and entertainment for members and friends. As membership grew, it rented additional space. By the summer of 1923 it was running a cafeteria, publishing a magazine, and operating a 250-acre campground in upstate New York.[3]

In 1925, work began on permanent housing. As at its other projects, United Workers undertook the Coops on a nonprofit basis, at cost. Combined with economical design, the low price of land in the Bronx, and creative (but ultimately risky) financing, cash prices were just one-third of those at places like Jackson Heights: $250 a room with monthly maintenance charges of $13 to $18, depending on the configuration and floor. In practice this meant $750 down and $45 a month for three rooms ($31,000 and $1,900 in 2010 dollars) to $1,250 down and $70 for five ($52,000 and $2,900). The apartments sold out before opening. A second section, which more than doubled the number of homes to around seven hundred, also sold quickly. This phase, designed by Herman Jessor, was so well equipped that affordable-housing activist Louis Pink concluded in 1928 that the "needle trades are no longer sweated and starving. They are well-organized, well-paid and powerful. These buildings provide an outlet for radical idealism in constructive endeavor."[4]

For the United Workers and other housing reformers in the 1920s, the co-op proved not just a third way between the suburban house and the city rental, and between the "public" apartment and the "private" home, but between the laissez-faire real-estate market and full state ownership of real property. In the previous two chapters we saw how collective homeownership represented a spatial manifestation of a uniquely American dialectic between urban and suburban desires, expectations for privacy and community, and concerns about rootedness and mobility. In projects like the Coops we also see co-ownership as a strategy—chiefly on the part of the left, but also appealing to some on the right—for improving worker housing, especially among those otherwise excluded from mainstream housing options, such as Jews and, to a lesser extent, African Americans and working women. We also see how, in stripping co-ownership of its social pretensions and repurposing it as a tool for liberation and social progress, the co-op challenges any characterization of the politics of homeownership as inherently conservative.[5]

Producing, marketing, and sustaining low-cost co-ops presented several challenges in the 1920s. Many workers lacked the means to make down payments and the secure, steady income necessary to sustain homeownership. More importantly, if they were to own at all, most preferred whole houses, either because the apartment—especially in low-cost peripheral locations—seemed at odds with ownership, or because houses could better generate income from boarders and accessory units than could compact, one-family flats. Many workers too seemed to bristle against restrictions on resales that developers imposed to ensure long-term affordability (conversely, workers showed little interest in social restrictions). Despite these limitations, the low-cost co-op idea captivated many, and by the 1930s the "nonprofit" co-op became central to national debates on housing.

Limited-equity Ownership

Collective homeownership emerged in the 1910s and 1920s as a characteristic dwelling type among the metropolitan middle classes. As one observer punned, the age-old housing dilemma of owning a house or renting an apartment had become now a "trilemma." And while that writer acknowledged that co-op living was not for all, "for certain classes of people it provides as satisfactory a refuge as either of the other two" options.[6] Co-ownership also came to be used for worker housing in the 1920s. In the U.S., where government provision of housing (common in many parts of Europe) was unlikely, many came to understand it as a better way to produce high-quality, low-cost housing than the prevailing methods of building codes and philanthropic development, which had proven ineffective for addressing the great mass of worker housing in cities like New York.

Philanthropic housing first appeared in the U.S. in the 1870s but had produced only a few isolated examples.[7] As early as 1914 housing reformers like Edith Elmer Wood were calling for government aid to replace it.[8] Given how unlikely this was, many in the 1920s came to see the limited-dividend as a best hope. Like philanthropic projects, co-ops such as the Coops reduced costs by replacing developers and landlords with low-profit, or "limited dividend," entities which took just three to seven percent return on their investments. (Most real-estate investors, by contrast, required a potential return of fifteen or twenty percent, given the volatility of the market.) Co-ownership, however, promised to improve on "philanthropy and five percent." Ownership gave residents more of a stake in their homes. This, many believed, would encourage better behavior and longer tenure, and, as a result, reduce physical wear. More importantly, it offered the possibility of empowering groups of wage earners to undertake projects themselves.

There were several precedents for employing co-ownership to improving ends. One was the long tradition of mutual-aid "cooperative" housing societies (which had evolved into savings and loan societies that operated more like banks than self-help groups). Another was the British garden-city movement, outlined by Ebenezer Howard in 1898, and the related idea of "tenant co-partnership." Under Howard's plan, poor housing conditions were eliminated by strong, centralized land-use controls achieved, in part, through co-partnership, a corporate model developed in the 1880s under which property was owned jointly by tenants and outside philanthropic investors, with profits reinvested in the community.[9]

Yet more important was the related consumers'-cooperative movement which had been devised in U.K. textile towns in the early nineteenth century. Rather than revolution as later called for by Marx and Engels, Robert Owen and others argued for a system of mutual self-help that eliminated producers' and retailers' profits. These ideas were codified in the Rochdale Principles, drafted by the Rochdale Society of Equitable Pioneers in 1844. The system spread throughout Western Europe, especially Scandinavia. It succeeded foremost in the arena of cooperative stores, such as groceries. By the late nineteenth and early twentieth centuries some cooperative societies in Europe were also experimenting with providing housing for members, primarily in co-owned apartment buildings.[10]

To ensure that housing remain nonprofit, by-laws typically prohibited owners from profiting from their equity investment. In limited-equity co-ops, as they came

to be called, it was forbidden to rent out one's apartment at a profit or to sell it
for more than the price initially paid (plus any additional equity accrued through
amortization of blanket mortgages). To ensure that rules were followed, most
buildings handled resales centrally. Prospective buyers did not look in the classified
ads but applied to the cooperative corporation, often joining a waiting list. Northern
European immigrants brought this model to the U.S. Others, especially working-
class Eastern European Jews, soon embraced it. Apart from a limited effort in
Milwaukee to develop small houses on this basis, U.S. activity in this field was
concentrated in New York, and in apartment buildings.[11]

The limited-equity co-op was far removed ideologically from the standard, or
"market-rate," co-ops discussed in the last two chapters. The two shared a basic
corporate-title plan of ownership but were distinguished by fundamentally different
interpretations of co-ownership and of individuals' status as co-owners. In a standard
co-op one had a long-term, all but perpetual proprietary lease, running twenty, ninety-
nine, or sometimes a thousand years. It was one's right to remodel as one wished and
to resell for however much money one could get. This latter promise, in particular, had
always been a leading incentive to co-ownership. The limited-equity plan, by contrast,
all but rejected the idea of private property ownership as commonly understood in
the U.S. Limited-equity proprietary leases were far less permissive. Often they were
very short; some just three years. One could not usually remodel. Apart from ability
to participate in community governance, one had few private rights at all.[12]

Advocates of the limited-equity model celebrated these differences. They
positioned the limited-equity in opposition to "so-called" and "fake" co-op plans that
permitted speculation and profit.[13] As Edith Elmer Wood wrote, in the "interest
of clarity, real coöperative housing should be carefully distinguished from joint
tenant-ownership . . . also, unfortunately . . . called coöperative." On Park Avenue
or in Jackson Heights, she continued, one "buys his apartment single or duplex,
absolutely as he would buy a house and lot" along with "joint ownership" of common
elements. He joins with co-owners in management, but "what he leases or sells it *for*
is nobody's business except his own." While this is a "perfectly legitimate and often
a convenient form of ownership," it is not cooperative. Reflecting the longstanding
conviction that poor conditions in worker housing were caused by the laissez-faire
real-estate market, she concluded: "Members of a real housing coöperative are
home-seekers," she concludes, "not profit-seekers."[14]

Early Experiments

The first consumers'-cooperative apartment house in the U.S. was Alku, a four-
story walk-up building in Sunset Park, Brooklyn, developed in 1916 by a group of

Fig. 37: Riverview, 673–83 Forty-first Street, Brooklyn, 1923. Eric O. Homgren, architect.

sixteen Finnish immigrants with a five-room apartment for each family. Within a decade Finns and a handful of other Scandinavians owned and operated as many as fifty small buildings in Brooklyn (with about six hundred apartments) and another four in Northern Manhattan, some of which they bought and converted, some of which they built (fig. 37). With blanket mortgages covering sixty percent of costs, apartments, by the mid-1920s, typically cost $100 to $150 a room down and $10 per room in monthly maintenance. For a five-room apartment this might mean $600 down ($25,000) and $50 a month ($2,100).[15]

During the housing crisis after World War I these experiments attracted the attention of housing reformers. Chief among them was the architect Clarence S. Stein. Stein (1882–1975) devoted much of his career to improving low-cost housing and neighborhoods. During the war he had worked on the federal government's first foray into housing production, a series of beautiful, well-planned communities in wartime shipping and industrial centers. After the war he and several others involved in the federal program hoped to see their developments sold to co-partnership groups. While this did not happen, Stein emerged as a staunch advocate for co-ownership as part of a larger program of limited-dividend housing. When appointed, alongside Andrew Thomas, to a postwar "reconstruction commission" by New York governor Al Smith, in 1919, he drafted a report encouraging the state to adopt an earlier proposal by Edith Elmer Wood for direct low-cost loans to limited-dividend groups for production of both U.K.-type garden cities and Finnish-type co-op apartments.[16]

Stein's idea for a state housing corporation did not materialize in the 1920s. His efforts did, however, encourage New York to publicly endorse limited-equity co-ownership after the war. In 1917, in part at the request of Finns in Sunset Park, the New York State Department of Farms and Markets had established a Bureau of Co-operative Associations to encourage cooperative effort in farming and other arenas. In 1920, the bureau began promoting consumers'-cooperative housing. Co-ownership, it advised, was an "effective way to meet the housing crisis" so long as, pursuant to Rochdale principles, "it is not operated for private profit."[17]

Despite this encouragement, no worker co-ops were built in the early 1920s outside of the Finnish neighborhoods, perhaps due to lack of financing, perhaps due to lack of interest. Among the few limited-equities built, in fact, nearly all were developed by and for reform-minded white-collar workers: socially engaged types with more education than money who used limited-equity ownership to live better, or in better areas, than they otherwise could. Following new tastes among the post-college set for charming Manhattan neighborhoods like Washington Square, these groups bought and renovated several sets of old houses. In 1921, for example, a group of young "professionals"—mainly women employed at a YWCA—organized the Beekman Hill Cooperative Association, remodeling four East Side row houses into four-room owned apartments. Around the same time some of the middle-class staff at Greenwich House, a settlement house in Greenwich Village, converted their old rooms to co-op after the organization built new headquarters.[18] In a similar vein, in 1923 a small group formed the Consumers' Cooperative Housing Association, which, after a year of discussions, bought and converted seven Greenwich Village row houses into the Bedford-Barrow Cooperative Apartments, with Stein as

Fig. 38: Bedford-Barrow Cooperative, Bedford and Barrow Streets, northwest corner, New York, reconstruction of older structures, 1924. Clarence Stein, architect.

architect (fig. 38). Most of these men and women were affiliated with Greenwich House or its neighbor, the Co-operative League of the U.S.A., a national umbrella group started in 1916 by a rich retired surgeon named James Peter Warbasse to promote the cooperative commonwealth. In marked contrast with buildings on the East Side and at Jackson Heights, the group made a point of not discriminating on the basis of race, religion, or ethnicity.[19]

Gradually, the idea of the limited-equity co-op began to reach poorer families. The most promising early project was a conversion undertaken by the pastor of an East Harlem church. Seeing his congregation pushed out of that neighborhood by rising rents, the Reverend Dr. H. M. Tyndall bought and renovated five old houses and sold the new apartments to his parishioners. Tyndall soon became an advocate for co-ownership, which he believed could not only arrest rising rents but cure slum conditions.

Tyndall believed that if residents "had owned their own homes and could have stayed in the neighborhood, governing and directing the conditions in which they were living, these great changes" in the neighborhood "never would have come about." As he argued in the *New York Times* in 1924: "If every church started some such plan . . . and housed in as short a time as we have taken as many people as we do," the city's slum problem could be solved permanently. "We have seen a remarkable difference in the attitude of the people themselves. When one owns a home it is to one's advantage to see that the neighborhood appears always to the best advantage. . . . They have lost their feeling of impermanence, the here today and gone tomorrow attitude that makes it so hard for civic interests to prosper."[20]

Tyndall's model was impractical financially. Apartments in these kinds of converted buildings tended to cost $1,500 to $2,500 down ($62,000 to $100,000), with $50 to $70 a month in maintenance ($2,100 to $2,900). These prices were far too high for most workers—as much as a typical annual salary. But where families could afford the cost of shares, or where financing could be arranged, these buildings offered a new idea in city real estate. Like standard co-ops they eliminated the problem of the landlord and helped protect owners against rising rents. They also allowed further savings by facilitating cooperative provision of other goods and services, such as milk and ice. Perhaps most importantly, they promised to channel workers' savings into improved living conditions.[21]

Inspired by Tyndall, housing reformers continued to advocate for wider adoption, and for state support. To "point out to the working people the necessity for cooperative housing," the United Neighborhood Houses of New York, a settlement-house group, held a six-day exhibition on the limited-equity co-op in 1924. As part of the event, the group led tours of the Finnish and East Harlem co-ops and hosted lectures by leaders of the Co-operative League of the U.S.A., co-op board presidents, city officials, mortgage lenders, limited-dividend developers, and architects. Among the speakers were Clarence Stein and Alexander S. Bing, partners in the Regional Planning Association of America (RPAA), an advocacy group that Stein helped establish in 1923, in part to promote good housing design through nonspeculative development. The closing talk treated visitors to stereopticon views of co-op housing in Europe.[22]

The exhibition failed to convince New York State lawmakers to fund the low-cost co-op loan program that Stein and Wood had envisioned. But it did help secure passage of a more modest bill: the Limited Dividend Housing Companies Law of 1926, which permitted cities to waive property taxes for limited-dividend housing, including co-ops. The program enabled significant savings. In tax-exempt limited-dividends costs could be as much as twenty-five percent less than in typical rentals, and the tax abatement alone lowered maintenance costs by about $2.10 per room per month, or $430 in 2010 dollars for a five-room apartment. In part as a result of this law— but also simply as the postwar crisis abated and more money became available for housing—New York began to see a steady stream of limited-equity co-ops.[23]

Jews and the Co-op

Most of these projects were developed by and for left-wing Jewish fraternal groups like United Workers' Cooperative, or by labor-union groups comprising primarily class-conscious Jews. In addition to the Coops they include the Shalom Aleichem Houses, the Farband Houses, the Amalgamated Cooperative Apartments (fig. 39), and the Amalgamated Dwellings. All were completed between 1926 and 1930 in the

Fig. 39: Amalgamated Cooperative Apartments, Van Cortlandt Park South, Gouveneur and Hillman Avenues, Bronx, 1926–27. Amalgamated Clothing Workers of America, developer; Springsteen & Goldhammer, architect. Photograph by Wurts Bros., ca. 1928.

Bronx, with the notable exception of the Amalgamated Dwellings, which was built as a slum-clearance demonstration project on the Lower East Side.[24]

For Jewish groups the limited-equity co-op was not just a way to lower the cost of housing: it was also a way to do away with the landlord and to create an engaged, urban community that cultivated specific cultural and political agendas, including Zionism, communism, and preservation of secular Yiddish culture. With their organization and financial resources these groups of prospective homeowners could have developed small single-family houses. But as architectural historian Richard Plunz notes, "the public emblems [they] associated with their new status were not private cottages surrounded by lawns" but something "closer to a people's palazzo, involving a monumentality not possible through individualism."[25]

This is not to suggest that most Jews chose to live in co-ops. To the contrary, in the city's myriad Jewish sections—by the 1920s Jews made up a quarter of Manhattan, a third of Brooklyn, and nearly half of the Bronx—co-ownership was, in fact, rare. In the "strictly 'American,'" Protestant world of the East Side and Jackson Heights co-ownership thrived. Affluent, conservative, and wary of the city's heterogeneity, those who could afford homeownership sought protection in "private" co-op buildings. In Jewish and other "ethnic" circles this imperative did not exist. Immigrants and their children also, perhaps, were more conscious of their geographic and social mobility, and therefore less inclined to tie themselves down with an equity stake in housing, even in good second-generation neighborhoods like Eastern Parkway, the Grand Concourse, and West End Avenue. (It is telling that in the Jewish limited-equities resales—back to the cooperative—were far easier, if less lucrative, than in high-class co-ops.) Hundreds of thousands of Jews and other ethnic groups moved to new apartments and houses in New York in the 1920s, but by and large it was only the more radical, politically engaged among them who pursued the alternative of co-ownership.[26]

The greatest advocate for limited-equity co-ops in the 1920s was a Jewish immigrant from the Ukraine named Abraham E. Kazan. He arrived in the U.S. as a teenager in the early 1900s; like most in his social milieu he was a socialist. In New York, however, he met a Scottish anarchist named Thomas Hastie Bell who introduced him to the alternative of the international consumers'-cooperative movement. Convinced that it was a more viable, and politically expedient, way to achieve social equality than revolution, Kazan (1889–1971) joined Bell's Co-operative League (not to be confused with the more influential, and enduring, Co-operative League of the U.S.A.). Although Bell's group struggled to run cooperative businesses on the Lower East Side, Kazan succeeded in one arena: buying up bulk supplies of sugar, matzos, and other staples for sale at cost to members of Local 35 of the International Ladies Garment Workers Union (ILGWU), where he worked as an office boy and handyman.[27]

Ironically, Kazan arrived at the co-op apartment as much through the left as through the right. Although he was likely aware of some of the early experiments with owned housing for workers both in New York and in Europe, Kazan credited Andrew Thomas with introducing him to the limited-equity. Thomas, in turn, seems to have gotten the idea from John D. Rockefeller, Jr.

After designing several middle-class complexes for Edward MacDougall in Jackson Heights, as well as large-scale low-cost rental projects in Brooklyn (for the philanthropic City and Suburban Homes Company) and in Queens (for the insurer Metropolitan Life), Thomas approached Rockefeller about building a similar complex in Manhattan on land that the oil baron owned on the far East Side. Rockefeller was interested, but preferred that the project be organized as owned housing rather than a rental.[28]

As a staunch conservative, Rockefeller (1874–1960) was opposed to government assistance for housing. In philanthropic housing, and especially the co-op, he saw an alternative to the kind of government-aided housing proliferating in Europe which U.S. housing reformers were eager to emulate. He not only financed Thomas's project, which he called Rockefeller Garden Apartments, but also a larger complex in Bayonne, New Jersey, for workers at his nearby Standard Oil refinery. Although the Bayonne project, also designed by Thomas, was rental and the Manhattan project attracted mainly white-collar staff of the nearby Rockefeller Institute, Rockefeller—and Thomas—became convinced that the savings and security offered by co-ownership could be extended to workers.[29]

Kazan met Thomas when the architect approached the ILGWU about developing a co-op. (Thomas was always in search of new opportunities to improve low-cost housing and the union was already operating a women's boarding house on a nonprofit basis.) Although Kazan had left ILGWU for a new job at the Amalgamated Clothing Workers of America, his old colleagues turned to him for advice. Under Kazan's and Thomas's lead, the ILGWU, the Amalgamated, and two other garment-trade unions began planning a joint project in 1924 (fig. 40). According to Abraham Baroff, general secretary-treasurer of the ILGWU, the workers he represented "suffer probably more than any other single group from the slum evils and high rents." In this project, he continued, "we can help ourselves and provide the decent homes to which we are entitled and which individual speculative effort has failed to provide."[30]

Thomas helped the group select a site on the Grand Concourse, a leafy section of the Bronx being rapidly developed with modern, middle-class apartment houses. Ground was broken. When costs ran over, however, the unions began to argue and

Fig. 40: Thomas Garden Apartments, 840 Grand Concourse, Bronx, 1925–27. John D. Rockefeller, Jr., developer; Andrew J. Thomas, architect. Photograph by George Van Anda, 1927.

Fig. 41: Thomas Garden Apartments, garden view, February 12, 1927.

construction stalled. To rescue the job, Thomas arranged for an investment from
Rockefeller. The philanthropist disliked the unions and they disliked him. But
Rockefeller feared that the project's failure might convince lawmakers of the need
for public housing. He assumed control and completed the building in 1927—and
beautifully so, with an elaborate Japanese-style courtyard (fig. 41). He named it the
Thomas Garden Apartments. For his next project, the Amalgamated Cooperative
Apartments, Kazan vowed to work alone.[31]

Rockefeller and the Dunbar Apartments

Rockefeller went on to help develop three additional low-cost co-ops, all designed by
Thomas, in pursuit of the idea that homeownership, even limited-equity, promoted
better citizenship and could "prevent the spread of socialism and bolshevism." One
project was the Van Tassel Apartments in the Westchester County town of Sleepy
Hollow, near Rockefeller's weekend estate; another was Brooklyn Garden Apartments,
sponsored by a group that included Rockefeller. These opened in 1930 and 1929,
respectively. The third was the Paul Laurence Dunbar Apartments in Harlem, which

opened in 1927 (fig. 42). As if to prove that
the 1926 state housing law was unnecessary,
Rockefeller refused its benefits.[32]

The Dunbar, begun in 1926, was the
most extraordinary of all the Rockefeller
developments. One reason for this was its
large size: 513 apartments in six, five- and
six-story walk-up buildings occupying
an entire block. More importantly, it was
built for New York's burgeoning Black
population. Dunbar was not the city's only
Black co-op. New York, like Washington,
D.C., seemed to have at least a handful of
Black co-ops by the mid-1920s, and the
success of Dunbar, in turn, prompted a
small wave of conversions and proposals
for new buildings in Harlem in the late
1920s, the largest of which was to have
been called Lincoln Mansion (fig. 43). But
Dunbar was the best-equipped of them, with
spacious, modern interiors. It attracted much
of the city's Black middle class, including

Fig. 42: Paul Laurence Dunbar Apartments,
Seventh and Eighth Avenues, West 149th and 150th
Streets, New York, 1926–27. John D. Rockefeller, Jr.,
developer; Andrew J. Thomas, architect. View of 246
West 150th Street façade. Photograph by Dynecourt
Mahon, 1979.

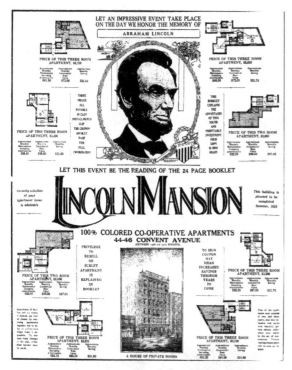

Fig. 43: Lincoln Mansion, unbuilt, 44–46 Convent Avenue, New York. Bonmar Construction, developer. Advertisement, *New York Amsterdam News,* February 8, 1928.

W. E. B. Du Bois, Paul Robeson, and A. Philip Randolph.[33]

As in every northern city, severe discrimination left Black families with few good housing options and virtually none in modern buildings. Furthermore, Black people had to pay more for housing than whites due to the limited supply, and were generally even more at the mercy of their landlords. Dunbar helped address all of these problems. Its sales literature emphasized, in particular, the fact that ownership put the resident in control: "If you've been shunted from place to place, time and again, in search of a livable home, you'll appreciate cooperative apartment-homes that have been built for beauty, comfort and permanence." The complex sold quickly.[34]

Thanks to a liberal thirty-year blanket mortgage from Rockefeller, apartments at Dunbar, which ranged in size from three rooms up to seven, cost $50 down per room. An installment plan allowed payment over three years. Average monthly maintenance, which varied with one's financing, ran $14.50 per room. For a six-room apartment (with three bedrooms, two baths, living room, kitchen, and dining room) this meant $300 down and $70 a month ($12,500 and $2,900), with no installment plan. These expenses were in line with other Thomas buildings and, by comparison, about half that of market-rate projects like Jackson Heights. (They were, however, fairly high for middle-class Black families. Average income at Dunbar was only $150 a month [$75,000 a year in 2010 dollars].)[35]

Community Life

Life in limited-equity co-ops was socially and materially different than in market-rate buildings. In standard co-ops, privacy was of paramount concern. As one writer claimed, "My lady of millions need no more associate with the other tenants in her house than you or I, fellow-pauper, with the people in the flat upstairs. Each apartment has its separate and private elevator [landing]; often, its separate and private entrance."[36] And while developers of projects in less central areas, like Jackson Heights, lured buyers with extensive common amenities, many gradually let these kind of things go, with owners happier to entertain privately than carry the communal expense of tennis courts, skating ponds, and putting greens.[37]

Private rights in property were emphasized, too, in market-rate co-ops. Many owners, for example, made it a point to express their individuality through physical customization, and they spoke proudly of the changes they made to their apartments. In the most expensive buildings developers learned to install only minimal partitions and fixtures, since nearly every buyer remodeled. All this activity in co-op renovation came to support what one critic characterized as an entire "colony of prosperous craftsmen" on the Upper East Side.[38] One cartoonist imagined this sort of personalization taken to the extreme in a co-op whose exterior reflected the individual tastes of each owner (fig. 44).

In the limited-equities, things were different. Residents took pride in their status as homeowners; some even refused, at first, to sign proprietary leases on grounds that the documents referred to them as tenants.[39] The basic fabric of the system, however, emphasized the group over the individual. Designs emphasized physical privacy for the family but apartments were expected to be returned to the corporation in their original condition. In some buildings there was no right of inheritance: at death, stock reverted to the corporation, although survivors were offered first right to repurchase it.[40]

Socially, limited-equities like the Coops emphasized a rich community life. "Cooperators" did not play golf and tennis like at Jackson Heights. They established and ran preschools, playgrounds, libraries, summer camps, cafeterias, and adult-education classes, and they produced and consumed a wide array of community programming, from newsletters and journals to lectures, concerts, and plays (fig. 45). At the Amalgamated Cooperative Apartments, the complex acquired a bus to carry children three-quarters of a mile to school. High-energy leaders like "Brother Kazan" worked tirelessly to maintain engagement and to cultivate commitment to the consumers'-cooperative political economy. The result was a tremendously rewarding experiment in congregant living.

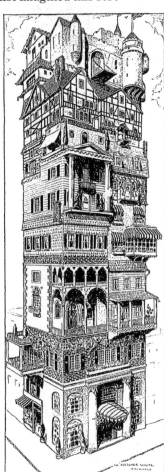

A 100 PER CENT. CO-OPERATIVE APARTMENT
BUILT TO SUIT THE INDIVIDUAL TASTES OF THE OWNERS.

Fig. 44: W. Fletcher White, *Life*, January 10, 1924.

Fig. 45: Amalgamated Cooperative Apartments, view of kindergarten. Photograph by Wurts Bros., 1929.

The different community orientation in limited-equity and market-rate co-ops was further reflected in how each was governed. In standard co-ops every share voted so owners with larger, more expensive homes held more power. Meanwhile, developers and managing agents made it a priority to reduce formal interaction among neighbors. Like new labor-saving appliances, well-crafted by-laws, propriety leases, and paid-management contracts aimed to minimize potential for conflict between owners, and the amount of effort required of them. One developer pushed so far in the direction of individual freedom that he jettisoned the corporate-title co-op plan entirely in favor one he called the deed plan. Under this system, which came to be known as the "own-your-own," title remained with an association comprising the owners. But rather than a proprietary lease, owners received individual deeds conveying an undivided share in the entire property along with the right to occupy a particular space in perpetuity.

The builder was Lionel V. Mayell, a young Angeleno who had given up study of the law after spells at USC and Stanford. According to one biography, while in Palo Alto he "became enthralled with the great co-op apartments being built in New York City" and dropped out to develop expensive high-rises in Los Angeles and in Long Beach, California, a rapidly growing resort area (see fig. 96).[41] Although he clearly saw promise in co-ownership, Mayell believed that Californians would bristle against the co-op as practiced in the East. He objected, in particular, to the custom of group approval of resales and left screening provisions out of his by-laws (he did, however, retain racial restrictions). Because of the symbolic value of the deed, because of the greater emphasis on private rights in property, and because Mayell was so effective at promoting his plan, the own-your-own quickly came into widespread regional use. At least half of Southern California's co-owned apartment houses before the Great Depression were own-your-owns rather than stock cooperatives. The system became so well known that a young Maxwell Shane wrote a script in 1925 (not produced) about modern apartment living called *Own Your Own*. Shane, like Mayell, studied law at USC. He went on to become a successful film writer in the 1940s.[42]

At the limited-equities, by contrast, by-laws followed Rochdale principles. Each apartment had one vote regardless of the size. (New York State even

AT THE DUNBAR YOU ENRICH YOURSELF—NOT THE LANDLORD!

CORNER OF GARDEN

Five perfectly good reasons why a man's wife and children as well as his property are safe at the Dunbar

PAUL LAURENCE DUNBAR APARTMENTS Inc.

2594 SEVENTH AVENUE · EDgecombe 4-3181 · New York, N. Y.

Under personal direction of

ROSCOE CONKLING BRUCE
and
CLARA BURRILL BRUCE

AT THE DUNBAR YOU ENRICH YOURSELF—NOT THE LANDLORD!

Fig. 46: Paul Laurence Dunbar Apartments, pages of *Paul Laurence Dunbar Apartments,* prospectus.

allowed limited-equities to incorporate under a special corporations law set up for consumers' cooperatives, since the one-member, one-vote system conflicted with standard business laws.) Paid management was rare and people actively engaged in, and helped manage, community activities.[43]

Although participation was encouraged in these respects, limited-equities were not necessarily more democratic. Their roots in philanthropy and the need to fortify the community against the temptations of privatism resulted in paternalistic management. Most limited-equities came also with other strings which compromised the autonomy of the collective. In tax-exempt complexes like the Amalgamated Cooperative Apartments, for example, a seat on the board was reserved for a New York State appointee. At Rockefeller's complexes, the philanthropist retained preferred shares of stock until mortgages were paid off, which afforded him absolute power. At Dunbar, this meant strict centralized management by a resident director named Roscoe Conkling Bruce, an African American Harvard graduate selected by Rockefeller. Bruce had full charge of screening tenants and enforcing by-laws, and employed a security patrol to police the property (fig. 46). Like a settlement-house director, he and his wife, Clara, also staged improving classes for the "tenants" on parenting, decorating, and etiquette.[44]

Rent Mutualization and Other Models

Several speculative developers also tried to produce housing for wage earners through co-ownership in the 1920s. Rather than limited profits and self-help, however, they relied on cheap land and economical designs to lower costs. In 1920, Frederic F. Culver, who went on to build several expensive co-ops in Manhattan and Westchester County's Bronxville, commissioned Andrew Thomas to design a garden apartment in Flushing, Queens, with units priced from $4,300 ($160,000). Another firm offered "Portional Purchase" co-ops in Flatbush, Brooklyn. The artist-developer Walter Russell also produced similar co-ops in Kew Gardens and Woodside, Queens, and in Jersey City, New Jersey. Russell's buildings promised buyers the "charm of an English Village[,] . . . proximity to the station," and "all of the comforts and safety known in a Park Avenue Type Apartment" at much more modest prices.[45]

Another strategy was to radically reduce the size of apartments. Borrowing from Los Angeles examples of modern buildings with well-equipped one- and two-room apartments, Russell proposed, in 1922, to develop a series of "California Efficiency Apartments" in Manhattan, to be designed by Jackson Heights architect

Fig. 47: New Versailles, Port Washington, New York, unbuilt. Walter Russell, Versailles, Inc., developers; Carrère & Hastings, architect. *New Versailles*, prospectus, 1916.

George H. Wells. Fitted with space-saving built-ins, like fold-up Murphy beds, the idea was to furnish small households with compact homes: six rooms (living room, library, Pullman kitchen, breakfast room, two bedrooms with dressing areas, and bathroom) in just 759 square feet. A model was erected at the showroom of the White Wall Bed Company. Although there was some initial interest in a proposal for Greenwich Village, no Russell Efficiency Apartment house was ever built.[46]

Russell also developed a more unusual plan: rent mutualization. It combined very small apartments with the old idea of reserving many units for rent to offset costs. The hope was that as rents rose and blanket construction mortgages were paid off, income would eventually cover all costs and return steady dividends to the homeowners. Convinced that this arrangement could permanently lower housing costs for wage-earners, he promoted the "Russell Rent Mutualization Plan for National Rent Relief; Universal Home Ownership Through Normal Rent Paying." In 1923 he established the National Rent Mutual Company, won the endorsement of President Coolidge, and found a number of investors to commit $1,000 ($44,000) toward his goal of a $10 million ($440 million) capitalization. Those contributing included Mrs. Harry Payne Whitney, architect Thomas Hastings (of Carrère & Hastings), the architecture firm of McKim, Mead & White, and the sculptor Alexander Calder.[47]

Several of these individuals had been involved with Russell in unsuccessful earlier attempts to construct a resort for artists on a similar financial model. The first of these proposals, in 1916, was New Versailles. It called for twenty-five hundred apartments—as well as theaters, stables, a range for trap-shooting, a landing strip, tennis courts, golf areas, swimming pools, and yachts for commuting to Manhattan—on a campus of 182 acres in Port Washington, New York, on Long Island's North Shore (fig. 47). At least one critic found the design by Carrère & Hastings far more compelling than the garden-city model at Forest Hills Gardens. It was doomed, however, by its $30 million cost ($2 billion). After the war the group tried again, proposing the more modest Grassy Sprain Manor for Bronxville with 250 apartments in a building (also by Carrère & Hastings) based on the Palace of Fontainebleau (fig. 48). It, too, went unbuilt.[48]

Fig. 48: Grassy Sprain Manor, Bronxville, New York, unbuilt. Walter Russell, developer; Carrère & Hastings, architect; Shreve, Lamb & Blake, associated architect. *Architectural Review*, January 1921.

The only rent-mutualization project to gain real traction was Beekman House, an unbuilt ten-story "300 Room Club-Residence for Women" to have been designed by Warren & Clarke and Thomas Markoe Robertson for Manhattan's far East Side.

Fig. 49: Advertisement for Beekman House, Beekman Place near East Forty-ninth Street, New York, unbuilt. Walter Russell, National Rent Mutual Corporation, developers; Warren & Clarke and Thomas Markoe Robertson, architects. *New York Times*, November 4, 1923.

Like under the California Efficiency plan, apartments were to be extremely small with a built-in Murphy bed, dressing room, and bath (fig. 49). Each floor was to share a single common kitchen. Specifications also called for a swimming pool, common lounges, and a cafeteria. The apartments were to cost $800 down ($35,000) with monthly maintenance charges, including financing, of $12 ($525). The idea enjoyed significant initial interest. Thousands of women were reported to have organized clubs to support rent mutualization and the New York League of Business and Professional Women demanded recognition of the plan by the federal, state, and city governments. Nevertheless, Beekman House and rent mutualization stalled. Likely as a result of the unconventional financial plan, no project was ever realized.[49]

The Limits of Co-operation

Russell's were not the only moderately priced co-ops to go begging for buyers. In fact, except where buyers were ideologically committed to consumers' cooperation or where they were otherwise excluded from the mainstream housing market, limited-equities and other low-cost co-ops struggled. Some workers hated, or could not afford, to make an equity payment. Others seemed to dislike paternalistic management. Yet others simply found the idea of co-ownership conceptually difficult. If and when working- and middle-class families did buy homes in the 1920s, most chose a house and grounds.

Thomas Garden Apartments—begun by the unions and completed by Rockefeller—illustrates some of these troubles. Although critically acclaimed for its design (see figs. 40, 41), the 166 units languished on the market. Some suggested that the problem was physical: it had too many large apartments and lacked elevators, which had become a standard feature in new buildings. Others pointed to cost, although the four-, five-, and six-room apartments sold for just $1,200 to $1,940 down ($49,000 to $80,000) and a twenty-five-year installment plan was available. Monthly charges ($64 to $100 with full financing) were comparable to going rents. Early buyers included policemen, firemen, clerks, and salesmen. The larger problem was that few among these groups wanted to own an apartment. To sell the place out, Rockefeller had to all but waive the equity requirements, reducing prices to as little as $300 ($12,000).[50]

Fig. 50: Our Cooperative House, 433 West Twenty-first Street, New York, 1929–30. Consumers Cooperative Services, developer; Springsteen & Goldhammer, architect.

Low-cost white-collar co-ops suffered similarly. The young bohemians who developed the Bedford Barrow Cooperative in Greenwich Village in 1924, for example, failed to realize a second project, in Brooklyn Heights. And in Manhattan, a thirteen-story tower called Our Cooperative House was unable to sell, even though it was developed by Consumers Cooperative Services (ccs), the largest consumers'-cooperative group on the East Coast (both in membership and annual sales).

Unlike trade unions, whose members were mostly Jewish leftists ideologically committed to living in a progressive, communal setting, ccs was, according to one co-op advocate, composed of "middle class, white collared native bourgeois Americans." ccs's business was also far from radical. The group had begun in 1919, when two women opened a café on East Twenty-fifth Street. To finance expansion, they incorporated as a co-op, selling shares to customers. Within a few years they had at least eight locations, in Greenwich Village, Irving Place, Midtown, and Lower Manhattan, selling cooked food in to-go containers, as well as baked goods and dairy. In 1926 they founded a credit union. Then they turned to housing, inspired by the success of the garment workers. They surveyed members for interest and settled on the idea of a modern high-rise on West Twenty-first Street in Chelsea (fig. 50). But sales were slow. When it opened ccs had no choice but to operate it as a rental.[51]

Sunnyside Gardens

The most significant failure of a co-op in the 1920s was at Sunnyside Gardens, the model suburb in Queens sponsored by Clarence Stein and the RPAA. Stein had started RPAA as an informal arena for socially engaged designers, builders, critics, and conservationists to rethink the metropolitanized American city by planning alternatives to the ordinary, speculatively developed built environment. Sunnyside was their first project. To construct it, Stein and the community-minded developer Alexander Bing (1879–1959) created City Housing Corporation.

From the start, the directors of the City Housing Corporation professed a desire to experiment with a variety of ownership structures, including the kinds of consumers'-cooperative co-partnership models advocated by Ebenezer Howard in the U.K. They anticipated that "genuine Rochdale co-operative groups" might buy blocks of row houses (some one-families, others with one or two accessory apartments) for operation on a nonspeculative, nonprofit basis. Early on, however, it became evident that common ownership of the row houses was not going to succeed. Although consumers'-cooperative groups were given first preference, none came forward and City Housing did not help establish them. (Its best efforts, to the contrary, went toward lowering the cost of individual ownership through a new system of long-term, low-cost mortgages devised by Bing. With Bing's generous, long-term financing Sunnyside attracted moderate-income American dreamers rather than groups of workers.)[52]

Fig. 51: Colonial Court, Forty-seventh and Forty-eighth Streets between Forty-third and Skillman Avenues, Sunnyside, New York, 1924. City Housing Corporation, Sunnyside First Cooperative Housing Association, developers; Clarence Stein, Henry Wright, architects. View of southeastern apartment block.

City Housing devoted somewhat more attention to cultivating consumers'-cooperative ownership of Sunnyside's small apartment buildings. According to one member of the organization, co-owned apartments were "one of the first experiments that commended itself to the company." Stein saw great promise in co-ownership for workers and anticipated much unmet demand. Sunnyside's first phase, called Colonial Court, was built in 1924. It included eight, one-family row houses; forty, two-family row houses; and forty apartments arranged in six, three-story buildings. The apartments and most of the houses were placed around the perimeter of a full block, with a common garden at the center that included tennis courts and a playground.[53]

The apartments were small, plain, and modern (fig. 51). Thanks to extensive financing, which attempted to mimic what Bing had arranged for the row houses, they sold for just ten percent down, or $480 for four rooms ($20,000 in 2010 dollars), with just under $50 a month in maintenance ($2,100). (Comparable market rentals were $65 a month.) Five-room units cost $580 ($24,000), while those in the basement went for $360 ($15,000). The apartments were harder to market than the houses. Nevertheless, they sold—to teachers, nurses, social workers, and other white-collar types, mainly with small households. Few had children.[54]

Although slow sales and the lack of larger families raised concerns, Stein and Bing remained committed to the limited-equity. A primary interest of RPAA was experimenting with design, including multifamily types, and members continued to believe that collective ownership was superior to tenancy. As one staff member explained, in a co-op "economies . . . accrue to the tenant . . . because of greater care in property maintenance, greater length of tenure, and responsibility of each tenant for his own apartment repairs." Additionally, selling apartments promised to be of greater short-term benefit to the corporation, which was short on capital and needed cash to continue building.[55]

As a result, the second phase of Sunnyside, built in 1925, also included a co-op: Carolin Gardens, a pair of more elaborate walk-up buildings with sixteen apartments each (fig. 52). Hoping that larger apartments might sell faster—and to a broader clientele than "women and older people who cannot maintain their own properties or who do not want to tend furnaces or climb stairs"—the number and size of rooms were increased.

Fig. 52: Carolin Gardens, east side of Forty-seventh Street between Queens Boulevard, Forty-third Avenue, Sunnyside, New York, 1925. City Housing Corporation, Sunnyside Second Cooperative Housing Association, developers; Clarence Stein, Henry Wright, architects. View of northern apartment block.

The new strategy failed. Carolin Gardens sold even more slowly than Colonial Court had. After six months a majority of units remained on the market.[56] One reason seems to have been cost. More generous dimensions meant higher prices: $600 for four rooms, and monthly maintenance that was on par with, rather than below, going rents. The more general reason for the failure, however, was that City Housing never sought out or cultivated a market for the co-ops.

Jackson Heights sold apartments because it promoted the idea relentlessly in newspapers, on billboards, on the radio. The Coops sold well because it was sponsored by a group which constituted a ready market. City Housing Corporation, by contrast, had no pool of prospects and did virtually no advertising. Word-of-mouth, cheap prices, and innovative financing worked well for Sunnyside row houses. But people wandering into the sales office in suburban Queens had little interest in owning apartments, and no amount of evidence, according to sales staff, seemed to "convert" the "would-be renter . . . to the advantages of cooperation." Rather than sell the idea, City Housing gave up, concluding that the "low-priced cooperative apartment idea has certain disadvantages and presents special problems and difficulties." The company rented out the remaining unsold apartments (over the protests of the people who had bought). Sunnyside's later phases included new apartments but all were run as rentals. The same was true of Andrew Thomas's Abbott Court Apartments at the RPAA's next development, Radburn, in northern New Jersey.[57]

Lewis Mumford expressed the group's frustration most forcefully. Mumford was a prolific cultural critic, intensely interested in urban form. He was part of Stein's innermost circle and had helped shape RPAA's ideals and activities from the start. He demonstrated his commitment to Sunnyside by buying a co-op there and moving in with his wife and son, in 1925. He did not like it. "Three-, four- and five-story apartment houses with every modern improvement," he wrote, "are not permanent homes for women and children; they are dormitory slums." After eighteen months he moved to a Sunnyside row house.[58]

The unequivocal success of the Jewish trade-union projects and of Rockefeller's Dunbar Apartments soon forced a reassessment. The new conclusion, which became conventional wisdom among housing reformers, was that only where there was "some bond of friendship, of race, occupation, trade union or religion" was co-ownership viable. This formulation was wrong. In fact, it was not necessarily the "homogeneous fraternal or racial group" that allowed low-cost co-ops to work.[59] It was people who were actively opposed to mainstream capitalism and people who had few other housing options, such as middle-class African Americans. It was, in other words, intense ideological commitment or lack of alternatives that brought most middle- and working-class families to co-ownership in the 1920s. For most everyone else, the decade offered an array of more appealing choices.

Once the wartime housing crisis eased, new housing flooded the market: between 1926 and 1928, for example, two new homes (mainly apartments) were built in the U.S. for each new household formed. Steam heat, elevators, and reasonable rents could now be had by families of average income without any equity investment or long-term commitment. For those who preferred to buy, inexpensive houses appeared by the hundreds of thousands at the urban edge, which became easier to reach than ever thanks to improvements in transit and

Ford's Model-T. Projects like the Thomas Garden Apartments and Carolin Gardens had trouble competing.[60]

Opposing Co-ownership

Many Americans were not just ambivalent about co-ownership, they were hostile toward it: because it conflicted with the ideal of a detached, fee-simple house; because it seemed too financially complex to be of genuine benefit to ordinary buyers; and perhaps because of the radicals and modern social types, like working women, whom the co-op tended to attract. In 1926, for example, a woman wrote to the *Chicago Tribune* "wondering why in the world they don't build some small coöps . . . for the young married couples who are both working and do not want or need any more room . . . [like] me and my husband."[61] Her plea elicited vitriol, at least from one reader who signed his reply as "A Real Daddy." He advised her to buy a suburban bungalow, "quit your job and put on an apron and be a nice little housewife. . . . That's the way to be a real good American citizen. A couple that gets married and both keep on working and don't have any nice little kiddies, blah!"[62] Never mind that, for some, co-ops were ideal for rearing children, full, as they were, of "well-meaning Dutch uncles and aunts," as one child of a co-op later recalled.[63]

For others, "co-op"—especially the high-class co-op—became synonymous with modernity, the market, and the often unsettling pace of change in the city. *Century* magazine regretted how all too often the "residence of an aristocratic family is sold to a ten-year-old construction company and a coöperative apartment is erected on the site. In a few weeks, a patina that three generations of conservative living imparts to a building, is shattered by impersonal"—and presumably immigrant Jewish or Italian—"hands that know neither piety, nor impiety, but only efficiency and realty values." A short story published in *Scribner's* magazine described the co-op as one of the "worst crimes ever perpetrated against humanity."[64]

Similarly, a Greenwich Village artist railed against plans for a "super-modern" co-op with "as many Gothic excrescences as a porcupine, or the Woolworth Building; as much window space as an automobile factory; all the hygienic, sanitary, modern, white-tiled splendors of a model ice box." As a renter, he offered, perhaps he had "no right to protest if the tumbledown picturesqueness of Washington Square South is to be 'improved' (save the [quotation] mark) by the erection of fourteen-story buildings." But, he warned, "picturesque dilapidation cannot be made in a day." And anyone whose "visions of beauty" helped nurture "America's first home for iridescent souls, first real art centre . . . [and] sacred ground to every free spirit in America," he felt it important to protest this "atrocity." "Is it only commercial values . . . [and]

real estate that is to be protected?" he wondered. "Will none raise a hand to save from profaning modernization the temples of the soul?"[65]

Occasionally opposition to co-ownership came from within real-estate circles, usually from owners of rental buildings. While national trade journals like *Apartments* offered regular, favorable reports on the co-op beginning in 1920, local organs like San Francisco's *Apartment House Journal* disapproved. Fewer than two dozen co-ops (or "community homes," as they were initially called there) were built in the 1920s, following their introduction in 1912. Nevertheless, the Apartment House Owners and Managers Association, which represented landlords, waged a campaign against the idea, albeit principally to its own members. In 1925, for example, an article reported alleged difficulties associated with co-ownership, including declining resale values and physical and "moral" deterioration stemming from wont of harmony among owners.[66]

Economists (and economics writers) also voiced concerns about collective homeownership, especially market-rate. These centered on the challenges of self-governance and on suspicion of profit motive. Both reservations were colored by incredulity that anyone could like apartment living enough to want to own her own unit. Land-use economist Coleman Woodbury advised: "Coöperative apartments have been advocated. . . . But, at present their use is distinctly limited by legal uncertainties, bad promotion, unsound finance, and the annoying difficulties which arise among most classes of people in the management and control of such enterprises."[67] A more skeptical voice, in a book of advice to young men, argued (erroneously) that the co-op "started as a strictly business attempt of real estate vendors to exploit a new idea—not as an idealistic effort to abolish the landlord." While he conceded that "coöperative ownership seems capable of establishing new and better home conditions," he also warned that "sometimes the plan is used by shrewd operators as a means of selling out a property to a group of owners for a larger aggregate price than they could get from an individual buyer."[68] Such price differences were often the case, but this was a function of the fact that a rental property and individually owned homes were different kinds of commodities, not profiteering.

Satisfied co-op owners thought little of these critiques. Mabel Helen Urner's popular serial "The Married Life of Helen and Warren," which ran from 1914 to 1944 in more than a hundred North American and U.K. newspapers, was a fictionalized account of her life with her husband. After marrying in 1912, they had bought an apartment at 36 Gramercy Park East; later they lived in another co-op, 1 Lexington Avenue.[69] The characters of Helen and Warren were relatively well off, like Urner and her husband, and they lived in the city. But unlike the real Urners, Helen and Warren were very provincial in their tastes. Warren, in particular, expressed constant disapproval of the new.

Warren, an attorney, time and again expresses a good deal of skepticism toward the co-op. In one 1920 episode, entitled "Warren Is Enraged at the Hold-up Methods of Profiteering Landlords," the couple hunts for an apartment. After a long day looking Warren is ready to give up:

> "Shall we knock off?" asks Warren.
>
> "We ought to look all we can while we're out," demurred Helen. "There's a sign on that house over there." But when they had crossed the street they found it read, "Apartments for sale on the cooperative plan."
>
> "Nothing doing! They'll not work that game on me. We may have to pay a good stiff rent for a few years—but we're not buying any gold bricks," replied Warren. Helen does not pursue the matter.[70]

Two years later, as their landlord tries to convert their fictional building to co-op Warren remains just as hostile. As a dinner conversation turns to co-ownership, their guest, a judge, declares, "I wouldn't touch them." In his view the system existed only as a way for developers to secure enough cash to build—"Nothing but a third mortgage"—and could not, as such, be of benefit for the homeowner. Warren agrees: "'Exactly what I've always said. . . . They've been trying to sell me this apartment—but as an investment I can't see it.'"[71]

Co-ownership in the New Deal

Although built examples were few in the 1920s, limited-equity co-ownership had a substantial, if indirect, impact on housing policy in the 1930s. During the Great Depression housing became a national policy concern. Not only did many families lose their houses through foreclosure but housing and construction came to be seen as central to economic recovery. Beginning with Herbert Hoover's President's Conference on Home Building and Home Ownership in 1931 and continuing through the protracted debates over public housing that resulted in the Housing Act of 1937, developers, designers, critics, economists, housing reformers, mortgage lenders, real-estate agents, and elected officials and policymakers competed to shape American housing through public action.

Individual ownership of apartments was largely ignored. When brought together at the President's Conference, for example, all sides overlooked co-op living, even when discussing the very tangible achievements of the Amalgamated Cooperative Apartments and the Dunbar Apartments. These projects were admired for their low "rent," limited-dividend status, good design, and for catering to underserved housing markets. But much to the frustration of the Co-operative

League of the U.S.A., virtually nothing was said about their co-ownership and self-governance.

Left unspoken seems to have been the idea that co-ops were fine for the rich but not for the middle class, let alone the working class—as though co-ownership would encourage the bad habits of apartment and city-center living. This antipathy toward ordinary families remaining in the city is particularly vivid in the volume *Home Ownership, Income and Types of Dwellings*, which was undertaken specifically to address the rise in apartment construction in the 1920s. "How much of that trend," the authors wondered, "resulted from . . . an unconsidered adjustment to the line of least resistance by speculative builders, concerned primarily to get the greatest profit in the shortest time?" "The trend toward apartment house building in the larger cities and in some of the suburban areas," it continued, "should not be misconstrued as indicating that the desirability of the ownership of homes built for single-family occupancy has decreased."[72]

While silent on co-ownership, policymakers did frequently discuss the consumers'-cooperative movement and limited-dividend housing. A central objective of housing reformers in the 1930s was to create a system of "public housing." This was not initially envisioned as state-built housing for the poor (as public housing later became), but as a new, noncommercial, nonspeculative housing sector controlled by forward-thinking housing experts rather than the market, and developed and operated on a limited-dividend basis by unions, government, and consumers'-cooperative groups. Edith Elmer Wood had first proffered something of this idea before World War I and Clarence Stein had argued for it in New York State after World War I. Now, New York reformers took to Washington to ensure that this kind of program be included in the New Deal.

State-aided housing had never engendered much interest outside of New York City and most developers were adamantly opposed to it. The limited-dividend's dual appeal to left and right, however, ensured it a privileged place in federal policy. Even before the New Deal, the Reconstruction Finance Corporation (established under President Hoover) offered loans to limited-dividend housing companies. One of President Roosevelt's first initiatives, in 1933, was an expansion of this program under the auspices of a new Public Works Administration. PWA's Housing Division was also authorized to make grants and loans to local public-housing authorities, but since none yet existed, limited-dividends remained the focus. Seven rental projects were funded nationally, including the Hillside Homes in the Bronx, designed by Stein, and the Carl Mackley Houses in Philadelphia, sponsored by a trade union. Working with myriad limited-dividend developers proved cumbersome for PWA, however, and in 1934 it decided to work exclusively with municipal agencies.[73]

Although PWA abandoned limited-dividend for state-built housing, new provisions for them were included—perhaps to neutralize demands for public housing—in 1934's National Housing Act, which created the Federal Housing Administration (FHA). Under the new law, FHA was responsible for two main programs. One covered construction-loan and mortgage insurance for "houses," which included structures with up to four dwelling units. The other covered "large-scale" housing: in particular, low-cost apartment complexes, which the law required to be developed and operated on a limited-dividend basis.

The program got off to a slow start. FHA was conceived of by the real-estate industry and its leadership and staff were drawn mainly from that field. Their primary interest was single-family housing and there seems to have been little sense of urgency about apartments. One advantage of this lack of interest was that FHA faced few of the problems that PWA had. It patiently rejected the kinds of amateur proposals that had dismayed PWA. More crucially, it took the time to cultivate entirely new kinds of limited-dividend projects that would, ultimately, come to be of great appeal to developers and tenants for decades. In its first two years, FHA produced even less limited-dividend housing than PWA had. But with codification of the new best practices it helped devise—and with the ear of mainstream developers—the program grew quickly thereafter.[74]

Most advocates for low-cost housing were skeptical of FHA; none believed its multifamily program was a substitute for public housing. Underlying this mistrust was a great ideological divide: reformers believed that mainstream developers *were* the problem—that speculative housing markets were the cause of poor housing conditions, and that except for the well-off, private developers could produce only slipshod, unhealthful homes.[75] According to architect Stein, developers could at best produce "little rows of ugly" houses that did "not meet the needs of the people for a healthy and sane community life. The urge for profit demands the use of every bit of space legally available." Mumford was even more dismissive. For a family of ordinary income, he wrote, developers built only semidetached houses "whose surrounding open spaces are covered by a multitude of auto drives and garages—that is Flatbush. Rows of mean little single-family houses, backed by wretched little drying-greens and alleys—that is West Philadelphia." Or apartments "lacking in sunlight, fresh air, beauty, freedom from noise and privacy—that is Boston, Chicago, and the Bronx."[76] By definition, then, FHA could never be part of the solution. Some, in private, referred to FHA as "Fuck Housing Altogether."[77] To really provide for the nation's low-cost housing needs, reformers believed they needed to create a permanent public housing program.

"Modern Housing" and the Co-op

Although various factions of reformers advanced competing ideas for public housing, all agreed on the need for funding to go to city housing authorities as well as to "alternative implementation agencies," including unions, consumers'-cooperative groups, and other nonprofit and limited-dividend housing societies.[78] The most ardent supporter of the alternative-agency provision was Catherine Bauer (1905–1964), a young protégé of Mumford. She helped draft the National Housing Act and ensured its success by persuading the powerful American Federation of Labor to support it over competing proposals.

Bauer's interest in the alternative agencies was shaped, like Edith Elmer Wood's and Clarence Stein's, mainly by the example of Europe. As Bauer wrote in her influential book *Modern Housing* (1934), the collapse of housing markets after World War I allowed for a broad program of state-funded construction in Frankfurt, Berlin, "Red Vienna," and other progressive cities, geared not just to the poor but to the middle class. The bulk of construction, which centered in Modernist garden-apartment complexes on low-cost suburban land, had been undertaken by limited-dividend companies, including consumers'-cooperative groups. Bauer's public-housing bill, drafted in 1935, provided for a similar system of architecturally progressive, suburban multifamily housing for the U.S., to be funded through sixty-year, low-interest loans to municipal and nongovernmental agencies, covering eighty-five percent of construction costs. Although Bauer's bill focused on limited-dividend housing in general, the nonprofit-sector provisions were of special importance. Bauer believed that without them the whole system would languish. In particular she worried that public agencies would be too focused on slum clearance and that a system operated only by government would result in excessive bureaucracy and paternalism.[79]

Yet more strident was the Amalgamated's Kazan, who not only continued to support co-ownership but insisted that it be the *only* form of low-cost housing. Kazan agreed with Bauer's assessment that private developers were not capable of producing well-equipped, low-cost dwellings. But even if they were, he argued, rentals led to poor conditions. The tenant, he noted, regards the situation as temporary and therefore cares little about quality or appearance, and therefore permits the landlord to let things go. Without a robust consumers'-cooperative sector Kazan also worried that more Americans would be tempted to own market-rate houses and apartments. Not only would this encourage speculation, but standard homeownership, he liked to point out, burdened workers with the "great difficulty of disposing of a house in the event of being compelled to seek employment in other cities."[80]

At the same time, Kazan was also wary of limited-dividend companies that "neglected the task of creating greater respect for and consideration of property . . .

[and] failed to teach their tenants the idea of self-help and the possibility of mutually building a better and finer community." He saw state-built housing as yet worse in this respect. Low-rent housing, he argued, should be provided to people "only on condition that they make an effort to improve their own living conditions." Otherwise, he warned, government housing would destroy the "idea of self help." Furthermore, he predicted, the lack of equity stake would lead to "carelessness and destruction of property. Subsidies now needed to lower the cost of housing may be needed to make operation of the project possible."[81]

Kazan's dream was not entirely unrealistic in the mid-1930s. During the Depression, consumers' cooperation enjoyed new currency as a model for empowering producers and consumers to effect "social change without revolution." This was true both in Washington and in the field, where the decade saw, among other things, new activity in agricultural co-ops and the emergence of "co-op" housing on college campuses as a way to lower the cost of room and board. Interest was further stimulated, perhaps by Upton Sinclair's 1936 *Co-op: A Novel of Living Together*, set in a fictional Hooverville in California, and by Marquis W. Childs's rosy reports on Sweden and Denmark in the *St. Louis Post-Dispatch*, published, also in 1936, as a book, *Sweden: The Middle Way*.[82]

Nevertheless, the housers failed to persuade Congress to support alternative-agency provisions. Despite the tireless national campaign, most in Congress, left and right, did not seem to agree that the nation was as poorly housed as Bauer, Stein, and Mumford imagined, and they were uncomfortable with the idea of using state funds to transfer control over middle-income housing to professional designers. Of equal importance, many on the left were reluctant to authorize funds for those with other options, no matter how dreary. Senator David I. Walsh of Massachusetts, who had grown up poor, believed that any and all money the nation could muster for housing ought to go to those most in need. He backed the idea of a public-housing program limited to slum clearance and to building low-rent, state-owned apartments for people in poverty. When he eliminated alternate-agency sections from Bauer's bill in 1936 and again in 1937, few objected.[83]

The FHA Program

Another reason for the failure of the alternative-agency provisions was that many saw little material difference between Bauer's program and what FHA was already accomplishing. The housers took the removal of the alternate-agency sections hard and continued to fight for low-cost federal financing for limited-dividend "middle income" housing. Critics, however, were in some sense correct. Despite FHA's reputation, its Rental Housing Division was staffed by many advocates for housing

Fig. 53: Colonial Village, Wilson Boulevard, Lee Highway, Veitch Street, Arlington, Virginia, 1935–37. Ring Construction, developer; Harvey H. Warwick, Sr., architect. Photograph by Theodor Horydczak.

reform who, after a tentative start, aggressively marketed the program to developers, ensuring it a great impact. By the start of World War II, FHA had insured 391 limited-dividend rental complexes, in thirty-eight states. This was more than all previous efforts in the limited-dividend and philanthropic fields, combined, since the Civil War.[84]

The first complex to begin work under FHA was Colonial Village in Arlington, Virginia (fig. 53). The developer, Gustave Ring, was a young engineer-contractor who had built several of Washington, D.C.'s, expensive high-rise apartment buildings in the late 1920s. During the Depression the city filled with new government workers to staff New Deal agencies. As vacancy rates fell, Ring decided to develop moderate-rent apartments. When he had trouble finding financing, however, he turned to FHA. At first, the agency rejected his project. But Ring and his architect, Harvey H. Warwick, Sr., met with Rental Housing Division staff and they worked together to reshape it. The collaborative proposal was approved in early 1935. Ring secured a large mortgage. By late summer the first families moved in. Rents were $12.50 a room ($490 in 2010 dollars)—less than in most of New York's limited-dividend projects. The project was not just a financial success but also a social one: fifteen thousand applications were received for 276 apartments. Second and third phases followed.[85]

Much of Colonial Village's appeal derived from the innovative physical form that FHA helped Ring and Warwick to devise. Rather than five- or six-story buildings enclosing courtyards as at Jackson Heights or the Amalgamated Cooperative Apartments, the project took the form of a sprawling suburban campus of forty-five, two- and three-story buildings, clothed in a reassuring garb of Colonial Revival red brick.

Ironically, Colonial Village, whose model quickly became standard for FHA-insured apartments, was shaped in large part by RPAA prototypes. Chief among the design and technical staff of the Rental Housing Division were architects Eugene Henry Klaber, a lifelong friend and former colleague of Clarence Stein's, and Cloethiel Woodward Smith, who had also been associated with RPAA. Furthermore, when Ring and Warwick met with FHA staff, it seems clear that Klaber insisted that they draw from his work in Chicago on the limited-dividend Michigan Boulevard Gardens, which, in turn, had drawn explicitly from Andrew Thomas's work and from RPAA projects such as Sunnyside Gardens and Chatham Village, in Pittsburgh.[86]

The new formula also drew from a local garden-apartment tradition, realized most fully at Hampshire Gardens. Hampshire Gardens was a co-op completed in 1929 in Northwest Washington's modest Petworth neighborhood, with 102 apartments in nine, two-story Tudor Revival buildings designed by James E. Cooper and George T. Santmyers (fig. 54). Initial inspiration came when an anonymous

Fig. 54: Hampshire Gardens, New Hampshire Avenue, Third Street, Emerson and Farragut Streets NW, Washington, D.C., 1929. Edmund J. Flynn, developer; James E. Cooper, George T. Santmyers, architects. Advertisement, *Washington Post*, August 25, 1929.

"philanthropist" (speculated to be Met Life) approached Secretary of Commerce Herbert Hoover about developing a limited-equity co-op for federal workers. Longtime Washington co-op sales agent Edmund J. Flynn was confident that he could realize such a project through efficient construction and design, without sacrificing a profit. In partnership with a local developer, Flynn achieved prices of $230 down ($9,200) per room with $12.50 ($500) in maintenance. Although the Depression forced him to stop work with fewer units than he had hoped, Hampshire Gardens made a great impact for its spaciousness and economy. Flynn himself moved there from the Hoyt, which he had converted to co-op after World War I. He lived in the new complex with his wife and children until after World War II.[87]

Toward a New Co-ownership

Although FHA staff contributed much to the field of low-cost multifamily housing in the 1930s, the agency, like President Hoover's conference, all but ignored co-ownership. Working to change this was Herbert U. Nelson. Nelson was national secretary of the National Association of Real Estate Boards (NAREB), the real-estate industry's leading trade group. Real estate was hostile to the RPAA's vision of public housing broadly conceived. But NAREB believed in homeownership and Nelson (ca. 1886–1956) was quick to see that the co-op, even limited-dividend, was preferable to many of the other alternatives in discussion. Over the course of the public-housing debate in the 1930s Nelson became the nation's leading advocate for multifamily homeownership.

Real-estate interests had long supported market-rate co-ownership. Developers had defended it after World War I, and by 1923 NAREB had established a cooperative-apartment section. At meetings, which included tours of co-ops in Washington, Chicago, New York, and Philadelphia, the group discussed design, best sales and management practices, and legislation. Not only was there money to be made developing, selling, and managing co-ops, but cooperative ownership could be just as effective as fee-simple ownership of a house in encouraging neighborhood stability—a major concern of real-estate groups in the 1920s. As Jackson Heights developer Edward MacDougall had suggested as early as 1920, "home ownership, be it a single family house or an apartment" helps "stabilize labor and industry, and will make for better citizenship."[88]

Of particular importance to the field in the 1920s had been amending the tax code to allow co-op owners to deduct property taxes and mortgage interest from their federal and state income taxes. NAREB went to Congress in 1926 and 1927 to argue that co-ops be given the same status in this regard as houses. Its position was that multifamily homeownership was full homeownership even without separate titles for each unit. There is "probably no doubt," its general counsel told Congress, that if the individual-title system were used in the U.S., "as they do in Scotland, where I investigated this matter," and each apartment were taxed on its own, deductions could not be denied. But since such a system was not used he sought a specific amendment "which shall provide that where these corporations are organized for the sole purpose of providing homes for the people who are going to live in them" each owner "should be entitled to the same exemption" as in a house. New York State began permitting such deductions in 1931; Congress followed in 1942.[89]

As part of a campaign to neutralize the possibility of Bauer's middle-class public-housing program, Nelson worked to disprove the idea that restricting profits (the limited-dividend) effected meaningful savings. In the summers of 1936 and 1937 he made his own tours of the Continent, meeting with local housing officials in at least ten countries. In 1937 he and his wife published a response to Bauer's *Modern Housing*, called *New Homes for Old Countries*. Here and in his other frequent writings Nelson argued that Europe's housing achievement resulted not from grants to limited-dividend companies in a handful of socialist cities but from widespread availability of low-interest, long-life mortgages and low property taxes. He acknowledged that the "co-operative societies" were doing terrific work in many places. But he believed that any developer with access to their financing could match it in terms of quality and cost. What the U.S. required, he concluded, was better financing for everyone. Specifically, he outlined the idea for a federal "homestead registration system" that would permit buyers of any kind of home—apartment or house, limited-equity or market-rate—to qualify for a ninety-percent, thirty-year mortgage at the submarket interest rate of three percent, to be insured either by government or private capital, with the requirement that property taxes be limited to one percent of value.[90]

Including co-owned apartments in this proposal was unlikely an afterthought. Nelson had made favorable comments about the co-op as early as 1934. By summer of 1937 he was writing in the *New York Times* that in Europe co-ops "are proving a very useful plan to make homes, fitted comfortably to modern conditions of living, possible for families in the lower income groups, to own." In the United States, he urged, "governmental authorities concerned with housing and housing groups generally should not overlook the possibilities of the cooperative apartment plan."[91]

Nelson continued to cultivate his interest in co-ownership even after the Housing Act of 1937 passed. He maintained that small detached houses were the best way to meet America's housing needs because in most places they were less expensive to produce per unit than were multistory apartment buildings. But he recognized that many people preferred apartment living and that the co-op offered city dwellers a "stable home at low cost" and the opportunity to build equity. In 1938 he and Edward MacDougall successfully lobbied Congress to liberalize FHA's rental-housing program, in part, it seems, with the co-op in mind. Under Nelson's lead NAREB also continued to compile information on best practices to ensure that "this form of home ownership [has] an opportunity for the best use."[92]

On later tours of Europe Nelson made additional visits to co-owned apartments. He remained impressed by work in Sweden and by low-cost and middle-class complexes in Florence. He was especially taken by new upper-class "co-operatives" in Rome, which, he noted, were organized not through corporations but through partnerships called *condominios*. He liked these Italian examples because, unlike in the U.S., local custom permitted individual mortgages for each unit, which, he imagined, helped to account for the surge in homebuilding there.[93]

By 1940, Nelson had become so convinced of the merits of collective homeownership that he, along with Abraham Kazan, began arguing *for* Bauer's vision: in particular, that federal public-housing funds go to Swedish-style limited-dividend mutual-housing groups rather than state-owned housing.[94]

Little happened to advance any of these ideas. Co-ops continued to fail in the 1930s—including the Coops and several other limited-equities—and the few proposals for new co-ops in New York and Washington that emerged beginning in 1935 were not realized. Nevertheless, by 1937 an active resale market was emerging in some places, and in 1939 sales resumed at some long-stalled projects. Although the Coops remained a rental, other co-ops began creeping back toward owner-occupancy, and in New York and Chicago one-time owners in at least some foreclosed buildings began establishing new cooperative corporations and buying their apartments back from lenders. By the 1940s even the "white elephant" building on Park Avenue in John Marquand's novel *Point of No Return*, which we visited at the end of chapter two, had turned around. Whereas our narrator last reported worried looks on the faces of building residents and staff, now "the hall attendant . . . wore an expression of unctuous triumph, and he was justified. God was in His heaven again. The building was solvent."[95]

CHAPTER 4

Vertical Subdivisions

Bell Park Gardens in Bayside, Queens, was in many respects a prototypical postwar suburb. Like Levittown, fifteen miles farther out on Long Island, Bell Park was conceived of in the late 1940s and developed with FHA-insured financing. It followed FHA design guidelines and featured wide green lawns, thirteen playgrounds, and an up-to-date suburban mixture of Early American architectural elements, in this case red brick, white clapboard, and gabled roofs (fig. 55). As at Levittown, most of the homes had four rooms: a living room, kitchen, and two bedrooms, as well as one bathroom. (Bell Park also included some larger homes, with separate dining rooms and three bedrooms, as well as some smaller ones.)

Socially, like Levittown, Bell Park Gardens appealed to veterans and their families. Most were second-generation Americans and first-time homebuyers. As at Levittown, they understood their new homes as more "American" than the rented city apartments they had grown up in. Certainly they saw them as improvements over the living arrangements they had suffered immediately after World War II. The cost of living at each community was also comparable: a home with two bedrooms at Bell Park, after a small down payment, cost $65 a month.[1]

Families bought at Bell Park because they perceived it as beneficial to their children, and because they expected its suburban atmosphere would be pleasant, comfortable, and safe. They reported that they chose Bell Park because they wanted "to be free from the tensions, haste, crowding and crime of the city," they believed ownership would afford them greater control over their surroundings and greater security of tenure, and they hoped "their children will find more pleasant playmates coming from more controlled homes and families."[2] One Bell Park buyer spoke of how the "cooperative and friendly" neighbors would benefit her children. Another, moving in with her husband and three children from a Bronx basement (following a cramped stay with her mother), explained: "It will be wonderful to see the sun in the morning."

Fig. 55: Bell Park Gardens, mixture of materials and child's bicycle.

A third elaborated: because her old home was in a tall building, the children could play outside only if she went too, for reasons of safety. Doing housework meant denying them fresh air and sunshine. Bell Park would correct this problem.[3]

Once they moved in, in 1950, Bell Park homeowners found life was not perfect. By and large, however, it met their expectations. As in many new postwar developments, men faced long commutes. From Bell Park it took ninety minutes to get to Manhattan by bus and subway. It took somewhat less time to go by Long Island Railroad, but one needed to drive to the station and most men left the family car with their wives. Fathers rarely made it home before their children went to bed. Women had to adjust to living farther from transit, shops, and their extended families. Bell Park's physical form, however, made it easy for mothers to watch their children—not that children were generally required to remain in sight: the relaxed community which quickly formed was such that everyone knew one another. Parents let their children roam, confident that another adult was looking out.[4]

Community also emerged in other ways. As in new middle-class developments everywhere, Bell Park families were active in neighborhood and civic affairs. They arranged for the public library's book bus to stop, organized a blood bank, and argued for a zoning variance to block construction of a shopping center, which they worried would generate traffic. Of special concern were schools. Thanks to the efforts of Bell Park parents—and the huge numbers of children—the city built a public elementary school adjacent to the complex in 1952. The average age of Bell Park homeowners at first occupancy was thirty-one; among the eight hundred homes were 760 children, ninety percent not yet in kindergarten. More atypical for a postwar tract, Bell Park homeowners also engaged directly with national problems like racial segregation in housing. Although the complex was all white (predominantly Jewish), a group of residents formed in 1951 to push for integration, arranging for a Black family to rent a home.[5]

Another important reason for resident satisfaction at Bell Park was control. This was especially true for women. Andrea Krest, who grew up in the complex, later recalled how "crucial to their suburban existence and sense of self-worth was the interior design." This was all more so because for most women it "was the first chance they had to control their surroundings; they were no longer guests in their parents' already furnished homes or transients in rented rooms." Because exteriors were similar, the "interior assumed great importance." Many women displayed "well-tended flower gardens, window panes of stained glass, stylish draperies, or vases on window sills, [but] the interior of the house was the focus of decoration." As another Bell Park child recalled, "Mom spent her days pulling apart the home and we all fantasized about putting it back together. Stripped cabinets waited for paint and instant meals waited to be popped into the oven."[6]

Despite these parallels with conventional suburbia, Bell Park was different in one critical respect: it was a limited-equity garden-apartment co-op. Its eight hundred homes were not in eight hundred single-family detached houses but in thirty-nine, two-story apartment buildings on a leafy campus of sixty-five acres.

The decade after World War II was the golden age of the American suburb: ticky-tacky boxes with picture windows and "split-level children."[7] After fifteen years of depression and war, millions embraced homeownership and nuclear-family domesticity. For the most part, this was in single-family suburban houses. In the 1920s, rates of homeownership had climbed from forty to forty-six percent but structural forces channeled capital toward apartments (relatively few of which were owned). Things began to change in the 1930s, thanks in large part to FHA. Between 1933 and 1941 FHA financed tens of thousands of apartments. Eighty percent of new homes, however, were single-family houses—the highest share ever. During the war there was a limited return to multifamily construction. But between 1946 and 1956, which saw a record seventeen million new homes, eighty-four percent were houses. Postwar prosperity, broad distribution of wealth, innovations in home production and financing, improvements in access to the urban periphery, decentralization of jobs, cultural focus on the house and child-rearing, a shifting racial landscape that brought millions of poor African Americans from the rural

South to metropolitan centers, and, above all else, the baby boom contributed to this trend. Homeownership rose from fifty-one to fifty-nine percent.[8]

Because of the role that government played in nurturing the single-family suburb and in steering capital away from urban neighborhoods through redlining, many imagine that the postwar American system all but precluded development of middle-class housing apart from the suburban house. It did not. Only one-quarter of postwar U.S. houses were financed with FHA. More importantly, the 1940s, 1950s, and 1960s saw a small but significant expansion of low-cost co-op living at places like Bell Park.

The co-op countertrend was generated in part by revived demand among cosmopolitan types for co-ownership. It was also fueled by a new willingness on the part of at least some ordinary middle-class families to own what they might otherwise have rented, either as a compromise between the lures of Levittown and the familiarity of apartment living, or as a steppingstone toward buying a house. This new phenomenon was concentrated in metropolitan New York, where myriad middle-class families—mainly Jewish, but far from ideologically committed to the cooperative commonwealth—embraced co-ownership. For yet other postwar co-op buyers, ideology did matter. Bell Park and its successors were, in certain respects, at the vanguard of a different set of hopes for the postwar metropolis than embodied by single-family suburbia. Relatively few Americans chose housing for ideological reasons and life at co-ops could be as defined by privatism as in any suburban subdivision. But for many, the co-op served as an important site of political engagement.

Another reason for the quiet revival of the co-op after World War II was government. As many as eighty or ninety percent of co-ops built between the 1940s and 1960s were produced with government support from Washington or in New York, City Hall or Albany. These welfare-state programs were critical to the spread of the low-cost co-owned apartment at a time when apartments never truly rivaled the house for American affections. At the same time, perhaps paradoxically, government policy also limited the appeal of low-cost co-ops. Terms of purchase were rarely as favorable as for houses. Moreover, most low-cost co-ops came with limited-equity restrictions, which, as in the 1920s, were at odds with mainstream ideas about homeownership. As a result, no more than a quarter of a million low-cost co-ops were built nationally by the early 1970s. As an alternative to suburbia, however, they represented a powerful experiment in postwar optimism.

Housing Crisis Redux

World War II, like World War I, generated housing problems that many people attempted to solve, in part, through collective homeownership. The specific issues were new. With memories of the post–World War I economic crisis in mind, Washington established an Office of Price Administration (OPA) in 1941 to control inflation, and in 1942 Congress authorized OPA to control rents. At first rent control applied only in a limited number of critical defense-industry areas. But as tenants' groups in larger cities like New York threatened to organize rent strikes, OPA extended controls there too, in 1943. Federal rent controls remained in place for the rest of the 1940s in most cities, continuing even after OPA was disbanded in 1947.[9]

Rent control had multiple effects on the co-op. On the one hand, it eliminated the most compelling wartime incentive to co-ownership for consumers: steep and frequent rent increases. On the other, it made conversion extremely appealing to landlords. In 1944 and 1945 hundreds of tenants reported to OPA that their landlords were asking them to buy their apartments. Most tenants bristled. Rather than see this as an opportunity, they interpreted the cost of co-op shares as a "bonus for the privilege of living in the apartment" they already had. To protect tenants and preserve rental units, in 1945 OPA introduced the requirement that eighty percent of residents consent before a conversion could go forward. Although many building owners continued to pursue conversion, sometimes aggressively—prompting investigation by the Securities and Exchange Commission, the Better Business Bureau, and the New York State Attorney General—few succeeded. In all, only about two dozen conversions happened in the 1940s in the entire U.S. The majority were on Park and Fifth Avenue buildings in New York.[10]

Even in these buildings co-ownership could be a difficult sell. Most had been built as co-ops and had failed during the Great Depression. Tenants were naturally hesitant to make a second investment in the same apartment. Furthermore, it was far from clear in the late 1940s that resale values would ever rise again. More importantly, with rent frozen at 1943 levels (sometimes just one-third of peak rates from the 1920s) rising wartime and postwar wages made apartments so inexpensive that other benefits of co-ownership, including exclusion, came to seem less important. When landlords circulated rumors about pending anti-discrimination laws that would have opened buildings to Jewish and Black families, even tenants in some of the most "restricted" first-class buildings resisted overtures to convert.[11]

Ironically, of the few conversions to happen in the 1940s outside of Manhattan, most were in wartime housing developments where the landlord was the federal government. In the 1930s, as the debate over public housing had unfolded, several New Deal agencies began experimenting with limited-equity cooperative production and ownership of single-family houses. The objective was not to achieve multifamily homeownership but to use consumer's-cooperative principles to lower costs. These highly limited experiments were conceived of at the federal Resettlement

Administration by Lawrence Westbrook, under the leadership of Rexford Guy Tugwell, who had been an affiliate of the RPAA. Westbrook called his program the Mutual Ownership Plan (MOP). When Congress began building war-related apartment complexes in the early 1940s it was understood from the start that they would be divested after the war, with MOP a possible model. The government disposed of as many as fifty projects on this basis between 1947 and 1955, including Aluminum City Terrace, outside of Pittsburgh, and Naylor Gardens, in Washington, D.C. An additional eight complexes were organized as MOP from the start between 1940 and 1942.[12]

The Veterans' Projects

After the war, the co-op—and, especially, consumers'-cooperative production of houses—briefly became a popular idea among veterans. High rates of family formation, a buoyant economy, and several years of low production meant that there was a huge shortage of housing after demobilization, especially well-equipped housing in up-to-date neighborhoods. To help overcome this problem, the international consumers'-cooperative movement, organized labor, and MOP encouraged groups of veterans to become their own developers. In books, pamphlets, and speeches these groups promised that by undertaking projects "the co-operative way," prospective homeowners not only could break the "log jam" in construction and get the housing they wanted sooner, but they could get better housing for less money than offered by developers. Before the market began producing large volumes of new speculative housing in the late 1940s, dozens of small veterans' groups, from New Jersey and Maryland to Detroit and L.A., announced plans to build.[13]

Most failed. Small, inexperienced groups struggled to plan developments that met FHA's standards for mortgage insurance even with technical assistance from groups like the Co-operative League of the U.S.A. When they did, work was often slow. Meanwhile, costs could rarely compete with those achieved by merchant builders like Levitt & Sons. Nationally, only a few such veterans' projects were completed, including small groups of houses and row houses in Washington, D.C., and California, before the housing market recovered.

Rather more successful were co-ops initiated on behalf of veterans directly by government. Virtually all were in New York City and were conceived of by the city's construction czar, Robert Moses, or by the New York State Division of Housing, an office created in 1926 to administer the state's limited-dividend housing program. The first of these projects was Hillman Houses, announced in the fall of 1946 for a Lower East Side slum-clearance site. To undertake the project, Moses recruited Abraham Kazan and the Amalgamated Clothing Workers of America. Moses, like most housing reformers, had little interest in fostering co-ownership.

But he recognized that Kazan had the experience and know-how to get things done. The power broker helped Kazan secure favorable financing from a large insurance company and an extended property-tax exemption from the state. Kazan built and sold the project.[14]

Yet more important than Moses was Herman T. Stichman, head of the state's Division of Housing. As housing commissioner it was part of Stichman's job to promote limited-dividend developments. He did so tirelessly during his tenure (1944–54). A career lawyer with little previous experience in housing, Stichman (1902–1967) began promoting the co-op idea shortly after the war. By 1947 he was at work on Bell Park Gardens, recruiting leaders of several trade unions to sponsor it. Under his direction they incorporated under the name United Veterans Mutual Housing (UVMH) (see fig. 2), bought the land in Queens, and hired

Fig. 56: Bell Park Gardens. Advertisement, *New York Times*, May 31, 1949.

William M. Dowling as architect. (Dowling had previously worked with Stichman as the Division of Housing's senior designer.) Stichman also helped the group get an FHA-insured mortgage and hired Roth-Schenker, an experienced local developer, as contractor, persuading the firm to accept even lower fees than specified by FHA for limited-dividend jobs.[15]

To market the project, UVMH opened a sales office at the Veterans Service Center in Midtown Manhattan. More than half of the apartments sold quickly by word of mouth. When sales stalled, advertisements were run. They suggested that buying at Bell Park Gardens was a patriotic act of self-help, as heroic as planting the American flag at Iwo Jima. Images showed four men raising an I-beam in emulation of Joe Rosenthal's iconic photograph (fig. 56). The caption reads: "Triumph on the 'Home' Front!"[16]

Bell Park eventually sold out and the first families moved in by 1950. Two additions followed: Bell Park Manor and Bell Park Terrace. Stichman also pursued several other projects, including a co-op for a meat-cutters' union in Brooklyn and

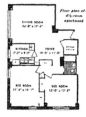
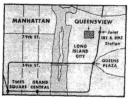

Fig. 57: Queensview, Crescent to Twenty-first Streets, Thirty-fourth Avenue, Thirty-third Road, Long Island City, New York, 1949–50. Louis Pink, Gerard Swope, developers; Brown & Guenther, architect. Advertisement, *New York Times*, April 17, 1949.

one for an electrical-workers' union in Queens, called Electchester. In addition, Stichman helped develop Queensview, a racially integrated complex in Long Island City sponsored by a group of housing activists under leadership of attorney Louis Pink, who had served as an early administrator of New York State's limited-dividend housing program. The project was conceived by Robert Moses as a life-insurance-company rental but no insurance company was willing to undertake a project in gritty Long Island City at the scale Moses envisioned. Pink, who sat on the board of a different insurance company, convinced it to make a mortgage for a smaller limited-equity co-op. The project began in 1948 and opened in 1950 (fig. 57).[17]

While generally successful, the postwar veterans' co-op fell somewhat short as an alternative to conventional suburbia. Strict limits on developers' profits, tax abatements, cheap land, constant oversight, and economical designs helped produce newsworthy low-cost housing. But sales were often slow. One reason may have been the apartment format. Houses were still hard to get in 1949 and 1950, but for most families they were worth the wait. Design and location may also have been a problem, especially at projects like Queensview, with its semi-industrial site and stark, high-rise form (fig. 58). Another reason for hesitancy among buyers was, presumably, that in the late 1940s the GI Bill's housing credits did not yet extend to FHA-insured co-ops. At Bell Park, for example, down payments were modest—$1,150 to $1,300 ($18,000 to $20,500 today)—but enough to make one consider a house. This discrepancy stemmed from the fact that the Veterans Administration (VA) had little experience with co-owned housing and was slow to figure out how to apply housing vouchers to co-ops, which had blanket, rather than individual, mortgages.

To take advantage of these vouchers, a handful of co-ops in New York, Washington, D.C., and Connecticut were organized between 1946 and 1948 on the individual-title plan of co-ownership (later known as

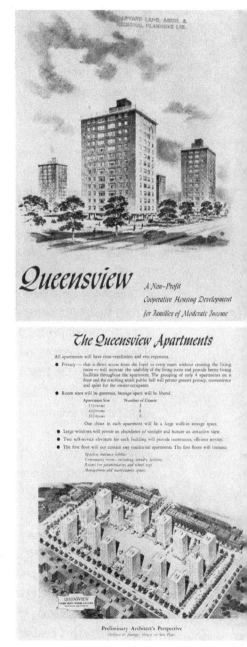

Fig. 58: Queensview, pages from *Queensview*, prospectus.

condominium in the U.S.). To comply with bank requirements, however, by-laws had to allow more individual rights in property than was customary in U.S. co-ops, and the projects could not, as a result, operate on a limited-equity basis. This ensured that the plan did not enjoy the support of housing reformers. What's more, the developers found the legal work required to establish individual fee-simple titles for each unit burdensome. Once the va worked out new formulas to reduce down payments for veterans at corporate-title co-ops, the deed plan was abandoned.[18]

A third problem with the veterans' co-op was the slow pace of development—and that home-seekers had to buy from plans in advance of construction (see fig. 2). To ensure that there was no speculative element in its co-ops, fha withheld approval (and therefore delayed construction) until ninety percent of apartments were sold. Direct union sponsorship, which provided a reservoir of workers as buyers could speed things up. But at other projects the delay could be a serious handicap. Rare was the homeowner willing to invest in a blueprint and wait a year or two for occupancy, when single-family houses and rental apartments were available for immediate move-in.[19]

Middle-income Housing

These limitations were far from clear at first. As work began on places like Bell Park—and as Congress wrestled over reauthorization of public housing in advance of the National Housing Act of 1949—housing reformers mounted a campaign for a greatly expanded federal program for limited-dividend middle-class housing, chiefly in the form of "middle-income" co-ops.[20] Although a similar idea had failed in Congress in the 1930s, Catherine Bauer, Clarence Stein, and groups like the Co-operative League of the U.S.A. and the American Federation of Labor remained optimistic in light of deep public concern about the shortage of well-equipped housing, and the success of many wartime housing projects. Joining the old guard in support were nareb's Herbert U. Nelson, as well as new figures like Stichman.

Nelson's interest continued to derive chiefly from his opposition to direct state construction of housing. As the *Washington Post* noted in 1948, "nareb's 45,000 realtors will use the cooperative plan as their last line of defense in a prolonged fight against any public housing measure." As before the war, Nelson believed that low-income co-ownership was a desirable and viable alternative. To bolster his argument, he made a new tour of Europe in the summer of 1948. He wrote widely of what he saw, especially in Sweden, where by the late 1940s consumers' cooperatives were producing nearly twenty percent of new housing. It was in part as a result of these efforts that postwar policy discussions began to focus on the co-op specifically rather than on limited-dividend housing generally. By 1949 U.S. lawmakers were using the terms "middle-income" and "cooperative" interchangeably.[21]

Like Finland, whose émigrés had helped bring the limited-equity co-op to New York in the 1910s, Sweden had had an active Rochdale movement since the 1880s. Frustrated by the lack of capital for building after World War I, tenants'-rights groups in Sweden established a network of building-and-loan societies in the mid-1920s to develop limited-dividend, limited-equity co-ops. About ten percent of urban housing built in Sweden in the 1930s had been done this way. After World War II, the Swedish government began offering cooperative groups favorable treatment in the form of long-term, low-interest loans covering ninety-five percent of costs. The primary rationale was less a desire to foster homeownership than the co-ops' proven record of producing high-quality, low-cost homes.[22]

After his trip to Europe, Nelson promoted the idea of a Swedish-style system of long-term, low-cost loans to cooperative groups for owner-occupied housing developments. In a press release in late 1948 he declared that co-ops were the "only road to home ownership for millions of Americans." On national radio he announced that Senator-elect Hubert H. Humphrey of Minnesota would propose an amendment to the pending housing act to provide more mortgage insurance as well as direct long-term, low-interest loans for co-ops. Unlike public housing, Nelson explained, which made tenants "become permanent wards of the government," the "Swedish system . . . leads to home ownership."[23] Many of his real-estate colleagues were skeptical. They insisted that anything less than fee-simple ownership, including co-ops, was "socialistic." Eventually NAREB's leadership forced him to withdraw his support for the amendment. The landmark National Housing Act of 1949—like that of 1937—passed without special provisions for middle-income co-ops.[24]

Still convinced that the program was necessary, the Truman administration immediately introduced a standalone Middle-income Housing Bill; John Sparkman of Alabama did the same in the Senate. The bills variously called for, among other provisions, a Cooperative Housing Administration to operate as a limited-dividend sibling to FHA and a National Mortgage Corporation for Housing Cooperatives to offer financing. Consumers'-cooperative groups, veterans' groups, and organized labor rallied behind them. No vote was taken that fall, however, and the bills were resubmitted in 1950. In the interim, Sparkman and most of the rest of the Senate Subcommittee on Housing and Rents followed Nelson's lead and sailed for Europe to make their own tour of low-cost housing.[25]

The primary justification for the middle-income co-op program was the idea, advanced by generations of housing reformers and colored primarily by the experience of Manhattan, that there was a large group of "forgotten" or "middle" families who were too well paid to qualify for public housing but not comfortable enough to buy or rent market-rate housing, including FHA (fig. 59). These families were said to earn between $2,500 and $4,000 a year ($40,000 and $63,000 in 2010 dollars) and to be able to pay $50 or $60 a month in mortgage, maintenance, or rent ($790 to $950). The best way—and, some suggested, the only way—to provide for them was with a Swedish-style system of co-ops.[26] The face of such families in congressional hearings was Donald Monson, an architect from Detroit who was involved with plans for a large co-op (unbuilt) called Schoolcraft Gardens. The complex—and public subsidies for it—was necessary, claimed Monson, because the FHA apartments and houses that he could afford were too small for his family in the neighborhood in which he preferred to live.[27]

Fig. 59: "Union Members Locked Out of New Homes," American Federation of Labor, Housing Committee, *Homes for Union Members*, 1950.

Although this premise enjoyed wide currency, others saw it as flawed. The National Association of Home Builders (NAHB) argued in congressional hearings that there was no basis for the claim that co-ops could be built more cheaply than other kinds of apartments or houses. Harvard legal scholar Charles M. Haar similarly pointed out that the "evidence offered for such claims" in support of the unique benefits of the limited-equity co-op "falls short of the burden of persuasion." Most of the savings claimed for such co-ops were in fact "attributable to large-scale enterprise" or "substitution of one type of effort and money for another," while in practice "the chief saving . . . is due to the financing technique of . . . long-term mortgages at a low rate of interest and amortization—savings that have no relation whatsoever to the cooperative form of organization."[28] Even Sparkman's extensive report on conditions in Europe conceded that while his group was "impressed by some of the good results obviously achieved by the housing cooperatives," this was "not to say that they could not possibly have been achieved except by the cooperatives" and that the primary benefits attributed to consumers'-cooperative housing resulted chiefly from "various kinds of subsidies, direct and indirect."[29]

Of equal weight in opposition in the age of Cold War and McCarthyism was NAHB's claim that the $2 billion ($30 billion in 2010 dollars) proposed for direct loans for the production of co-ops was "another excursion into Government-subsidized socialism, involving inevitable mismanagement by inexperienced people which would subject the Government, and, in turn, the taxpayers, to losses of unpredictable magnitude." Congress, the homebuilders warned, ought to not "underwrite another housing fiasco like the Lustron deal without knowing all the facts." (Lustron was a highly touted but unsuccessful postwar reconversion scheme to use steel to build prefabricated houses.) Even federal housing chief Raymond M. Foley expressed doubt that below-market-rate loans to middle-income groups was an efficient use of public funds.[30]

Yet more persuasive as an argument against the middle-income program was that half of FHA-insured homes—co-op, rented, and single-family—were already being bought and rented by families earning between $2,000 and $4,000 a year. The "forgotten third," in this light, was as much a political figment of reformers—committed to the idea that people deserved better-designed communities in better locations than the market supported—as it was an actual constituency that FHA was neglecting. No dedicated co-op bill passed.[31]

FHA's *Cooperative Housing Division*

The first federally aided co-ops took shape even before Bell Park Gardens. Following Colonial Village—the rental complex of 1935 whose example was codified in FHA design guidelines (see fig. 53)—most were low-density campuses of small, two- or three-story buildings surrounded by green space and parking. Like Bell Park Gardens, most also followed Colonial Village's Early American style, which took on a new symbolic importance after the long foreign war. Typical of these projects was the Warwick Gardens apartments in Red Bank, New Jersey, a Colonial Revival complex developed by the architect Erwin Gerber in 1946 (fig. 60). Although navigating FHA was never easy, its generous financing enabled anyone with a moderate amount of capital, including architects, to become developers. Less characteristic was the conversion by a determined veteran of a large

VETERANS
HERE'S YOUR APARTMENT!
▶ *Occupy it immediately;* ▶ *Less than an hour from New York*

WARWICK GARDENS, RED BANK, NEW JERSEY
Limited number
New 3 and 4 Room Cooperative Apartments For Veterans,
Veterans' Widows, Members of the Armed Forces.

COMPARE THESE VALUES!

Size of Apts.	Cash Required	Estimated Monthly Charges
3 Rooms & Bath	$2111.40	$51
4 Rooms & Bath	$2525.40	$61

AGENTS
RAY STILLMAN & ASSOCIATES
EATONTOWN, N. J.
Telephone: NEW YORK CITY—WHITEHALL 3-2380   EATONTOWN, N. J.—EATONTOWN 3-0007

Fig. 60: Warwick Gardens, Pinckney Road, Red Bank, New Jersey, 1947. Erwin Gerber, developer and architect. Advertisement, *New York Times*, January 19, 1947.

Fig. 61: 16 East Eighty-fourth Street, New York, reconstruction of older structures, 1947–48. Robert Freifeld, developer; James E. Casale, architect.

row house off of Fifth Avenue in Manhattan to eleven apartments, also in 1946 (fig. 61). Many East Side mansions had converted to apartments beginning in the early 1930s, but none, until 16 East Eight-fourth Street, had been organized on an ownership basis.[32]

Because it did not insure them under a separate program, it is difficult to tabulate the number of co-ops that FHA helped finance in the 1940s. It appears, however, that no more than a dozen or two were completed before 1950, including those sponsored by Stichman and Moses. Meanwhile, hundreds of thousands of rental units were built. Rentals appealed to people who saw their tenure as short term, had no money to put down (or were saving it for a house), or who saw ownership of an apartment an unnecessary risk after a very long decline in resale values. They also appealed to developers. During the war Congress created an emergency housing program at FHA which offered favorable terms for production of rental apartments. Like rent control, it was extended after the war to help ease the housing shortage. By 1950, when the program ended, seven thousand rental complexes with nearly half a million units had been built, blanketing swaths of metropolitan New York, Chicago, Washington, Los Angeles, and beyond with up-to-date garden-apartment complexes (fig. 62).

In 1950, this balance toward rentals began to change. The emergency rental program expired amid a glut of cheap apartments. More importantly, from the ashes of the failed Middle-income Housing Bill, Congress established a Cooperative Housing Division at FHA. It was accompanied by a new program, Section 213 of the National Housing Act, specifically for insuring mortgages on limited-dividend, limited-equity co-ops. It covered ninety, and sometimes up to ninety-seven, percent of costs.[33] In part because FHA programs sent important signals to developers about what was best to build at a given moment, the number of co-ops grew substantially (fig. 63).[34]

The new program was far more modest than what reformers had fought for. "Two-thirteens" (projects built under Section 213) had to be incorporated as consumers'-cooperatives rather than as joint-stock enterprises, and had to follow Rochdale rules: one vote per apartment, regardless of size or price. Owners had to offer their apartments back to the cooperative before they could sell to others, and

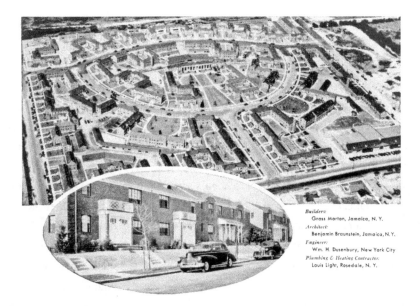

Builder:
Gross Morton, Jamaica, N. Y.
Architect:
Benjamin Braunstein, Jamaica, N. Y.
Engineer:
Wm. H. Dusenbury, New York City
Plumbing & Heating Contractor:
Louis Light, Rosedale, N. Y.

Fig. 62: Glen Oaks, section one, Union Turnpike, Commonwealth Boulevard, 249th Street, Seventy-sixth Avenue, Bellerose, New York, 1948–49. Gross Morton, developer; Benjamin Braunstein, architect. Detail of advertisement for Bell & Gossett. *Architectural Forum*, May 1949.

Fig. 63: Mitchell Gardens, Union Street, Whitestone Parkway, Twenty-fifth and Thirtieth Avenues, Bayside, New York, 1951–52. Benjamin and Harry Neisloss, developers; Benjamin Braunstein, architect. Advertisement, *New York Times*, February 18, 1951.

only for the price paid plus any additional equity accrued through the repayment
of a project's blanket mortgages. Proprietary leases were short term, usually just
three years. Unlike the failed bills, however, Section 213 did not offer direct loans at
below-market interest rates. Also, as with low-cost rentals FHA allowed speculative
developers to participate so long as they abided by its rules. Critics, by contrast, not
only hoped for subsidized financing, but believed that to ensure quality construction
and create wholesome, stable communities, co-ops had to be initiated by prospective
homeowners or nonprofits.[35]

Even more at odds with reformers' ideals were provisions for what FHA called
"sales-type cooperatives." These allowed production of single-family houses on a
consumers'-cooperative basis and then conversion of each to separate fee-simple
ownership after construction. While this system could lower some production costs,
it met few other goals of the consumers'-cooperative movement, especially at projects
sponsored by speculative developers where the "cooperative membership consists of
people brought . . . by means of advertising and a regular sales campaign" and projects
"involve[d] speculative and profit-making aspects on the part of the initiators."
Lakewood, California, the first major project to use the program, was precisely of this
sort. It was a massive single-family tract in L.A. County with more than seventeen
thousand houses, built between 1951 and 1954. To secure favorable financing, the
developers organized several sections as sales-type cooperatives. Because in every
other respect Lakewood was an ordinary subdivision many argued that it had
violated the spirit of the provision. FHA rarely permitted such projects thereafter.[36]

Bay Terrace

More typical of FHA's new co-op program was Bay Terrace, a garden-apartment
complex begun in 1953 in Bayside, Queens. The developer was Norman K. Winston,
who had spent most of the 1940s and early 1950s building single-family houses on Long
Island. The architect was Bell Park's William M. Dowling (ca. 1899–1954). Like Bell
Park, Bay Terrace was suburban in character. It was, however, much larger: initial
plans called for thirty-seven hundred apartments in 220, two-story modern Colonial
Revival buildings (fig. 64). To speed production while satisfying FHA requirements
that co-ops be ninety percent sold before beginning work, Winston divided Bay
Terrace into several smaller sections, each with its own cooperative corporation.
Even so, construction was slow and the project was not completed until 1966. Early
phases closely resembled Bell Park. As work progressed, plans were revised to include
modernistic six-story elevator buildings designed by Alex Danin (fig. 65). Both types
of structures included a mixture of four-, five-, and six-room apartments that sold for
$1,100 to $1,700 ($13,000 to $20,000) with maintenance of $80 to $120 ($950 to $1,400).[37]

Fig. 64: Bay Terrace, Bell Boulevard, Twenty-sixth Avenue, Cross Island Parkway, Clearview Expressway, Bayside, New York, 1953–66. N. K. Winston-Holzer, developer; William M. Dowling and Alex Danin, architects. View of garden apartments.

Fig. 65: Bay Terrace, elevator building.

Prices at Bay Terrace, as at most other FHA co-ops, were competitive with rentals, as well as with comparable single-family houses. Although the first for-sale houses at Levittown were under $8,000 ($120,000), prices for most new single-family houses in metro New York immediately after the war were $9,000 to $11,000 ($135,000 to $170,000) for basic models in similarly "basic" locations. By the early 1950s even the cheapest models at Levittown cost $9,000 with $1,000 down for veterans ($1,900 for civilians), and small ranch houses by other developers ran at least $11,500. Three- and four-bedroom houses in more established places such as Manhasset or Far Rockaway sold for at least $15,000 to $20,000 ($235,000 to $315,000) in the late 1940s, and half again more by the 1950s. Larger houses (for which there were few comparable co-ops) sold from $30,000 after the war and from $40,000 or more by the 1950s (both roughly $500,000).[38]

Marketing for Bay Terrace was done in partnership with Gimbels department store, which erected full-scale models of two apartments on the tenth floor of its Manhattan flagship. Store ads for the project suggest some of the appeal (fig. 66): "Gimbels believes the Bay Terrace Co-operatives are . . . a bargain! Just [$]77.80 a month carrying charge (after your down payment) buys you a spacious 4-room garden apartment. . . . You could hardly rent room in Manhattan to swing a cat for that. . . . Above all, you won't be paying 'rent' any more; you'll have eliminated the ordinary landlord relationship. The carrying [maintenance] charge takes care of upkeep, pays for your gas and electricity. You'll live on a wooded site flanked by 2 golf courses and the sailboat-dotted water of Little Neck Bay. Good schools are in walking distance. A new bathing beach is being developed just a stone's throw away. And all this is a bare half-hour from Times Square." The apartments sold well. Many, according to the sales manager, were bought by households that had previously owned detached houses.[39]

FHA-insured co-ops like Bay Terrace appeared all over metro New York in the 1950s, with the greatest concentration in suburban Queens, followed by Riverdale in the Bronx, and the thickly settled towns of southern Westchester County, including Yonkers, New Rochelle, and Mount Vernon. Manhattan and Brooklyn also saw several each, including a large high-rise at 1270 Fifth Avenue facing Central Park. FHA cost limits made the high price of land a challenge, however, and most projects in Manhattan and Brooklyn appeared in out-of-the-way sections like Inwood and Coney Island. FHA-insured co-ops also began to appear in other cities by the late 1950s, including Chicago, Los Angeles, Philadelphia, and Miami. By the mid-1960s, half of all FHA co-ops were outside of metro New York. In many places these were the first co-owned apartments built since the 1920s.

Fig. 66: Bay Terrace. Advertisement for Gimbels, *New York Times*, April 19, 1953.

United Housing Foundation

While FHA was a leading force in diffusing the low-cost co-op in the 1950s, it was not the only program or organization working toward this end. First among the others was the United Housing Foundation (UHF). UHF began in 1949 as the Council for Cooperative Development, convened by Abraham Kazan after passage of the Housing Act of 1949. Title I of the new law offered liberal provisions for "urban

Fig. 67: Kingsview, Myrtle Avenue, Ashland Place, Willoughby and St. Edwards Streets, Fort Green Urban Renewal Area, Brooklyn, 1955–57. Louis Pink, Gerard Swope, developers; Brown & Guenther, architects. Advertisement, *New York Times*, September 19, 1954.

redevelopment" (renamed "urban renewal" in 1954), which, unlike the Housing Act of 1937, allowed city governments to clear slums for projects other than public housing. Based on the success of the Hillman Houses, Robert Moses, who led the city's "Title I" program, invited Kazan to draft new proposals. Joining Kazan were a group of longstanding New York housing reformers. As a first project, Moses asked Kazan to develop a fifteen-acre site on the Lower East Side called Corlears Hook. Following first approvals of that project, Kazan incorporated the group as UHF, with Clarence Stein, Louis Pink, and other community leaders on the board.[40]

UHF's goals were twofold. One was to develop and construct union-sponsored co-ops in both Title I slum-clearance areas and beyond. The second was to help other groups develop and operate limited-equity co-ops. UHF did both well. In the 1950s and 1960s the group built more than thirty thousand apartments. In addition to the Corlears Hook project (called East River Houses), these included the Seward Park Houses on the Lower East Side; Queensview West in Long Island City; Kingsview in Brooklyn's Fort Greene Urban Renewal Area (fig. 67); Penn Station South, a Title I project near Manhattan's Garment District sponsored by the International Ladies Garment Workers Union (fig. 68); and the James Peter Warbasse Houses and Rochdale Village in Brooklyn. In the mid-1960s it also began Co-op City (fig. 69) in the Bronx, which would have more than fifteen thousand apartments alone when completed in the 1970s. UHF also assisted smaller groups to develop tens of thousands of other co-ops around the city, including Morningside Gardens near Columbia University, and Chatham Green and Chatham Towers, in Chinatown.[41]

Aiding UHF and its offshoots were three city and state programs designed, at least in part, to foster low-cost co-ops. The first, of relatively minor importance, was the New York State Redevelopment Companies Law of 1942, which empowered municipalities to use eminent domain to condemn land for new housing developments. The major achievement of that program was Stuyvesant Town in Manhattan. Like all of Met Life's projects in the 1940s, however, it was a rental. The second program, which was even smaller, directed New York City's public-housing authority to construct projects for sale (or lease) to consumers'-cooperative groups.

Fig. 68: Penn Station South, West Twenty-third and Twenty-ninth Streets, Eighth and Ninth Avenues, Penn Station South Urban Renewal Area, New York, 1958–62. International Ladies' Garment Workers Union, United Housing Foundation, developers; Herman J. Jessor, architect. President Kennedy at project opening, 1962.

Fig. 69: Co-op City, Baychester Avenue, Co-op City Boulevard, Bronx, 1968–72. Riverbay Corporation, United Housing Foundation, developers; Herman J. Jessor, architect. Aerial view of construction, August 12, 1969.

This program was discussed as early as 1955 and was implemented in 1959; by 1965 eight co-ops had been developed this way.[42]

The third and by far most effective program was New York State's Limited Profit Housing Companies Law of 1955, commonly referred to as Mitchell-Lama, after its sponsors. This law replaced the state's 1926 housing program with one closely resembling what housing reformers had been fighting for for more than forty years: direct, low-interest loans from the state to limited-dividend developers. It also authorized municipalities to make similar loans. Many rentals were developed under Mitchell-Lama. The majority of units, however, were co-op. Altogether, the state and city financed around sixty thousand co-op units through these programs.[43]

Foundation for Cooperative Housing

Outside of New York, UHF's efforts were paralleled by a sister organization called the Foundation for Cooperative Housing (FCH). FCH was established in 1950 by an overlapping group of housing reformers, including Clarence Stein, to take advantage of the new FHA co-op provisions. To run it, the trustees hired Roger Willcox, a young land planner out of Stein's office at Kitimat, a new town the architect was designing in British Columbia. Willcox was committed to consumers'-cooperative housing. He had grown up in Bleecker Gardens, a block of row houses in Greenwich Village that a group of progressive families had bought, renovated, and outfitted with a communal garden in 1929. More recently, Willcox (b. ca. 1920), his parents, and siblings had developed a subdivision in suburban Connecticut on a consumers'-cooperative basis. Motivated by an opposition to ethnic restrictions in many suburbs and by the conservative design of most speculative houses, they formed a group in 1949, selected a site, and recruited other likeminded families to build Modernist houses on the community's sixty-seven lots.[44]

FCH's initial focus was on preserving pet projects of trustees through conversion to co-op. These included a government-built World War I community, in Bridgeport, Connecticut; Greenbelt, Maryland, developed by the Resettlement Administration under Rexford Tugwell in the mid-1930s; and, somewhat later, Clarence Stein's and Henry Wright's Chatham Village, in Pittsburgh. Early new-build projects included a co-op for U.N. employees in New York and co-op apartments and "sales-type" houses on vacant land at Greenbelt. FCH also offered technical support to other developers. The first major client was Reynolds Metals, which sponsored several limited-equity co-op complexes in Title I urban renewal areas to showcase aluminum building materials (fig. 70).[45]

Fig. 70: River Park Mutual Homes, Fourth Street between N and O Streets SW, Southwest Urban Renewal Area, Washington, D.C., 1963. Reynolds Metals Company, developer; Charles M. Goodman, architect.

Fig. 71: Eastwyck Village Towne Houses, 2892 Eastwyck Circle, Decatur, Georgia, ca. 1965. Foundation for Cooperative Housing, developer.

In the early 1960s FCH shifted emphasis. It began working in partnership with small-scale local builders in college towns, blue-collar suburbs, and small cities as co-developer of low-cost garden-apartment complexes (fig. 71). By the 1960s new FHA incentives to low-cost co-ownership and burgeoning demand among baby-boom households for smaller, more highly serviced kinds of homes was generating new demand for co-ops. In larger centers, developers had enough savvy to meet demand on their own. In places where the co-op had little or no history, small-scale builders turned to FCH to navigate FHA paperwork and for assistance with things like design.

Most of these builders were unaware of, and uninterested in, FCH's consumers'-cooperative vision. Willcox helped them all the same. Through these partnerships, FCH developed several dozen complexes in Michigan, and smaller numbers in Puerto Rico, Indiana, Illinois, Kentucky, Maryland, Georgia, Kansas, Nebraska, Ohio, Arizona, and Virginia (fig. 72). They accounted for the bulk of postwar co-ops built outside of metropolitan New York. Perhaps under similarly cross-ideological premises, FCH also took on the U.S. Agency for International Development as a client in the 1960s. As part of its antirevolutionary efforts, USAID became involved in slum-clearance projects in Brazil and Argentina and wanted to redevelop them with owner-occupied housing, including co-owned apartments.[46]

Fig. 72: Irongate Townhouses, Newport News, Virginia. Foundation for Cooperative Housing, developer. Foundation for Cooperative Housing, *Cooperative Housing in the USA*, ca. 1973.

Community Life

The lived experience of postwar co-ops varied widely with geography and design. In particular, it depended on the kind of people drawn to a complex. As sociologist Herbert Gans argued in his 1968 essay "Urbanism and Suburbanism as Ways of Life," the "behavior and personality patterns ascribed to" a community, whether single-family houses or an apartment building, "are in reality those of class and age."[47]

A 1955 report in the *New York Times* by Herbert Mitgang underscores this idea. Mitgang investigated why for every four families with children moving from New York City to Westchester County or Long Island, one similar family moved back. There were obvious differences between life in each place: Manhattan meant smaller quarters, walking to work rather than taking the commuter train, and playing in parks rather than the backyard. Some people said they found the city less isolating; others that it offered more privacy. Yet others, however, observed that many aspects of life were surprisingly similar. One father, for example, noted that his "conversations . . . in the suburbs. . . . were always on two subjects: obstetrics and houses." Back in Manhattan, it turned out, "the conversations among our friends are still obstetrics and houses," although relieved, from time to time, by "a few other subjects, too." Meanwhile, he elaborated, the "life ambition" of everyone in suburbia "was to have a bigger house . . . in an excellent school community where the people were 'their kind.'"[48]

These same aspirations animated many co-op families. In 1955, a New York nonprofit concerned with early child development called the Play Schools Association (PSA) began a pilot program in new middle-class co-ops—some in Manhattan, some in Queens; some state-aided, some FHA; some in elevator buildings, some in garden apartments. The objective was unremarkable: to improve children's opportunities for recreation. The methods were extraordinary: preoccupancy training and ongoing workshops to teach co-owners how to work together. PSA reports offer a rich record of why people bought apartments and what life was like in the developments.[49]

Echoing the experience at Bell Park—and places like Levittown—the group found that people bought co-ops for more and better space than they had before, for the satisfaction and stability of owning their own homes, and for a "decent community": a controlled social environment of likeminded families, where their children could make friends with "nice—not rough—people," and where there were "no bad gangs or a lot of juvenile delinquents." The result were tight-knit, homogeneous communities more like vertical subdivisions than anonymous apartment buildings.[50]

Inwood Terrace

Exemplary of the vertical subdivision was Inwood Terrace. Inwood Terrace was the first of three Mitchell-Lama co-ops developed in the steep, rocky hills of Northern Manhattan in the late 1950s and early 1960s by the socially progressive architects George D. Brown, Jr., and Bernard W. Guenther (fig. 73). Brown & Guenther had designed the limited-equity Queensview for Louis Pink and Herman Stichman in the late 1940s and become specialists in middle-income co-ops, designing more homes of this type nationally than perhaps anyone except Herman Jessor, Kazan's architect of choice.

Physically, Inwood Terrace was quite apart from suburbia. Like most Mitchell-Lama and UHF co-ops—and, increasingly, many FHA co-ops by the late 1950s—it was a freestanding high-rise, with more than two hundred apartments in a twenty-one-story tower slab. It also eschewed the historicist signifiers of domesticity and the optimism of Miesian and California Modernism which characterized suburban architecture in the 1950s. Defined primarily by a drab but pragmatic utilitarianism, Inwood Terrace rose as a sheer mass of plain red brick, relieved only by hyphenated ribbons of small windows. At a distance there was little to distinguish it from any number of low-rent public-housing projects.

Like Bell Park Gardens, Inwood Terrace was designed to accommodate a somewhat greater variety of families than most suburbs; apartments ranged in size from three rooms to six. A majority of buyers were young families with children but there were also families with teenagers, as well as some seniors. All were middle-class. Mitchell-Lama required income ceilings of roughly $7,000, and down payments and maintenance costs were set to accommodate households earning between $4,000 and $6,000 a year ($38,000 to $56,000). To meet these limits—much to the frustration of some buyers—Brown & Guenther withheld many features that had become standard in market-rate housing by the late 1950s, including hardwood floors, individual washers and dryers, and dishwashers. But the result was an equity investment of $450 per room with projected maintenance of $23. For a five-room apartment this meant $2,250 down and $115 a month ($21,000 and $1,100).[51]

Despite the building's physical form and relative diversity in terms of age, the community that developed in Inwood Terrace was not so different from that of the suburban Lakewood, California, of D. J. Waldie's memoir *Holy Land*—or even, for that matter, the middle-class Stuyvesant Town of Corinne Demas's *Eleven Stories High*.[52] Owners worked together to buy a rooftop TV antenna and new playground equipment. At Halloween, mothers organized parties while fathers patrolled the building and neighborhood. Residents organized weekly dance classes and bridge and canasta nights. Attracted to the building, according to PSA, by ads that "promised to fulfill their dreams of . . . an ideal suburbia planted within the city," Inwood Terrace families made this dream a reality with enthusiasm. Similar kinds of community formed at other middle-class co-ops. At Bell Park Gardens, owners carpooled and published a yearbook. At Merrick Park Gardens, an FHA-insured African American garden-apartment complex in Queens, they threw Fourth of July parties. At Colonial Square, an FCH project in Ann Arbor, Michigan, owners swapped babysitters and wrote a monthly newsletter.[53]

Fig. 73: Inwood Terrace, 99 Hillside Avenue, New York, 1957–59. Brown & Guenther, developer and architect.

Although "suburban" in these respects, the communities that took shape at middle-class co-ops distinguished themselves from mainstream suburbia, especially in their politics. In New York, at least, most of the homeowners were Jewish, and most were quite liberal. Yet more popular than canasta night at Inwood Terrace was a weekly discussion group that attracted as many as sixty-five people to confront issues such as nuclear disarmament, the migration of Puerto Ricans to New York, and modern art. Cooking and sewing groups were failures.[54]

Also atypical were the owners' views on race. Following Rochdale principles, New York State had prohibited discrimination in new state-aided limited-dividend projects in 1939. New York City extended this commitment to fair housing in a series of postwar laws that prohibited segregated projects from using tax abatements and eminent domain. Eventually, the city prohibited segregation in all government-aided projects. Racial homogeneity remained the overwhelming norm, however, because the laws were difficult to enforce. As at other progressive co-ops, such as Bell Park Gardens and Queensview, homeowners at Inwood Terrace readily embraced integration, with many parents hoping their children would "learn tolerance." Unfortunately, as had happened at Queensview a decade before, only a handful of Black families bought. This was particularly disappointing to the Black homeowners, whose children, especially teenagers, could feel isolated. As one woman told PSA, "I am very happy here, but I do not know if I would have moved here if I had known that so few Negro families were to be my neighbors."[55]

Co-op Conservatism

Despite the commitment to racial liberalism, life in middle-class co-ops could also be characterized by streaks of suburban conservatism. PSA found that above all else, co-op mothers wanted their children to be materially successful and popular. It observed tremendous pressure on children to perform in school and gain admission to prestigious colleges, and that children were overscheduled, with insufficient time to explore the world on their own. Although children took dance and music, their parents did not want them to become artists, dancers, or musicians. PSA staff also encountered social conformity: "In a cooperative tastes are often adapted to the prevailing 'norm.' To be like one's neighbor means to be safe, means to be assured a place in the group." In one building, they noted, "there was a period when almost everyone bought a spinet [piano] because his neighbor had one; naturally this led to piano lessons for all of the children. This pattern repeats itself over and over." PSA also found that status concerns "predominate even in the more 'intellectual and culturally oriented' groups, who may choose to purchase hi-fi sets, or original oil paintings, rather than ostentatious television sets or bigger automobiles."[56]

Yet more surprising given the broad support for integrated housing was hostility to desegregation of schools. At one complex in Jackson Heights, Queens, built in 1958 and 1959, a 1963 proposal to pair the local school with one a few blocks away in a lower-class African American neighborhood provoked intense opposition. According to two sociologists who lived in the complex, a majority of the homeowners, whom they characterized as "middle mass, not middle class," had moved there to escape from mixed-income neighborhoods, especially "deteriorating" sections of Brooklyn and the Bronx. They felt they had worked hard to leave "shabby and rundown ghetto[s]" and wanted nothing to "spoil" their new neighborhood, which they "frequently spoke about . . . as if it were a part of suburbia." Higher-status owners tended to support the school-pairing program, but they were less invested: many anticipated moving to a larger home in a better neighborhood after a few years. Those less secure in their middle-class status—and more intent on staying put—remained wary of anything that might compromise their children's upward mobility.[57]

Some degree of this inward focus may have been a result of neighborhood conflict. Most of the PSA-assisted co-ops, for example, had been built on greenfield or country-club sites at the urban periphery, adjacent to established suburban communities. The gentile old guard in surrounding neighborhoods "resented and feared" the newcomers on account of their Jewishness, working-class origins, and generally liberal politics. At one FHA co-op whose eighteen, six-story buildings contrasted markedly with the surrounding one- and two-family houses, there developed the "familiar pattern of resentment toward the cooperative," which intensified when groups of teenage boys from the older suburban neighborhood began terrorizing children and teens from the apartments. Even where there was no such conflict, however, middle-class co-ops tended to have an intense inward focus.[58]

A Limited Market

Although multifamily homeownership appealed to many middle-class households and, as FCH's Roger Willcox notes, there were "virtually unlimited funds" for co-ops thanks to FHA, co-op living remained fairly uncommon in the late 1940s, 1950s, and early 1960s with the exception of metro New York. Even in New York City there were, by one count, only fifty-five thousand co-ops by 1962 (up from a Depression low of approximately five thousand), with another thirty-eight thousand in development. Beyond New York there were, perhaps, another fifty thousand. Half of these were in New York suburbs. Most were the product of government incentives. No more than a quarter, in any jurisdiction, were financed privately with "conventional"—that is, non-FHA or Mitchell-Lama—mortgages. As a share of new homes co-ops were only

slightly more common than they had been in metro New York in the 1920s; outside of
New York they were less common.[59]

A major reason for modest demand was demographics. Although household size
continued to fall in the postwar era—from an average of 4.0 persons in 1928 to 3.4
in the mid-1950s to 3.3 in the mid-1960s—more than forty percent still comprised
married parents with children. These kinds of families overwhelmingly preferred
houses. And now, for the first time in history, most could afford them. Meanwhile,
among those still unable to afford a house, or who did not want or need whole houses,
renting continued to make the most sense. Until the number of households without
children grew, co-op sales would remain flat.

Even in New York this larger preference for the house was an issue. Below-
market prices at Mitchell-Lama, UHF, and FHA co-ops kept them full in middle-class
areas like Manhattan, Riverdale, and northern Queens. But elsewhere, sales often
languished. At Kingsview, for example, which was a complex of well-equipped high-
rises designed by Brown & Guenther in Brooklyn's Fort Greene, the apartments
struggled to sell (see fig. 67); so did the red-brick high-rises at University Towers in
nearby Clinton Hill, designed by Kelly & Gruzen.

Many in the 1950s hoped that housing preferences could be changed to reverse
the socio-economic decline of cities and to curb suburban sprawl. To explore the
viability of additional middle-class housing in city centers—a strategy widely
embraced by city governments in the 1950s—*Fortune* magazine helped finance a
study of middle-class households in Center City Philadelphia, downtown Chicago,
and Manhattan. (*Fortune* was home to urban-affairs reporter William H. Whyte, a
leading critic of suburbia.)

Conducted in 1957, the study investigated why middle-class and well-to-do
people—people who could afford to live in suburban houses—chose to be in town.
Large new apartment buildings and old-stock row-house sections were analyzed, and
the homeowners and tenants surveyed. The prognosis was not promising. Contrary to
expectations, the authors found that the market was meeting, rather than distorting,
demand. Families with children liked houses, they discovered, while only households
without children liked apartments. More discouraging was that well before starting
to shop, people knew exactly what kind of area they were after. Location was so
important that more than half bought or leased the first place they saw: the particular
dwelling hardly mattered, just its social identity, and that of the neighborhood.[60]

The study pointed out, for example, that just twenty percent of city-center
households had children, and only six percent had school-age children. Far more
common were older couples and older singles, eighty percent of whom were women.
Also common were younger career-oriented singles, half men and half women, many

living with "similar people of the same gender" (presumably as roommates and as gay couples). The sample also revealed major differences between the apartments and row houses. High-rise residents were fifteen years older, even less likely to have children at home, and three times as likely to be Jewish. No matter the housing type, however, the implication was clear: that there was little immediate hope of convincing large numbers of middle-class families with children to live in city centers.[61]

Evading Paternalism

Apart from these large structural hurdles, the low-cost co-op faced additional problems. One was confusion surrounding cooperative ownership. Another was hostility to limited-equities' restrictive by-laws, even among populations with few good housing options, such as middle-class Black people.

Merrick Park Gardens, in Queens, was one of the first racially integrated co-ops insured by FHA's Cooperative Housing Division. It was developed by a white lawyer named William Brafman in 1952 on farmland once owned by Homer and Langley Collyer. It comprised seven, two-story buildings designed by Erwin Gerber, along with four playgrounds and garage space for forty-three cars. Like Queensview and Inwood Terrace, however, it attracted little interest. In editorials, the *New York Amsterdam News* pleaded with the paper's Black readers to buy. And in an unprecedented move, FHA allowed Brafman to make personal loans, at no interest, to buyers for their down payments. His contribution of nearly $80,000 ($1 million in 2010 dollars)—presumably made through arrangement with a local bank rather than out of pocket—lowered down payments from an initial range of $675 to $1,150, to just $175 to $275 ($2,300 to $3,700). Only then did enough families come forward to save the project. They included salesmen, teachers, engineers, bus drivers, and clerical workers, of whom many worked for state, federal, and municipal government.[62]

According to Brafman, the biggest obstacle to reaching this clientele was "explaining the co-op principle"—that is, convincing ordinary people of the benefits of owning what one might otherwise rent. Another appears to have been the limited-equity format, which seems to have struck many as anathema to homeownership. At its projects, for example, the New York State Division of Housing not only demanded that homeowners suffer asphalt-shingle floor tiles and live without dishwashers, but it told homeowners that they were not, in fact, owners: "The apartments in a cooperative are owned by the housing corporation." Buyers at most limited-equities could not choose which unit they received—they indicated preference of size and location but took what was offered on a first-come, first-served basis. No "improvements" could be made to apartments without consent of the board. Often, no animals were permitted. Worst of all, to many, were restrictions on resales.[63]

While it is difficult to find record of these critiques, it is clear that where possible, homeowners devised tactics to evade restrictions they found onerous. The boldest of these was black-market resales. These were not possible in every limited-equity. UHF, FCH, and the New York State Division of Housing kept close watch on homeowners and mandated use of centralized waiting lists and buy-back programs to enforce prohibitions on individual profit. In FHA-insured projects, however, homeowners routinely ignored these guidelines.

As noted by the New York State Assistant Attorney General responsible for co-ops, "stockholders of Section 213 cooperatives have demonstrated rather widespread . . . disapproval of FHA procedures in connection with the resale of apartments."[64] In practice, as another expert noted in 1961, it is "generally recognized that almost every one who has bought a co-operative apartment during the last 20 years has sold it for more than he paid for it."[65] The *New York Times* reported that four-room apartments which initially sold, in the early 1950s, for $1,800 ($24,000) commanded $4,000 ten years later ($33,000). At particularly attractive projects, like Bay Terrace, apartments were said to have tripled in price between first sales, in 1953, and 1960. FCH disapproved, warning that selling "merely to make a profit" was "threatening the stability" of co-op organizations, but to little effect. FHA was aware of the controversy but had little interest in enforcement. It did not, after all, restrict resales in houses.[66]

Limits of Cooperation

Another problem in limited-equities was that despite the emphasis on collective rights in property, the system often failed to cultivate requisite feelings of proprietorship. In the 1920s, the cooperative spirit was engendered by the intense political engagement of the co-owners; the genuine thrill of worker-led organizations having created better housing at lower prices than the market; and, most importantly, by the tireless efforts of dedicated, highly spirited leaders like Abe Kazan. There was only one Kazan, however, and without someone of his talents, projects suffered. Contributing to this problem was the large size of postwar complexes. Inwood Terrace, with two hundred units, was not unmanageable. Bell Park Gardens, on the other hand, had eight hundred units; Queensview seven hundred; Electchester twenty-two hundred; and Bay Terrace, thirty-seven hundred. In some, separate cooperatives were established for each section. But in most, control remained unified. With boards of directors of just seven or nine people, and rarely more than thirteen, no number of volunteer committees could ever engage more than a token share of owners. As a result, most residents experienced these places less as owners than as tenants, much to the frustration of self-appointed leaders who felt their neighbors treated them as paid management or, worse, the landlord.[67]

In UHF, FCH, and Mitchell-Lama co-ops, some effort was made to circumvent these tensions through preoccupancy training. But without continual support from an individual like Kazan or counselors supplied by the Play Schools Association, things could deteriorate. Perhaps in recognition of this structural limitation, UHF began to tentatively deemphasize the communal nature of its brand of co-ownership in the 1960s. In one sales prospectus, for example, it explained that the "purpose of a cooperative is to provide home ownership, not just apartments to rent." In rental buildings, it continued, the "landlord's interest was in financial gain," so, as a consequence, there is "no common interest between the tenants" and little sense of community. "The common bond of collective ownership which you share makes living in a cooperative different," it promised. "Home ownership, common interests and the community atmosphere make living in a cooperative like living in a small town."[68]

This shift in rhetoric coincided with a new focus at UHF in developing not just very large projects like Penn Station South, with twenty-eight hundred households, but mega-projects like the James Peter Warbasse Houses, initially planned for fifty-two hundred apartments (although completed with half that), and Rochdale Village, with nearly fifty-nine hundred units, all under a single corporate umbrella. UHF recognized these sizes were less than optimal, but it had become so effective at redeveloping otherwise difficult sites that city leaders pressured it to build more, faster, and larger. Unfortunately, the limited-equity model collapsed under such heavy weight.[69]

Co-op City, in particular, was so large and unruly that even UHF leaders questioned whether such a project was sustainable. Co-op City was conceived of by Robert Moses and New York State Governor Nelson Rockefeller as a way to help the site's previous owner, developer William Zeckendorf, escape financial trouble. Although Kazan had reservations, he agreed to take the job on. From a distance, many thought the project's problems stemmed from its design, which included fifteen thousand apartments in thirty-five towers (and a small number of row houses). Like many state-aided limited-equity co-ops of the 1950s and 1960s, Co-op City was widely critiqued for its repetitive forest of utilitarian high-rises (see fig. 69). The reporter and activist William H. Whyte, a longtime champion of middle-class apartment living in cities, characterized Title I co-ops as "bleak towers, which stretch to an infinity," no better than the slums they replaced. Architecture critic Ada Louis Huxtable agreed, describing Co-op City's design, by Herman Jessor (1895–1990), as far inferior to the new towns built in Scandinavia and the U.K.[70]

The real trouble, however, stemmed from the large size and the alienating structure of governance. Even before the project's completion, Vietnam-era inflation led to runaway costs. By the time the buildings opened, between 1968 and 1972, maintenance charges were far higher than UHF had promised in the original sales prospectus, in 1965. By the mid-1970s stagflation meant they were more than triple initial estimates. As at other limited-equity projects facing similar difficulties, the frustrated and effectively voiceless homeowners reacted like aggrieved tenants rather than homeowners, organizing a "rent" strike. They also sued UHF for stock fraud. The financial—and symbolic—damage, coupled with Kazan's death in 1971, led UHF to permanently leave the field of development. After the Co-op City debacle, as one historian has written, UHF "died of a broken heart."[71]

Structural Problems at FHA

While housing reformers and government sought to expand access to co-ownership only to be hampered by market demand for suburban houses and resistance to paternalistic governance, other forces were also at work against the co-op. Chief among them were ambiguities within federal policy. Formulated as a political compromise between real-estate interests and housing advocates after the collapse of the middle-income housing bills in 1950, FHA's co-op program was designed primarily to discourage speculation in housing by empowering groups of prospective homeowners to become their own developers.

As a result FHA required co-ops—whether apartments or "sales-type" houses (as at Lakewood, California), and whether twelve homes or twelve hundred—to be nearly sold out before construction. If the market was slow this could force developers and buyers to abandon a project. Even in strong markets there were problems. According to Maurice R. Massey, Jr., who developed high-rise FHA co-ops in Philadelphia and Detroit in the mid-1950s, "the minute an apartment is sold . . . [the buyer] takes a proprietary interest . . . and pretty soon he is around to tell you how to build the building and pretty soon he goes to the FHA and tells them how to build the building, and pretty soon the FHA tells you," putting the whole project "at jeopardy."[72]

Meanwhile, as late as 1955 FHA remained focused on stimulating "consumer-initiated" co-ops, and its regional officers were instructed to assist these kinds of groups either directly or by referring them to organizations such as FCH. To help, Congress lowered down payments on most co-ops from ten percent—the standard for single-family houses—to just five percent. In 1959 it lowered them again, to three percent. This policy change stimulated sales to some degree, but it did not address a more fundamental issue: not only were most FHA co-ops initiated by speculative developers or organizations like FCH rather than prospective homeowners, but groups of homeowners did not make good developers.[73]

According to David Krooth, a seasoned attorney long involved with co-ops (and FCH), the original ideal of "bringing consumers together who were going to hire an architect and plan and build a project themselves" proved a "most disastrous procedure." One could not, he continued, "bring a group of amateurs together and expect them—just because they want and need a home—suddenly to get the background and experience to know how to design projects and produce housing at a price they can afford. I've represented such groups; so I know whereof I speak. These groups become debating societies. They waste money needlessly, preparing plans which ultimately are not used. In preparing the plans, everybody has their own idea of what they want and they all want everything. Then when the prices are obtained, the people find they can't afford the housing, so the groups often end up in disillusionment."[74] Other supporters of limited-equities agreed. New York attorney Max Tretter, a longtime advocate for low-cost housing, warned Congress in 1955: "It is somewhat naïve to believe that the ultimate consumer can develop a cooperative housing project with all its complexities in the law of finance, administration, planning, construction. The driving force, the know-how, must come from someone outside the ultimate consumer."[75]

At the insistence of advocates like Tretter and, more influentially, homebuilders and architects, in 1956 Congress introduced an "investor-sponsor" program that allowed "corporate investors" (that is, real-estate developers) to build in advance of sales so long as they promised to transfer title to a cooperative corporation within two years of completion. This measure was only halfhearted, however. To not alienate those who disparaged the quality of developer-built projects, the program received far less preferential treatment than other kinds of housing: rather than five percent down as in pre-sold co-ops, or ten percent down as in houses, buyers of prebuilt co-ops had to pay fifteen percent down. As a consequence the program had little impact. And when buildings using it ran into financial trouble due to slow sales, it came be seen as a failure.[76]

An additional structural problem was FHA's method of processing applications. The regional offices that did this work were understaffed and overwhelmed. This meant that new programs that required mastering complex new standards got low priority. Even after staff learned to navigate programs, pressure from Washington to speed through applications for single-family houses meant that apartments often had to wait. Further complicating things was that most staff were drawn from local real-estate circles who, according to Krooth, were "accustomed to looking backwards to determine the value of property and the marketing experience. When they look back in a community which had no housing cooperatives, they assume there must be a reason for the lack of cooperatives." In metropolitan New York this was not a problem, but developers hoping to build co-ops in L.A., Detroit, Atlanta, and elsewhere reported onerous delays.[77]

Middle-income Housing, At Last

The number of government-aided co-ops grew substantially in the 1960s and early 1970s despite these challenges. FHA's original co-op program fell out of favor with builders and homeowners as more flexible—and less restrictive—avenues for financing co-ownership emerged, like the condominium. But in New York, Mitchell-Lama and UHF continued to produce tens of thousands of apartments, culminating in Co-op City. Of equal importance, after more than forty years' struggle housing reformers secured passage, in 1961, of a national program for long-term, below-market-interest-rate (BMIR) loans covering the entire cost of limited-dividend apartments. The program—Section 221(d)(3), and, beginning in 1968, Section 236—was administered by FHA rather than an independent agency, as advocates in 1950 had hoped. But it did much to stimulate the low-cost co-op.[78]

As in earlier eras, the question of federally subsidized middle-income housing was polarizing. At base, the debate betrayed opposing ideas about what the French writer Henri Lefebvre described, in the late 1960s, as the "right to the city." According to Lefebvre, whether housing was built privately or by the state, as in France's *nouveaux ensembles* after World War II, advanced capitalism "literally set itself against the city and the urban to eradicate them" in favor of new suburban forms—but at the cost of social equity and spatial (and architectural) coherence. The right to the city was, he argued, the right to enjoy "the city and the urban."[79]

Like Lefebvre, BMIR was animated by the idea that people had a right to space in "the city"—in particular the high-demand city center. By rendering expensive space affordable, BMIR could counter these centrifugal impulses. As future New York mayor John Lindsay argued in 1961, BMIR was necessary because the "greatest housing need in this country is for moderate or middle-income housing, particularly in cities."[80]

Many saw this idea as absurd. According to Chicago real-estate analyst James C. Downs, Jr.: "Advocates of middle-income housing subsidies are sentimentalists. Almost any middle-income family that wants a three-bedroom house can find one that is decent, safe and sanitary—and perhaps new—if the husband is willing to commute, say, 40 minutes."[81] The homebuilding trade press further argued that "housing liberals . . . have been overstating the so-called need for vast amounts of new low priced housing for years." It also pointed out that income data used to justify BMIR were shaped to overstate the number of "middle-income" families by masking the fact that many were small, younger, or older households that did not require the family-size homes presumed in program calculations.[82]

Debate over BMIR also encompassed other concerns. In the 1920s it had also been about curtailing jerry-building, in the 1930s about the promise of architectural Modernism, and in the 1940s and early 1950s about the extent to which the U.S.

would embrace the liberal welfare state. In the 1960s it came to be about the shifting socioeconomic landscape of the American city and, especially, race. The rapid migration to cities of African Americans during and after World War I and, especially, World War II, combined with restrictions on foreign immigration between the 1920s and 1960s, radically transformed the ethnic composition of low-rent sections of American cities. Meanwhile, continual suburbanization—of middle-class families, of department stores, of offices and factories—made it seem by the 1960s like slums were encompassing more and more of the urban field. Urban renewal, conceived in the 1930s in part to aid owners of outmoded slum property, became a program of violent "Negro removal" designed to protect business districts and pockets of wealth from encroaching racialized poverty.

Initially, BMIR was employed to reverse these trends. It emphasized housing in cities designed to match that of the suburbs in terms of size (large), price (low), and age (new). As with many urban renewal projects, policymakers hoped to appeal to middle-class white households, to bring them "back" to the city. Soon, however, aspirations for BMIR shifted. The War on Poverty and five summers of urban race riots in the mid-1960s led many to the new hope that BMIR could raise rates of homeownership among disenfranchised African Americans, both through new construction and though conversion of rented buildings, as a palliative for the problems of the racialized city and, to a lesser degree, to generate Black wealth through property ownership. These goals were paralleled by renewed discussions (rarely realized) in the 1960s about converting public housing and troubled privately owned buildings to limited-equity co-ops through BMIR.[83]

In practice, BMIR fell short of both goals. Because even in greater New York many were reluctant to live in apartments, because of resistance to the limited-equity format, and, perhaps, because of FHA's sluggishness, BMIR never attracted significant numbers of middle-class white families to city centers. And while it eventually produced many appealing projects in working-class neighborhoods, including Washington Park in Boston's Roxbury and in Wooster Square and Dixwell in New Haven, the program often ended up financing middle-class apartments in college towns like Ann Arbor and Tempe, Arizona, and in small, low-cost cities like Omaha, Des Moines, and Newport News (see fig. 72)—many of which were devised by FCH.

In these projects, there was often little ideological commitment to consumers' cooperation on the part of either developers or buyers. To the contrary, the idea was mainly to take advantage of low interest rates and low prices, and to offer residents some assurance of good neighbors. As home-seekers and builders in leading BMIR states like Michigan and Indiana became more savvy about co-ownership and learned of alternatives to the limited-equity, they quickly abandoned BMIR for less restrictive forms of ownership like the condominium. Exemplary of this transition was Eli Broad, a young Detroit developer whose firm, Kaufman & Broad, built four of country's first BMIR co-ops, all in partnership with FCH. Within a year, however, Broad moved to Los Angeles, where he developed similar complexes but on a strictly market-rate basis. Within a few years this formula made Kaufman & Broad one of the nation's largest homebuilders.[84]

The End of the Low-cost Co-op

By the mid-1970s, UHF, Mitchell-Lama, and FHA had together produced around 250,000 limited-equity co-ops, half by UHF and related groups, and three-quarters in metropolitan New York. Then production all but ended. UHF stopped building entirely after Co-op City. Mitchell-Lama was effectively bankrupted by city and state fiscal problems by 1970, and it too stopped work by the mid-1970s. BMIR fell out of favor with developers. FCH shifted focus to mutual-aid housing in the developing world. Spiraling costs, high interest rates, and a deep recession—precipitated by the Vietnam conflict and by the unraveling of the postwar political (and industrial) economy—extinguished any reasonable hope for the limited-equity co-op as a mass, mainstream form of housing.[85]

Despite this collapse, the limited-equity left a solid legacy of well-built, well-managed housing that continued to inspire many.[86] Pittsburgh's Aluminum City Terrace stayed vibrant well into the 1980s, four decades after it converted to limited-equity under the Mutual Ownership Program—faring far better than several similar projects which had converted to public housing. Rochdale Village, by the 1990s, became a stable, even glamorous, enclave for middle-class Black families in the New York area. Many of FCH's BMIR co-op complexes, too, survived intact and were well cared for into the 1990s, although some languished half empty, unable to compete with other low-cost options. Bell Park Gardens remained a suburban oasis of inexpensive housing for a new generation of first-time homeowners, including many recent immigrants.

In the city center, meanwhile, Kazan's co-ops proved so popular that many buildings abandoned their limited-equity mission, converting to market-rate ownership. Apartments at UHF's Lower East Side projects, for example, sold for up to $1.5 million by the first decade of the twenty-first century. Yet other limited-equities rejected this temptation. At Penn Station South—in the heart of Manhattan, on some of the nation's most expensive land, surrounded by some of the nation's most expensive homes—well-kept, spacious apartments cost just $12,000 a room (after a ten- to fifteen-year waiting list). Decades after the low-cost co-op all but disappeared as a policy goal, they served as isolated reminders of the great possibilities of the cooperative commonwealth.[87]

CHAPTER 5

Leisure Worlds

For all the experiments by artists, the Manhattan rich, the Jewish left, working women, African Americans, and others over the previous hundred years, it was the elderly, primarily in Florida, who first made co-ownership a truly mainstream dwelling practice in the U.S. Before World War II, relatively few Americans owned second or retirement homes. If people went on vacation, they stayed in hotels. Most older people lived with their grown children, in institutional homes for the aged or infirm, or in residential hotels; seldom did they maintain, let alone own, homes of their own. By the 1950s this was changing. Along with a house, car, and television set, the postwar American dream increasingly came to include a summer cabin, trailer, or beach apartment. Although figures are unreliable, by the early 1950s around fifty thousand second homes were being built each year in the U.S., and by the early 1960s, double that. A huge, vital part of this resort market was older families. Increasing longevity coupled with trade-union pensions and Social Security (introduced in 1935) made the postwar era the first in which ordinary Americans could enjoy a comfortable, independent retirement.[1]

In his 1955 guide to "finding what you seek in Florida," travel writer Norman D. Ford suggested that most any "oldster" could afford to retire in the Sunshine State so long as he or she avoided popular tourist areas like Miami and paid for a home in cash. Rented homes were plentiful, he noted, but no less expensive than in many northern cities. Trailers were somewhat more economical, but not trailer-park rents. "Believe me," he insisted, "nothing, absolutely nothing, offers a cheaper way of life in Florida than outright ownership," especially given statewide property-tax exemptions on the first $5,000 of a home's value. To underscore his message, he concluded with a frightening list of alternative housing options: sanatoriums, convalescent homes, nursing homes, and rest homes.[2]

Ford had a specific kind of home in mind: the small freestanding house. Most U.S. developers after World War II focused on single-family houses for young GI Joes of modest income. Some, however, catered to another new segment of the housing market: retirees, especially retirees moving to the Sunbelt to make new, warm-weather lives for themselves. Physically, these retirement communities, which concentrated in Florida and Arizona, resembled other low-cost FHA-insured complexes, with large tracts of all but identical houses. Apart from grab bars in the bathtubs, they differed from Levittown prototypes only in terms of materials (uninsulated concrete was common), size (many houses had just one bedroom), and location. Low-cost postwar subdivisions for young families were often built outside of cities but within the suburban ring. Retirement subdivisions of the late 1940s and early 1950s were usually much farther afield, allowing for house prices as low as $5,200 ($65,000 in 2010 dollars).[3]

While Ford reported that some 250,000 retirees already owned houses in Florida (the U.S. state with the highest share of older families), his vision of "outright ownership of a concrete block or asbestos siding home assessed at under $5,000" was not as broadly appealing as he imagined. Several of the largest among these projects had already stopped work by the mid-1950s or shifted emphasis to larger, better-equipped houses for younger families. Leisure City, for example, sold only a quarter of its six thousand houses in seven years. The developers abandoned one-bedroom models selling for $5,280 in favor two- and three-bedrooms selling from $11,250; they began mentioning schools in ads.[4]

One problem was geography. Like most holidaymakers, retirees favored more established locations near the ocean. Many preferred cities, especially St. Petersburg and Tampa on the Gulf Coast, and Palm Beach, Fort Lauderdale, and, most of all, metropolitan Miami and Miami Beach on the Atlantic "Gold Coast." This was particularly true of Jewish families from New York, Philadelphia, and other northern cities, who migrated by the tens of thousands a year to Florida. By the early 1950s Miami Beach was, according to one local historian, "the gayest, richest Jewish city in the world."[5]

More importantly, many retirees preferred multifamily to single-family housing. They wanted to live where the burdens of maintenance were shared, and where close quarters nurtured conviviality, easing the transition away from old homes, friends, and family. As one 1950s transplant to Miami noted, a house required too much effort and was too isolating. Giving up their house, she said, meant that she and her husband could always find an informal get-together, a fourth partner for bridge, or a poolside conversation. "I don't know how to explain it exactly . . . but there seem to be more people to do more things with."[6]

Fig. 74: Eden Roc Hotel, 4525 Collins Avenue, Miami Beach, 1955–56. Ben Novack, Harry Mufson, developers; Morris Lapidus, architect. Photograph by Ezra Stoller, 1956.

At first, vacationing retirees in search of this kind of community chose hotels, or, for those of more limited means, a furnished rental apartment. Beginning in the late 1930s, Miami and Miami Beach filled with glamorous new hotels, motels, and small apartment buildings. Many were designed by Midcentury Modern architects like Lawrence Murray Dixon, Roy F. France, Sr., Igor Polevitzky, Norman Giller, Charles McKirahan, and Morris Lapidus (fig. 74). Between 1945 and 1954, thirteen thousand hotel rooms were built in Miami and Miami Beach, and thirty-five thousand apartments. Most of the apartments were in small, low-rise buildings away from the beachfront, and rented by the week, month, or season.[7]

As more people spent more time in Florida—encouraged by air conditioning and inexpensive flights back home—year-round multifamily dwellings followed. Some were unfurnished rentals with annual leases. Many, however, were owner-occupied. By the late 1950s there was a small boom in co-ownership. Then, in the 1960s and 1970s, there was a mass migration of middle-class retirees to warm-weather apartments. Although Ford never mentioned the co-op—the trend was still nascent in Florida in the early 1950s—the owned apartment made perfect sense for the reasons he outlined: rentals were expensive and, more importantly, the "majority of responsible northerners past fifty own their own homes outright. These can be sold at a price that will purchase a small new Florida home." On a typical union pension, he maintained, this arrangement left enough money for all expenses and allowed one to enjoy an independent, financially stable retirement.[8]

As retirees adopted co-ownership, they adapted it, echoing earlier efforts by workers and housing reformers to bend it to meet their particular needs. Unlike these earlier groups, who pulled co-ownership more toward common rights in property, postwar retirees favored a more liberal framework—so liberal that they not only rejected the limited-equity co-op, but the corporate-title co-op altogether. Many retirees moved to apartments in search of a community. Most, however, had little time for the clubbiness of the luxury co-op or the moralism of the limited-equities. More importantly, neither system suited their financial needs. The individual-title condominium plan did. This more commoditized system of ownership brought some unforeseen problems, but its greater financial flexibility and less restrictive ownership policies were more in line with mainstream American ideas about homeownership. It caught on quickly. By the 1970s much of South Florida had been transformed into a new kind of mass condoscape.

The Beach Clubs

Before World War II, nearly all visitors to American resorts—including those staying for an entire season—lived in hotels or furnished rental apartments. Limited experiments with co-ownership of resort apartments appeared during the real-estate boom of the 1920s in Florida, as well as in Asheville, North Carolina, and Pasadena and Long Beach in California (see fig. 96). Among the half dozen or more co-ops proposed in Miami, however, only one or two seem to have been realized. Left unbuilt were plans for several massive co-op resorts, including Villa Biscayne, designed by New York hotel architects Schultze & Weaver, which called for more than two hundred apartments; and the Urmey Arms, a twenty-five-story tower proposed for Coral Gables by Villa Riviera developer, and originator of the California own-your-own plan, Lionel V. Mayell, with more than three hundred units. Both were advertised in New York, Chicago, and other northern newspapers, but neither sold enough units to begin work before a great hurricane, in 1926, destroyed the Miami real-estate market.[9]

After World War II, interest in the resort co-op began to grow, although the trend was statistically negligible until the 1960s. Apart from "turnkey" convenience, one appeal of co-ownership was presumably the ease of renting units to other vacationers to help cover expenses. Another, for many, was the ability to police social

boundaries as hotel living was being superseded by the apartment. As the fair-
housing activist Charles Abrams noted at the time, resort towns like Fire Island,
New York; Laguna Beach, in Orange County, California; and coastal regions of
Florida and New England—places where vacation co-ops first became common—all
regularly excluded Jews and other ethnic groups well into the 1950s.[10]

In Florida, the importance of exclusion is suggested by the fact that the first
significant clusters appeared not in the largest centers, Miami and Miami Beach,
where social codes were so relaxed that Jews had come to predominate by the
1950s, or in the most expensive ones, like Palm Beach, where codes were so fixed
that social change was unlikely. Rather, co-ops appeared in the in-between areas of
Broward County, centering on Fort Lauderdale. First platted by the railroads and
other speculative promoters in the 1920s, Fort Lauderdale and nearby towns like
Hollywood and Pompano Beach remained largely undeveloped until the 1940s, when
they became popular with middle-class, mostly gentile families from the Midwest.[11]
While evidence that these groups explicitly prohibited Jews is difficult to find,
ethnic exclusion was commonly implied. As *Holiday* magazine reported in 1954, its
"spiritual geography . . . places the real location of Fort Lauderdale somewhere in
Ohio, Illinois, Indiana, Michigan or Wisconsin . . . [making it] more of a 'home town'
to most tourists than any of the other resorts towns along Florida's Gold Coast."[12]

Because their development was so private—without ads, without developers
to promote them—the trend was unnoticed by the local real-estate press and their
emergence is not well documented. The first postwar co-op in South Florida appears
to have been built at Pompano Beach in 1946. Rather evocatively, it was called the
Cloisters. More than sixty other small co-op complexes followed over the next ten
years, nearly all in neighboring areas of Broward. Socially these complexes operated
as small clubs. Like early co-ops on the East Side of Manhattan and in other cities,
many were developed as such, often by groups of acquaintances from Midwestern
cities such as Chicago and Pittsburgh.[13]

Physically, these Florida co-ops resembled the region's small rental apartments
and hotels. Nearly all were low-rise buildings or groups of buildings, typically of two
or three stories, with twelve to forty units arranged in a wide U- or C-plan, with
a pool, cabanas, and "sundeck" at the interior court (fig. 75). They almost always
faced the ocean, Biscayne Bay, or a manmade canal. More were one apartment deep,
and units on upper stories were accessed through open-air corridors, widely known
in Florida as "catwalks." This arrangement allowed each home a minimum of two
exposures and good cross-ventilation. Elements of this typology had been employed
as early as the 1930s by Miami Beach architects like Lawrence Murray Dixon at
small apartments and hotels. After World War II, it became standard.

Fig. 75: Bay Harbor Towers, 10141 East Bay Harbor Drive, Bay Harbor Islands, Florida, 1956. Bernard J. Flood, developer; Charles Foster McKirahan, Sr., architect.

Typical of this genre of co-op was Sea Club, in Hillsboro Beach near Fort Lauderdale (fig. 76). Built in 1955 on ten acres, Sea Club had ninety-two apartments arranged in three long, low modernistic buildings served by catwalks, and in several smaller buildings, including eight modest one- and two-family bungalows with ziggurat Bermuda roofs. All the buildings shared a private beach, swimming pool, nine-hole golf course, yacht basin, and clubhouse. Nearly every apartment occupied a corner. The designer was the Fort Lauderdale architect Charles Foster McKirahan, Sr. (and perhaps his professional partner and wife, Lucile W. McKirahan). McKirahan (ca. 1919–1964) is most remembered for his hotels, especially the Polynesian-shipwreck-themed Castaways (1958). Between 1954 and his death, however, he designed at least sixteen co-ops and condominiums, more than any of his contemporaries. In a practice that would be adopted by virtually all future large-scale Florida co-ops, Sea Club's developer, Gilbert Edwards, advertised the development in northern newspapers and national magazines, including the *Chicago Tribune, New York Times, Time*, and *U.S. News and World Report*. The units cost from $10,900 for one bedroom and $14,900 for two ($120,000 and $160,000). They sold quickly and Edwards developed several additional co-ops.[14]

Fig. 76: Sea Club, 1221 Hillsboro Mile, Hillsboro Beach, Florida, 1955. Gilbert Edwards, developer; Charles Foster McKirahan, Sr., architect.

The Miami Co-op

Well after co-ownership became common in Fort Lauderdale, life in Jewish Miami remained grounded at hotels. Although at least two small co-ops were completed in the late 1940s in Dade County (which included Miami and Miami Beach), two larger proposals failed. One of these was Continental Square, slated for Miami's Brickell district. It called for more than seven hundred apartments in three towers designed by Edwin T. Reeder. The other was an "ultra luxury" tower for Bal Harbour called the Gold Coast Apartments, designed by Roy France, Sr. Apartments were to be expensive: $25,000 to $35,000 ($380,000 to $530,000). Few who could afford them, however, seemed to care to forgo life at large resort hotels. Neither was built.[15]

Things began to change in the mid-1950s, when a new generation of co-ops began to appear. The first were small, as in Fort Lauderdale. Among them was Bay Harbor Club, built in 1955 on Bay Harbor Island, a man-made island in Biscayne Bay, between mainland Miami, which fronted the bay, and Miami Beach on the Atlantic Ocean. Bay Harbor Club was modest, with twenty-four, one- and two-bedroom apartments clustered in a two- and three-story L-plan building, arranged around a lawn that culminated in a swimming pool and boat dock on the Intracoastal Waterway. Like Sea Club, it was designed by McKirahan. Its

Fig. 77: Sea Tower, 2840 North Ocean Boulevard, Fort Lauderdale, 1957. Terrell J. Murrell, developer; Igor B. Polevitzky, architect.

physical formula—modest size and intimate atmosphere—distinguished it from a resort hotel. At the same time, it was larger and better-equipped than most rented apartments. The project proved popular: it was announced, built, and sold in the course of just one season. Over the next two years two sister projects (see fig. 75), and at least a dozen similar ones built by other developers, appeared in Dade County.[16]

As the apartment gained traction, buildings grew larger. By 1957, co-ops as tall as ten stories were appearing in Fort Lauderdale (fig. 77). Miami also saw its first high-rises. In early 1957, contractor Frank J. Walker began developing Coral Sea Towers, a modernistic high-rise designed by Carlos Schoeppl (fig. 78). Though unprecedented in physical form—and taller than perhaps any other building north of Miami Beach's main hotel district—the apartments sold quickly. Borrowing from the residential towers of Latin America, the building featured a geometric façade of white and turquoise stucco that served as a brise soleil to protect exposed elevator landings. Windows were glass and aluminum jalousies. Though arranged as a slab, floors had only four units, each with two or three outside exposures and a rear balcony facing the Intracoastal Waterway.[17] Within five years, South Florida had more than fifty tall co-ops.

The popularity of the co-op was attributed in the press to the tranquil, less burdensome lives they allowed their occupants to lead. Commenting on the "construction vogue" for co-ops in Miami in 1957, the *New York Times* observed "both a trend toward longer vacations and a change in the clientele itself." It noted that most buyers were longtime seasonal visitors "in or near senior-citizen class" who, after many years of hotel life, "seem nowadays to be seeking a quieter way of life."[18] According to the *Miami Herald,* the draw of apartment ownership also "involved responsibilities": namely that management promised to open and close homes for the season and to prepare for hurricanes in the summer, when most homeowners were away. For "luxurious Florida living," the paper reported, "more and more of our moneyed visitors are choosing co-operative apartments" because their ownership "requires no maintenance effort on the part of

Fig. 78: Coral Sea Towers, 10300 East Bay Harbor Drive, Bay Harbor Islands, Florida, 1957. Frank J. Walker, developer; Carlos Schoeppl, architect.

its owner."[19] As *Florida Building Journal* noted about Sea Club in 1955, "For prospective Floridians, it is a retirement dreamworld."[20] The press also attributed another factor to the co-ops' success: location. "Owners can live in a stylish apartment in a fashionable neighborhood," noted the *Herald,* "for much less than it would cost for an equally stylish home [house] in the same area."[21]

Social homogeneity was also surely a draw, even when ethnic exclusion was not a priority. Ads were dominated by the language of privacy (private porches, private parking, private pool) and exclusivity ("carefully selected clientele," "selected neighbors," "quiet atmosphere"). As Coral Sea Towers announced in 1957, it was a place for "people of refinement . . . who are accustomed to and can afford the finest in luxury living. They will know that their neighbors have been selected—without regard to creed—for their integrity, congeniality, financial responsibility and respected position in their home communities."[22]

Some people, meanwhile, chose to own retirement apartments, at least in part, for socially progressive ideological reasons. In contrast to the conservative

impulses at most co-ops, homeowners at the Sherbrooke, the Galaxy, the Golden
Dreams, and the FDR-inspired Four Freedoms emulated the by-laws of New York's
limited-equity complexes. Most of these co-ops were created through conversion
of older hotels and rental buildings—which was less expensive than building
anew—and were located in older, less fashionable parts of town, like Art Deco
South Beach. Owners were primarily working-class Jews moving from limited-
equity buildings in New York. Although conversion was not common in postwar
Florida, at least a dozen buildings underwent this transition in the late 1950s and
early 1960s.[23]

Co-op City, California

As homeowners and small-scale developers transmitted the co-ownership idea
incrementally, the resort and retirement co-op grew slowly but steadily. There was,
however, a deeper latent demand. This gap became apparent in 1961 at a project
called Leisure World, an "active retirement" community of nearly seven thousand
co-op apartments in Orange County, California, where occupancy was restricted to
households in which one person was age fifty-two or older (fig. 79). Public response
was enormous: 255 people bought homes in the first eight hours of sales and twenty-
five thousand people visited model apartments the first week. Over the next eighteen
months, an average of ninety units sold each week—an astonishing rate for any

Fig. 79: Leisure World, Seal Beach Boulevard, Westminster Avenue, San Diego Freeway, Seal
Beach, California, 1960–62. Ross W. Cortese, developer; Ross W. Cortese, Burt Nicolay, Charles R.
Hills, architects. View of main entrance, Seal Beach Boulevard at Golden Rain Road.

development, anywhere. Eighty percent of buyers were from California, but people also came from thirty-seven other states.[24]

Leisure World's developer, Ross W. Cortese, was perhaps an unlikely pioneer in the field of retirement housing. A high-school dropout from Glendale, California, who may have had some training as a draughtsman, Cortese (1916–1991) began working as a homebuilder around 1939 with a pair of speculative houses done with the help of more established builder Ben Weingart. When Weingart and his partners went on to develop the mega-suburb of Lakewood in the early 1950s, Cortese was invited to build several hundred houses there. With a partner from that project, he began doing his own tracts in Long Beach and Anaheim. Then, in the late 1950s, he developed the Walled City of Rossmoor (today Rossmoor City), with nearly thirty-five hundred houses on twelve hundred acres. While notable for it size, the main innovation was restricted access: Rossmoor was one of the nation's first gated communities for middle-class families.[25]

As he completed that project, Cortese bought two adjacent tracts. On the smaller parcel, north of Rossmoor, he continued to develop houses. But for the larger site, with more than five hundred acres, he conceived of Leisure World. When completed in 1962, it was the largest co-op complex in the world, with 6,750 apartments—nearly a thousand more than UHF's Rochdale Village in New York. Overnight it more than doubled the number of co-owned homes in Southern California. More importantly, it brought the need for affordable, easy-to-maintain retirement housing into national focus, revealing the retirement co-op as a major new housing trend.

Leisure World's active-retirement model was not original. Trailer parks in Florida had been experimenting with highly programmed living for decades, and as early as 1949 Del Webb had begun work on a subdivision of three thousand houses called Pueblo Gardens, in Tucson, that may have been directed, if not limited, to seniors. The mid-1950s had seen several additional efforts, such as Youngstown, Arizona, and Leisure City, Florida. Then, in 1959, Webb began a new project: Sun City, twenty-five miles northwest of Phoenix.[26] At Sun City, Webb (1899–1974) made substantial refinements, including an array of leisure facilities and programming designed to allow retirees to make friends and combat homesickness. At the center of Sun City was a large recreation center with a circular (and thus more social) swimming pool, dozens of shuffleboard courts, lanes for lawn bowling, and a building full of hobby workshops and meeting rooms for clubs. Surrounding the rec center, among the homes, were four golf courses, three shopping centers, and several neighborhood pools. Sun City also improved upon earlier examples by offering a mixture of dwelling types, including semidetached houses and co-op garden

Fig. 80: Sun City co-op apartments, east side North Del Webb Boulevard between West Buccaneer Way and West Topaz Drive, Sun City, Arizona, ca. 1961. Del Webb, developer.

Fig. 81: Leisure World, tricyclists. Photograph by Bill Ray, 1963.

Fig. 82: Leisure World, Ross W. Cortese surveying construction from the air. Photograph by Bill Ray, 1963.

apartments in addition to freestanding houses (fig. 80). In its first year, Sun City sold 1,300 houses and 250 apartments.[27]

Cortese, recognizing that many people did not care to move to exurban Phoenix, imported Webb's model to metropolitan Los Angeles. Leisure World included golf (in the form of a compact "executive" course for putting), three clubhouses, a 2,500-seat theater, an Orange County branch library, and hobby rooms for woodworking and arts and crafts. In advertisements Cortese promoted the complex as a "country-club city for happy people over 52."[28]

Leisure World's promise of community was more than a sales gimmick. As *Life* magazine reported, "In Leisure World there is no leisure." Residents joined clubs for "reducing" (dieting), singing, hiking, collecting stamps, dressmaking, investing, and playing pinochle, bingo, and chess. There were groups for Democrats, veterans, and members of Hadassah (the Jewish women's volunteer organization). There was community theater, and there were classes in ceramics, bridge, square dancing, and ballroom dancing. Tricycle riding became popular (fig. 81). Nine college courses were available. And, for widowers, at least, there was an active dating scene (2,400 of the 8,000 residents were single women).[29]

Leisure World's thousands of apartments were arranged in approximately 550 nearly identical one-story buildings. These were of varying lengths, some in geometric groups of four on an X-plan but most in informal rows, with none

Fig. 83: Leisure World, typical unit with customized patio and landscaping.

parallel to the next, which prevented the appearance of barracks (fig. 82). The units were modest in size: just 604 to 759 square feet, with one or two bedrooms, an open-plan kitchen and living room, one bathroom, and a small private patio at the front (fig. 83). Each also had a private one-car garage in a separate parking structure, usually just behind the apartment. Apart from a smaller number of two-story buildings done later, the complex had no stairs. To further accommodate seniors Cortese placed power and telephone outlets two feet above the floor and gave bathrooms shower stalls with seats instead of tubs. Finishes were expedient and easy to maintain, including linoleum flooring throughout. The architects of record were Burt Nicolay and Charles R. Hills, but Cortese may have been the primary designer.[30]

In addition to its metropolitan location (secured, like Cortese's earlier project, with an elaborate network of walls, gates, and resident guards), low prices, and all-co-ownership format, Leisure World offered an additional innovation over Sun City: collectivized primary medical care. A great attraction of co-op living had always been that it spread the cost of physically maintaining the home. Cortese extended this to maintaining the homeowners themselves. Along with taxes, landscaping, recreational facilities, and common utilities, monthly maintenance charges funded an on-site medical clinic that was to be staffed with ten doctors, twenty-six nurses, and a lab with X-ray equipment, all available free of additional charges.

In the postwar era most Western nations introduced systems of nationalized healthcare. In the Cold War U.S., by contrast, employers assumed this responsibility, leaving many—especially seniors—vulnerable. In 1965, President Johnson oversaw the introduction of Medicare despite widespread opposition to "socialization" of medicine. Cortese pioneered his system several years before the Great Society. In doing so, he claimed: "This is free enterprise's solution to the nation's problem of housing for the elderly. It also indicates there are better solutions . . . than socialized medicine."[31] The clinic was popular. The Leisure World theme song, performed by the complex's men's chorus, included the verse "If you need a pill or two, see your clinic doctors, they'll make you feel like new."

While Medicare made the collective provision of medical services redundant, the homeowners retained the clinic, and Cortese included similar facilities in subsequent projects.[32]

While Cortese's multifaceted solution to the problem of how to live well as a retiree in postwar America won over many, others were skeptical. The *Los Angeles Times* was undoubtedly referring to the project when it noted, in 1963: "Critics of retirement communities have compared them with concentration camps and likened their residences to rabbit hutches."[33] Cortese appears to have taken these objections seriously. For later Leisure Worlds and Rossmoors, in southern Orange County, the Bay Area, and suburban Chicago, Washington, and Phoenix, he hired skilled architects and landscape architects like Charles Warren Callister, and Mott and Hayden, to produce much richer designs.[34] To focus on physical form, however, is to ignore Leisure World's primary innovations, which were social and economic: providing affordable, fixed-cost, permanent, low-maintenance homes for one of the nation's fastest-growing marginal-status groups. Fifty years after opening it continued to enable people to live modest but dignified and independent lives. And with time and mature landscaping, Leisure World's vibrant community defied the physical uniformity, transforming it into a green, spacious place, with broad lawns, wide streets, and big skies enveloping the low-slung buildings.

Finding Horizontal Property

As the market for retirement co-ops emerged in the late 1950s and early 1960s, many developers and lenders came to see the prevailing methods for establishing and financing co-ownership as too restrictive. In particular they took issue with the emphasis on common rights in property. While there were advantages to this balance, several limitations became apparent as more people, and more kinds of people, bought apartments.

One drawback of the corporate-title co-op system was that everyone had to finance a purchase in the same way. At FHA-insured buildings this meant that everyone was heavily leveraged, with low equity payments but high ongoing costs. At Leisure World, which was financed under FHA, one-bedroom apartments sold for just $680 but maintenance, at $92 to $103 ($750 to $830 today), was high given the location and small size of the apartments.[35] At most Florida co-ops, by contrast, there was no blanket mortgage at all. This meant that, as Norman Ford advised, one could buy one's home outright. But it also meant a cash payment of at least $7,000, in 1959, for a modest one-bedroom unit at an out-of-the-way garden-apartment complex ($63,000), or $20,000 or more at places like Sea Club, Bay Harbor Club, and Coral Sea Towers ($200,000). Monthly maintenance, however, was often under $50 ($500)—

the cost of a single night at a first-class Miami Beach hotel.[36] Neither system was capable of appealing to broad numbers of retirees.[37]

Some developers began to recognize that eliminating the blanket mortgage while allowing large long-term loans, preferably on an apartment-by-apartment basis, would enable each homeowner to put down as much or as little equity as she liked. But so long as ownership arrangements emphasized the group over the individual, lenders resisted this idea. Developers, as in the 1920s, could use installment plans, but these did not apply to resales. The solution was to introduce the condominium.

Although several developers later claimed to have pioneered the condo in Florida, credit belongs to Brown L. Whatley, the state's leading mortgage banker. In the late 1950s, Whatley became aware of *condominio*, a plan of co-ownership in Puerto Rico that reversed the American emphasis on common rights. Of equal importance, the condominio system conveyed ownership of individual units through a unique deed and title rather than a proprietary lease. (Proprietary leases were just as powerful as titles at conveying exclusive rights to housing, but few lenders understood this.) In its technical arrangement, the Puerto Rican plan operated by dividing a single property into multiple "fees," each corresponding to a cube of air, with common elements owned collectively through tenancy-in-common. Under the condominio plan multiple parties owned distinct undivided (and undividable) shares of a single property. Although banks in Puerto Rico had not yet made any mortgage loans for individual units, Whatley (ca. 1904–1982) was confident they could be persuaded to—and that Stateside lenders would too.[38]

Legal historians trace the roots of Puerto Rico's plan to medieval Europe, and to Napoleon, who included provisions for condominios in his Civil Code of 1804. In practice, the condominio was a product of Interwar Europe. World War I generated a housing crisis there yet worse than in U.S. cities. Just as many Americans and Scandinavians turned to co-ownership to solve the problem of high rents (and the lack of capital for construction), so too, albeit to lesser degree, did the rest of Continental Europe. But whereas the consumers'-cooperative limited-equity model prevailed in Scandinavia and the socialist cities of Central Europe, the fee-simple *co-propriété, propiedad horizontal, condominio,* or "story property" predominated everywhere else. The idea of "horizontal property" derived from the fact that one owned a horizontal slice of a building rather than a vertical column of space. (This concept is also reflected in "strata title," the legal term that came to be used instead of condominium in Australia and parts of Canada.) Condominio, which seems to have been coined in Italy, was a Latin neologism meaning co-, or joint, dominion. After World War I, national governments, starting with Belgium in 1924, began updating

Napoleonic laws to cope with postwar surges in construction. Rich urban families and developers pursued co-ownership of apartments for many of the same reasons their counterparts did in New York, Chicago, and Washington in the 1920s. By 1939, France, Spain, Italy, Greece, Sweden, Poland, Rumania, and Bulgaria had revised or added condominium statutes.[39]

In Latin America, governments followed European examples, updating laws originally transmitted through colonial civil codes. In 1928, Brazil modernized its code, and by 1940, Mexico and Chile followed. By 1950, Peru, Uruguay, Argentina, Colombia, Bolivia, and Cuba all had new condominio or propiedad horizontal laws. After the Inter-American Bar Association hosted a special conference on co-ownership at Montevideo in 1951, Venezuela and Puerto Rico also added them.[40]

Laws of this sort had never been necessary in the U.S. because of the co-op's stronger emphasis on common rights in property. With powerful boards and restrictive by-laws, American buildings were well equipped for long-term upkeep. Under the European plan, by contrast, the basic ownership structure was so independent that without laws mandating specific deed restrictions and by-laws—including that the owners form an association to maintain the property—there was little to prevent a building from falling apart. To illustrate the importance of such laws old French legal texts recalled the example of a building in Grenoble where the owners could not agree on a color for the façade. Each painted the exterior of his unit as he wished. While this example was benign—recalling the varied windows and balcony enclosures still common in co-owned buildings in Europe, and occasionally the U.S.—without well-crafted laws the potential for more serious hazards remained. As a result, virtually every jurisdiction that had known this system, going back to the twelfth century, had regulated it, at first through misinterpretations of ancient Roman law and later by specific statute.[41] (In the early twenty-first century, by contrast, weak condominium laws in Asia and Israel made early physical obsolescence a serious problem.)[42]

Puerto Rico and the Condominio

When Puerto Rico's lawmakers passed the updated Horizontal Property Act of 1951, it was largely an aspirational measure. The island had remained predominantly rural until after World War II, when it began to enjoy sustained industrial growth. Greater San Juan's population, which had expanded from 70,000 in 1920 to 170,000 in 1940, reached 430,000 by 1960. Most construction, especially middle-class, concentrated in FHA-insured single-family subdivisions at the city's periphery. The first of these, Puerto Nuevo, started in 1948. Beginning as early as the mid-1930s, a handful of San Juan's rich families came to prefer apartments, and several well-

Un Paso más de Avance
PARA SATISFACER UNA NECESIDAD SOCIAL

Los Directores de
CONDOMINIUM ENTERPRISES, Inc.
en ocasión de haber llevado a feliz término la
construcción del • • • •

Condominio
San Luis

desean hacer constar su reconocimiento por la colaboración brindada, a todas las
entidades gubernamentales, en particular al BANCO GUBERNAMENTAL DE FO-
MENTO y a la JUNTA DE PLANIFICACION DE PUERTO RICO, así mismo al
BANCO DE PONCE y sus oficiales, quienes otorgaron el financiamiento para la
construcción de la obra. También extendemos nuestros reconocimientos a demás
particulares que con perseverancia y entusiasmo ayudaron a dar feliz realización
al proyecto.

CONDOMINIUM
ENTERPRISES, INC.
Oficinas Generales
Hotel La Rada
TELEFONO 3-0850

Fig. 84: San Luis, Calle Palmeras
54, San Juan, Puerto Rico. Luis
Esteban Julía, Luis J. Rodríguez,
developers; René Ramírez, architect.
Advertisement, *El Mundo* (San Juan),
July 6, 1957.

appointed buildings appeared in the city, mainly in
the fashionable oceanfront neighborhood of Condado.
All were rental. Only in the mid-1950s did better-off
families become interested in owning apartments,
"walk-up" garden apartments, and semidetached
casas duplex.[43] The first co-owned building, the San
Luis apartments, was completed in 1957, in San Juan's
Puerta de Tierra (fig. 84). It was an immediate success.
By the spring of 1960 sixteen condo complexes (several
with more than one building) were built or under way.[44]

Brown L. Whatley, Florida's elder statesmen of
home finance and a former president of the Mortgage
Bankers Association of America, closely followed
the growth of the retirement co-op in the 1950s. As
he expanded his firm's operations in Puerto Rico
he became convinced that the Latin condominio
alternative was superior to the U.S. model. He was
not alone. Herbert U. Nelson of NAREB had described
Rome's condominios in favorable terms in the late
1930s. American developers and real-estate writers
working in Scotland, France, and Mexico had also
returned, over the years, with similar tales.[45] There
had been little incentive to introduce the new system,
however, mainly because in New York, the leading
market for co-ownership, the corporate-title co-
op plan was very familiar. New York lenders had,
in fact, already devised an "outright deed plan" of
ownership in 1946 for Sixteen East Eighty-fourth
Street so the project could comply with VA regulations.
Homebuilders, however, rejected it once the VA
figured out how to work with co-ops. As the real-
estate attorney who devised the 1946 plan later recalled, the system was "very
cumbersome, very tedious and very particular."[46]

Florida in the late 1950s was different from New York in the 1940s. As Whatley
explained in a pamphlet that his firm distributed to developers and lenders, "Florida
attracts many permanent and part-time residents who prefer the convenience of
apartment living over the responsibilities entailed in private home ownership.
Among these are a large number of retirees. . . . Living on fixed incomes for the most

part, retirees are usually interested in investing as much cash as possible on the down payment of a home to assure themselves of a permanent Florida residence at relatively low monthly housing expense."[47]

In 1959, Whatley proposed a state horizontal property act modeled on Puerto Rico's. (It passed, four years later, as the Condominium Act of 1963.) With the aid of several developers and lenders from Puerto Rico, Whatley also persuaded the island's Resident Commissioner, Dr. Antonio Fernós Isern, to introduce a bill in the U.S. Congress to establish FHA insurance of "individually owned units in a multiple family structure." In 1960—and, when no housing act passed that year, again in 1961— Whatley and five lenders and developers from San Juan testified in Washington. When the next housing act passed, in 1961, a special section for condominiums was included, alongside the one for below-market-interest-rate co-ops.[48]

New and Improved Co-ownership

The condominium as imported from Puerto Rico solved three major problems in housing. One was financing. Lenders, even in metro New York, were accustomed to issuing mortgages only for houses. As a result, they believed that the only true proof of ownership was a unique title. The emphasis on common rights in co-owned buildings—and perhaps even the very term "cooperative"—did little to persuade them to think differently. As a rule, then, they regarded proprietary leases as not proprietary enough. The condo, by contrast, with its more familiar deeds and titles, immediately met mortgage bankers' expectations. After eighty years of co-ownership in the U.S., the individual apartment was transformed in a single legal leap from an untouchable liability into a desirable, liquid asset.

A second problem the new format solved was cumbersome restrictions on resales. A chief appeal of co-ownership in the U.S. for many had always been the closed environment: that ownership made the "public" apartment house "private." This had been achieved, in part, by screening resales. But approvals took a huge amount of time and were a great source of frustration for both sellers and buyers. By the 1960s, neither bankers nor most homebuyers believed that restrictions were essential for maintaining resale values. In part this was because it had become clear by the 1960s that formal limitations were unnecessary for maintaining a homogenous atmosphere. The housing market already had so many subtle barriers to entry, financial and social, and there was so much self-sorting before buyers even looked at an apartment, that board screenings were hardly required to police most boundaries. Indeed, most Americans, quite correctly, continued to understand the co-owned apartment house as "private" even after the switch from co-op to condo, simply by virtue of the ownership (fig. 85). At the same time, the condo seemed to signal a new degree of

THIS is the private world of *Fountainhead*

17 STORY OCEANFRONT CONDOMINIUM RESIDENCE
TOP O'THE GALT OCEAN MILE / FORT LAUDERDALE / FLORIDA

A classic expression of the art of residential building.
Architect-designed apartment homes, lavishly spacious,
meticulously detailed... set in the completely private world
of a landscaped park at the ocean's edge.

*Now displayed for your inspection,
a selection of furnished 1-2-3 bedroom apartment homes
and penthouses with oceanfront balcony terraces.*

$31,000 to $73,000

Condominium Purchase *provides individual apartment ownership
with warranty deed. Eliminates cooperative and mutual ownership problem.*

An illustrated brochure and further information
may be obtained by writing.
FOUNTAINHEAD
3900 north ocean drive, Fort Lauderdale 15, Florida
Phone LOgan 5-3900

Conceived, created and developed by
RADICE REALTY AND CONSTRUCTION CORPORATION OF NEW YORK AND FLORIDA / INVESTMENT BUILDERS SINCE 1920

GEORGE J. SOLE, A.I.A. ARCHITECT / H. J. ROSS ASSOCIATES, CONSULTING ENGINEER

Fig. 85: Fountainhead, 3900 North Ocean Drive, Fort Lauderdale. Radice Realty and Construction, developer; George J. Sole, architect. Advertisement, *Florida Architecture*, 1964.

openness in housing. In a reversal of the conventional wisdom of the 1920s, many in the 1960s came to see restrictions as inconvenient, distasteful, and a drag on sales.

As the condo had been shaped in the more socially rigid countries of Europe and Latin America, there seemed to be no need to burden homeowners with the tyranny of unlimited, arbitrary power to vet neighbors that rich Americans demanded of the co-op. In originally justifying board screening of resales, in 1881, Philip Hubert noted that "in no country in Europe are the upper-classes so exclusive as with us [Americans] in their social intercourse or so jealous of preserving their social distinctions. . . . In the old countries. . . . [a] gentleman may be forced to content himself—and thousands of French gentlemen do—with a small apartment up in the very attic of some dingy Parisian house; his immediate neighbors are mechanics, quite as well off as himself, and yet his social position remains distinct, and is recognized by all around him. There is no desire or even thought of familiarity. He is a gentleman who has no money, that is all. How is it with an American family compelled to seek refuge in one of our New York tenement houses?—Many have been driven to do so during the past few years, and their own silent but aching hearts alone can tell what they have suffered."[49]

By the 1960s, things had changed. The condo's symbolic embrace of difference had a special importance in South Florida, where many retirees were Jews who were keenly aware of their prohibition from the best-equipped buildings in New York, and of Miami Beach's own long history of racial and ethnic covenants. (Until they organized to fight such policies after World War II, Jews had been barred from many Miami Beach hotels and apartment buildings, and prohibited from buying houses in several of the city's neighborhoods.) Even outside of Miami, however, the condo was received well. This quick acceptance of the condo precisely as "white flight" was accelerating and American cities burned with Black frustration complicates some basic assumptions about the conservative nature of homeownership.[50]

Indeed, when mainstream media reported the introduction of the condo, articles typically stressed the freedom from resale approvals, positioning the condo as open, equal, and more in step with postwar American values than the co-op. *Time* opened its first story on condos with the example of Peter and Patricia Lawford, who had recently been prohibited from an East Side co-op building in Manhattan because of their Democratic politics and unconventional jobs. "This one-man veto," it reported, "was a dramatic demonstration of one of the differences between a cooperative and a new form of communal housing . . . the condominium." That the rejection was absurd was taken by the writer as entirely self-evident.[51]

That the condo represented a meaningful, if tepid, advancement in the politics of American housing was further underscored by the fact that the elimination

of restrictions was not inherent to the format, but a strategy on the part of
homebuilders. From a legal standpoint, in fact, exclusion was entirely possible in
condos. For generations, deeds on single-family houses in the U.S. had prohibited
occupancy on the basis of race, ethnicity, and faith. When racial covenants were
declared unenforceable in the late 1940s, single-family communities devised any
number of other tools to restrict occupancy, including screening committees. Already
Sixteen East Eighty-fourth Street, Manhattan's "outright-deed" co-op of 1946, had
included language subjecting subleases to approval. According to the architect of that
plan, the only reason for not including yet stronger restrictions was the assumption
that they might have made the apartments less attractive to the mortgage lender.[52]

Meanwhile, many early condos offered homeowners the collective right of "first
refusal." As inherited from Europe and Latin America, condos typically allowed the
association a period of time, usually thirty days, in which to match any legitimate
purchase offer, or to find another buyer who would. In L.A., a small number of
condos actually used this provision in the 1960s to block sales to Black families, most
notably in Baldwin Hills as it became popular with middle-class African Americans.
It was also nearly used by a Fifth Avenue building in New York in the 1970s to
prevent Richard Nixon from buying an apartment. These situations were extremely
rare, however, and many developers soon dropped the first-refusal provision.[53]

Emotional Appeal

A third limitation of the co-op that the condominium solved was emotional.
Condominiums promised homeowners individual deeds for their suites, and deeds
held tremendous symbolic value (fig. 86). Southern California builders like Lionel
V. Mayell had long recognized this fact, and ads for own-your-owns, both before
and after World War II, nearly always stressed the importance of the deed and the
great individual freedom that it conferred. When Whatley and other Americans
encountered the condo they immediately recognized this benefit. As one leading
South Florida developer declared: "Condominium will replace co-ops because
people like the idea they're getting a deed to the apartment. New Englanders and
Midwesterners coming down to Fort Lauderdale are meat-and-potatoes types. 'Give
me my deed,' they say. Condominium has tremendous appeal."[54]

The sentimental appeal of the condo clouded all but the most informed discussions
of the new format and was reflected in constant rhetorical comparisons of the
condo to ownership of a house and the co-op as something less. In his statement
before Congress, for example, Puerto Rico's Resident Commissioner Fernós noted:
"Many persons desiring apartment homes do not wish merely to own an interest in
a cooperative organization but prefer to own outright a family living unit in such a

building." Dr. Rafael Picó, president of the Government Development Bank for Puerto Rico, made a similar point, arguing, "There is a difference between these individually owned apartments and the co-ops. We believe that the cooperative . . . is fine for certain groups that can form that type of tenure, but our type of apartment is individually owned. It is not like owning a share in a cooperative apartment. It is an apartment that can be disposed of like all property owned in fee simple. It is something that you can mortgage, you can rent, and act as though you owned an individual house. That is a great incentive for our people who just love individually owned homes." Whatley went so far as to declare that the condominium "is much to be preferred over our so-called cooperative."[55]

Coverage of the condominium system in the trade and mainstream press, which was overwhelmingly

CONDOMINIUM . . . at last a way to really own your apartment home in Florida

SPACIOUS LUXURY of a *Landmark* living-dining area adds a touch of genuine distinction to Florida entertaining.

COMFORT is the keynote of the *Landmark*'s floor plans, with one or two bedrooms, and a separate bath for each.

The *Landmark*, in Daytona Beach, is your first Florida opportunity to really *own* an apartment home. The *Landmark* is not a cooperative—you purchase no shares in a corporation that may restrict the future use, alteration, or transfer of your property.

Instead, the *Landmark* offers all the advantages of a new concept in apartment ownership called "condominium." This means that you get full and complete legal title to the *Landmark* apartment you select. You get a recordable, transferable warranty deed, just as if you were buying an individual dwelling. And, the title to your apartment is fully insured through Lawyers' Title Insurance Corporation of Richmond, Va.

The *Landmark* graces the shores of the Intercoastal Waterway in downtown Daytona Beach. Fast, reliable *Eastern Elevators* will whisk you to any of 11 floors, where you may select a one- or two-bedroom apartment with the finest of appointments. Each apartment opens onto a spacious balcony overlooking the exquisite Halifax Yacht Basin. Yet the purchase price—which may be as low as $18,000—includes wall-to-wall carpeting by *Bigelow*; appliances by *General Electric*; plumbing fixtures by *Crane*. And you'll have covered parking for your car, along with enjoyment of the *Landmark*'s private putting green, olympic swimming pool, and luxurious Plantation Lounge.

Write today for complete information including the details of conventional financing available on individual apartments. Remember, your only opportunity for condominium ownership in Florida is at the *Landmark!*

the LANDMARK
CONDOMINIUM APARTMENTS
By Halifax Enterprises of Daytona, Inc.
404 South Beach St., Box T, Daytona Beach, Florida
(Located in Downtown Daytona, opposite the Halifax Yacht Basin)

Fig. 86: The Landmark, 404 South Beach Street, Daytona Beach. Halifax Enterprises, developer. Advertisement, *Florida Trend*, July 1962.

favorable, relied on similar turns of phrase. After decades of promoting the co-op as nothing less than absolute homeownership, the real-estate industry now characterized the condo as a "true" system of ownership and the co-op as something partial and inferior.

The very word "condominium"—to which homebuilders and reporters immediately gravitated—similarly served to promote the system. Despite its awkwardness, it was more succinct than legal terms such as the Spanish "horizontal property" and the French "co-property." More importantly, it sounded as new and exotic as "cooperative" sounded stuffy and communitarian. That few Americans could pronounce it was part of its appeal. Its novelty suggested the system was innovative and, therefore, superior. Like earlier terms, including "cooperative" but also "French flat" and "apartment," "condominium" also helped to distinguish the well-equipped and highly serviced multifamily dwelling from more ordinary residences. In a culture where the advantaged gravitated so heavily toward houses—and where everything was always being renewed and improved—there was a continual need to coin glamorous new terms for multifamily housing.

The marketing seemed to work. Although for a brief time condominiums were described as a "new type of co-op" or a "condominium co-op," within a few years one regional business magazine noted that "like Spiro Agnew, condominium has become a household word."[56] As a developer reported in 1965, on "many occasions" prospective buyers "walk into our sales offices and ask: 'Is this a condominium?' . . . After being told that it was, he would then say, 'All right, now I will talk to you.' He had no idea actually of what a condominium was, other than to know that it was good."[57]

In rare candid moments, real-estate analysts acknowledged that the differences between co-op and condo were, at core, immaterial—grounded in style and spin as much as legal contracts. Ultimately, each was a slightly different way to achieve an essentially identical end. As NAREB noted in 1961, "The 'new' cooperatives, while basically the same as the co-ops that had such a vogue 30 years ago, are dressed in different clothes to create a new sales appeal." In public, however, the changes in co-ownership that were bundled with the new name—the deeds, the more open screening policies, the financing—were presented as entirely fresh.[58]

Questioning the Condo

Although much heralded and an effective solution to several limitations of corporate-title co-op ownership, the condominium solved only some of the complexities of co-ownership. It had no effective way, for example, to cope with troublesome owners. In a co-op, occupancy was dependent on compliance with the proprietary lease; when owners violated conditions by engaging in noxious activities or not paying monthly maintenance, the corporation had the right to evict. In a condo, the association could sue an owner or have a lien placed on her property but lacked the right to have the owner removed.

Another problem concerned physical decay. While only two-thirds of owners in typical co-ops had to approve of major expenditures, the first generation of condos required unanimous consent and was therefore all but impossible (this provision was soon relaxed). Similarly, while a co-op corporation could take out a new blanket mortgage to cover unexpected expenses, condos had to rely more frequently on an unpopular device called the special assessment, leaving each owner to come up with her share individually, which could be difficult for many, especially those living on fixed incomes.[59]

An additional problem was that individual-title ownership cost more, in aggregate, than corporate-title. In a co-op, initial purchase required one mortgage, one survey, one title-insurance policy, and one set of closing documents for the entire complex. For resales there were no closing costs at all, just the cost of paperwork to transfer the stock. In a condo these expenses accrued to each unit, and again for each resale.[60]

As a result of these weaknesses, some in real estate declared the condominium inferior and predicted that it would, at best, come to share the market for owner-occupied apartments with the co-op. Others anticipated that well-to-do homeowners would continue to favor the co-op while middle- and lower-income families would choose the condominium. Both sets of critics agreed that the condo, with its multiple fees and titles, was cumbersome and unnecessary.[61]

Among the most ardent opponents of the condo were leaders of the limited-equity movement. When mortgage banker Whatley and the delegation from Puerto Rico testified before Congress, Dwight D. Townsend, director of the Washington office of the Co-operative League of the U.S.A., spoke against the idea. Critiques generally centered on the condo's emphasis on individual rights in property and its higher costs. According to Abe Kazan, individual deeds made it too difficult for the several owners to evict an "undesirable" homeowner. In his limited-equity co-ops, he explained, "we have *collective* ownership. If we encounter a bad egg, we give him back his money and tell him we don't want him here."[62]

More objectionable, UHF told the *New York Times*, was the fiction of "absolute" ownership proffered by developers. For this reason, it argued, the condominium "can never be more than a selling gimmick" because of the "hard, real fact that the dwelling unit is part and parcel of a building that houses the dwelling units of co-tenants."[63] Kazan also critiqued homeowners' ability to accrue personal equity. In the limited-equity, what the "tenant-owner puts in, he takes out. We don't treat this as an investment. The tenant-owner joins the collective organization to get better housing."[64] For many Americans, however, this line between exchange value ("an investment") and use value ("better housing") was blurred: part of what made housing better was its reliability as a vehicle for generating equity.

Embracing the Condo

Americans adopted the condo and abandoned the co-op—market rate, FHA, and limited-equity—with terrific speed. One reason was that the condominium's more commoditized arrangement made bankers keen on it. They were so enthusiastic, in fact, that FHA, which had propped up the middle-class co-op since World War II, became largely immaterial. Roughly half of all postwar co-ops were insured by FHA, and most of the rest by New York City or State. By contrast, only one percent of condominium units built in the U.S. between 1961 and 1974 were insured by FHA. The rest found lenders happy to finance construction and sales without federal guarantees.[65] Most planners and policymakers also embraced the condo, regarding it—like the limited-equity co-op in earlier generations—as an ideal vehicle for increasing the supply of low-cost, owner-occupied housing. In New York, for example, elected officials—including state senators Mitchell and Lama—began discussing the possibility of building condos under their submarket interest-rate program as early as 1961.[66]

Similarly, the condominium attracted the interest of many national real-estate industry leaders. Along with Whatley, Albert M. Cole, a former federal housing administrator and an executive at Reynolds Metals; Miles L. Colean, a national housing consultant once in charge of FHA's Rental Housing Division; William K. Kerr, an insurance executive; and Raymond O'Keefe, vice president of the Chase Manhattan Bank in charge of real estate and mortgages, all became convinced of the condo's benefits.[67] Largely as a result of their enthusiasm, glowing reports appeared in mainstream newspapers and magazines, from the *New York Times* to *House Beautiful*. More crucially, these men undertook demonstration projects, including two of the FHA's first condominiums, Condominio Atlantico in San Juan, financed by Kerr's Equitable Life Assurance Society, and Hartshorn Homes, an urban renewal project in Richmond, Virginia, developed by Reynolds, which was also at work on the River Park co-op in the Southwest Urban Renewal Area in Washington, D.C. (see fig. 70).[68]

Another reason that the condo took hold so rapidly was that homebuilding had become quite centralized in large corporations by the 1960s. These operators standardized and disseminated new practices far and wide, and often all at once. There had been national dialogues about co-ownership in the 1920s, but production was so small scale and local that, outside of the cities where the ideas emerged, new practices were adopted slowly. Beginning in the late 1950s several large regional "merchant builders" went public; several others were bought by large multipurpose, multinational conglomerates like International Telephone and Telegraph and Westinghouse, often because they saw large-scale builders' stocks of suburban land as a favorable investment. Other companies, like Castle and Cooke, which already owned land, saw development as a new business opportunity. When these firms experimented with the condominium format they did so at multiple projects in multiple markets.[69]

In the 1960s there were also more avenues for trade discourse. Industry groups such as NAREB had been publishing journals and hosting conferences since at least the 1920s. But in the 1930s, 1940s, and 1950s new groups, such as the National Association of Home Builders and the Urban Land Institute, were formed. New regional and national real-estate and homebuilding magazines began publication, including *Florida Builder* in 1946, McGraw-Hill's *House & Home* in 1952, and *Florida Trend* and *California Builder*, both in 1959. The condominium was discussed extensively in all beginning in 1960. In the early 1960s trade groups also staged conferences whose purpose was to disseminate information to homebuilders about the condominium mechanism.

Of equal importance, by the early 1960s homebuilders were intently focused on multifamily housing. The percentage of multifamily units among new housing starts nationally had fluctuated greatly in the 1940s and 1950s, peaking in most markets right after the war, then falling precipitously. But in the late 1950s, apartments had grown from eight to thirty percent of new housing construction. Rising land prices in most metropolitan markets, and the demographic bubble created by World War II, made it clear that the 1960s, like the 1920s, would be a decade in which apartments flourished. The debate over the condo was part of a much larger discussion about this impending growth in multifamily living.[70]

Most importantly, wherever buyers faced a choice, they overwhelmingly opted for the condo. In southeastern Florida, the number of co-ops had grown dramatically in the early 1960s; by 1963 and 1964, however, the volume stabilized and then fell, even as the total number of co-owned buildings rose. Virtually no new buildings were sold as co-ops after 1966. Exemplary of this dynamic were twin buildings in Hallandale developed in 1966: Paradise-by-the-Sea, a condo, and Paradise Harbour, a co-op. The developer had built several co-ops in Broward and Palm Beach Counties, including four others at the Paradise Island complex in Hallandale. Presumably to test the market, he now organized one on the condominium plan. Prices were $400 ($2,900 in 2010 dollars) more than at the co-op ($9,900 rather than $9,500 for one-bedroom units). Nevertheless, they sold better. After nearly a decade of building co-ops, he, like all Florida developers, abandoned the old system.[71]

Condominium Coast

The introduction of the condo coincided with a new epoch in American social history and an accelerated phase in the development of Florida and other resort centers. By the mid-1960s half a million Americans were retiring each year; as many as one in five moved to Florida. The Gold Coast alone, in the 1960s and early 1970s, grew by around 100,000 people a year, from a full-time population of 1.5 million in 1960 to 2.7 million in 1974. In 1950, five thousand people over age sixty-five lived in Broward County; by 1970, more than a hundred thousand did. At times it seemed as though whole sections of northern cities, especially New York, were migrating together. "It is not uncommon," the *Los Angeles Times* reported, for a Miami Beach building to have "a substantial portion of its residents come from a single neighborhood in Brooklyn, Flushing or the Bronx."[72]

Most of the newcomers bought condos. Retirees of the most slender means continued to stay in Miami Beach hotels—smaller, older, run-down operations, which one official of the Southern Florida Hotel and Motel Association characterized as "obsolete hotels . . . almost apartment houses." The most affluent sometimes bought houses or leased well-equipped apartments in modern high-rises, where rates were as high as $375 to $650 ($2,400 to $4,200 in 2010 dollars) a month by 1968, unfurnished, on an annual lease.[73] Hundreds of thousands, however, became multifamily homeowners in the late 1960s and 1970s.

Several broad social and economic forces stimulated this mass migration to the retirement condo. One was the empty nest. The Greatest Generation's children, born between 1945 and 1960, left home between 1963 and 1978. A second reason was inflation. As prices for everything, including housing, continued to escalate with the war effort in Vietnam, many families hoped to minimize future uncertainty by securing their retirement housing early. They sold their old houses at substantial profits—average U.S. house prices doubled between 1966 and 1972—and bought smaller, less expensive condos, adding the difference in equity to their savings while continuing to enjoy low ongoing costs. By the early 1970s, for example, few single-family houses in any part of metro New York sold for less than $50,000 ($260,000), while a new two-bedroom apartment in Florida typically cost $15,000 to $35,000 ($80,000 and $180,000), depending on size and location.[74]

The retirement condo also represented a next stage in white flight. Many older condo families were motivated to come to Florida because of the unfolding urban crisis in their home cities. As the *Los Angeles Times* noted, mention of New York in Florida "brings much resentment; many say the city has become so violent that they had no choice but to move." According to Miami Beach writer Polly Redford, the city's new residents "want all the excitement of city living with none of its problems—no slums, no smog." *Life* likewise observed in a 1970 article on Sun City, Arizona, that residents regarded it as an "oasis in a world that grows nuttier every day. The town has no hippies, no smog, no race problem (since, in fact, it has no Negroes), no riots, no bombings, no LSD and no relief rolls."[75]

These factors, combined with the sun, fun, and collectivized physical maintenance that developers promised at sales centers, led to an unprecedented (and unrepeated) wave of condo construction. Between 1946 and 1962 around two hundred co-op buildings were built in southeastern Florida; over the next ten years, more than seven hundred condo buildings went up. In 1969, more apartments were permitted in Dade and Broward Counties than in New York and Chicago combined. This mass migration became even more frenetic in the early 1970s. By 1970 there were more than fifty-five thousand co-owned apartments in Florida, in thirteen hundred complexes—three-quarters of them in Dade, Broward, and Palm Beach Counties. By 1975 there were nearly four hundred thousand—nearly as many as there had been nationally five years before. At least eighty percent of buyers were retired, virtually all were over the age of fifty, and, as Norman Ford advised, between forty and seventy percent of buyers paid cash. "Florida's Gold Coast," speculated one business journalist, "might well become [the] 'Condominium Coast.'"[76]

Morris Lapidus and Aventura

Mass condo living in Florida helped generate a new kind of built environment in Florida. Through the early 1960s most new residents could be accommodated near the beach, and co-ops concentrated along the oceanfront. As the sections between Miami Beach and Fort Lauderdale and Palm Beach filled in, developers began to devise new kinds of neighborhoods at inland sites. The program called for places that reflected retirees' role as year-round holidaymakers, whose primary responsibility was leisure rather than social or economic production—that is, a landscape almost entirely structured around consumption. What emerged, beginning around 1963, was a new kind of hybrid urban form, suburban in location but whose basic unit of building was not the one-family house or the workplace, but the resort apartment and the country club.

The bulk of new buildings were freestanding towers—as they had been since the late 1950s. Now, however, they appeared in clusters at large master-planned developments that, like Leisure World, had thousands of apartments and could support extensive common facilities. Physically, this new condoscape resembled Modernist architects' prescriptions for the city: widely spaced towers in the park (see fig. 10), with malls, medical clinics, banks, and synagogues and churches connected by broad, easy-to-navigate boulevards in a frictionless, auto-friendly space. Unlike many Modernist developments, however, where the client was the state and the residents young and poor, the middle-class retirement complex was a social and economic success.

A key figure in giving physical form to this ad hoc modern urbanism was the architect Morris Lapidus. Although he could be dismissive of Florida, describing it to the *Miami Herald* in 1973 as "the ass-hole of the world . . . when it comes to architecture," more than any other postwar U.S. designer he deeply considered the architecture of leisure.[77] In the 1950s, at ostentatious Miami Beach hotels like the Eden Roc (see fig. 74), Lapidus (1902–2001) had created the world's premier stages for the performance of conspicuous vacationing, with choreographed entrances, dramatic stairways, and movie-set historicism and lighting—devices he became acquainted with as a child at Coney Island. By the 1960s, however, the market for such hotels was in decline. Between 1959 and 1963, Miami Beach's oceanfront saw eight new apartment buildings but just one new hotel. Lapidus began to focus on apartments. By 1971, he had designed at least eighteen. Most were at large-scale complexes.[78]

The very largest of these, and exemplary of Florida's new retirement-city paradigm, was Aventura. While Abraham Kazan was building Co-op City with fifteen thousand high-rise apartments on three hundred acres of marshland in the northernmost reaches of New York City, Donald Soffer began Aventura, an even larger community of high-rises on nearly eight hundred acres of submerged land in the northernmost reaches of Dade County (fig. 87). Soffer's firm, Oxford Development, was a major builder of shopping centers in Pittsburgh. When visiting Florida in 1967, he noticed the site. Halfway between Miami and Fort Lauderdale, it seemed ideal for a large regional mall. The parcel could accommodate other uses, too. With scores of co-op and condos in surrounding areas, housing was an obvious choice. Soffer (born ca. 1933) formed a partnership with a high-rise New York homebuilder and bought the land in 1968. They commissioned a master plan for "Biscayne Village" from Monterey, California, architects Hall & Goodhue, later amended by in-house engineers (fig. 88).[79]

Like other luxurious, large-scale high-rise developments of the postwar period such as Century City in Los Angeles and Washington's Southwest, Aventura was quiet, elegant, and spacious. Gulfstream Mall (eventually built as Aventura Mall) fronted the main boulevard, at the inland side. Surrounding the mall were commercial buildings and a new avenue which connected to a marina at the opposite side of the complex and then the ocean, a mile to the east. Looping through the rest of the site was a winding ring road enveloping a double golf course lined with dozens of tall buildings. The total projected community was to include twenty-four thousand apartments, the maximum permitted under county density limits.

Visually, Aventura was distinguished by its vast green voids. To engender a sense of domesticity, buildings were grouped in inward-facing clusters. Each "neighborhood," which typically comprised two or three buildings, included its own clubhouse with meeting rooms, library, locker rooms, sauna, gym, pool, shuffleboard courts, and auditorium. Some also included tennis courts. Within buildings, Lapidus eliminated elements that recalled hotels, such as large lobbies and long interior corridors. Instead, apartments were accessed through outdoor catwalks, which offered each unit an outside entrance (see fig. 10), or, in taller, more expensive buildings, multiple banks of elevator, which allowed small numbers of apartments

Fig. 87: Aventura, Biscayne Boulevard, NE 192nd and 207th Streets, Intracoastal Waterway, Aventura, Florida. Donald Soffer, developer; Hall & Goodhue, initial site plan. Aerial view of construction progress, 1974.

Fig. 88: Aventura, development plan indicating initial phases of housing (top and at center left of golf course), ca. 1970.

Only a tiny part of Aventura will ever have apartments.

That's why it's so nice to own a condominium here.

AVENTURA

Fig. 89: Aventura, advertisement, *Miami Herald*, July 4, 1971.

to be arranged off of intimate landings rather than long anonymous hallways. Interior plans were compact and efficient.[80]

Although oriented more toward private space than the hotels, Aventura also embraced community. As one anonymous developer told *Florida Trend*, "People moving to Florida, especially in retirement, leave their old associates and they find it hard to make new friends. . . . Here in the [larger co-op] developments the social initiative is assumed for them."[81] Shared spaces, in this social context, were just as important as the apartments themselves. Aventura recognized this. Ads proclaimed that the community was "The condominium with a country club complex," and "If you don't play golf you can enjoy the view. And our yacht club. And our tennis. And our exciting enclosed shopping mall. And our etcetera."[82] Visual representations emphasized golf courses, the clubhouse, sailing, cycling, tennis, and swimming, while rendering the residential buildings as small gridded abstractions (fig. 89). It was this marketing emphasis on recreation and leisure that seems to have prompted Soffer to change the community's name, in 1970, from Biscayne Village to Aventura. "Village" connoted small-town domesticity. "Aventura" was not only Spanish for "adventure" but it sounded exciting, modern, and exotic.[83]

The importance of community spaces was also reflected in Aventura's architecture. Lapidus's most polished statement was the Aventura Country Club (later renamed Turnberry). The building comprised two cubic masses, one with a dining room and the other with locker rooms, connected by a glass reception lounge with a thirty-foot travertine waterfall. To further impress, the entire structure was placed high on a manmade hill. Lapidus's apartments were, by contrast, expedient. His hotels had been wonders of stagecraft, but condos served a different purpose and had little need to dazzle, especially in a robust sales market. Executed by a young associate in his Miami Beach office named Robert M. Swedroe, the

visual language was a reserved tropical
Modernism of white stucco, plate glass,
and screen doors, which became the
architectural lingua franca of high-rise
resort condos in the 1960s and 1970s.
Swedroe enlivened this at Aventura with
contrasting trim, and on some buildings,
vaguely mansard decorative roofs whose
bright colors (blue, yellow, brown),
distinguished one complex from the next.

Perhaps embarrassed by their
simplicity, Lapidus later distanced himself
from Aventura. As he told the *Herald*
Sunday magazine: "My buildings are
designed to make money for the client,
they are designed to be money-making
machines." That they were profitable,
however, does not take away from the
fact that they embody, in concrete form,
a triumphant culmination of the Fordist
system, which brought the American
worker from the shop floor to Levittown

Fig. 90: El Dorado, 3675 North Country Club Drive,
Aventura, Florida, 1973–74. Donald Soffer and Arlen
Properties, developers; Morris Lapidus, architect.

and, finally, to a comfortable retirement at resort buildings like the El Dorado (fig. 90).[84]

Turmoil in the real-estate market, overbuilding, and enmity between Soffer
and his business partners meant that Aventura did not sell twenty-four thousand
apartments by 1980 as planned—actual sales were under four thousand. The project
was the best-selling complex in Florida for much of the 1970s, however. And unlike
several competing projects, it continued construction, with the help of new partners,
over the next quarter-century, resulting, eventually, in something like what one of
the earliest ads promised: "The compleat condominium community."[85]

Meanwhile, similar but smaller complexes proliferated in Florida. Retirement
co-ops and condos also began to appear in and around many northern cities. Metro
New York, for example, saw projects like Princeton Manor House, a five-story co-op
on 180 acres on the outskirts of Princeton, New Jersey, built around 1963. Residency
was restricted to those age fifty-five or older (with preference said to be given to
Princeton and other Ivy League alumni). Among other amenities were a common
dining room, a library, card rooms, "hobby shops," a music room, individual garden
plots, riding stables, nature paths, and a number of partial golf courses. This project

was followed by a dozen others. By the 1970s, mainstream developers like Levitt &
Sons began marketing senior-only communities in suburban New York and beyond.[86]

Vacation Condos

Vacation condos for younger families also proliferated in this era. By the 1960s,
middle-class Americans had more time and money for vacations and second homes
than ever before. Many found it more convenient and practical to own an apartment
than a house. In addition to buying for their own use, many also came to see
vacation condos as a good way to invest surplus equity. As one 1975 study reported,
"Potential for unit appreciation appears to be the principal economic component of
demand for these units," and buyers regarded them, "either explicitly or implicitly,
as investments." By 1975 twenty to twenty-five percent of the 1.7 million co-ops and
condos in the U.S. were owned as second homes.[87] Among the ten housing markets
with the highest share of co-op and condo units in 1970, six were resort areas: Fort
Lauderdale, West Palm Beach, Miami, Honolulu, Phoenix, and Tampa. Important
concentrations also appeared at Ocean City, Maryland, Lake Tahoe, and Rocky
Mountain ski towns like Aspen and Vail, as well as at more isolated resorts such
as Hilton Head, North Carolina, and Sea Ranch, California, whose Condominium
Number One, designed by Charles Moore, was the first example of serious,
innovative architecture in the new ownership format, and whose example was
imitated endlessly in resorts in the late 1960s and 1970s.[88]

One way in which buyers explicitly employed ski and beach condos as
investments was to buy them to operate as rental properties. By-laws sometimes
limited this sort of activity, but in many buildings, especially in resorts, boards did
not enforce them. Co-ownership, which eased the burdens of physical maintenance,
served small landlords well. At resorts like Lake Tahoe, which was an extreme
example, nearly ninety percent of condos were bought as second homes, and among
these, two-thirds of owners planned to rent them out some or all of the time.[89]
One Hallandale high-rise was even planned from the start, in the late 1960s, to
host small-scale landlords. More than half of the thirteen hundred units (arranged
in four high-rises) were bought by foreign businessmen, and building services
included a management-operated office for leasing them to visitors. The developer,
unfortunately, turned out to be a major white-collar criminal, Robert Vesco, and the
model did not prove well suited to maintaining the building. It was not repeated.[90]

A more successful real-estate instrument which emerged as part of the mania
for buying vacation apartments was the timeshare. This system of ownership,
which was pioneered in France, first appeared in the U.S. in its modern form at
Brockway Springs on Lake Tahoe. The site was home to an old resort hotel that

had burned down in 1961. Rather than rebuild the hotel, an Ohio-based developer erected for-sale apartments. But instead of marketing them to single owners for $40,000 to $115,000 ($190,000 to $550,000 in 2010 dollars), it sold eleven, one-month shares for $4,000 to $24,000 ($19,000 to $115,000). The twelfth month was reserved for two, two-week blocks of repainting, replacement of furniture, and other heavy maintenance. Financing allowed buyers to put twenty-five percent down and pay the balance over ten years.

Under this plan, a one-month share of a two-bedroom unit cost about $1,500 upfront, and then $720 a year in mortgage and $432 in maintenance. This averaged out to $288 ($1,300) for each week of ownership, or $40 ($180) per night. Presumably this was cheaper than a hotel, and the cost could be offset by renting out the place for some of the weeks owned. As in the failed Hallandale project, a management-operated rental office—operated, in this case, by a subsidiary of Hyatt hotels—handled scheduling and operations. This system was lucrative for the developer, who sold the apartments for more than he could have done to single buyers. It was also a boon to owners, who could vacation at a popular spot, in a two-bedroom apartment, at reasonable rates.[91]

Full Disclosure

Collective homeownership was billed by homebuilders—and embraced by retirees and second homeowners—as a modern, sensible alternative to the hotel and the rented apartment. Co-ops and condos offered alluring prices and appealing combinations of privacy and community. With the pleasures of condo living, however, came costs.

One set of difficulties concerned the challenge of self-governance. Retirement condos brought together scores, sometimes hundreds, of owners, few of whom had any experience with collective homeownership. As one study of Fort Lauderdale reported, "The concept of communal living and shared responsibility is often unfamiliar to unit owners, who may make demands on the association officers as they would in a tenant-landlord relationship. This has often caused experienced unit owners to avoid service on the governing board."[92] Problems were magnified by the fact that many owners were often absent; at the other extreme, many had so much time for building affairs that governance could get bogged down by an excess of opinion. Apathy, however, was rare. As one study in the mid-1970s revealed, Florida condo owners were very engaged: three-quarters of owners reported that they regularly attended building meetings, and half that they frequently spoke at them.[93]

A more difficult set of challenges concerned practices pioneered by developers to keep initial—but not ongoing—costs low. In the 1950s and early 1960s it was common for developers to retain ownership of common elements, usually the recreation complexes. These recreation, or "rec" leases, they argued, allowed lower sales prices. But terms were generally unfavorable to homeowners and, in practice, rec leases served as a way for developers to continue to profit long after they had sold all the apartments. Included in the deeds, which unsuspecting buyers rarely scrutinized in advance, were requirements that owners pay rent for these facilities whether or not they used them. Additionally, many developers included escalation clauses that tied rents to inflation. Worse yet, many developers also locked associations into unfavorable, long-term, binding contracts for paid management, usually from the developer or a subsidiary, as detailed in John D. MacDonald's 1977 disaster novel *Condominium*. These agreements similarly tied maintenance charges to inflation or allowed increases to be determined at management's discretion, without approval of the association.[94]

When buyers discovered that they had unwittingly assumed these obligations, they protested. At first they directed their anger at local elected officials. Later they turned to the State of Florida, and by the early 1970s to Congress and the Federal Trade Commission, which had jurisdiction over interstate real-estate sales. At the core of demands for new consumer protection was "full disclosure": that developers fully reveal to prospective buyers the complete terms of an offering, including all by-laws. New York State had begun requiring that homebuilders fully disclose the terms of co-op (and later condominium) plans of ownership (or "offerings") in 1961, so these types of abuses were unheard of there. But elsewhere, as Senator Joe Biden argued, there ought to be aid for the buyer "confronted with a bewildering set of documents." Otherwise, he continued, "I don't know how anybody expects to move into a condominium and have it be a house." In 1974, the U.S. Senate held hearings on two bills to protect buyers by requiring homebuilders to offer all buyers full disclosure and mandating that the Secretary of Housing and Urban Development regulate condominium sales.[95]

Point East

The first reports of abuse surfaced in the late 1960s at North Miami Beach's Point East condominium. Point East was developed by an unscrupulous operator named Leonard Schreiber beginning in 1966, following the sales success of two low-cost co-ops, both of which he named for himself: Ro-Len Gardens, in Hallandale, and Mar-Len Gardens, in North Miami Beach. The new project (which included a Leonard Drive) was much larger, with 1,400 apartments on sixty-two acres.[96] Buyers were typical of those for Florida retirement apartments: the average age was around fifty, thirty-five percent were already living in Florida, and thirty-seven percent were moving from greater New York.

Among the New Yorkers was Ernest Samuels. In an affidavit given to the Federal Trade Commission in 1974, Samuels explained that he had decided to buy based on promises made in ads that Schreiber ran in the *Herald* in the summer of 1966. These variously promised a wealth of community amenities, including "a Community Clubhouse, Health Pavilion with Medical Clinic, two full size Gyms, Olympic Swimming Pools, Full time Social Director, two Sand Beaches, Boat Rides, Water Shows, Fashion Shows, Coffee Shop open daily, Weekly Lecture, Forums and Instructional Classes, Golf Instruction, Weekly Stage Shows and Dancing, and many other amenities including a 1200 seat auditorium." Samuels signed a purchase agreement.[97]

Only after closing, a year later, was he given full documentation, in the form a book with 105 pages of small type. Only then did he read the project by-laws and learn of the ninety-nine year rec lease, the twenty-five year management contract (with fees determined as a share of the association expenses). And only then did he learn of the "funding fee." This was said to serve as security deposit for monthly maintenance charges and to finance an initial reserve fund. After several years, however, when Schreiber raised monthly maintenance by more than forty percent, it emerged that the actual purpose had been to artificially lower monthly maintenance costs during sales. In fact, the complex was operating at a massive loss, mainly due to the medical clinic, which turned out to cost $10,000 a month to run—despite being equipped only to examine owners for fitness to use the gym.[98]

As the scandal at Point East unfolded, prompting CBS television's Mike Wallace to investigate Schreiber on his *60 Minutes* program in 1974, a few industry leaders, like Brown L. Whatley, began to align themselves with aggrieved homeowners. Whatley lobbied tirelessly for the state to ban rec leases and long-term management contracts. Most developers, however, opposed this plan. Only after aggrieved homeowners gained the attention of Congress did Florida enact full disclosure laws.[99] (Sadly, later studies showed that even when full disclosure was required, eighty-five percent of buyers remained unfamiliar with or unaware of their by-laws.)[100]

While disclosure laws in Florida forestalled federal action, the rec-lease scandals compelled national real-estate leaders to address these problems immediately. To this end, the Urban Land Institute and the National Association of Home Builders established a new organization, the Community Associations Institute (CAI), in 1973, dedicated to improving the condo and other forms of co-owned housing on a voluntary basis, by working with lenders, developers, and local and state lawmakers. As concerns mounted about the challenges of self-governance CAI also began serving as a clearinghouse for information to assist boards. Meanwhile, secondary mortgage

Fig. 91: "The good life ... relaxing leisurely beside Sea Towers' superb four-acre lagoon," Cove Circle, St. Petersburg, Florida. *Florida Builder*, January 1972.

lenders like Fannie Mae and Freddie Mac developed new requirements for the buildings it did business with. More generally, the real-estate industry worked to standardize practices, professionalize management, and manage buyers' expectations (and excessive costs) by eliminating unsustainable amenities.[101]

Promised Land or Slum?

In addition to rec leases and management contracts, mass condo ownership generated problems that reform efforts were unequipped to cope with. One was financing for resales. Another was cyclical overbuilding. Bankers were happy to finance new construction and make initial mortgages for individual units, but well into the 1970s they were reluctant to finance "spot" mortgages for second-hand sales. The reason provided was that it was too difficult to appraise apartments on a unit-by-unit basis.[102] This situation was exacerbated by the vast quantity of new construction in the 1970s, which continually undercut the sales appeal of last year's models. In Florida, in particular, this led many in the 1970s to question whether the condominium was not the slum of the future rather than, as one Aventura ad boasted, "the promised land delivered."[103]

Reflecting on the question of whether condos were ultimately good or bad for retirees, an attorney for Point East homeowners told the *New York Times* that condominium living "is a useful social experience offering the retired people perhaps the first opportunity to live by themselves with a feeling of dignity and self-esteem." Aaron M. Sweeman, a retired accountant from New Jersey, added, "We do many things we have never done before. We swim, we play golf, we go on trips, and generally we have a lot of fun. And we don't have to worry about cleaning the swimming pool or cutting the grass" (fig. 91).[104] The condo, for all its growing pains, served as an efficient and generally happy way to house the retired mass-middle-class in an age of unprecedented abundance. A 1975 survey showed that ninety-six percent of Fort Lauderdale co-op and condo owners were satisfied with their homes. As *Florida Trend* declared in 1970, a "new life-style is evolving in Florida and with it, a new habitat, the condominium."[105]

CHAPTER 6

California Townhouses

I n 1962, as bankers in Florida were working to introduce the condominium to
retirees, the Santa Clara County, California, Planning Commission published a
briefing to "stimulate interest" among developers in this "third type of cooperative
housing" (after the stock co-op and the California own-your-own, a unique West
Coast model pioneered in the 1920s). Much of the material in this enthusiastic
dossier came directly from a recent conference on the condo organized by a regional
trade group and *California Builder* magazine. The housing that most captured the
imagination of these suburban Bay Area planners, however, was not the high-rise.
Rather, it was what they called "common green": a "form of site planning which
clusters dwelling units"—mainly attached row houses—"in and around open space."
They were talking about suburban townhouse complexes.[1]

Common green was patterned in part on the site-planning experiments of
Clarence Stein and Henry Wright in the 1920s and 1930s, and on the FHA-style
garden apartment. More specifically, it looked to two recent projects by Eichler
Homes, one of the Bay Area's more prolific homebuilders. One comprised three
small groups of attached row houses along the edge of Greenmeadow, an otherwise
single-family subdivision that the firm was developing in Palo Alto. The other, called
Pomeroy Green, was a larger townhouse subdivision in a leafy section of the City of
Santa Clara (fig. 92).

According to Eichler's multifamily project coordinator, Donald Stofle, these
common-green townhouse complexes were conceived of in response to new
conditions in the field of housing. Eichler's innovative single-family houses had
defined the Modernist look of Northern California suburbs in the second half of the
1950s. But rapid suburbanization meant that land costs were rising, generating new
pressure to conserve. It also meant that much of the space that remained for new
housing in the Bay Area—as well as in Southern California, where the firm also

Fig. 92: Pomeroy Green, northeast corner Pomeroy Avenue, Benton Street, Santa Clara, California, 1960–62. Eichler Homes, developer; Claude Oakland, architect; Sasaki, Walker & Associates, site planning consultants. Model.

worked—was hilly or "otherwise difficult." Both things meant single-family houses were becoming more difficult. Multifamily designs, Stofle explained, would allow more freedom to "place the housing units in locations that are appropriate and leave the other areas undisturbed." Also of concern were new patterns of demand. Eichler households, Stofle noted, seemed to be "tired of mowing the lawn and painting the fascia and trimming the hedge and this sort of thing." In the new common-green projects, he explained, homeowners "now have an opportunity where all they have to maintain is the interior."[2]

In response to these changing conditions, Eichler began experimenting with several kinds of multifamily communities, from garden apartments to high-rises, both rented and owned. The common-green complex, as designed by architect Claude Oakland at Palo Alto and Santa Clara, was one. Given customers' preferences for suburbia—for quick access to the outdoors and to the car, for indoor-outdoor living and ample physical privacy—their townhouses proved popular. As a result,

Stofle wrote that the "typical condominium I predict that we will see in this area is going to be the row-house type of development, sharing common landscaped grounds, sharing play facilities."[3]

When lenders began promoting the condo in the 1960s in Florida and then nationally, many in the housing field expected that it would be used as a form of "horizontal property," especially for moderate- and lower-income city-center households. In his research on Europe, for example, New York State's assistant attorney general, David Clurman, an expert on co-ownership, determined that the condominium had been specifically designed for multistory buildings. In the U.S., he noted, it had been introduced to help Puerto Rico, which he imagined as "distressingly in need of high-rise[s]" because of its compact size. Condos had already succeeded in San Juan as a form of expensive housing. He hoped federal provisions secured in 1961 would help it "receive acceptance at lower levels of the income strata," where the limited-equity and FHA co-op had met resistance. He was optimistic that condo ownership would help middle-class families in other cities, too. The condominium, he wrote, "offers the first genuinely effectual opportunity since the mid-1930's to provide an adequate supply of middle-income housing."[4]

The condominium did come to be used for middle-class housing, but not in city-center high-rises. In practice, outside of resorts and retirement complexes most condos took the form of medium-density, often suburban housing, especially in townhouse clusters like Eichler's. Even in New York State, Clurman recalled, "first thing" after his office began accepting applications for condo offerings, "builders and bankers came in and they started talking about formulating plans for cluster housing in the suburbs."[5] Although Clurman was concerned about this unanticipated application, in other parts of the country developers and planners quickly understood the townhouse as an appealing new alternative to mainstream suburbia.

Among those who embraced this mode of dwelling were Mr. and Mrs. Carl Mattos, who bought a row house at Pomeroy Green during initial sales, in 1962. Mrs. Mattos, in particular, was so enthusiastic that she volunteered as a "hostess," leading tours for prospective buyers. As a "resident manager" she continued to show apartments for resales for many years. (Although a model "condominium" complex, Pomeroy Green was, in fact, an FHA-insured co-op, and resales were handled through the cooperative rather than outside agents.) Mattos wrote to Eichler Homes in 1970 that the units "were easy to sell—they sold themselves" and that eight years later the complex remained a "thriving, prosperous and financially sound townhouse development" with a waiting list. She was "completely sold" on what she described as the "Eichler way of townhouse living" (fig. 93).[6]

Fig. 93: Pomeroy Green, community swimming pool.

Communities like Pomeroy Green did not thrive only because middle-class families were tired of mowing the lawn and the cost of land was rising. They also succeeded because they appealed to baby boomers. Young adults in the 1960s and 1970s established more households, smaller households, and more varied households than had earlier generations. These new household types included divorced families, single-parent families, dual-commute families, small families, and single-person households—homes in which working adults typically had little time for such chores as exterior and ground maintenance. By 1960 the number of families nationally with working women reached fifty percent, and by 1970 nearly sixty percent. The share of single-person households grew to eighteen percent in 1970 from under eight percent in 1940. The number of single-parent families grew similarly. In 1960, eight percent of U.S. children lived with a single mother, while in 1970 nearly twelve percent did.[7]

Baby boomers were better off financially than young people in earlier eras which meant they could afford to own their own homes even when they did not yet need whole houses. Spurred on by Vietnam-era inflation and rapidly rising resale prices, this cohort became just as eager as its parents had been in the 1940s and 1950s to build equity through homeownership. New genres of housing, like the common-green townhouse, catered directly to them. With a widely appealing mixture of privacy, economy, and community, the townhouse caught on rapidly coast to coast. By the 1970s it had become an exciting—if sometimes vexing—element of the metropolitan landscape (fig. 94). Perhaps for these reasons—or maybe simply because of its visual novelty—it was explored by young artists, including Joel Sternfeld and James Casebere, and became the subject of films like *Over the Edge* and primetime sitcoms like *Condo*.

Fig. 94: Westover Plantation, DeFoors Ferry Road at Westover Plantation and Middle Plantation Roads NW, Atlanta, ca. 1979.

Since the 1970s many critics have attacked the common-green complex on grounds that its private governance represents a withering of the public sphere and, in turn, the democratic state. This perspective privileges just one side of the condo story. Townhouses and other "private" communities were informed by conservative impulses. But they were also shaped by progressive ideals and served new, smaller kinds of households, including many women, in a way that older kinds of neighborhoods did not.[8]

According to Suzanne Keller, a Princeton sociologist who bought a suburban New Jersey townhouse in the early 1970s, co-ownership served a

Fig. 95: Strawberry Square, Moorpark Avenue at Periwinkle and Junipero Serra Lanes, San Jose, California, 1971–76.

practical, forward-thinking purpose in a post-Levittown era: mediating an awkward but growing gap between preferences for the pastoral isolation of suburbia and the new social realities of "divorce, single-parenthood, and smaller families." Writing in the 1980s, after fifteen years in residence, Keller argued that townhouse complexes differed from single-family neighborhoods in their efforts to "break down the splendid isolation of suburban life and move toward some form of shared living that constitutes a compromise between urban conviviality and suburban privatism" (fig. 95). They also reflected, in her view, an attempt by both the producers and

consumers of housing "to foster a new sense of collective responsibility" in an era
of smaller households, when more people felt a great need to "reach beyond the
cocoon of the family to a wider social terrain" to avoid "suburban isolation and
vulnerability . . . to loneliness."[9]

Apartments in Freewayland

Collective homeownership was an elastic, shape-shifting container that could
accommodate a variety of physical forms and legal arrangements. As it grew in
popularity after 1960, homebuilders and designers transformed and adapted it to
fit an increasing variety of social, economic, and physical conditions. Outside of
Florida, where the condominium format was introduced, some of the most innovative
experiments—both in terms of legal arrangements and physical form—were in
Southern California.

In certain respects this might have been unexpected. Southern California was
the prototypical suburban city, the first great metropolitan region anywhere to
have a residential fabric overwhelmingly stitched of single-family detached houses.
Although freestanding houses had long predominated in many parts of American
cities, it was not until the 1950s, when L.A. supplanted Philadelphia as the nation's
third-largest city, that there was a major urban area whose residents lived mostly in
freestanding houses. Generations of Americans had moved to L.A. to enjoy its good
climate and modern, relaxed way of life, and most everyone—designers, politicians,
and voters—made efforts to ensure that L.A. did not come to resemble the more
congested, centralized cities of the East Coast and Midwest.[10] Wartime and postwar
industrial growth in aviation, aerospace, and automaking brought millions more
people to the region. The city's superior road network, ample undeveloped land,
and success in mass-producing modest houses in large, cost-efficient developments
(coupled with federal programs designed to make homeownership more accessible),
helped white Angelenos achieve the American dream of a detached suburban house.
Most did.[11]

Even in L.A., however, the supremacy of detached houses did not last. Beginning
in the 1950s and 1960s a growing minority of middle-class and well-to-do households
began to seek medium-density, owner-occupied multifamily housing. In doing so,
they turned away from older and often more transient alternatives to the detached
house, such as rental apartments and residential hotels. By the mid–1970s as many
as one in seven owner-occupied homes in Los Angeles, Orange, San Bernardino,
Riverside, and San Diego Counties—more than a quarter of a million units—were
multifamily. By the 1980s, metropolitan Los Angeles surpassed metropolitan New
York in population density.[12]

Unlike people in New York or Miami, however, Southern Californians eschewed tall apartment buildings in favor of homes that preserved privacy, offered outdoor space, and readily accommodated the automobile. The formula was in many respects suburban. The result was a transformation of "Freewayland," as the architectural critic Reyner Banham described the region, into a new kind of hybrid built environment that by the 1970s defied the conventional categories of city and suburb.[13]

To meet the needs of smaller, relatively affluent households, beginning in the late 1940s and 1950s small-scale speculative homebuilders and architects began to experiment with new kinds of garden apartments. By the early 1960s they were pioneering the modern townhouse community. In planning these projects, architects and developers built upon local housing traditions and borrowed and adapted models from cities such as New York, where owner-occupied, suburban multifamily housing had first appeared in the 1920s. Within a decade of the completion of Lakewood, in 1954—the iconic FHA project near Long Beach with more than seventeen thousand detached houses—a majority of new homes that were under way in Southern California's fourteen counties were multifamily. In L.A. County the share was two-thirds, and in the city of L.A., three-quarters.[14]

This dramatic shift to multifamily housing challenges popular conceptions of postwar Southern California—and, by extension, postwar middle-class America—as a TV-land of picture windows, picket fences, and stereotypically gendered, nuclear-family domesticity. This was the era of regional and national merchant builders, such as Levitt & Sons, and mass-built, large-scale, visually homogenous suburban subdivisions, such as Lakewood, whose advancements were often limited to efficiencies of speed and cost. Local developers, however, aided by modern financing mechanisms which kept barriers to entry low, tested new kinds of housing, including owner-occupied multifamily housing. Larger companies could build and sell homes for somewhat less than local builders because of greater economies of scale, but these savings were not so great that new, smaller firms could not compete.

Own-Your-Own Apartment

As in Chicago and Washington, the owner-occupied apartment emerged in Southern California after World War I. Its popularity, however, remained intermittent until the mid-1950s. The Southern California housing market suffered far less during the 1910s and early 1920s than those of large industrial centers such as New York and Chicago, and the government center of Washington. As rents rose during the war, writers in the *Los Angeles Times* urged readers that the best protection against these increases was to move to "own your own" houses in "the country."[15] Many families did. But others, as in New York, Chicago, and Washington, became interested in apartment ownership. At the time, the apartment house had long enjoyed a limited popularity in Southern California, particularly in Los Angeles, often as a form of itinerant housing for seasonal visitors.[16]

The first co-op planned in L.A. appears to have been the Figueroa Arms. It opened for sales in early 1920. Within months the developer, a Chicago salesman, had announced three other buildings. Unfortunately for buyers he disappeared with everyone's deposits.[17] It was several years before another project in L.A. succeeded in attracting enough initial interest to get built. In 1921, for example, a group of East Coast investors bought a twenty-acre site along Wilshire Boulevard adjacent to the city's largest, most lavish hotel, the Ambassador. They hoped to build a project called the Barcelona Apartments, a vast twelve-story complex with six wings and more than two hundred units. The promoters claimed it would be the largest residential building west of New York. Certainly it was the most expensive, at least west of Chicago, with the apartments priced at $50,000 and more ($2.2 million in 2010 dollars). The architect was Aleck E. Curlett of Curlett & Beelman, one of L.A.'s most prolific designers. Launched around the time of the Figueroa Arms scandal, it took just two months for the developers to abandon the plan.[18]

Fig. 96: Villa Riviera, 800 East Ocean Avenue, Long Beach, California, 1928–29. Lionel V. Mayell, developer; Richard D. King, architect. Postcard, ca. 1929.

Far more successful than city-center co-ops in this emergent suburban metropolis were the well-equipped high-rise resort apartments developed by Lionel V. Mayell at Long Beach (fig. 96). At least sixteen buildings of this sort went up along this oceanfront in the 1920s, and it was for these projects that Mayell devised his "deed plan." Most people called it "own-your-own." Although some buildings organized as traditional co-ops were also marketed as "own-your-owns" in Southern California, the true own-your-own followed Mayell's plan. Like the condo, this relied on the legal doctrine of tenancy-in-common to convey, via deed, an undivided share of a building to each owner. Although this plan meant that neither blanket nor individual mortgages were available, it was used widely, from

San Diego to Santa Barbara, until the early 1960s, when the condo and townhouse superseded it.

Pasadena Apartment Courts

Through the Depression and World War II, into the early 1950s, co-ownership existed only at the margins of the Southern California housing market. New development was primarily horizontal, with vast tracts of houses built near the region's new industrial plants at the urban periphery. Some multifamily housing was built, but little of it catered to families who could afford homeownership; most was rental. Immediately after the war a small number of low-cost co-ops appeared. Some were built by speculative developers, some by groups of prospective homeowners. The best known of these was Avenel Homes, a ten-unit complex of striking row houses designed by the politically progressive Modernist Gregory Ain, completed in 1948. Co-op living among ordinary middle-class families, however, failed to catch on.[19]

Somewhat more popular were better-equipped, conventionally financed own-your-owns. Among the first of these was Orange Grove Manor in Pasadena, developed by Mayell (fig. 97). Pasadena, like Long Beach, had been a winter resort

Fig. 97: Orange Grove Manor, 168–80 South Orange Grove Boulevard, Pasadena, 1949–50. Lionel V. Mayell, developer. Northeast building.

and had many expensive hotels and
mansions, which centered on South
Orange Grove Boulevard. After
World War II the town became
more of a year-round center. As new
sections developed, primarily with
detached houses, the old business
district, and many of the older
middle-class areas, became run
down. The city's overall population
grew from around eighty thousand
in 1940 to more than a hundred
thousand in 1950, and its African
American community grew from
around four thousand to eight
thousand. Well-do-visitors stayed
away, leaving many of even the best
houses unoccupied. Nevertheless,

Fig. 98: Studio, North King's Road between West First
Street and Beverly Boulevard, Los Angeles, ca. 1936.

South Orange Grove retained social cachet. What it required, however, was smaller,
more manageable kinds of housing. Mayell (1897–1978) was among the first to
discern this and in 1948 took a permit to replace a mansion with a modern Mission
Revival apartment court.[20]

Orange Grove Manor represented a great advance in the evolution of housing
in the region because it was among the first owner-occupied multifamily complexes
to appeal to year-round residents. In most other respects it was unexceptional. Its
hybrid design motif was not new. The stylistic treatment, which, to paraphrase
Reyner Banham, was what expedience extracted from the Spanish Colonial Revival,
had come into vogue in the 1930s.[21] Its apartment-court plan—which included five,
two-story buildings, each with four apartments, grouped around a landscaped
garden—was also familiar.

Historically, the most common kind of multifamily housing in Southern
California was the low-rise rental complex. These tended to come in two varieties:
the apartment or bungalow court, and the "studio" apartment, a local typology in
which three or four (sometimes more) apartments were arranged in a structure
that read from the exterior as a large single-family house (fig. 98). Both types were
relatively inexpensive to construct and offered tenants a way of life compatible with
the good climate and automobility. Unlike high-rises, most included outdoor space
in the form of private patios or common gardens, which in some complexes might

include a swimming pool. Each suite also typically had a private entrance leading directly to the outside, allowing for quick access to the car. Many of these complexes were quite elaborate, but most were simple and inexpensive. They often served as temporary housing for tourists, seasonal residents, or retirees.[22]

Mayell's project, which required a change in zoning, faced resistance from longtime residents. Only after extensive debate did city leaders approve of the necessary change.[23] As Orange Grove Manor rose in the spring of 1949, the *Times* reported with a hint of nostalgia that "in the midst of disdainful mansions and the frowning ghosts of a thousand blue-blooded memories, the first units of an apartment colony are being erected. A big sign beckons to those who would invade 'Millionaire's Row,' which is reserved for millionaires no more."[24] Within a few years, however, the paper had reversed its position. In 1954, a society columnist reported, in an article subtitled "Residents of Crown City Forsake Own Homes for Apartment Life," that "many people who have lived in their own homes [houses] for years are moving into 'own your own' apartments." The writer noted in particular that one local matron was "getting settled in her spacious apartment on S Orange Grove," having sold her house to a younger family.[25]

The own-your-own way of life fanned out from Orange Grove Boulevard. Between 1950 and 1961 Mayell completed as many as ten additional complexes in Pasadena, each better equipped with richer materials and newer technologies than the last. At 1954's Villa San Pasqual, for example, which comprised fifteen modernistic buildings grouped around two courts, each of the sixty suites had a kitchen finished in natural birch with copper hardware, sixteen-foot-wide sliding plate-glass balcony or patio doors, and optional central air conditioning (fig. 99). Green slate roofing from Idaho complemented the buildings' stucco façades, which were painted flamingo pink.[26] Mayell also developed similar projects in La Jolla and Santa Barbara, as well as in Phoenix, Houston, and Florida. His acquaintance Charles E. Carpenter began building similar complexes in nearby, if less exclusive, Glendale, signaling a broadening market for multifamily homeownership in metropolitan Los Angeles. By 1963 Carpenter had completed ten own-your-owns in Glendale, as well as others in La Jolla and Los Angeles's Los Feliz neighborhood.

Specific information on owners at these own-your-owns is scarce but prices and the size of apartments—typically nine hundred to seventeen hundred square feet—suggest that most were small, well-to-do households, perhaps retirees. Typical units at Villa San Pasqual, for example, sold for $18,900 in 1954 with $31 per month in maintenance charges ($210,000 and $350 in 2010 dollars). At buildings with larger apartments, the smaller units often sold better, further suggesting that buyers

Fig. 99: Villa San Pasqual, 1000 San Pasqual Street, Pasadena, 1954. Lionel V. Mayell, developer. Details of *Villa San Pasqual*, prospectus.

were smaller, older families.[27] These prices were low relative to those of houses. In the 1950s, houses typically sold for $15,000 to $25,000 in outlying sections of the region, $25,000 to $50,000 in more central areas (including Glendale), and as much as $300,000 ($3.4 million) for the largest houses in the most desirable neighborhoods, such as Beverly Hills.[28] The apartments were far from inexpensive, however, because no financing was available.

Although most own-your-owns took the form of apartment courts, by the late 1950s mid-rise and even high-rise buildings also began to appear. The first was Wilshire Terrace, an expensive co-op announced by New York developer Norman Tishman in 1956 and completed by 1959 (fig. 100). The twelve-story building was designed by Victor Gruen Associates and featured two-story duplex suites, each with a two-story balcony with a built-in barbecue pit. It was a popular subject with artists (both Ed Ruscha and Julius Shulman photographed it), and those who bought were among the city's cultural and business elite. Taller own-your-owns and co-ops followed, especially in the Wilshire corridor.[29]

FHA *in L.A.*

As the expensive own-your-own spread in the late 1950s and early 1960s, other developers began to experiment with owner-occupied multifamily housing catering to middle-class families who required financing. The leading developer of such projects was Ardmore Development Corporation, which built nearly twenty projects between 1957 and 1964. Unlike Mayell's buildings, the units were sold on the co-op

Fig. 100: Wilshire Terrace, 10375 Wilshire Boulevard, Los Angeles, 1957–59. Norman Tishman, developer; Victor Gruen, architect. Photograph by Julius Shulman, 1959.

plan of ownership, using loans insured by FHA. Among the first proposals for an FHA co-op in L.A. was the unbuilt Braemar Towers, a thirteen-story building planned by Paul J. Broman for West Hollywood. Broman unveiled the project by way of a model apartment at L.A.'s annual Home Show in June 1955. Ads pitched one-bedroom apartments to "career women" (two- and three-bedroom units were also available). Although the building seemed to sell well from plans, it appears that by the time FHA was ready to permit construction to begin, the project was no longer financially feasible. Broman refunded deposits and in 1962 erected a rental building on the site.[30]

Ardmore emerged from this failure. The firm's principal, Leonard B. Schneider (not to be confused with Miami's Leonard Schreiber), had worked in Broman's sales department. When forty of the two hundred buyers initially refused to accept refunds and insisted on waiting as long as required to get an apartment, he became convinced that he could make a project work. With the help of a local attorney he established Ardmore and began work on one of postwar California's first

Fig. 101: 6400 Primrose Avenue, Hollywood, ca. 1958. Ardmore Development Corporation, developer.

successful middle-class co-ops: 6400 Primrose Avenue in Hollywood's Beachwood Canyon (fig. 101).[31]

Recognizing the limitations of existing physical forms, Ardmore developed a new typology. Unlike Braemar Towers or most FHA co-ops on the East Coast, 6400 Primrose was neither a high-rise nor a conventional garden apartment. A large high-rise such as Braemar Towers could pose unforeseen problems with financing. Furthermore, despite the occasional sales success of tall co-ops, the high-rise had never proved especially popular in Southern California. Standard garden-apartment models were also not quite right. One constraint was that the market for owner-occupied multifamily housing in 1955 remained quite small. Own-your-owns in Pasadena and Glendale contained a few dozens suites at most, and a New York type FHA project, with hundreds of apartments, would have been too large. Another factor seems to be that typical middle-class households in Southern California in the 1950s had different expectations for quality in housing than in East Coast cities, requiring more privacy, better-equipped outdoor space, and more convenient parking. A third factor was that the cost of land was higher in Beachwood Canyon than in areas where homebuilders typically erected FHA-insured co-ops. A standard garden apartment development, with multiple structures and wide-open lawns, required too much land.

Shaped by these conditions, 6400 Primrose, whose designer remains unknown, broke from national models. Its twenty-four, one-story suites were arranged in

Fig. 102: 6400 Primrose, courtyard and pool.

a single, two-story G-plan building, with a swimming pool and landscaped patio at the center (fig. 102). Apartments were accessed from the courtyard through ground-floor front doors or through exterior staircases placed in recessed alcoves, each of which led to two upstairs units. The project also broke visually from East Coast examples, rejecting Colonial Revival in favor of a contemporary California vernacular that borrowed from generic ranch and split-level houses, as well as recent designs by such well-known architects as Frank Lloyd Wright, Marcel Breuer, and Harwell Hamilton Harris. Like them, the designer of 6400 Primrose employed an asymmetric plan; horizontal massing and fenestration; low, pitched roofs with deep eaves; and contrasting exterior materials, in this case panels of light stucco and dark clapboard, accented with vertical panels of aluminum and beige glass. In its use of inexpensive applied decoration over stucco, the project also recalled the region's "dingbat" and "stucco box" rental apartments of the 1950s.[32]

Ardmore also included amenities rarely found in FHA co-ops. Some of the apartments had private patios. More importantly, the complex had a swimming pool. While neither small middle-class houses nor Mayell's own-your-owns included pools, Schneider seems to have believed that this sort of luxury was necessary to make the homes attractive. Because of these features and the high cost of land in Hollywood, the project was more expensive than typical FHA co-ops. (FHA insured projects only up to a certain cost, and buyers had to make up the balance with their down payments.) Apartments sold for $4,980 to $5,300 down ($49,000 to $52,000), with $141 to $148 per month in maintenance ($1,400 to $1,450). The building opened by 1958.[33]

San Fernando Valley

The sales success of 6400 Primrose led Ardmore to begin nineteen additional FHA co-ops over the next five years. While these included two high-rises—one in Hollywood and one in Westwood, both longstanding centers of apartment living—the rest were suburban in scale; many were also suburban in location. Eleven were in the San Fernando Valley, including one in remote Reseda.[34]

These projects, which were designed primarily by the young architect Robert Charles Lesser, were larger and more strictly Modernist than was 6400 Primrose. Most comprised compact, symmetrical groups of two to ten long, horizontal I-, L-, or C-plan buildings with aluminum-frame ribbon windows and flat roofs. The spare aesthetic recalled many of the area's progressive low-income rental projects of the 1930s and 1940s, including the RPAA's Baldwin Hills Village and the wartime projects of Richard Neutra, Channel Heights and Pueblo del Rio.[35] Lesser distinguished his co-ops by providing lush landscaping and enlivening flat stucco façades with colorful contrasting trim, iron screens, and decorative panels of painted brick, tile, dark wood, and natural stone (fig. 103). Side and rear elevations remained unornamented stucco. Lesser (b. 1931) also offered custom-design services to buyers, who were free to rearrange suites to fit their needs and had a choice of several optional features.[36]

Lesser's designs improved on Ardmore's earlier project by providing homeowners with more privacy. Although multifamily homeowners tended to prefer projects with shared amenities, they also seemed to select those that offered the most privacy. To that end, Lesser gave every apartment its own fenced patio or balcony. He also included individual carports in parking structures placed at the back or side of the complexes. 6400 Primrose, by contrast, had a surface parking lot. Privacy was also achieved by orienting buildings perpendicular to, or entirely away from, the street, and by obscuring entrances. 6400 Primrose had a clearly articulated front entrance (although most homeowners approached from a side gate by the parking lot; see fig. 101). Lesser, however, pushed entryways—which also housed mailboxes, directories, and way-finding maps—to corners, and he obscured them with gates, deep trellises or canopies, and other visual screens.

Information on buyers is also difficult to find for these projects. The size and prices of apartments suggest that Ardmore homeowners included larger, middle-class households, including families with children. According to Schneider,

Fig. 103: Queensland Manor South, 11121 Queensland Street, Los Angeles, ca. 1960. Ardmore Development Corporation, developer; Robert Charles Lesser, architect.

apartments with three and four bedrooms sold more quickly than those with one or two. As trade journal *House & Home* noted in 1961, this trend "suggests there is not only a social need but also an effective market demand for family-size apartments even in the middle of a traditionally one-family-house area."[37] The relatively modest price of land in places such as the Valley kept construction costs lower than at 6400 Primrose, and well within FHA limits for blanket mortgages. At several projects that began sales around 1960, for example, prices ranged from $950 down with $99 in maintenance ($8,200 and $860) for one-bedroom units to $2,500 with $250 ($22,000 and $2,200) for three. These prices were competitive with those for small detached houses.[38]

Although Ardmore seems to have primarily catered to younger families, it also found a market with older ones. Leisure World, announced in 1961, with its nearly seven thousand co-op apartments, revealed a huge new market for apartment ownership in L.A. But not all seniors wished to live in a sequestered community. To best accommodate this mixture of older and younger families—and minimize disturbances from noise—Ardmore began segregating projects by age.

At Coldwater Ardmore it divided the two-and-a-half-acre site in half and built one section for families with children and one in which residence of children was prohibited by the co-op's by-laws. Each had a separate pool and recreation area. Communities segregated by age were not new, but Coldwater Ardmore was among the first to cater to old and young by explicitly separating them. This technique became common nationally in the 1960s.[39]

Row House Revival

After more than decade of incremental growth in multifamily homeownership, 1962 saw a shift away from apartment-court and garden-apartment typologies to another physical form: the suburban-style row-house complex. Widespread use of the condominium plan, which quickly superseded the own-your-own and co-op, coincided with this design shift. As a result, many in Southern California came to use the term "condo" to refer to row houses and cluster site plans, regardless of arrangements for ownership (row houses were also commonly sold on the own-your-own and co-op plans, as fee-simple common-interest developments, or operated as rentals). Meanwhile, by the 1970s at least one homebuilder nationally began to market "California townhouses."[40]

In contrast to the urban row houses common before World War I (which in a few cities continued to be built through the 1950s), this new generation was developed almost exclusively on suburban campuses or large superblocks. Housing reformers began introducing this arrangement to the U.S. at Forest Hills Gardens in Queens and at wartime housing projects during World War I. Some of the architects who worked on these projects further experimented with this model in the 1920s under the auspices of the RPAA at Sunnyside and Radburn, and in the 1930s at the Greenbelt towns, Chatham Village in Pittsburgh, and Baldwin Hills Village in Los Angeles. In the interwar years a handful of private developers also experimented with this model of semi-suburban housing, with several examples in Washington, D.C., with its "community houses," and in metropolitan New York, where builders promoted "closes," "courts," and "group houses" in Queens, Long Island, and Westchester County.[41]

After World War II many government-aided garden apartments—including FHA projects, rented and owned, but also some public-housing complexes—came to include row-type units, although typically as just one of several available floor plans. Presumably to encourage this trend, FHA's Cooperative Housing Division, established in 1950, introduced new design guidelines in 1952 that recommended two-story row-type units that included private parking spaces and patios. When New York's Bay Terrace began the following year it included a mixture of four- and six-room simplex apartments, arranged above and below one another, and five-room duplex units, arranged side-by-side. According to the sales manager, the row-type units were the most in demand. As the *New York Times* observed, these "parallel the conditions of private home ownership, inasmuch as they offer not only two separate living levels and the room layout of a private home, but also two private entrances, front and rear." As a later survey confirmed, owners appreciated the greater "individuality" of the row house, with its private patios and front doors. In the 1950s, however, only ten to twenty percent of FHA apartments were in row units.[42]

The second half of the 1950s saw further experimentation with this format. Urban renewal projects like Washington's Southwest included row houses in the Capitol Park complex designed by Chloethiel Woodard Smith (and, somewhat later, at the River Park complex designed by Charles Goodman; see fig. 70). Eastwick and Mill Creek in Philadelphia, designed by Constantine Doxiades and Louis Kahn, respectively, included row houses, as did Lafayette Park in Detroit, designed by Mies van der Rohe. In California, architects Vernon DeMars and Donald Hardison pioneered their own variants at Easter Hill, a public housing complex, and the Plaza, a privately financed urban redevelopment, both in Richmond, California.

Around 1959, developers began to pioneer a new generation of row houses. That year, a group called Dudley Square opened in Shreveport, Louisiana, and *House & Home* featured another set, in Bakersfield, California, on its cover.[43] 1959 also saw the architect Victor Gruen propose a widely publicized (but unbuilt) group of nearly three hundred very expensive three-story "town houses" for the former Long Island estate of Cornelius Vanderbilt Whitney. This project in particular seemed to engage critics' interest in what planners soon came to call "cluster" and "planned-unit development" design.[44] The term "town house" began to surface as early as 1952 to recast row houses as up-to-date and middle-class rather than old-fashioned and working-class. After 1960 the term became ubiquitous, along with such variants as "townhouse" and "townhome."[45]

Toluca Townhouse

The first contemporary row-type project in Southern California appears to have been built in 1960. That fall, K. L. van Degrift Corporation, a small-scale homebuilder, advertised a complex of "patio town houses" called Bundy Place on Los Angeles's West Side. The ad copy suggested that the idea derived from "more than a year's study of row-housing in Washington, D.C., Baltimore and San Francisco." Despite this claimed pedigree, the compact project, whose designer is unknown, was innovative, comprising two parallel rows of eight, two-story units oriented inward toward a narrow walkway. Each unit had a patio facing the walkway and a garage at the rear fronting either the street or an alleyway, recalling the parking arrangements at RPAA's Chatham Village. The garage was accessible via interior staircases.[46]

Bundy Place remained an isolated experiment in Southern California for two years. Then, in 1962, several new projects appeared. Like Bundy, these tended to feature modern designs, and appealed to affluent, sophisticated households, including many older, childless families. One of these was Toluca Townhouse, an elegant condominium complex of crisp geometric row houses in Burbank, in the San Fernando Valley. The initial project had thirty-six units, although later phases would bring this number to more than two hundred by 1967. The developer was Barclay Hollander Curci, a new local firm that was buying up old movie-studio ranches from Warner Brothers and Columbia Pictures for conversion to residential use. (Since the 1920s and 1930s, major studios had owned large back-lot sites in remote sections of town; as the city grew, they sold them for redevelopment.)

Fig. 104: Toluca Townhouse Two, 4310–44 West Kling Street, Burbank, ca. 1963. Barclay Hollander Curci, developer; Richard D. Stoddard, architect; John R. Spahn, site planer. View of walkway and private patios.

Toluca's architect was Richard D. Stoddard, with a novel site plan by civil engineer John R. Spahn, who became a regional expert in townhouse-complex design. The project was inward-facing, with five virtually identical buildings of five or six units each arranged symmetrically around a small courtyard with a swimming pool. At the front of the complex were four buildings running perpendicular to the street; the fifth sat behind them, parallel to the street at the back of the site. The front buildings were paired around two landscaped walkways (fig. 104). At the rear of each unit, fronting alleyways, were private two-car garages. To mask the alleys and to save space, living areas and the walkways were elevated half a story above the street, and the alleys were sunk half a story, providing each home with a basement. The style was modernistic. Walkway façades were faced with floor-to-ceiling plate-glass windows framed in white.[47]

Toluca Townhouse catered to relatively affluent older families. The site was near the production facilities of Universal, Disney, Warner Brothers, Columbia Pictures, and NBC, and the developers hoped to provide convenient, carefree housing for single people, older families, and childless couples. Children under the age of thirteen were prohibited (a prohibition that the condominium association strictly enforced). Units contained either two bedrooms and two baths (one thousand square feet) or two bedrooms, a den, and three baths (fifteen hundred square feet). Stoddard arranged them on a split-level plan over two-and-a-half stories, with tall (one-and-a-half-story) entrances facing the walkways. Each had a private patio, and many an upstairs balcony that projected over the patio. Standard built-ins included wall-to-wall carpeting and a central vacuuming system. Prices ranged from $20,500 to $26,500 ($160,000 to $210,000). The least expensive units required $4,000 down ($31,000) with a twenty-four-year mortgage. A majority of the residents had previously owned houses.[48]

Gramercy Park and the Working Mother

The townhouse also came to appeal to working- and middle-class families with children, often because it afforded them more housing, in better locations, than single-family houses. The first large complex to explicitly court young parents was Scottsdale Town House, begun in 1963, which had six hundred condominium row houses in eighty buildings on forty-four acres in Carson, near the port of Los Angeles and the South Bay industrial belt. The developer was Raymond A. Watt, who had built dozens of single-family subdivisions in the 1950s. Planning was done by Spahn, who included a five-acre recreation area with a seventy-six-hundred-square-foot community center, Little League baseball and Pop Warner football fields, swimming and wading pools, tennis courts, handball courts, and two playgrounds, all overseen by a full-time "director of activities." The units came in a variety of three- and four-bedroom configurations. Original plans envisioned modernistic rows of buildings as at Toluca Townhouse but were revised to offer a choice of several exterior themes, including "ranch," "rustic," "contemporary," and "Hawaiian," which, presumably, were thought to be of greater appeal to young families of moderate income. The project sold quickly and Watt went on to develop several additional multifamily projects for a similar clientele.[49]

Even more accommodating to families of modest means was Gramercy Park, a group of about two hundred units developed by Ardmore in Anaheim, in Orange County, beginning in 1962 (fig. 105). Like Ardmore's earlier complexes, this one was organized initially as an FHA-insured co-op, although perhaps in response to customer inquiries it was soon reorganized as a condominium. The first phase, called

Fig. 105: Gramercy Park (end of West Gramercy Avenue) and Anaheim Village (West Glenoaks and Greenleaf Avenues, west of North Fairhaven Street), Anaheim, 1962–64. Ardmore Development Corporation, developer. View of Gramercy Park houses and walkway.

Anaheim Village, contained a mixture of one- and two-story row houses. The larger two-story units sold best. Later phases, which Ardmore called Gramercy Park, were all of this type. The new name referred to West Gramercy Avenue, which ran through the neighborhood.[50]

Promotions stressed the ease of maintenance and the excellent community facilities. At the sales office, Ardmore screened a twenty-minute color film, "Better Living for Less Money," about its earlier projects. In the film, according to an advertisement, the "'dramatic conflict' . . . is provided by the home-owner's losing war against hand-to-hand combat with the tyrannical lawnmower." "The film shows," it continued, "how rescue from his plight is provided by a cooperative apartment project, in which the resident is completely freed from the cares and responsibilities of yard upkeep, pool cleaning, repairs and maintenance."[51] Other advertisements asked readers, "Why maintain a house?" and promised "more leisure time for yourself and your family."[52]

More important than these promotions were, perhaps, the services that Ardmore promised to young families, especially those in which all the adults worked outside the home. The typical American family was changing by early the 1960s. At projects like Scottsdale and Gramercy Park a new age of working mothers and latchkey kids was already in evidence. Services at Gramercy Park included vans to take commuters to major local employers such as Hughes Aircraft, Northrop Corporation's

Nortronics, and North American Rockwell's Autonetics for a monthly fare of $4 ($31 in 2010 dollars). There was also an all-day nursery school for $35 a month ($280); an after-school program operated with Anaheim's Park & Recreation Department for $10 a month ($79); a free evening study hall supervised by certified teachers; and babysitting at competitive rates.[53] Advertisements spoke directly to women workers ("Perfect for Working Mothers!") and to employees of the larger companies—for example, "A Fabulous Deal for People Who Work at Hughes" (fig. 106).[54]

Like Scottsdale Town House, Gramercy rejected the symmetry and clean, Modernist imagery of Toluca Townhouse in favor of a diluted historical vocabulary, in this case vaguely French. The design also emphasized the individuality and privacy of the row house's physical form by articulating each unit with various widths, setbacks, and decoration.[55] All roofs were flat, but many of the houses featured exaggerated mansard-style false fronts at the second story. The exterior cladding was a mixture of stucco, brick veneer, and, for the mansards, clapboard and what appears to be enameled steel; fenestration was irregular, with casement windows of varying widths and heights. Wholeheartedly embracing this formula's playfulness, Ardmore chose a palette of Disneyesque colors, including baby blue and pink, which it splashed with abandon on trim and mansards.

This decorative scheme was a variety of L.A.'s Hollywood Regency, whose loose combination of early nineteenth-century English, American, and French revivals had emerged in the 1930s as an alternative to the ubiquitous Spanish Colonial (see fig. 98). Exaggerated mansard-style rooflines began to appear around 1940 and became popular in house renovations in the mid-1950s. Speculative developers began to use them in the 1960s as people tired of ranch and split-level styles.[56] Because the mansard evoked the urban sophistication of the Continental city it was seen as especially appropriate for what seemed a historic—and historically urban—typology such as the row house.

Varied row-house façades—which several RPAA and FHA projects had experimented with in a far more restrained, and monochromatic, way—masked the homogeneity of units' interiors. When combined with a variety of incongruous and often exaggerated historical styles in a single complex, the effect could be corny. The popularity of this combination had been tested at Colonial Park, a group of 116 low-income units built in an urban renewal area in Louisville, Kentucky, around 1960. The developer, George Clark Martin, said he was inspired by the row houses in Georgetown which he admired on visits to Washington for meetings of the National Association of Home Builders. That project sold out quickly and captured the attention of developers nationwide. In 1961, a color photograph of it ran on the cover of *House & Home*, showing five townhouses distinguished from

A FABULOUS DEAL FOR PEOPLE WHO WORK AT HUGHES

Consider these 9 special attractions of living at Gramercy Park (town house condominium) or Anaheim Village (garden-apartment condominium).

1. Ride To & From Work Every Day For $4 a month.

For every 9 Hughes employees who purchase a home here, Rowe Development Co. will provide a 9-passenger Volkswagen bus, to be used for transportation to and from the Hughes plant. Riders will take turns driving; cost per rider will be $4 a month.

Free yourself from the expense of a 2nd car, traffic, and parking problems.

2. Perfect for Working Mothers.

All-Day Nursery, $35 a Month

The Nursery School is part of Gramercy West—the completely separate section, 2 blocks away from Gramercy East, the adult section. The nursery school is directed by Mrs. Margery B. Taylor, one of America's outstanding child care experts. For children 2 to 6. Special reduced rates for residents: all-day care, 5 days a week, 7 a.m. to 6 p.m., including morning snack, lunch, and afternoon snack, $35 a month. Half-day care, $15 a month without lunch, $20 a month including lunch. These are about one-half the usual charges for nursery school.

3. For Ages 7 to 13, Anaheim's famous "Growth Through Recreation" Program.

Swimming, Tennis, Dramatics, Music, Softball, Basketball, Hobby Courses, Teenage Clubs, Excursions, Picnics—the Anaheim Park & Recreation Department sponsors a complete schedule of exciting activities that is unsurpassed anywhere in America. When you live in Gramercy West, your youngsters can join the fun—and you have no transportation problem. The transportation between Gramercy West and whatever park, pool, or playground the activity of the day is located will be provided. Transportation charge will not exceed $10 a month per child participating.

Give your children the benefits of this great Anaheim youth recreation program, with excellent professionally-qualified instructors for every activity ... no need for you to be tied down by "chauffeuring" chores.

SEPARATE ADULT SECTION AND FAMILY SECTION

Anaheim Village (the garden-apartment section) and Gramercy East (the adult town house section) are 2 blocks away from Gramercy West, the family town house section.
9 Swimming Pools—
Private Park . . . Recreation Building

4. Evening Study Hall.

For elementary, junior high, and high school students, a 7 to 9 p.m. study session will be held in the development's recreation hall, 4 nights a week (Monday-Tuesday-Wednesday-Thursday). One or more certificated teachers will be on duty, and will be available to assist students with study problems. There is no charge for the evening study hall. An inviting arrangement to make it fun to study.

5. Baby-Sitters.

You will always be able to obtain carefully-screened baby sitters at moderate rates by phoning the management office.

6. "Golf Cart Shopping".

One of these easy-to-drive electric golf carts will be provided for every 30 families in the adult sections. Available free on the premises for just-around-the-corner shopping at the big Broadway-Robinson's Shopping Center, or the adjacent Broadway Village-Crawford's Market.

7. Choice of Town House or Garden Apartment.

Prize-winning architecture, excellent design, finest quality construction —and, as the sound foundation of your property value—a central location that is unequalled in all of Orange County. Choice of 1, 2, 3, and 4 bedrooms. Refrigerated air conditioning included in many units.

8. Grant Deed. No Maintenance Chores.

You get Grant Deed and Title Insurance to your apartment-home or town house. You get deductions in full for all taxes and interest (in opinion of counsel). You never have to bother about exterior maintenance, the lawns, or cleaning the swimming pools. It's all taken care of under the condominium arrangement.

Isn't this better than paying rent month after month? Or pushing that lawnmower week after week?

9. Full Prices: $13,900 to $24,950. Only 5% Down.

Full prices range from $13,900 for a 1-bedroom residence in Anaheim Village to $24,950 for a 4-bedroom 2-bath town house in Gramercy Park.

GUARANTEED HOME TRADE-IN PLAN

SEE THE 6 FURNISHED MODEL TOWN HOUSES TODAY.

Anaheim Village Gramercy Park Sales Office

Directions: FROM SANTA ANA FREEWAY, SOUTHBOUND: North on Euclid, 1 block past the Broadway-Robinson's Shopping Center, turn left at Glenoaks. FROM SANTA ANA FREEWAY, NORTHBOUND: Exit Loara to Euclid, North to Glenoaks. FROM RIVERSIDE FREEWAY: South on Euclid, right at Glenoaks. Phone (714) 774-4605.

Sales Agents Rowe Development Co., 1177 W. Glenoaks Ave., Anaheim, Phone (714) 774-4605.

Rates quoted herein for services are guaranteed by Rowe Development Co. to January 1, 1966, and are subject to modification thereafter by the various Owners' Associations.

Fig. 106: Gramercy Park and Anaheim Village, advertisement, *Los Angeles Times*, August 16, 1964.

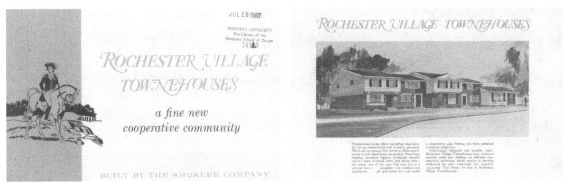

Fig. 107: Rochester Village Townhouses, Patrick Henry Street north of East Walton Boulevard, Oakland, Michigan, ca. 1965. Smokler Company, Foundation for Cooperative Housing, developers. Pages from *Rochester Village Townhouses*, prospectus.

each other by a variety of colors, window patterns, and a mixture of wood and brick facing.[57] By the mid-1960s this treatment had become standard for U.S. row-house complexes. Variations in visual language ranged from Early Colonial, with clapboard and leaded windows, in Michigan (fig. 107) to Norman farmhouses and Georgian plantations in Atlanta (see fig. 94) to Mediterranean ranches in Florida (fig. 108). Like the skin on a skyscraper, strip mall, or tract house, developers could apply any number of exteriors to a basic shell, as determined by local tastes and marketing imperatives. When U.S. homebuilders Levitt & Sons and Kaufman & Broad began working in France and Germany, this varied-façade phenomenon became international.[58]

To further appeal to families with children at Gramercy Park, which was among the first projects in Southern California to distinguish individual house façades in this way, Ardmore grouped the rows of houses around a wide common green. In an early phase units had faced the neighborhood's narrow streets. Then Ardmore created a superblock, with houses arranged at the perimeter facing inward toward a shared garden, as at the eponymous Manhattan development of 1831. Parking was accommodated in long sheds behind units, accessed by alleys. Each house also had a small rear patio surrounded by high walls for privacy.

These design strategies, coupled with the promised services, resulted in strong sales, and Ardmore planned two additional projects for younger working families. One was Fountain Park, in Woodland Hills, in the western San Fernando Valley, which advertised to employees of neighboring Rocketdyne and Litton Industries. The other was Concord Park, in South Central, the first major townhouse complex in Southern California marketed explicitly to African Americans. Its planning was reported extensively in Black newspapers and

President Johnson visited the site in March 1964. After the Watts riots in 1965, however, the project was no longer seen as feasible and was abandoned. Ardmore disbanded soon after. Fifty years later, however, Gramercy Park remained a model neighborhood. The carpool vans and study halls had long ended, but it was well kept and, more importantly, still home to the sorts of working families, by then mainly Mexican immigrants, for whom Ardmore had intended it.[59]

Fig. 108: Snapper Creek Townhouse, 11200 SW Seventy-first Street, Miami, ca. 1973–74.

Planned Unit Development

Although Gramercy Park's townhouse formula quickly became dominant, both regionally and nationally, multifamily housing remained a rich arena for experimentation in the 1960s and 1970s. This was especially true at master-planned "new town" communities which began appearing in Southern California in the late 1950s, with Irvine, and in other markets by the 1960s and 1970s. Especially in California, innovative land planning was often a priority—and sometimes a necessity—at these developments, since many encompassed difficult-to-develop waterfront or hillside areas where the high cost of site preparation demanded compact, efficient use of space. As architect Richard R. Leitch, who designed housing in many such communities, explained, "Some engineer used to spend about 20 minutes doing a subdivision plan for a development. The architects would then work for weeks to design houses. . . . But we were defeated before we started. Every house could be a jewel, but from a distance they were repetitious and dull." At the new communities, "the land development became interesting."[60]

Among early achievements in this realm was a relatively small Leitch project called the Bluffs in the Eastbluff section of Irvine Ranch, overlooking Newport Bay. Built beginning in 1963 by one of Orange County's largest developers, George M. Holstein & Sons, the original project called for a novel mixture of nearly twenty-six hundred apartments, attached houses, and detached houses on 345 acres. Steeply pitched red-tile roofs, rough-sawn lumber, and hand-carved front doors evoked the atmosphere of a Spanish Colonial village and marked the place as distinct from usual Orange County development. Although the site itself was flat, Leitch sculpted the land to enhance both views and privacy in what was considered an environmentally sensitive way.[61]

Support for projects like the Bluffs came in the form of a new kind of land-use code: "planned-unit development." Although rooted in experiments encouraged by FHA's land-planning division as early as the 1940s, the planned-unit idea emerged hand-in-hand with growing interest in more compact, highly serviced forms of housing in the late 1950s and early 1960s. Separate from the condominium and not necessarily multifamily, this model allowed developers freedom to play with existing zoned densities by clustering units together and preserving saved space for common use. On ten acres of land zoned for two houses per acre, for example, one could build twenty row houses in a corner and leave the rest of the land open for tennis courts, a recreation center, or gardens. Orange County introduced an enabling ordinance in 1962, in anticipation of the Bluffs. County planners, like planners and designers everywhere, understood it as a way to avoid the monotony of earlier postwar suburbs.[62]

Like in an apartment house, common areas in planned-unit communities were owned collectively, even when the housing was single-family. Co-ownership could be achieved through any of the existing systems: co-op, own-your-own, and condo. An increasingly popular option was to forgo these more intertwined mechanisms in favor of a modified fee-simple plan typically referred to as "common interest." This plan worked only where every unit sat directly on its own piece of ground. It conveyed to each family ownership of both house and the land beneath it, as in a conventional single-family neighborhood. As in a condo, however, everyone also owned an undivided share of common elements. Landscaping and exterior maintenance, including painting, was usually done collectively. Because this system was legally and conceptually simpler than co-op, condo, or own-your-own, it became a preferred method of co-ownership.

Quadrominium

The shift toward multifamily housing in California in the 1960s also generated creative new building types. The Bluffs, for instance, included duplex "patio homes" and "garden homes." Other projects in the 1960s and 1970s included "walled garden homes," "apartment cottages," "village green cluster-courts," "courtyard homes," and "zero lot-line houses." All were variants on the townhouse, garden

Fig. 109: Advertisement for McKeon Construction, detail, from *Los Angeles Times*, October 7, 1972.

apartment, and compact single-family house, engineered to deliver a strong sense of community—and community services like open space and recreation—while maximizing privacy.[63]

One of the most popular variants was the four-plex "quadrominium" (fig. 109). This uniquely suburban type, which grouped four units into a building that resembled a single-family house, was originated by Northern California developer George R. McKeon in the mid-1960s and brought to Southern California around 1970.[64] The four-plex apartment building was not new. Buildings with three, four, or six units had been a predominant housing type in working-class sections of many U.S. cities in the early twentieth century.[65] In California, many of L.A.'s "studio" buildings of the 1920s and 1930s had also contained three or four units. These, like quadrominiums, appeared at the façade as a large single-family house while offering each unit an outside entrance and, in many projects, private outdoor space in the form of a small patio or terrace.

McKeon's innovation, apart from ownership, was to arrange the apartments so that none was above or below any other, eliminating the noise from upstairs and down, which was one of the chief nuisances of apartment living. McKeon achieved this by placing two, two-story units at the front of the building, a single-story unit on the ground floor along one side, and another single-story unit above a shared garage and laundry room at the rear. Another innovation was that McKeon arranged quadrominiums in large clusters, grouping them in suburban-style subdivisions of approximately seventy-five buildings along curvilinear streets and cul-de-sacs. The three hundred homeowners undertook governance and maintenance together and shared a recreation center and pool.[66]

Quadrominium catered specifically to baby boomers. Like other fads, it spread with startling speed. By 1972, McKeon was one of the top developers of co-owned housing nationally and he came to be known as the "fourplex king." By 1973 he was developing quadrominiums in Nevada, Texas, Florida, Illinois, Minnesota, Maryland, and Virginia. Other leading operators, including Kaufman & Broad and Levitt & Sons, introduced their own versions.

According to Levitt, quadrominium was the "finest method of land planning currently available." Although these firms built other housing types, quadrominiums, with their unique formulation of privacy, community, and suburban living, sold best. As a leading real-estate consultant declared in 1972, it "has been to homebuilding what the Volkswagen was to the automotive industry."[67] Unlike the fascination with the Beetle, however, interest in the quadrominium soon faded. The underlying premise of owner-occupied, medium-density suburban housing for swinging singles and young couples endured, but changing tastes

Fig. 110: DeFoors Glen, southwest corner Glenn Avenue and DeFoors Ferry Road NW, Atlanta, ca. 1984.

Fig. 111: Decatur Square Condominiums, 1175–1231 Church Street, Decatur, Georgia, 1984. DRL Properties, developer.

and rising land costs meant that other arrangements, such as the standard four-plex (fig. 110), the six-plex (fig. 111), and, especially, the townhouse, quickly supplanted it.

The Magic Name in Ownership

Production of middle-class multifamily housing in the U.S. had begun to shift to suburbia in the 1940s and 1950s. The impact of this change, however, was limited because demand had been so modest in most places. With new household patterns in the early 1960s, the suburban condo became a generic metropolitan housing type. It also became the dominant form of new housing in Southern California. By the early 1970s Los Angeles County had around 108,000 owner-occupied apartments and townhouses, Orange County 64,000, San Diego County 53,000, and San Bernardino and Riverside Counties 36,000, for a regional total of 260,000.[68] Nearly all had been built since 1962.

In addition to site-planning constraints and the baby boom, a major reason for the paradigm shift away from single-family suburbia to the townhouse was cost at a time of rising prices. Although multifamily homes, especially on expensive land, cost more per square foot than houses did (because of expensive sound- and fire-proofing) the availability of smaller sizes meant that prices were typically lower. While the smallest, cheapest new houses in greater L.A. or New York commanded around $35,000 in the early 1970s ($200,000), two-bedroom units at suburban townhouses and quadrominiums, with a thousand square feet of space, sold, often in more central locations, for $20,000 or $25,000.[69]

Another reason was rising expectations for quality in housing and the neighborhood environment. Leading critics like William H. Whyte and Ada Louise Huxtable hailed this aspect of the new community planning. According to Huxtable, writing in 1964, cluster-type arrangements were an "innovation in residential development that may help to rescue the suburban dream from the nightmare of mass-produced housing." Not all projects were as well designed as the Bluffs, but critics believed that even mediocre examples were preferable to conventional single-family suburbia. More and more homeowners agreed. In one national survey, nearly eighty percent of townhouse and condo owners reported that a primary allure had been community design, including shared amenities and open space. In large-scale projects with well-known reputations for innovative planning, such as Reston, Virginia, more than ninety percent of owners ranked community first.[70]

Freedom from physical maintenance was also an important draw. As one highly mobile Douglas Aircraft engineer explained, "When we moved to California I bought a new house and put in a new yard. Then I was transferred to another California plant and again I struggled with a new yard and landscaping. Now I've just been transferred a third time, and I'm not going through all that again. I've bought a boat, and we want to spend our weekends sailing. Before, I couldn't afford a swimming pool. Now my two girls can use this $100,000 pool and I have no maintenance worries. This is better for all of us." At projects like the Bluffs and Pomeroy Green, homeowners felt the same. When asked, large majorities said they did not miss caring for a lawn. Condo owners all over California reported that they would recommend condo living to friends because of "no maintenance."[71]

Not everyone felt this way. As Herbert Gans noted at the time, critiques like Huxtable's were flawed because they prioritized physical form over "how well" the new communities "work and how their occupants feel about them." Ordinary homeowners tended to appreciate the savings afforded by townhouses, which enabled them to buy more home for the money. But, unlike critics, they were often indifferent, sometimes even hostile, to the unconventional site planning. Lower-income buyers—especially younger, first-time, and blue-collar families—tended to care more about the size of their units than about neighborhood design or shared amenities. Such families, especially on the East Coast, regarded the cluster-type project as a second-best alternative to the single-family house, and they yearned for *more*, rather than fewer, physical responsibilities—including yard work.[72]

A related problem with the new community types was that for some families, shared governance was unappealing. As one study argued, buyers "have traded

Fig. 112: Huntington Continental, northwest corner Brookhurst Street, Adam Avenue, Huntington Beach, California, 1962. Kaufman and Broad, developer. Advertisement, *Los Angeles Times*, March 3, 1963.

maintenance responsibilities for obligations to a community governing process which," for many, "violates their idea of" homeownership.[73]

Although anathema to the American dream in these respects, most townhouses were able to manage their affairs. One particularly successful experiment was Huntington Continental, Kaufman & Broad's first multifamily complex in California (fig. 112). Announced in 1962 and opened in 1963 in Orange County, the project offered one- to four-bedroom attached "patio houses," each with a private fenced yard at the rear and a private enclosed garage. The homes sold for $10,000 to $14,000 ($80,000 to $110,000), and in the first three weeks more than twenty thousand people visited the showroom and all four hundred units sold, making it, in the words of one ad, the "magic name in new home ownership." K&B quickly became one of the region's largest developers and repeated the model at half a dozen similar projects. The designer of most was architect Earl G. Kaltenbach.[74]

Many in homebuilding circles doubted that the project could succeed. In particular they worried that hundreds of moderate-income homeowners could not collectively manage the place and that it would quickly deteriorate. But after a dozen years, according to Byron R. Hanke, who had been chief of land planning at FHA in the early 1960s and was now head of the Community Associations Institute, "the project is in excellent shape" and "worked out far better than anyone had dreamed." The reasons, he explained, were hard work and, more importantly, well-written by-laws. The president of the homeowners' association for many years, Hanke explained, was an ordinary blue-collar man: a security guard in a bank. While in this respect he may have been ill-suited to run a housing complex, he selected a good managing agent and followed the association rules. "In doing so,"

Hanke argued, "he demonstrated that the community association concept does work for suburban moderate income housing."[75]

Tragedies of the Common-interest

Where by-laws were inadequate, however, trouble could arise. Most problematic were fee-simple projects, which many counties (and lenders) erroneously treated, at first, like ordinary subdivisions. Especially at lower-cost projects where buyers were more interested in their individual homes than in community, problems fulfilling collective responsibilities were endemic. As early as 1968 the Orange County Planning Department and researchers at California State University, Fullerton, reported that many of the new planned developments were in trouble, especially those with younger, less affluent families. Owners were behind on their monthly maintenance, cash reserves were low, and there was premature physical deterioration. Lenders, they warned, were already becoming wary of townhouses and were reluctant to make new loans. Some projects were converting to rental. Such failures were much less common in co-ops, with their community emphasis, and condominiums, which states (and lenders) required to have strong by-laws.[76]

A particularly egregious example was Bel Air Town II, a group of 149 fee-simple townhouses developed by Levitt & Sons in Bowie, Maryland, outside of Washington, D.C., in 1968 (fig. 113). The project was so dysfunctional that after six years the homeowners attempted to dissolve the association entirely, with each owner agreeing informally to take care of the common elements near his unit, and to do his own exterior and garden maintenance. In part, Bel Air Town II's trouble was that it lacked a leader like Huntington Continental's. The larger fault, however, lay with the developer and with the county planning department. The community had been organized under a recent, untested county ordinance for planned-unit development that contained insufficient standards for articles of incorporation, by-laws, covenants, and restrictions. To make matters worse, Levitt & Sons, which was just entering the field of co-ownership, did not inform buyers about their mutual obligations.

Few owners volunteered to serve on the board of the homeowners' association, few voted in elections or came to meetings, and many never paid maintenance. High turnover destabilized things further. Subsequent owners were rarely told by sellers that there was an association. Limitations on investment ownership were also ignored and by 1974 half of the houses were occupied by renters. Renters were not unusual in condos and townhouses. According to one survey, eighty percent of complexes had at least one renter, and twenty percent were at least half renter-occupied. Significant numbers of renters, however, tended to weaken a community.

Fig. 113: Bel Air Town II, Millstream Drive from Annapolis Road to (and including) Midwood Lane, Bowie, Md., ca. 1968. Levitt & Sons, developer.

Apart from the physical toll of more frequent turnover, absentee owners were more often late to pay maintenance, more reluctant to spend money for improvements, and rarely screened their tenants or informed them of by-laws. Faced with dissolution of the Bell Air Town II association, the county at last appointed a receiver to run things until the community could become self-sufficient. To avoid similar tragedies of the commons at future projects, the county substantially revised its planned-development ordinance.[77]

L.A.'s Growing Pains

The growth of condo and townhouse living also generated additional tensions. Many stemmed from friction between adjacent incumbent homeowners and developers proposing new projects. In Southern California these conflicts were exacerbated by the fact that—unlike in East Coast and Midwestern cities, where longstanding zoning restrictions ensured that suburban apartments and row houses were often concentrated in specific nodes—developers in the West understood the entire region as more appropriate for multifamily projects. But as the number multifamily projects swelled, so too did organized opposition.

The first major protest against a condo emerged in 1963. It concerned a proposal by a homebuilder to develop a "condominium-type apartment project" at Woodland Hills in the western San Fernando Valley, which at the time was still largely undeveloped. Owners of adjacent tracts, mainly investors living elsewhere in the region, supported the new development. But local homeowners, who organized as the Woodland Homeowners Organization and GRIPE—Group Representing Ignored Public Everywhere—filed a suit. The suit was ineffective. But that same year other citizens' groups successfully prevented development of townhouses at Orange, a "patio home" project at Northridge, and a small condominium apartment complex in West Covina.[78] Over the next several years, organized protest spread like a Southern California wildfire.

At every contested site opposition coalesced along similar lines. A single homeowners' association recruited others to support its cause. Typically they formed an umbrella group. Members attended public hearings. When city councils or planning boards ignored their demands, they collected signatures to place the matter on the ballot. More often than not homebuilders negotiated with land-use authorities to avoid cancellation of the project entirely. Typically, they revised designs to include fewer units. In several municipalities, including the City of Los Angeles and the City of Beverly Hills, protest also resulted in building moratoria and revisions to citywide zoning codes.[79]

Protest against development seemed to grow out of a sense of dissatisfaction that many Southern Californians began to feel in the 1960s and 1970s as the region transformed from the dynamic but socially homogenous suburban city of the 1950s to a congested, expensive, and racially diverse city bedeviled by the same social problems plaguing East Coast centers. This feeling grew especially acute after the Watts riots of August 1965. According to homeowners, multifamily projects crowded schools, made traffic intolerable, depressed resale values of existing single-family houses, and disturbed the visual character of a neighborhood, instantly transforming a place from "suburban" to "urban." As one opponent of a nine-hundred-unit condominium project scheduled for Chatsworth explained to the *Times*, he moved there "to find a place where his five children could grow up in the same kind of rural atmosphere he enjoyed in the [San Fernando] Valley as a youngster." He resented the area's further transformation.[80]

Association Nation

Paradoxically, perhaps, this same malaise also helps account for the popularity of multifamily homeownership. Although many believed community governance to be a burden, others embraced it. Part of the appeal concerned resale values. As the *Los*

Angeles Times noted, self-governance helped "retard deterioration of housing on a broad scale," presumably in comparison to rental complexes, and ensured that homes would stay "in better condition and keep going up in value." But of equal importance, perhaps, was that it offered homeowners "a return to grass roots, neighborhood government—a way for homeowners to gain a measure of control over their part of a confusing world."[81]

Some homeowners—and most critics—found the homeowners' associations "big brotherish." Most owners, however, were satisfied with the associations and their rules. "We thought the rules might be a thorn in the residents' side," said the director of one Claremont College study. By contrast, they "found out that people were not nearly so resentful of having controls as they were of not having the controls enforced."[82] Moreover, many appreciated the transparency of the self-governing associations and their ability to meet local needs quickly. In practice, the condo allowed groups of likeminded homeowners to create shadow local governments—albeit ones free of usual democratic safeguards, where participation was limited to property owners.[83] As one townhouse association president told the *Times*, "It gives government back to the people, where it belongs."[84]

By way of explanation, this board member elaborated how his group had recently solved a problem. The question was whether to buy new playground equipment and, if so, how to pay for it. It took just fifteen minutes to agree to order it and pay for it with voluntary contributions. "What governing unit could settle anything in 15 minutes—and then get residents to cough up the wherewithal on their own?" asked the *Times*. "The answer is a body called the homeowners' association." As a result of his positive experiences, this president—who was, by day, an engineer at North American Rockwell, continued—"we kind of look forward to the day when this kind of thing can be woven into the fabric of city government." As the *Times* quoted the head of another association, which typically met in members' living rooms, "it's pretty tough to get in a real fight with a scotch and soda in one hand."[85]

Many homebuilders also championed self-governance as a way to create community. As the real-estate trade group Urban Land Institute noted in its *Homes Association Handbook* in the mid-1960s, "The explosive growth of our cities, their trend to giantism, and the high mobility of their residents are rapidly destroying a sense of community among individuals in urban America. Constructive forces are needed to counteract these negative aspects and to utilize the opportunity that growth offers to build better communities. The best possible way to bring about—or to revive—a grass roots sense of community is for home owners to control nearby facilities of importance to them and through this to participate in the life of their neighborhoods. The homes association is an ideal tool for building better

1972   MOST CHANGE   1976

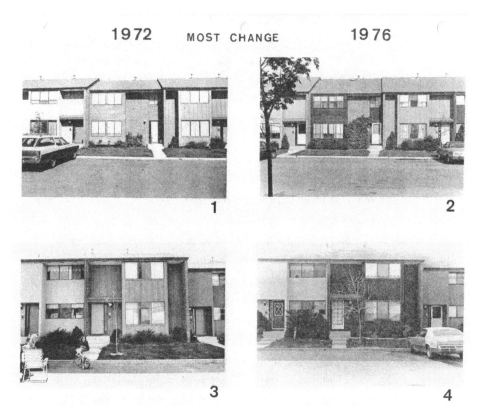

Fig. 114: Twin Rivers, Twin Rivers and Lake Drives, Probasco Road, East River Township, New Jersey, 1968–74. Gerald C. Finn, Herbert Kendall, American Standard, developers; Conklin and Rossant, preliminary architects; J. Robert Hillier, architect. Suzanne Keller, "Twin Rivers, Study of a Planned Community," TS, 1976.

communities." For this writer, the condo helped make the increasingly complex world more navigable.[86]

Twin Rivers

In her studies of Twin Rivers, Princeton sociologist Suzanne Keller agreed. Twin Rivers, in East Windsor, New Jersey, was among the first cluster-type housing developments planned in the Northeast (fig. 114). The complex was imagined in 1963 by developer Gerald C. Finn, who had become enamored of Reston, a new town going up in suburban Washington, D.C. with a mixture of housing types, including townhouses and apartments. As Finn recalled, "I thought that the Reston idea would be a great thing to bring to New Jersey in order that better development could occur in our state." He hired Reston's progressive architects, Whittlesey and Conklin (later Conklin and Rossant), to draw up preliminary plans. They called for approximately twelve hundred apartments, both rented and owned, and more than sixteen hundred attached row houses, on more than four hundred acres. Local leaders were skeptical. Existing zoning already permitted garden apartments, but members of the planning board and town council worried that the town might be forced to maintain common areas under the new plan. After years of deliberation and delay—and a bus tour of Reston—the project was approved in 1968. The first families moved in in 1970.[87]

Keller attended community meetings for fifteen years, starting before move-in. She also surveyed a thousand households through a Gallup poll, interviewed fifty families at a ten-year interval, and five hundred families on a one-time basis. Echoing the experience of homeowners at earlier prototypes like New York's Bell Park Gardens, Keller found that Twin Rivers was in most respects "suburban," despite its new physical form and its co-ownership. The population mix was typical of "modern suburbia," she wrote, mainly comprising young, upwardly mobile families with children. So too were the reasons families moved there, most of which concerned "land and space," and social reproduction: people wanted to own homes with private, safe outdoor space for their children. Indeed, most Twin Rivers owners, like many younger families on the East Coast, preferred the idea of conventional suburbia and maintained "attachment to the ideal of the detached house." They bought townhouses because in the inflationary 1970s the "average American's ability to own a free-standing single-family house on a substantial plot of land" had become compromised.[88]

Many critics at the time were concerned about the rise of—or retreat to, as some saw it—small, self-governed communities. In *America II*, a jeremiad against the contemporary American landscape, journalist Richard Louv singled out the condo as representative of a new, unwelcome postindustrial social and economic order. "The America we know is dying," he wrote, "but a second America is rising from the body of the first." This "America II," he suggests, comprised marginal social types: "condo dwellers and pot farmers, corporate utopians and private police, rural entrepreneurs and urban escapees, computer programmers and unemployed wanderers." He suggests the condo was particularly exemplary of a "new shelter." Most mysterious to him was why anyone would agree to live in a community with so few individual rights in property—that is, where a man must agree with his neighbors about what kinds of plants he may use in his own garden and where the "dictatorship of the condo proletariat" prohibits expression of "human individuality."[89]

Yet others, according to Keller, believed the condo weakened social and neighborhood ties, as a result of "transiency and brevity of social contracts in new developments that preclude a deeper interdependency." In his more recent *Bowling*

Alone, political scientist Robert D. Putnam echoed this critique. He interprets the rise of planned communities as evidence of people sorting themselves into "finely distinguished lifestyle enclaves segregated by race, class, education, life stage" where community governance served chiefly to reinforce more powerful social barriers. "One might expect the numbing homogeneity . . . to encourage a certain social connectedness," he concluded, but "surprisingly low rate[s] of civic engagement" among owners "actually points in the opposite direction." Homogeneity, his sources suggested, "reduced the local conflicts that engage and draw the citizenry into the public realm." As one social historian of housing noted elsewhere, "town houses need a town."[90]

Keller, however, found just the opposite: that "condominium living fosters social and neighborhood ties." At least in Twin Rivers, she witnessed an interconnectedness of homeowners' lives, "physically, visually, and aurally," as demanded by a townhouse plan that "makes every home owner automatically a land sharer bound up with the private and domestic space of unknown other residents." In this sense she found the condo to restore some of the "integration of 'family, house, and village'" that industrialization had pulled apart. In day-to-day life this meant not only functional, democratic self-governance, but deep satisfaction with the community, even among those most jealous of their physical privacy. Perhaps more importantly, she found community. Like the young families at Bell Park in the 1950s, for example, many at Twin Rivers socialized not in their private patios but in the common front lawns.[91]

The Best of Both

Despite the success of places like Gramercy Park, Huntington Continental, and Twin Rivers, both as experiments in self-governance and as places to live and rear children, media widely reported the suburban condo trend as a "crisis" by the 1970s. Rather than evidence of a new "cultural pluralism, different kinds of family life, and more diverse communities" or a "positive, realistic approach to economic constraints, energy problems, or demographic change," observed architectural historian Gwendolyn Wright, "townhouses and trailers and cooperative buildings were consistently presented as inadequate, makeshift substitutes for detached suburban dwellings."[92]

As an embodiment of recent social changes in concrete form; as the preferred home of single mothers (at least anecdotally) and swinging singles; as somewhere that required less money and physical effort to maintain than a detached house; as a form of "urban" housing outside the typical urban environment; and as a still unfamiliar form of ownership that seemed to make developers a lot of money without offering much more physically than a rented apartment, this "new" kind of housing struck many as suspect. According to Keller, Americans "fear that with townhouse living, privacy, that coveted nugget of well-being in an impersonal mass society, becomes an endangered species."[93]

At Twin Rivers, however, such worries rarely materialized. To the contrary, many families of the 1970s found new hybrid formats ideal, even utopian. As Marty Bernstein, an original resident of Twin Rivers, declared after twenty-five years in residence, "Our kids were raised in a perfect environment." Unlike in conventional suburbia—or Brooklyn, from which the family had come—the kids "never had to cross the street, they were able to make hundreds of friends. . . . We never had to mow a lawn or push snow. We weren't chauffeuring our kids everywhere, they simply walked out the door or rode their bikes." With "10,000 people living in a community that is 16 square blocks. . . . [y]ou have your cake and eat it too; you're an urban person in a suburban setting. . . . It made a huge difference in our lives."[94]

CHAPTER 7

Back to the City

Converting her West Side Manhattan building to co-op was not a project that Linda Grover had ever imagined taking on. A writer and homemaker, Grover moved to her apartment in the summer of 1959. At the time, she and her husband, Stanley, were living in a fourth-floor walk-up, also on the West Side. The walk-up had just one and a half rooms and they had been looking for a larger place from the time Grover became pregnant, a year and a half before. They could not, however, afford market-rate rents on Stanley's income as an actor and a singer, and it was a struggle to find a rent-controlled unit that was not a complete "horror." Controlled units were plentiful but tenants rarely gave them up; when they did, they often passed them to friends and family. In desperation, Stanley's manager promised a rental agent a free cruise if a suitable apartment could be found (cruise lines allowed performers' agents to send along a "manager" with acts). When the baby was ten months old the couple got word of a six-room apartment on Central Park, at 325 Central Park West; the rent was $117.70 a month ($1,050 in 2010 dollars).[1]

While the Upper West Side had many stately apartment houses, Grover's was not among them (fig. 115). Sandwiched between two much grander places, hers, she wrote, was the "least appealing house of the lot, a narrow dirty runt of a building," just fifty feet wide and seven stories tall, erected around 1899. And while it had been well maintained for many years—until recently it had had Oriental rugs in the lobby and a full-time elevator operator—things had quickly deteriorated after it changed hands in 1958. Denuded of staff and carpets, the lobby "smelled like semislum; not urine—not that bad—just dust and rotted curtain, musty and airless." Outside, the front steps were crumbling and the iron fence was warped and "missing teeth." Her "eternal quest for chic bungled again," worried Grover.[2]

The apartment itself had the six rooms, as advertised, arranged off a long corridor. Otherwise the place "was certainly no prize." Although she did not test the

Fig. 115: 325 Central Park West, New York, conversion and renovation, 1963–66.

plumbing, a leaky faucet and radiators promised at least some basic conveniences (although, as it turned out, there was no hot water in the kitchen). Given the dismal state of every other rent-controlled place she had seen, Grover (ca. 1934–2010) was happy to settle for it "no matter what it looked like." She picked a shade of pink paint at the landlord's office, moved in two weeks later, and set about making the apartment feel like home with hand-me-down curtains and carpets, and lots of Con-Tact paper.[3]

Then, shortly after moving in, one of Grover's new neighbors knocked on the door with bad news: their building was slated for demolition. As part of a Title I urban renewal project the area directly behind 325 Central Park West was to be cleared of—in Grover's words—a "crowded derelicts' hotel" and beyond it a "dismal" neighborhood of "people shouting and fighting, squatting on their fire escapes, throwing their garbage and beer cans out of the windows." While the grander adjacent buildings were to be spared, the city believed Grover's to be substandard and planned to raze it. Grover and her neighbor wrote to their elected officials and began attending neighborhood and city meetings in protest. City officials were pleasantly surprised by their interest and promised to reconsider their plans. By 1962, however, the building had been condemned. The only way out, the city offered, was for the tenants to buy it as a cooperative and bring it up to code at their own expense. Although hesitant and overwhelmed, they took the project on. Within a few years—and with much hard work—Grover and her fellow tenants became homeowners.[4]

In the 1960s and 1970s a fourth pole in collective homeownership emerged alongside low-cost government-aided co-ops, retirement condos, and suburban townhouses: market-rate city apartments. The co-op had been pioneered in Manhattan to accommodate well-to-do cosmopolitans. In the 1920s this mode of housing flourished, but it collapsed in the Depression. In the postwar era, amid widespread urban disinvestment and white flight, it began to recover, fueled by demand from a gradually expanding urban middle class and by structural forces that decreased the appeal of renting. By the 1970s, this countertrend toward ownership of city apartments became a national phenomenon as baby boomers, new ideas about city living, rising wealth, profit motive, interest in historic preservation, and, at times, equal doses of racial paranoia and communitarian sentiment generated "condomania": a great wave of co-op and condominium production, often through conversion of older buildings.

Many saw this surge in middle-class urban living, which defied the mainstream thrust toward suburbia, as the city's last hope. In the context of the postwar metropolitan crisis—whose culmination coincided with condomania in the 1960s and 1970s—condo living offered a great opportunity to save declining buildings and neighborhoods as a new generation found new uses for them. Others saw this shift as aberrant—even more so than the suburban townhouse. As we shall see, it represented a new, often tense, phase in the incremental, long-term restructuring of the great American city from a place of blue-collar to white-collar work, from a site of industrial production to one of offices and entertainment, and of one for those with the fewest choices to one for those with the most.

Postwar Modesty

The postwar resurgence of the city co-op was evident as early as the 1940s, even though federal rent controls had eliminated much of the incentive to co-ownership. Much of this early activity was in the field of re-conversion. During the Depression, lenders had foreclosed on an estimated ten percent of East Side buildings in Manhattan, and perhaps half of market-rate buildings elsewhere (as well as several

Fig. 116: 860–880 North Lake Shore Drive, Chicago, 1948–51. Herbert Greenwald, developer; Ludwig Mies van der Rohe, architect. Photograph by Wayne Andrews, ca. 1951–53.

of the limited-equity co-ops of the 1920s built by workers). Tenant-directed rent restrictions made even well-to-do families think twice about buying back their apartments. Yet by the close of the 1940s most high-class buildings in New York had reverted to co-ownership, along with a few that had been built as rentals.[5]

A small burst of new construction accompanied these re-conversions in New York. This was driven as much by demand, however, as by developers' aversion to rent control. Rent control poisoned the rental market, especially until new buildings were exempted from the program, in 1947. When new market-rate apartments went up in the 1940s, nearly all were co-op. Of seven apartment houses built between 1946 and 1948 on the Upper East Side, six were owned: a balance tilted more toward co-ownership than in the 1920s.

High-class postwar apartment houses, both rented and owned, differed from their pre-Depression neighbors physically, socially, and economically. One major change was that architects silenced historicist visual language. While well into the 1950s most garden-apartments and mass-produced single-family houses looked backward toward the Colonial Revival (or, in California, variants of Spanish

Colonial), city apartments rejected the sculpted terra-cotta trim and elaborate limestone and brass entrances that had signified high status before the socially tumultuous 1930s. Buildings of the 1940s and 1950s employed smooth, simple finishes and egalitarian restraint.

The most pronounced, if immodest, example of this turn was in Chicago: the twin co-op buildings at 860–880 North Lake Shore Drive, designed by Mies van der Rohe (fig. 116). Mies, who all but defined postwar U.S. Modernism, sheathed the structures, built between 1948 and 1951, in his signature taut skin of glass and steel. In contrast to their older neighbors they appeared to float, both because they were set back from the street on all sides and because their first stories were left open apart from small, glass-enclosed lobbies at the center.[6]

Although Miesian Modernism was emulated in other residential buildings from time to time, it evolved chiefly as a language for business. More common in housing were variants of the modernistic functionalism seen at the postwar limited-equity co-ops of Herman Jessor and Brown & Guenther (see figs. 68, 69, 73). Like these low-cost co-ops, many of the new "luxury" buildings included recessed balconies running the entire height, and sometimes width, of the structure, a strategy tested in New York at several moderne buildings in suburban sections in the 1930s. Market-rate examples were distinguished from low-cost projects by their irregular silhouettes, which helped to create visual variety, and by their cladding of plate-glass picture windows and new, fashionable shades of glazed brick, like buff and deep brown (and, by the 1950s, white; fig. 117).[7]

Top-end city apartments after World War II also differed from those of earlier eras in their modest size and appointment. First-class apartment houses of the 1920s typically included units of seven to fifteen rooms. In the Depression, co-op owners and landlords often divided large apartments into multiple smaller ones.

Fig. 117: 20 East Seventy-fourth Street, New York, 1947. Sam Minskoff & Sons, developer; Sylvan Bien, architect. Advertisement, *New York Times*, May 18, 1947.

Subdividing continued after the war, when as an incentive to increase the supply of apartments, newly subdivided units were exempted from rent control. Apartments in new buildings assumed a similarly reduced scale, most with just three to six rooms, perhaps with a handful of seven- or eight-room "penthouses" on the top floor.[8] In lieu of palatial dimensions, developers offered a range of impressive but relatively inexpensive features. Some, like balconies and custom artwork in lobbies, were innovations. Others, like subterranean parking garages, were old ideas exploited to a new degree. Many involved new technologies: plate-glass sliding doors, radiant heating, air conditioning, multiple phone jacks, television "outlets" connecting sets to rooftop antennae, and appliances like dishwashers, washing machines, and dryers.[9]

Like streamlined exteriors, smaller apartments also resulted from a diminished demand among the rich for ostentation and, perhaps, space in which to rear children. Of equal importance, they reflected new economic and racial realities. With foreign immigration all but prohibited since the 1920s, the cost of domestic workers, especially white ones, rose to a level inaccessible even to the ordinary rich. (The desirability of white workers was suggested by prohibitions in some co-ops in the 1920s against use of maids' rooms by non-whites.) Without large household staffs, and with fewer domestic workers to house, apartments shrank.

Steep, progressive income taxes—which climbed as high as ninety-one percent—also helped turn large apartments into white elephants. On the one hand, taxes helped stimulate interest in co-ownership; in 1942 Congress began allowing income-tax deductions for property taxes and mortgage interest.[10] On the other hand, they compromised the spending power of the rich and flattened patterns of consumption. The result was that Americans lived more alike in this era, regardless of social status or occupation, than ever before or since. This broad social equality, which all but excluded African Americans, was even more visible in the suburban landscapes of Levittown and Lakewood, where blue-collar and white-collar workers lived side by side in identical houses.[11]

Prices in these new, modest co-ops were extremely low. At 3 East Seventy-first Street, four-room apartments—which included two "master" (family) bedrooms, two bathrooms, "large galleries" (presumably a euphemism for a combined living and dining area), and wood-burning fireplaces—sold for $10,000 with $142 in maintenance ($160,000 and $2,200 in 2010 dollars). At 870 Fifth Avenue, apartments sold from $13,000 for three rooms, up to $24,000 for seven. These prices were comparable to mid-range single-family houses in the suburbs (although because mortgages were unavailable, they were effectively much more expensive). Low prices remained common until the early 1960s, when top income-tax rates were reduced.[12]

Rent Control

After 1948, new construction subsided and conversion became the predominant source of new market-rate co-ops in New York. On the Upper East Side, ten buildings converted in the 1940s (in addition to those reestablishing themselves as co-ops). But in the 1950s as many as two hundred buildings converted. In all, roughly two buildings converted for each new co-op built on the East Side between the war and the mid-1960s. By the early 1960s it was said that there were few "good" rental buildings left.[13]

In a reversal of earlier conditions, much of the impetus to convert by the 1950s derived *from* rent control, established in New York in 1943. Fear that demobilization would lead to rent profiteering prompted Congress to extend it into the early 1950s. In most cities, high rates of housing production and oversupply of FHA "emergency" rentals meant that control was soon unnecessary. In New York City, however, perpetually low vacancy rates and the political muscle of tenants' groups persuaded state lawmakers to extend it further. When state officials allowed it to lapse, in the early 1960s, New York City leaders extended it under a new municipal program. In 1969 the city also introduced an additional rent-regulation program to "stabilize" rates in more than four hundred thousand apartments never (or no longer) covered by the 1943 law.[14]

While initially rent control made tenancy more appealing than ownership, by the 1950s landlords cut back on services and maintenance. People in better buildings initiated conversions to ensure the quality of their housing. This practice generated so much interest that in 1956 NAREB published a book, *The Purchaser's Approach to Cooperative Apartments*, in which a leading New York sales agent walked tenants through the process. Although at first concentrated almost entirely on the East Side, by the late 1950s the long-term effects of rent control had begun to motivate tenants in other sections of New York, like the West Side, to convert. In cities where rent control was not extended past the early 1950s, by contrast, conversion was rare. In Washington, for example, there were at least ten conversions immediately after the war, but none, for many years, after 1953.[15]

In addition to pushing tenants toward ownership, rent control continued to pull developers and landlords out of the business of market-rate rented housing. Although new buildings were not controlled after 1947, developers remained wary. Many rentals were built. But typically this was done only to take advantage of tax benefits designed to stimulate their production, and after a few years buildings were converted. One element of the tax code that stimulated this pattern was that sales of apartments in a new project were characterized as ordinary profits and taxed at ordinary rates. Profits from the sale of an existing building to a cooperative corporation, however, were taxed as capital gains, at lower rates. An additional tax incentive to build as a rental before conversion was "depreciation." Depreciation allowed companies to deduct from their annual income a percentage of a building's original cost (whether a factory, shopping center, or apartment house) to compensate for a presumed loss in value due to wear, tear, and age. Many developers found it advantageous to take depreciation for a few years.[16]

Other developers and landlords left the field of housing entirely. The owners of the ultra-luxurious high-rise rental building at 300 Park Avenue, for example, sold the site in 1955 to investors who replaced it not with new market-rate apartments but with an office tower for the Colgate-Palmolive corporation. In the 1920s, when the building had opened, the palatial apartments rented for up to $8,000 a year ($200,000 in 2010 dollars, or $27,000 a month), with one penthouse going for $25,000 ($1 million, or $85,000 a month). Rent control, however, froze these rents at Depression-era lows of $3,500 and $6,000 a year, respectively. By 1955, these rates converted to just $37,000 and $64,000 in 2010 dollars, or $3,100 and $5,300 a month: a rent reduction, since the 1920s, of nearly ninety-five percent! As the economy recovered and costs rose, these deeply discounted rents proved insufficiently attractive to keep the building going. Many nearby landlords similarly converted to commercial use. By the 1960s this section of Park Avenue (see fig. 22) had been transformed almost entirely from apartments and hotels to corporate offices for companies like Lever soap and Seagram liquor.[17]

Concerns about landlords abandoning the rental market in this way led policymakers to rein in rent control from time to time. Piecemeal "liberation," however, often had the unanticipated consequence of further stimulating conversion. As a concession to the landlord and real-estate lobby, for example, New York State "de-controlled" "luxury" apartments in 1957. This affected only the six hundred apartments, all in Manhattan, with rents of $5,000 per year ($4,000 a month in 2010 dollars). Within a year, half the affected buildings were converting, since tenants feared dramatic rent increases and landlords were resigned to the fact that tenants preferred to buy than pay the rent required to maintain high levels of service. Not all tenants supported conversion and at several buildings there was struggle over the process. But in the end, virtually all such proposals succeeded. De-control of additional units in the late 1960s and again in the early 1970s triggered similar rounds of conversion.[18]

Open Housing

In addition to the push and pull effects of postwar rent control, co-ownership, at least in Manhattan, also came to appeal as a way to evade fair-housing laws. The fair, or open, housing movement that emerged during the Depression and World War II sought to outlaw discrimination by developers, agents, sellers, and landlords on the basis of race, color, religion, and national origin in the rental or purchase of housing, as well as in real-estate advertising and mortgage lending. New York was a leader in this struggle and in the related drive to desegregate public accommodations, such as theaters and restaurants. Local laws preceded federal ones by many years. Initial efforts, in the late 1930s, barred discrimination in public housing and in tax-exempt limited-dividend projects. By 1954 the city had also prohibited discrimination in housing developed with loans insured by FHA. As a "private" form of housing, however, co-ops were effectively immune.[19]

To some degree, co-ops were part of the solution to discrimination in housing. State-aided complexes like Queensview (see fig. 57) were open-occupancy from the start, and white prospective homeowners (overwhelmingly Jewish) literally applauded the first Black families there, in 1948. At low-cost, predominantly Jewish FHA co-ops like Bell Park Gardens, owners also pursued integration by the early 1950s.[20]

More often, however, co-ops served as barriers to the cause. Nationally, co-ops were not a priority for the fair-housing movement, which focused on the more egregious (and obvious) injustices of discrimination in state-owned housing and in suburbia. Nevertheless, New York City activists like Charles Abrams recognized the owned apartment as an important arena. He worked, in particular, to challenge the notion, originally formulated by progressive housing reformers in the 1920s, that co-ops—including limited-equity worker co-ops—required homogeneity to succeed. In 1946 he wrote that social or ethnic homogeneity "as a condition for co-operation is not only a baseless but a dangerous concept. . . . There may be more conflict in a housing project between an Irish Democrat and an Irish Republican than between either and a Swede. The binding force for co-operation arises not from similarity of skills or skulls, national origin or religion."[21]

The co-op's clublike admissions procedures made it a challenging place to fight bias. The unique problem of the co-op is suggested by "A Few Little Words," a short story by Francis Steegmuller published in the progressive magazine *Common Ground* in 1948. The story concerns prospective buyers who find that even the mention of Black acquaintances leads to threats of rejection of their application. The board's representative assures them that as "an owner here you would be legally entitled to receive anyone you wished." But "the directors . . . are legally entitled to reject the application of anyone *they* wish, without giving a reason." If the prospective owners will not promise to entertain Black friends outside of the building, she asks them to consider withdrawing their application. "It would have been approved automatically, on my recommendation," she explains. "But now I think I know what the decision of the directors will be, and I don't like to embarrass anyone whom we like as much as we do you." Echoing longstanding ideas in real-estate circles, the ostensible grounds for this policy were resale values: "There is nothing—*nothing*—that causes real estate values to go down more quickly than any question of Negro tenancy, or even any hint or rumor of Negro tenancy," she explained. "That is fatal to a building—absolutely fatal."[22]

Such fears marshaled substantial opposition to fair housing. In 1957, New York City lawmakers began considering a bill to end discrimination in all housing except family-owned rental buildings with four or fewer units. The bill enjoyed the universal support of civil-rights, religious, and education groups. The establishment, including the *New York Times*, fought it. According to the *Times*'s editors, "We do not think that the people of New York have been adequately prepared for the passage of this bill, and we fear that the consequences of its adoption in such circumstances would be a stopping of large-scale construction and a drastic depreciation of property values. We believe that the difficulties of enforcement are enormous, that nuisance cases would be innumerable and that intolerance might be aggravated rather than diminished. So, with the deepest regret, we oppose this bill as being the wrong way to a right end."[23] Real-estate interests also fought hard against it.[24] In advertisements, real-estate trade groups argued: "We abhor prejudice. . . . But we strongly object to this wanton invasion of basic property rights. This proposed law would *compel* the rental of apartments and the sale of cooperative apartments to persons whose occupancy could make *your* homes less attractive to *you*."[25] They warned that the law would curb mortgage lending by banks.

Despite the hostility, the bill passed and none of the predicted doom materialized. To the contrary, co-op construction surged. Between 1957 and 1964, more than four dozen towers—mainly on the Upper East Side—were begun. What's more, some of these buildings specifically courted Jewish and Black families. One was Butterfield House, a 1962 building in Greenwich Village with a striking design by William J. Conklin and James S. Rossant (who later planned Twin Rivers; fig. 118). Ads for the building featured testimonials by buyers clearly meant to be read as Jewish, such as "Dr. & Mrs. Seymour Felder" and "Mrs. Harry Lehman."[26] At Linda Grover's 325 Central Park West, meanwhile, the all-white tenants went out of their way during conversion to sell the building's vacant units to Black and biracial families.[27]

This spirit of integration was also evident in many co-ops in other cities. Outside of New York, in fact, co-ownership often seems to have served less to exclude than to create community among diverse groups of owners. At a hearing in 1967 in Detroit before the National Commission on Urban Problems, for example, a homeowner

Fig. 118: Butterfield House, 37 West Twelfth Street, New York, 1960–62. Dan Gray, developer; William J. Conklin, James S. Rossant, architects.

named Kathryn Maxwell spoke of the powerful integrative effects of ownership at her co-op, the Ranier-Hamilton. After living in a house for many years, Maxwell had moved to the building while it was still a rental. When the place began "to slip," it converted. Renovations associated with the conversion "gave a lift to the whole neighborhood." It also changed the social composition of the building.

Before conversion residents had been all white and mainly older, including many widows. "They were not delighted with the changes in the neighborhood," Maxwell testified. "And they were apprehensive about the fact that many Negroes were coming into the neighborhood, and particularly that there would be Negroes in the cooperative. Some of the people who lived there were . . . bigots." Maxwell, however, was determined to buy, and she persuaded others to as well. One friend of forty years "was most apprehensive and I, among others, persuaded her to stay." A young African American woman moved in across the hall. Now the two visited and enjoyed each other's company. "There have been many instances like this that . . . have changed the attitudes of people."[28]

Closed Housing

Despite these gains, opaque admissions procedures meant that the co-op also emerged as a tool for avoiding fair-housing requirements. This was especially true in New York after 1959. That year, a Jewish man sued a Park Avenue co-op board that had rejected his application to occupy an apartment whose shares he had contracted to buy. In its ruling, the state court found that co-op boards, while subject to fair-housing laws, did not have to disclose reasons for disapproval of resales. In other words, while co-ops could not exclude on the basis of race, ethnicity, or religion, they could for any other reason. Either way, boards had no obligation to disclose to applicants their reasons for rejection.[29]

With the burden of proof lying heavily on the applicants, claims of bias were difficult to substantiate. The result was effective virtual immunity. In one landmark case, for example, the City Commission on Human Rights determined, in 1962, that the president of one of the city's leading Jewish temples had been improperly barred from a co-op because of his Jewishness. State courts, however, overturned the decision, and the co-op's board went unpunished.[30]

There was, nevertheless, much evidence that many co-ops violated the law. Investigations begun in the early 1960s by the New York State and New York City Commissions on Human Rights and by the Anti-Defamation League of B'nai B'rith (a Jewish human rights group) revealed East Side co-ops to be "fortresses of anti-Semitism and monumental symbols of discriminatory exclusion."[31] In another case—prompted by a 1959 investigation by the U.S. Civil Rights Commission into the suburban town of Bronxville, in Westchester County, which showed it had not a single Jewish resident—the state attorney general filed a complaint against one of the town's co-ops. In an affidavit, a Jewish applicant declared that the board had told him that "people with dogs or people of the Hebrew faith" would not be permitted in the building.[32]

Despite these investigations, little was done to force co-ops to comply with the law. At Bronxville, for example, the building's board was simply made to agree to comply with state antidiscrimination laws and to amend its by-laws to prohibit discrimination. This sort of weak reprimand was typical. The best way to fix the problem was to require boards to disclose reasons for rejecting applicants—or to prohibit screening privileges altogether. Lawmakers and the courts, however, cowered before this obligation.

In their defense, co-op owners, developers, and agents frequently made the obfuscating—and historically inaccurate—claim that the co-op was chiefly a private

club rather than housing.[33] By this deeply flawed logic, any co-owned property—
condo, townhouse, or otherwise—might also have claimed exemption. The courts,
however, seemed to accept it. According to the *Columbia Law Review*, they were
"unable to develop standards capable of dealing" with the co-op's unique status
as both "personal" and "real" property. So while judges were willing to recognize
that the essential purpose of the co-op was to "approach individual home ownership
as nearly as is possible in a situation where the only practical solution is common
operation and management of many features," they also upheld the special privilege
of the co-op owner to "live among persons whose tastes, wishes, [and] standards of
comfort and living . . . are substantially the same as his."[34]

Despite continued reports of such behavior, co-ops were effectively given further
reprieve in 1968. Fair Housing provisions in the Civil Rights Act of that year
prohibited discrimination in the sale, rental, and financing of all housing nationally
on the basis of race, color, national origin, and religion (it was later amended to
include gender, disability status, and presence of children in a household). Like the
New York State courts, however, the federal government all but declined to enforce
the law for co-ops. In 1969, for example, the Justice Department investigated the
Washington, D.C. co-op Tilden Gardens, which had no Jewish or Black homeowners.
The corrective, as in Bronxville, was simply to require that a nondiscrimination
clause be added to the by-laws. National policymakers, too, seemed to accept the
myth that co-ops were not chiefly a form of housing.[35]

Policing Gender

Boards rejected buyers not only because of their ethnicity and religion. They
also excluded people because of their politics and social habits, in addition to
more legitimate concerns about job security, savings, and income. One of the
first arbitrary exclusions to be discussed widely in public, for example, was that
of Peter Lawford, an actor, and Patricia Kennedy Lawford, the slain president's
sister. Somewhat later, another co-op very publicly prohibited Richard Nixon (in
addition to the condominium which attempted to exclude him).[36] Many co-ops also
routinely rejected gay men, single people, and people with new money, and they
tried to limit, if not eliminate, children and dogs. According to one managing
agent, "We get memos from our buildings all the time saying, 'We have our
quota of divorcees, so don't show apartments to any more of them,' or 'No more
children,' or 'No dogs.' . . . One memo said, 'We have found new achievers not to be
satisfactory tenants.'"[37]

Many boards also policed gender boundaries. In 1969, Rita Berger and her
husband Ernie tried to buy an apartment on Riverside Drive. Rita worked as the

full-time assistant to a Broadway producer; Ernie was an actor. The couple was living in a three-room, rent-controlled building elsewhere in the neighborhood but wanted more space. They decided to invest their substantial savings in a co-op. The place they settled on was dark and run-down, but it had six rooms and cost $34,000 ($200,000); the maintenance was low, which would leave them money to renovate. The elderly seller was ill and eager to move. When Berger and her husband interviewed with the board—a group of seven middle-aged and elderly men—things seemed to go well. It was "not like formal East Side board meetings," she recalled, and there were few substantial questions. There was, however, one red flag: the board addresses only Ernie, all but ignoring Rita. "It is as if I am not there."

Rather than approval (or rejection), the coming weeks brought arbitrary, demeaning, and misogynistic demands. Suspicious that Berger was a secretary rather than an assistant, the board asked her to submit a second letter from her employer to assure them that his initial letter was accurate. Worried that Berger lied when she said she did not want children, the board demanded she sign a statement assuring them that she would not get pregnant or adopt. Having heard, through mutual acquaintances, that Berger's father was ill, the board asked for written proof that she was the primary heir. Berger and her husband refused on all counts. Indignant, they also contacted their elected officials and the state attorney general; all said there was nothing they could do to help.

Friends of friends, who lived in the building, called to suggest that the board president was a snob and that the rest of the group was fine but too busy with the rest of their lives to challenge him. These acquaintances urged Berger and her husband to give in to the board's demands and to "fight" to get in. Their agent was sympathetic. She confessed to Berger that "I can't place a single woman, a widow or a divorcee, even if they are very wealthy, in a co-op. They have a very difficult time passing the boards." Apparently couples in which the woman earned more than the man were also suspect. After months of negotiation, and of refusing to humiliate themselves to humor a capricious board, the Bergers were rejected.[38]

Glass and Steel and Suburbs

In the late 1950s and early 1960s, a small wave of co-op construction began in city centers nationally; it grew quickly. New York's lull in new market-rate construction, which began around 1950, broke early and fast as developers rushed to beat a 1961 zoning ordinance that they feared would make new buildings less profitable. Other cities, too, saw elegant new market-rate co-ops. Buyers included some younger families, but many older ones—empty nesters who wanted to move to apartments, but not to Florida or Leisure World. As *Fortune* magazine had found in the late

1950s when examining new buildings in Philadelphia, Chicago, and New York: "Suburbs may be considered an ideal place in which to raise children, [but] many aging couples regard center-city apartments as an ideal place to live when children are no longer a consideration. A number of these couples are 'returnees' from the suburbs." As early as 1959 one New York sales agent, in recognition of this market, established a "trade-in" service through which owners could "exchange" their suburban houses for co-ops.[39]

Architecturally, this second wave of postwar co-ops and condos was more adventuresome than the first. Embrace of the modernistic geometries of Mies's Lake Shore Drive apartments eventually led to expedient new formulas and the ubiquitous glass-and-concrete "cracker boxes" and "ice-cube trays" derided by critics. Along the way, many fine examples were built, such as Harrison & Abramovitz's United Nations Plaza in New York (fig. 119). Renewed interest in city living also led to many new experiments in what proved to be a highly creative period in apartment design, as developers competed for sales and as architects exploited new construction technologies. As in the 1920s, not all good buildings in this era were co-owned, but many were. Projects like Butterfield House in Greenwich Village, Charles Goodman's River Park in Washington (see fig. 70), Victor Gruen's Wilshire Terrace in L.A. (see fig. 100), were beautiful, sophisticated, and original.

Although market-rate co-ownership was concentrated in city centers, well-equipped and well-appointed buildings also began to appear in peripheral sections. This was especially true in New York. Higher-density suburban apartments had been common in metropolitan New York since the 1920s, but in the ten years after World War II they were largely forgotten in favor of the FHA garden apartment. The fashion began to change in the late 1950s when Alfred Levitt successfully rented Levitt House, a group of thirty-two, nine-story Modernist apartment buildings at Cryder's Point, an otherwise single-family neighborhood in northern Queens, fronting Long Island Sound (fig. 120).

For twenty-five years Levitt had been the designing partner in his family's firm, planning both the houses and the community facilities at Levittowns in New York and Pennsylvania. Around 1954, however, he parted ways with his brother, William, who was uninterested in multifamily housing. Levitt House apartments had three and a half to five and a half rooms and a balcony off the living room accessed by floor-to-ceiling sliding-glass doors. Community amenities included a private beach and clubhouse, swimming pools, tennis courts, a yacht basin, a "young folks television theater," and a small shopping center.[40]

Developers quickly followed Levitt's lead and started building higher-density, highly serviced market-rate apartments in outer boroughs and some suburban

Fig. 119: United Nations Plaza, East Forty-eighth and Forty-ninth Streets, First Avenue, FDR Drive, New York, 1963–66. Webb & Knapp, initial developer; Alcoa, developer; Harrison & Abramovitz, architect.

Fig. 120: Levitt House (today LeHavre), Twelfth Avenue, 162nd Street, Powell's Cove Boulevard, Whitestone, New York, 1956. Alfred Levitt, developer.

Fig. 121: Crescent Park Apartments, 320 South Harrison Street, East Orange, New Jersey, 1964. Tandy & Allen, developer; Morris Lapidus, architect. Photograph by Ezra Stoller, 1964.

centers. As with luxury city-center buildings, most were co-owned or quickly converted (Levitt House later went condo). By the mid-1960s, a dozen co-owned high-rises had been completed in Riverdale, Bronxville, Forest Hills, and northern New Jersey. Among the most distinguished of these was Crescent Park, a curving nineteen-story slab of 252 apartments designed by Morris Lapidus in East Orange, New Jersey, which opened in 1964 (fig. 121). Surrounded by single-family houses, the building offered sweeping, unobstructed views of city and country, which Lapidus captured with dramatic floor-to-ceiling windows. Like his apartment buildings at

Aventura (see figs. 10, 90), Crescent Park lacked the drama of his earlier Miami
Beach hotels (see fig. 74). Nonetheless, it offered the suburban homeowner a touch
of American glamour. By the early 1970s New York had a dozen more luxury
high-rises outside of Manhattan and similar buildings were built in many other
housing markets.[41]

"Co-op or Go Down"

While older families constituted much of the market for deluxe new high-rise
apartments, younger households helped fuel a nationwide explosion in conversion.
In New York City the number of conversions rose from a few hundred apartments a
year in the 1950s to more than fifteen hundred a year in the first half of the 1960s,
more than four thousand a year in the second half of the decade, and more than
eight thousand a year in the early 1970s. By 1975 more than eighty-five percent of
all conventionally financed co-ops and condos in New York City had been produced
through conversion. Nationally, the 1970s saw more than 360,000 conversions.
One-third were in Census-defined "central cities" and another third in suburbs.
(The remainder, presumably, were in more isolated resorts.) After Chicago and
Washington, D.C., which together accounted for a third of the total, the largest
numbers of conversions were in metro New York, followed by Miami, Los Angeles,
San Francisco, and more than thirty other metro areas, including Minneapolis,
Hartford, Cleveland, Denver, Dallas, and Houston.[42]

As at Linda Grover's building on the West Side, most early conversions were led
by tenants. This practice had originated around 1920 and became common, again,
in the late 1940s on the East Side. By the early 1960s an estimated three-quarters
of buildings there had converted. Things happened more slowly on the West Side.
West Sixty-seventh Street had been an important early center of co-ownership,
but, the story of Rita Berger notwithstanding, the neighborhood was more liberal
and middle-class than the East Side, and the tenants more forgiving of deferred
maintenance in exchange for low rents. But only up to a point.

The first major postwar conversion on the West Side happened in 1959. Tenants
at 300 West End Avenue—a 1917 building with thirty-seven units of three to twelve
rooms—became incensed when the landlord announced plans to replace full-time
elevator operators with automatic cabs monitored by closed-circuit television
cameras. There had been several recent muggings in the area, including one inside
an apartment-house elevator. The relatively well-to-do tenants, who included the
singer Harry Belafonte, were alarmed.[43]

Under state laws governing rent-controlled buildings, disputes between tenants
and landlords were made before the Temporary State Housing Rent Commission.

The commission decided in favor of the landlord. The tenants contacted Edward Sulzberger, a young Upper West Side management and sales agent. He arranged for them to buy the building, which included a sub-grade parking garage, in 1961. At the time, Sulzberger correctly predicted that a majority of better buildings in the area would convert within the next few years. Among other early conversions in the neighborhood were the Dakota, whose tenants bought it, also in 1961, when the landlord announced plans to replace it with a modern high-rise that would have been exempt from rent control (fig. 122).[44]

Efforts to fight decay and demolition reflected a new kind of community activism among middle-class city dwellers in the 1960s and 1970s, especially younger bourgeois bohemians. These efforts were stirred by opposition to rapid, impersonal change and reflected renewed interest in historic buildings and neighborhoods. Jane Jacobs's *Death and Life of Great American Cities*, published in 1961, forcefully articulated this emerging view. Jacobs wrote of the unique promise of older building stock, "small scale" urban fabric, and the "liveliness and variety" of older neighborhoods. According to Jacobs—whose outlook was as much that of architecture critic as activist—the "mingled building age" of these neighborhoods, their "functional mixtures" of land uses, and the heterogeneity of class, age, "taste and proclivity," and ethnicity conferred upon them an authenticity that the rest of postwar America lacked. She saw historic city architecture as more useful and pleasant than the "infinity and repetition which generally seem overwhelming, inhuman and incomprehensible" at large-scale, Modernist developments.[45]

All the Grandeur of the Glorious Past

THE DAKOTA

NUMBER ONE WEST 72ND STREET FACING CENTRAL PARK
THE NEW YORK TRADITION THAT IS NOW A COOPERATIVE

Because it is The Dakota, it is a cooperative of established worth. Because it is The Dakota, it is the original rather than an attempt at a revival. Because it is The Dakota, it is a tradition in elegance that remains unique in New York's social history. At long last, the great iron gates are open again to apartment seekers. Apartments of impressive size, each one with its own masterpieces of decoration. You are invited to inspect the few apartments still available, by appointment with the agent:

APARTMENTS OF 3 TO 13 ROOMS PRICED FROM $25,000 TO $65,000

SELLING AND MANAGING AGENT

110 East 56th Street • PLaza 5-0700 / Representative on Premises—TRafalgar 7-9456

This advertisement is not an offering. No offering is made except by the prospectus filed with the Department of Law of the State of New York. Such filing does not constitute approval of the issue by the Department of Law or the Attorney General of the State of New York. The stock is available only to residents of New York State.

Fig. 122: The Dakota, 1 West Seventy-second Street, New York, conversion. Advertisement, *New York Times*, February 18, 1962.

Grover and her neighbors at 325 Central Park West were typical of the new market for conversions. When arguing for the building they focused on its physical attributes. They spoke, for example, "of our high ceilings and fireplaces and charm; of the big kitchens, with windows; of our formal dining rooms and sixty-foot halls— great for roller skating on rainy days." Conversely, they criticized contemporary high-rises, suggesting that, despite the policy goal of stabilizing their area with middle-class families, "new construction will not replace the old in solving this problem. With their one small and one smaller bedroom," they exaggerated, "new apartments are large enough only until a family is unlucky enough to have their second child differ in sex from the first. Then off to Rye or Levittown." Unlike high-rise "ice cube trays of tomorrow," Grover emphasized, old age and low rents had also given them an "economic and cultural spread" that was "any sociologists's dream." Among the group, she pointed out, were a social worker, an artist, a composer, a teacher, clergy, and white-collar professionals, along with an "almost published" poet and a "sweet shabby old lady who took in boarders."[46]

In 1963, city officials gave them a choice: demolition, or buy their apartments and renovate them to comply with safety codes. At first the group resisted. Unlike at the Dakota or 300 West End, Grover and her neighbors had very little money. The project would cost $21,000 per apartment ($160,000). Even with an FHA-insured mortgage this would mean down payments of $1,500 ($11,500) and monthly maintenance (before utilities) of $160 to $190 ($1,200 to $1,450), nearly fifty percent more than they were currently paying in rent. On instinct, Grover "righteously" declared that "our tenants can't buy a building—they aren't interested in acquiring anything but peace of mind. They just want to keep the homes they've got, at rents they can afford." Could the building simply not be turned back to a private landlord? Yes, they were told, the building could be put up for auction. But the result would be subdivision of the apartments into much smaller ones, since this was the only way to liberate the building from rent control and cover the cost of required repairs. The choice was "co-oping" or demolition, or as Grover punned, "co-op or go down."[47]

It took just minutes for Grover and her neighbors to begin to see the benefits of ownership. In addition to preserving their bohemian way of life, ownership offered more control, including the right to customize. It would also allow owners to profit. If you decide to convert, one city commissioner advised them, "you will be in the very favorable position of owning real estate in an area of rapidly rising values." Another commissioner, nodding in agreement, affirmed that the project would "no doubt" prove "lucrative." "With these words," Grover recalled, she became convinced of the "whole warm delicious concept of ownership." "Could you believe it?" she wondered. "Two minutes ago we'd been agitating, downtrodden tenants; now there was a

totally new feeling. A heady brew—capitalism, aggrandizement." Meanwhile, once
the contractors had started work, Grover and her neighbors became consumed
with an "uncontrollable urge" to customize. Families once perfectly happy to live
with "bugs in the kitchen, rust in the water, the clank in the radiator, the chill of
a heatless day" now caught "Extra-Work Euphoria," suddenly finding thousands
of extra dollars to move walls, add baths, and stock realigned kitchens with
previously unimagined appliances. "How much closer could you get to heaven . . . ?"
wondered Grover.[48]

Gentrification

Gentrification in the 1960s and 1970s is often associated with the renovation of
individual houses and the incremental "unslumming" of neighborhoods like Boston's
North End and New York's Greenwich Village, both celebrated by Jane Jacobs.
But it was just as much about transforming multifamily housing, mainly through
conversion. Gentrification was stimulated by many factors: counterculture rejection
of the mainstream built environment of middle-class suburbia; a "rent gap" between
low-value land uses in slums and potential "highest and best" alternatives, such as
middle-class housing; new concentrations of specialized, high-paying service jobs
in finance, insurance, and real estate in "global" cities; expansion of the professions,
which also concentrated in central business districts; and a new impetus to urban
living among baby boomers enjoying an extended adolescence between college and
child rearing, and among women and gay men in the age of sexual liberation.[49]

This brew of forces greatly expanded the number of households that shared a
taste for, and the financial means to achieve, middle-class city living. These urban
middle-class clienteles, both professional and bohemian, were far from new. But in
the 1960s and 1970s they grew tremendously, and so too expanded the zone of the
city they inhabited: from East Side to West, and from a handful of older "bourgeois
bohemian" enclaves like Russian Hill, Georgetown, and Brooklyn Heights to close-
in tenement districts, boarding-house districts, and loft districts. What began in
the 1920s with projects like the Bedford-Barrow Cooperative in Greenwich Village
(see fig. 38) flowered in the age of Aquarius as tens of thousands of people like Linda
Grover used co-ownership to secure space for themselves in cities.[50]

Available data generally confirm impressions of urban co-op and condo owners as
fitting these stereotypes. According to a 1969 survey of co-op buyers in New York,
the typical family was "solidly middle-class in aspect" with an income of $19,500
($120,000). Sixty percent were between the ages of thirty-five and fifty-five; the
average size of household was three persons. Eighty percent were first-time co-
owners, seventy percent had previously lived in rental apartments in Manhattan,

and eighteen percent had moved to Manhattan from the suburbs. Sixty-two percent of buyers were businessmen, seventeen percent professionals, thirteen percent in the arts, and eight percent "other," including professional athletes and the "idle rich." A national study of converted units in 1980 found owners to be even younger and with yet smaller households. Thirty-five percent were under the age of thirty-six, and a similar share were thirty-six to fifty-four. A majority were single: twenty-one percent were single men, and thirty-six percent single women. (By contrast, just four percent of owner-occupied homes overall were owned by single men, and ten percent by single women.)[51]

Curiously, this second, larger study showed that conversion was less a cause of gentrification than a symptom. Before and after conversion, it found, most buildings were remarkably similar in terms of age, income, and family status. Many tenants in converting buildings chose not to buy, but generally this had less to do with demographics than with personal preferences. In other words, the buildings had already changed socially through a process of neighborhood succession before they changed ownership. These findings foreshadowed the work of urban planner Lance Freeman, who found similarly ambiguous links between gentrification and displacement a generation later.[52]

In addition to political, social, and economic factors, gentrification through co-ownership—as with retirement condos in Florida and townhouses in California—was also encouraged by larger-scale economic forces like inflation. High inflation fueled by the Vietnam War made people eager to own real estate for fear of missing out on later opportunities to buy, and because frequent rent increases, where permitted, made them feel that money spent on rent was "thrown away." As one planner observed in the late 1970s, "The customer pays over and over again for what he already has—i.e., access to an apartment that in the very nature of things is a little bit older and worse each month than the month before." As costs go up "the tenant must . . . pay more money for what he already had paid for over and over" to "someone whom he usually never sees . . . for something that the landlord already made." Many tenants, in this context, came to perceive ownership as a better choice.[53]

Of equal importance, inflation, like rent control, made it hard for landlords to make ends meet. As one developer explained in 1973: "Rental properties are obsolete in an inflationary economy. You simply cannot make any money on them because rents are too low and you can't raise rents fast enough to keep up with rising costs."[54] Another developer preferred the long-term income of rentals but found "market conditions didn't warrant it." As a result, lenders and corporate real-estate investors, like real-estate investment trusts, saw difficulties in the rental market and pushed money toward co-ops and condos.[55]

Ownership was not the only outcome. In neighborhoods appealing to middle-class bohemians and professionals such as Linda Grover's Upper West Side, where housing demand was strong and gentrification was under way, the mismatch between prevailing rents and rising costs was commonly resolved through conversion. In many marginal neighborhoods, by contrast, this gap resulted in abandonment. Beginning in the late 1960s, landlords in the Bronx, the South Side of Chicago, Detroit, and beyond began walking away from apartments. In the second half of the 1960s alone, eighty thousand to one hundred thousand buildings were abandoned in New York City. Arson became common. In Detroit, October 30th became Devil's Night, when hundreds of buildings were burned as entertainment. In New York, arson acquired the colloquial name "Jewish lightning," the unfortunate initial title of the 1977 film *Fire Sale*. The term reflected the ethnicity of many old-time owners.[56]

Decades of disinvestment left city centers in crisis by the 1960s and 1970s: strapped for revenue with decaying infrastructure and huge populations of the poor and disenfranchised. Crime and disorder were rampant. Ownership of an apartment—whether at snobby East Side buildings or at 325 Central Park West—offered city dwellers a measure of control. As one anthropologist found, owning a home mediated anxieties generated by social and economic turbulence.[57] As another reported in the early 1980s of her own experience, "I think co-op living is wonderful. It's not so much the ownership as it is having some control over where I live." Conversion helped make the chaotic city seem more navigable by arresting—and even reversing—otherwise inexorable changes, social and physical.[58]

State Support for Co-ownership

Market rate co-ownership in cities was stimulated by several public policies in the 1960s and 1970s. The federal urban renewal program permitted cities to include market-rate co-ops in their redevelopment plans, and many did. FHA discussed conversion as early as 1959 (declaring it had a "tremendous future") and by the 1960s was directing much energy to that end. The IRS, as already discussed, offered landlords incentives for conversion (on top of the usual deductions for individual homeowners). The Federal Home Loan Bank Board, under direction of Congress, also began making ever more generous loans for co-owned housing.[59]

New York State lent yet greater support. New York had been encouraging limited-equity co-ops since the 1920s. Beginning in the late 1950s it also worked to broaden market-rate ownership. At the forefront of this task were the state attorney general, Louis J. Lefkowitz, and, especially, an assistant attorney general named David Clurman. In 1958, Lefkowitz instructed Clurman to draft a law on real-estate syndication. Real-estate syndicates were partnerships that allowed groups of small investors to buy or develop property together. These had been used for decades, including to develop co-ops. In the 1950s they had become more common in New York and there had been several cases of fraud. Promoters lured investors with promises of impossibly high returns; many of the victims were elderly. Co-owned housing was not Lefkowitz's concern. Clurman, however, anticipated that it would be growing in importance in the 1960s and that there was similar potential for deception. He included provisions in the law he drafted that gave the state power to govern the sale of co-ops. It passed in 1961, against the protest of the real-estate industry.[60]

The new regulation affected collective homeownership in three main ways. First, it required the attorney general to review every co-op (and, after amendments in 1964, condominium) "offering" in the state, both new construction and conversion. Second, it required developers to give prospective buyers full disclosure of the facts of a project, including details of any financing charges (both individual and for blanket mortgages), profits to the developer, projected maintenance costs, a description of the neighborhood (including schools, shopping centers, tax rates and assessments), and a detailed description of the complex. The regulation also required advertisements for co-ops and condos to include a statement to the effect that the ad was neither an offering nor proof that the project had yet, or would be, approved of by the attorney general's office.[61]

Third, Clurman's law empowered the state to monitor sales practices and to enforce state and local laws designed to protect tenants during conversion, of which there were several. To discourage wartime profiteering, OPA's original rent program in the 1940s had required eighty percent of tenants to consent to conversion. When New York State took over the program, that requirement was relaxed to thirty-five percent approval. If developers failed to get this consent within six to eighteen months of the formal offering (the law shifted requirements from time to time) the conversion had to be abandoned. The law further specified that every tenant had between thirty and ninety days' exclusive right (again, the law varied over time) to buy her apartment once thirty-five percent had given approval, and, sometimes, another six months in which to match any offer made for her unit by an outside buyer. The law also permitted most tenants who did not wish to buy to stay on for two years, or at least until the end of their leases. Later, Clurman devised a waiver of the thirty-five percent requirement if the developer permitted rent-regulated tenants to remain in place for life. Under this plan, the sponsor could sell the units only after the tenant left, even if it took decades.[62]

Clurman (b. 1927) believed these protections were essential to making conversion fair. When New York City law weakened participation to fifteen percent of tenants in 1969, he vowed to continue to apply the more stringent standard of thirty-five percent. In letters to the mayor and city council, Lefkowitz warned that the lower threshold "would appear to permit excessive pressures" on tenants who did not join the plan and that it "presents a clear danger to the public interest, especially middle and lower income residents not in a financial position to purchase their apartments."[63] Were it up to him, Clurman would have raised the requirement to fifty-one percent, especially in buildings bought by third-party "flippers" specifically for conversion, presumably because Clurman saw this growing practice as predatory. He also persuaded lawmakers to permit him to reject conversions in poorly maintained buildings where plans did not include an ample reserve fund for capital improvements.[64]

Improved Financing

Clurman was also instrumental in democratizing market-rate multifamily homeownership. One of the primary reasons for importing the condo from Latin America to Florida and for pioneering the fee-simple townhouse was that lenders immediately recognized condo deeds as worthy of individual mortgages. This was of little help to New York, where there were already a hundred thousand co-ops built or under way by the late 1950s. Furthermore, many developers and lenders were wary of these new systems. But as demand for co-ownership grew, the unavailability of individual financing became a major problem.

Lack of mortgage financing restricted access to homeownership. It also kept people reliant on expensive, antiquated alternatives. The 1920s-type installment plan, for example, remained in wide use well into the 1960s, with some lenders charging premiums of up to twenty percent for them (exclusive of interest). Buyers also continued to use high-interest, short-term personal loans. For resales, many relied on risky private arrangements through which the buyer paid the seller over time according to a schedule established by contract.[65]

Clurman, by contrast, believed that New Yorkers deserved the same long-term, self-amortizing mortgages enjoyed by homeowners in the rest of the country, where fee-simple houses, townhouses, and condominiums predominated. To rectify this problem, New York State, at his recommendation, passed a law that offered banks a financial incentive to make co-op mortgages, or "share loans." Like most states at the time, New York regulated the rates of interest that banks could charge for mortgages. Clurman's law allowed banks to charge an extra one and a half percent interest for co-ops. To overcome lingering reservations, a new legal device called a "recognition agreement" was also introduced, which allowed co-ops to recognize the right of a lender to foreclose on an apartment.

With the stroke of a pen, co-ops in New York State now qualified for mortgages. The law required banks to lend only up to seventy-five percent of the sales price, and for just twenty years. But as co-ops proved themselves to be low risk, loans were offered for longer periods and larger amounts. Many boards required buyers to pay a quarter or more in cash and some East Side buildings prohibited mortgages altogether. But for hundreds of thousands of families, Clurman made homeownership possible. As one bank proclaimed in ads showing a young couple picnicking on an indoor rug (rather than a suburban lawn), "Our New Co-op Loans . . . could change your mind about moving to the suburbs."[66]

Forestalling the Condo

In part as a result of this policy, adoption of the condominium was forestalled in New York City. As in L.A. and Florida, the condo and common-interest townhouse quickly appeared in new construction in New York suburbs, and even in the outer boroughs. In Manhattan, however, the co-op dominated until the 1980s. The second reason for this slow transition was simply that there was little new construction in Manhattan in the late 1960s and early 1970s. The overwhelming majority of "new" apartments on the market in this era were conversions—and, because of lower legal costs, it was cheaper to convert to co-op than to condo. For this reason the co-op also enjoyed a modest resurgence in cities like Washington and San Francisco in the 1970s and 1980s, especially as mortgage lenders followed New York's lead and began offering co-op loans. The third reason for slow adoption was that Manhattan's first condominium, the St. Tropez, sold poorly, although this was mainly due to an awkward location; a generic, boxy design by Kelly & Gruzen; and the fact that the market was flooded with new buildings when it opened, in 1964. (Village House, Manhattan's second condo, sold quickly when it opened four years later, in Greenwich Village.)[67]

Another factor was that local lenders—while long reluctant to make individual share loans—preferred to finance construction for co-ops. Interest rates on mortgages to individual homeowners were regulated by the state. Those for cooperative corporations, which were treated like commercial landlords, were not. As a result, they could carry higher interest rates and were more profitable. Furthermore, like old-fashioned individual mortgages they were typically short-term balloon-type loans that had to be renegotiated every few years at interest rates which, in the late 1960s and 1970s, were constantly rising.[68]

A final reason for slow adoption of the condominium in New York may have been resistance on the part of consumers, although the evidence is mixed. According to Raymond O'Keefe, a senior vice president of Chase Manhattan Bank, a "very

significant factor" was that "people do want the exclusivity of a co-op." As another
real-estate executive, who wished to remain anonymous, told the *Times*, it was also
"probably a fear of minorities."[69] In more recent work, anthropologist Setha Low has
confirmed that many New York City homeowners, while not observably racist, took
"comfort . . . living with people like themselves" and "express relief that they knew
that all prospective buyers would have to go through a rigorous vetting process to
be a co-op member," even when they perceived this vetting as diminishing stated
preferences for socioeconomic diversity in their buildings.[70] That said, in subsequent
real-estate cycles, beginning in the 1980s, the condo format predominated and
condos came to command higher prices than co-ops. Additionally, as others have
found, comparable "geographies of inclusion and exclusion" also exist in condos,
despite their open occupancy.[71]

Condo Conspiracy

Going co-op or condo was nearly always controversial. At East Side buildings
in the 1940s and 1950s, and to a lesser degree West Side buildings in the 1960s,
sophisticated tenants, with the resources to buy, hired experienced agents and
attorneys and undertook conversion themselves. By the late 1960s and 1970s,
however, landlords and, increasingly, third-party developers who specialized in the
legal and financial complexities of conversion were commanding the process. Most
of the firms who undertook conversion were small, but larger ones also emerged.
These operators used conversion to quickly meet market demand for co-ownership
at a lower cost than could be achieved through new construction, especially given
the significant inflation in the 1970s in the cost of materials and labor. They often ran
into opposition. In New York, for example, tenants blocked between ten and fifteen
percent of conversion proposals.[72]

Despite the mounting popularity of co-ownership, many people still preferred
to rent. Opposition was most evident in modest neighborhoods. When Harry
Helmsley bought Met Life's Parkchester in the Bronx, in 1968, for example, few
tenants were enthusiastic about going condo. Helmsley became involved with
conversion in 1958, when he and his business partner, the attorney Larry Wein,
began selling furnished suites at the Ambassador Hotel in Palm Beach, Florida.
In a proto-timeshare arrangement, two buyers were to share ownership of each
room while management retained responsibility for maintenance and for renting
out the units as the owners wished. Conversion of hotel suites to co-op had been
tested at several expensive hotels in Manhattan, including the Sherry-Netherland,
Hampshire House, and the Pierre. Ten years later, Helmsley bought Parkchester
for conversion. Over the next several years he did the same at Fresh Meadows, a

similar project in Queens, as well as at a series of expensive buildings in Manhattan and Beverly Hills.[73]

Although the twelve thousand apartments at Parkchester were well maintained, much of the surrounding area was in decline and tenants saw little reason to invest their savings in it. The general sentiment was that if they were going to buy, they would prefer to do so in newer complexes with up-to-date conveniences such as air conditioning. According to one observer, "Look at it from the point of view of the guy who lives there. He's a guy who makes $12,000 [$58,000] a year and has been there 18 years. His rent isn't bad, and the Bronx is not the best investment in the world. Why should he buy? There's absolutely no reason for anybody to say yes." As one of the original tenants of the project asked: "After 31 years? Do I look crazy?" The conversion eventually went through, but only after Helmsley agreed to use Clurman's no-eviction plan.[74]

More affluent households also sometimes resisted co-ownership. When they did so it was generally on grounds of being forced to choose between two unwelcome and unsolicited options: buying or leaving. One of the more bitter battles in New York between tenants and a landlord over conversion was at Imperial House, a well-equipped 1960 building where, by 1970, rents were between $500 and $1,000 a month ($2,800 and $5,700). The asking prices proposed for the apartments, had the conversion gone through, were as high as $250,000 ($1.4 million). Although most could have afforded to stay, more than 270 of the building's 375 tenants contributed $100 ($570)—and promised an additional $150—to cover legal fees in a suit against the developer. These tenants disliked being told what to do and how to spend their money. As one tenant explained: "I'm not going to give up my clothes and cruises to buy this apartment."[75]

Having to make such a choice violated Americans' sense of themselves as powerful consumers. As *Playboy* magazine wrote in a long feature on the "Condominium Conspiracy" in 1979, "options are shrinking." It used to be, imagined the reporter, that one could rent an apartment wherever one liked for just a quarter of one's income. Now, "if you don't want to move, or you want to live near your work . . . or you just can't find another apartment to rent," you must buy.[76]

The *New York Times*'s architecture critic, Ada Louis Huxtable, was yet more unequivocal. After losing her rent-controlled apartment when the landlord sold her building, she and her husband "made the remarkable discovery that the only place we could afford to live" was a co-op. After paying $45,000 down from savings ($265,000), maintenance was only $200, about one-third of their previous rent of $550. "As New Yorkers reckon things," she acknowledged, this substantial economy put them "ahead of the game." But Huxtable felt compromised. As a self-proclaimed "bourgeois bohemian" she preferred living in the "sp[l]endidly slightly shabby architectural town house manner." Her new co-op, however, was "conventional": a 1920s high-rise without the "handsome architectural spaces and details" she enjoyed. That the Park Avenue building was "well-kept, well-staffed," with doormen, offered some compensation. But she was "a lover of the luster and luxuries of the city . . . [and] a passionate devotee of the right to . . . live as one pleases and flaunt a favored life style." In buying she felt that "what we have given up is the one thing that is supposed to go with New York success—choosing your own way of life."[77]

The Condo Disease

Freedom of choice aside, expansion of co-ownership brought many more concrete difficulties, especially in places with weak oversight and few protections for existing tenants. Conversion may have followed rather than initiated social change in most neighborhoods. But there were always some who could not afford to buy or did not care to do so. Especially vulnerable in this regard were the elderly. Unlike retired homeowners who could swap houses for condos, many elderly renters did not have the cash to buy outright and it made little sense at age seventy or eighty to take a thirty-year mortgage. Furthermore, the elderly had little interest in potential appreciation, unlike younger buyers.[78] As the head of one tenants association explained, the landlord "would have us believe they are offering us the American dream. I am living through it, and actually it is more like a nightmare. There are many senior citizens who are on fixed incomes." The building, she continued, "is our home. Many of us have lived there since it was built. Now we are told that we must buy or move."[79]

This particular landlord, a company called American Invsco, became notorious when the media began reporting these disruptions. The firm was started in the late 1960s by the young, glamorous sister-and-brother team Evangeline and Nicholas Gouletas as a small sales and management agency. They converted their first building in 1972, and by the end of the 1970s had converted more than thirty-two hundred units in Chicago. They began buying and converting buildings in other places, including suburban Washington, D.C., and New York. More than anyone else, the Gouletas were the public face of conversion in the 1970s. Sentiment was rarely in their favor.[80]

For the elderly, forced moves could prove traumatic. In 1973, while recovering from cancer, Kathryn Eager received notice that her building, in Northwest Washington's fashionable Connecticut Avenue corridor, was converting. Rather than buy, she moved across the street to another rental. Four years later, that building converted as well. Worried about the effort of moving again—she was by then in her early seventies—and hoping to "secure a permanent place to live," Eager bought. Witnessing two conversions convinced Eager that the process was toxic. As far as she could see, it was to no one's benefit except the speculator's, and, worse yet, it was destroying the "ambiance of old neighborhoods." She was especially worried about the emotional hardship on friends who faced the "sadness of leaving . . . familiar faces and places." The inevitable results, she warned Congress in 1979, were depression, diminished will to live, and, all too often, suicide. "Doctors tell me," she claimed, "that they are treating more senior citizens for heart attacks and strokes. They call it condo disease."[81]

A second set of problems for many renters—elderly and otherwise—was the high ongoing cost of owning an apartment. Buying not only required an equity payment, but monthly costs were often steeper than in all but the newest, best-equipped rentals—at least before property taxes and mortgage interest were deducted from the owner's income. At Linda Grover's building, maintenance was nearly fifty percent higher than rent had been, and the average increase nationally was nearly seventy percent. Some writers reported increases of more than two hundred percent. (Conversely, others buyers reported ownership a bargain compared to going rentals.)

These increases defy simple explanation. Contributing factors included the cost of legally separating a single property into multiple ones, the cost of physical improvements, and rising interest rates, which meant that new mortgages were inevitably more expensive than the one the old landlord had used to buy the building. Perhaps most critical, according to economists, was an "asset pricing" gap between what "rental investors" (landlords) and "appreciation investors" (homeowners and third-party converters like American Invsco), would pay for the same property.[82] At a time of swelling condo demographics and rapid inflation, the for-sale value of an apartment—where ownership included the right to profit from future resale—was significantly higher than its rental value. Rents reflected last year's costs; sales prices reflected expectations for the future.[83]

A third set of problems with conversion concerned high-pressure, sometimes fraudulent, sales practices. According to *Playboy*, developers in Chicago sent staff to large buildings to pose as tenants, signing contracts conspicuously in lobbies and elevators in view of the tenants to suggest high demand. Some developers secretly withheld blocks of units from sale for similar purposes. A related problem was that developers sometimes sold blocks of apartments to investors. This practice was reported in San Francisco, Houston, and other cities as soon as the condo format appeared in the early 1960s. By the late 1970s groups of investors were buying as many as fifty or seventy apartments at a time in larger buildings in cities like

Chicago. The idea, presumably, was to hold them until prices rose, and then sell at a profit. Whether held by the developer or third-party investors, "warehousing" of units not only distorted prices but it delayed the establishment of self-governance, since boards became active only once sales had closed on a certain number of units, usually three-quarters.[84]

A related problem was purchase of single units as income property. Nationally, as many as one in five condominium units was operated as a rental by the 1970s (a figure somewhat higher than the one in seven single-family houses). Owning individual apartments was a boon to small-scale landlords in an era of large-scale complexes. But higher turnover among tenants, disregard for long-term physical maintenance among both the tenants and landlords, frequent failure of landlords to explain community by-laws, and absenteeism on the part of landlords in matters of project governance could cause problems that most boards were ill equipped to handle. These problems intensified as the share of renters increased and, it was suggested, when landlords owned and operated multiple units. For these reasons, most buildings began to limit the number of renters, and many management agents came to encourage by-laws prohibiting ownership of multiple units.[85]

Regulating Co-ownership

Abuses, especially in the field of mass conversion, led to serious discussions about the wisdom of co-ownership and to new efforts to regulate it. The most thorough inquiries happened at the federal level. Following an initial investigation, in 1974, into problems with the condominium in Florida, Congress staged additional hearings, in 1976 and 1979, that focused specifically on conversion. And in 1980, as directed by Congress, HUD produced an exhaustive study on the topic. Although HUD found nothing untoward in condomania overall, Congress was sufficiently concerned to pass the Condominium and Cooperative Conversion Protection and Abuse Relief Act in 1980. This law addressed earlier concerns about rec leases and management contracts, and more recent worries about the impact of conversion on "low- and moderate-income and elderly and handicapped persons." Its primary provision was to permit associations to terminate "unconscionable" rec leases and management contracts. But it also discouraged lenders from financing conversions where vulnerable populations were adversely affected, and it recommended that state and local governments require that tenants receive "adequate notice" before a conversion and the right of first refusal to purchase their units.[86]

Yet more effective in preventing hardship were improvements to state laws governing the formation and sale of co-owned multifamily housing. In Illinois, for example, the state Condominium Property Act of 1963 was amended in 1978 and again in 1981 and 1982 to require such measures as written notice to all tenants of the conversion, the right to remain a tenant for 120 days or until the end of one's lease, a full offering detailing the price of each apartment, and the right of first refusal to purchase one's unit. Calls by some in Chicago to require approval of at least some of the tenants, however, were not addressed. Many of these changes were modeled on a series of sample laws drafted by the nonprofit National Conference on Uniform State Laws. These included a "Uniform Condominium Act" in 1977, which was subsumed by a broader act covering all common-interest developments, in 1982.[87]

Local leaders also responded to mass conversion. At least twenty suburban towns in New York, for example, took advantage of a state law allowing them to offer special assistance for the elderly in converting buildings. Washington, D.C., and Los Angeles introduced requirements that developers aid tenants with relocation by contributing toward moving expenses and, sometimes, first-month's rent in a new apartment. Yet more common were moratoriums. Moratoriums were part of a larger wave of new interventions in housing markets introduced to cope with rapid social and economic changes in the 1960s and 1970s. Others included sweeping limits on all multifamily construction (rented and owned) in parts of California and Florida, and rent control, which, after decades of operation only in New York City, spread to scores of places in the 1970s, from Boston to L.A.[88]

By 1980 moratoriums on condo conversion had been deployed in Chicago, Philadelphia, San Francisco, and Washington, D.C., among other large cities, as well as in many suburban jurisdictions, including Evanston, Illinois; Fort Lee, New Jersey; Montgomery County, Maryland; and Riverside, Palo Alto, and Mountain View, California. Most moratoriums were brief and were designed to allow frenzied markets to cool for a few months. Some were enacted preemptively, like in Santa Monica, which imposed one in 1974 after just 162 units converted, most in a single high-rise. Elsewhere, longer-term prohibitions were introduced. In Washington, for example, limits were in place from 1976 through 1980. In San Francisco, a short-term ban on most condominium development in 1974 grew into a permanent system of caps on condo conversion, managed through a lottery system, accompanied by onerous renovation requirements.[89]

Regulation helped mitigate many of the problems associated with conversion and forced developers to operate more responsibly. Of equal importance, it helped ensure better distribution of the benefits of conversion. By 1980, for example, perhaps as a result of regulations, HUD found that ten percent of converted units were owned by Black people—relatively far more than the seven percent of homes overall.[90]

Conversion and Community

Exemplary of a large-scale conversion gone well was Parkfairfax, a Met Life rental project built in the 1940s outside of Washington. The insurance company sold it in the mid-1970s to a local developer named Giuseppe Cecchi. According to Cecchi—who had helped develop the Watergate complex, which included three co-ops—Met Life had reduced and deferred physical maintenance, and the seventeen hundred garden apartments were deteriorating. During the conversion Cecchi performed work that prevailing rents could not support. He also added swimming pools, tennis courts, and community buildings. Even with these improvements the sales prices were lower than for new construction in metro Washington: from just $36,000 ($120,000) for a two-bedroom row-type unit.[91]

With low prices, favorable press, and good word of mouth, the apartments sold quickly. As each section went on sale, hundreds of buyers appeared, many camping out overnight. Among the campers were Elaine and Dennis Dorsey. The couple were renting an apartment in Washington but had been hoping to buy for at least a year. According to Elaine, it was "expensive to buy" in their current neighborhood. Parkfairfax, she felt, was "the most convenient place to D.C. that we could afford." Additionally, she noted, "I love the trees and landscaping." Although waiting overnight struck some as extreme, as another woman hoping to buy said, "I spent six hours in line to see King Tut [at the National Gallery of Art]. I guess I can sacrifice one night to buy a home."[92]

Cecchi offered even better prices to the existing tenants, and more than sixty percent of them bought. To those who did not buy, he offered five-year leases—a generous term given the era's rapid inflation. An additional ten percent of the tenants participated in this program. "At Parkfairfax," Cecchi told Congress in 1979, "we proved that a properly done conversion . . . can be a blessing for all parties involved." Congress, perhaps, hardly needed convincing: among the buyers were at least four members of the House of Representatives.[93]

Linda Grover would have agreed with Cecchi that conversion could be a blessing. But unlike a developer, she also acknowledged the hard work involved in sustaining a building. Community, after all, did not form automatically; governance in particular could be rough going. After buying their building from the city, for example, Grover and her neighbors had to fill five vacancies. In accordance with standard co-op procedures they formed a screening committee—or "screaming committee" as Grover characterized it. The committee received more than a hundred applications for the five apartments, including one from a social worker who had been assigned to the building when it was condemned, and one from the old landlord who had helped run the place down![94]

The process immediately turned sour. When choosing complete strangers "to spend twenty years with," Grover noted, "you find yourself crazy with indecision. . . . It's like choosing a marriage partner, and when you form a committee to do it, it's mayhem." "Can they pay the rent?—that's all you should care about. If you're all going to play God, then I quit!" would insist one member, only to be immediately drawn into a debate about whether it would be better to write "for an extremist newspaper out of commitment or simply out of hunger."[95]

Fortunately, Grover found that, unlike in suburbia, where "people living side by side . . . can ignore each other for years . . . the intimacy of a shared plumbing leak" in a co-op "frequently produces *detente.*" In the end, the experience helped bring Grover to the idea that co-op living was not just about owning the "best and cheapest housing anywhere around," new kitchens, and profiting from resales. (Although by 1970 at least one owner had sold for $20,000, netting a gain of $15,000 [$85,000] over the cost of equity and custom renovation.) It was about creating community. For her—as for generations of co-owners—ownership allowed "impersonal New York apartment dwellers" to form a "warm haven in this cold armed camp of a city." "If our contact with our fellow residents is sometimes abrasive," she reflected, "so be it: it's contact. In a city where most people merely live next to one another, somehow we manage to live together."[96]

Not everyone relished this intimacy. Grover's husband was eager for the renovation and "enforced togetherness" to end. "Then," he explained, "most of us will be glad to go back to being New Yorkers—and seeing just the people we want to see." For Grover, however, hopscotch, barbecues, ice skating, hand-me-downs, and the "certain knowledge that anyone in the house will take in a package, look for a lost cat, or warn of an impending parking ticket" were worth the effort, and the conflict. "For all the bickering and battling," and certainly for the money and years of hard work, concluded Grover, "life in our collective has more to recommend it than just being cheaper and more lively. It's also better."[97]

Epilogue

The condomania of the 1970s—and the panic that enveloped it—quickly evaporated. One reason was oversight. New federal, state, and local regulations, while imperfect, kept many abuses to a minimum by the 1980s. Another reason was that as better data were collected it became clear that some concerns had been overblown, especially surrounding the "end" of rental housing in cities. Careful accounting revealed, in fact, that rental housing had far from ended in cities: just two percent of rental housing in the three dozen largest metropolitan markets was converted in the 1970s. In Chicago and Washington, the share was higher: five and half percent and nearly seven percent, respectively. In both, however, the phenomenon concentrated not in the city center, but in suburbia, where the rates were nine and eight percent. At the same time, the 1970s saw more than three million new rentals, or nearly ten for each unit lost to conversion. Given that nearly twenty percent of co-owned units were rented out, the small loss disappeared entirely.[1]

Condomania also subsided for demographic reasons. Baby boomers and retirees generated a huge, unprecedented market for co-ops, condos, and townhouses in the 1960s and 1970s. But the younger cohort soon began marrying and having children. When they did, most moved to houses. The entire field of multifamily housing stabilized. Annual construction of new co-ops and condos peaked at 160,000 units in 1974 but remained above 100,000 nearly every year through 1987. Then production declined. Between 1990 and 2003, fewer than fifty thousand new units were built each year; most years saw only around thirty-five thousand. Many boomers continued to live in co-owned housing, and the condo continued to serve as a popular form of housing for the next generations of yuppies, single moms, divorced dads, and other small households, but demand was much reduced from the 1970s.[2]

That said, by the millennium earlier patterns began to repeat. Aging baby boomers and "echo boomer" twentysomethings generated new demand for owned apartments and townhouses (fig. 123). Production increased, and conversion once again became commonplace in competitive housing markets, at least until the real-estate collapse of 2007. During that downturn, when many new suburban subdivisions fell into distress, some urban planners and real-estate analysts even claimed the *cause* of the downturn was this demographic shift and, beyond it, a new preference on the part of all Americans for more compact forms of settlement.

Fig. 123: Town Village at New Haven, State Bridge Road at Magenta Lane, Johns Creek, Georgia, ca. 2004. Centex, developer.

Homebuilders, they argued, failed to gauge this turn, resulting in a disastrous glut of suburban houses. History suggests these claims are overstated. The suburban century saw fundamental changes in American households and in patterns of housing consumption, but there remain many kinds of families for which the house is ideal. It is clear, however, that forty years after the condomania of the 1970s, co-ownership is more central than ever to the way Americans live and when housing construction resumes, the condo will enjoy renewed prominence.[3]

Crisis of Confidence

Since the 1970s, critics have raised serious concerns about co-ownership. The leading one has been that co-ownership is unsustainable—socially, financially, and physically. Well-to-do families in relatively small buildings on Park Avenue or Gramercy Park might succeed in running their homes well, it was implied, but the job was too complex for ordinary Americans to handle in a satisfactory manner.

Some who attacked multifamily homeownership were aggrieved owners. Fed up with rec leases and management contracts, and government reluctance to prohibit them, condo owner David Osterer warned Congress in 1974 that the whole system was unworkable. Osterer was president of the Condominium Executive Council of Florida, which represented nine hundred complexes. All, he reported, were "victimized and . . . suffering from the condominium laws of Florida." Angry and frustrated, he asked, "What gives anybody the impression a condominium can work in the first place?" He continued, "I just don't think it can work without a lot of strife and a lot of problems. . . . I propounded that question to HUD and they resented it. I propound it to you now. The question must have an answer before we go any further. Can a condominium actually work? Is it a service to the people or is it a disservice to the people that are involved?" Even with paid management, he argued, "people fight amongst themselves." Self-governance, as a result, was impossible. The end result, he predicted, could only be widespread financial failure—and ruin for all the individual homeowners. With another decade like the 1970s, he concluded, "you are going to wipe out half the middle class."[4]

These concerns were echoed in much of the professional and scholarly literature on condos in the 1980s—as well as in writing on the broader phenomenon of common-interest communities (and their governing homeowners' associations) that subsumed the condo discourse in the 1990s. In their pioneering studies of condominiums in California, for example, Carol J. Silverman, a sociologist, and Stephen E. Barton, an urban planner, argued that the condo was inherently flawed because it was a system of collective homeownership being sold to a public unwilling to accept mutual obligations. In the condo they saw a fundamental chasm between "the values associated with homeownership and the realities of condominium life," or, put differently, "the ethics of private property and those of community." An equally fundamental problem, they believed, was that condo owners often looked at their tenure as temporary and, like renters, were unmotivated to pay for necessary upkeep.[5]

To blame for this gap, they argued, were developers who sold condos as a form of "carefree" living without explaining the burdens of governance. In the 1920s, co-ops were marketed as a "continuous vacation"; in the 1950s, as offering the life of a "millionaire" (fig. 124); in the 1970s, "for people who want a 1-family home . . . but don't want to be married to a lawnmower."[6] Elsewhere condo ads promised youthfulness and sex, typically in the form of a woman in a bikini. These sales campaigns, according to Silverman and Barton, offered a contradictory "understanding of property rights that recognizes only rights and not obligations." But once he was a homeowner, they argued, the unsuspecting buyer found that he had "traded maintenance responsibilities for obligations to a community governing process which violates their idea of private property rights." As one board member

Fig. 124: Salisbury Manor, Salisbury Point, South Nyack, New York, 1958–61. Palmbrook Investing, developer; Joseph S. Riggio, architect. Advertisement, *New York Times*, September 21, 1959.

volunteered in a research interview, "My original intention in purchasing a condominium was not to be concerned with maintenance. . . . I now have that concern for 125 units" thanks to neighbors who, in Silverman's and Barton's analysis, "often did not understand, questioned, or even rejected the legitimacy of the collective dimension of association life."[7]

Although reflective of "general tensions between individualism and community in American society," Silverman and Barton saw these problems as specifically troublesome for condos because they believed the inevitable outcome would be "strain and conflict." Of equal importance was a systemic failure to emphasize the "obligations of the owner to use the property in a way which is responsible to the surrounding community," which they feared would result in physical neglect.[8]

As private governance in housing spread in the 1990s—driven in large part by rising demand for shared amenities, a weakening of local government, and market preference for extensive deed restrictions—other critics worried that "heightened aesthetic" sensitivity and "preferences for uniformity and regimentation" were threatening "personal identity."[9] As evidence, they pointed to specific condos struggling with apathy; to litigation among homeowners and between homeowners and developers; and to new sets of legislation focused specifically on improving maintenance or resolving conflicts through mediation and other alternatives to the court.[10]

A more worrisome trend, some suggested, was not only that condo living did not enlighten ("lead to larger public awareness") but that by serving homeowners who did not always participate in community governance it "weakened public life."[11] As a Canadian scholar concluded in a study of women condominium owners in Toronto, the condo represents an "accelerated process of commodification, privatization, and securitization that threatens the potential for democratic or equitable citizenship." In this model, buying an apartment substitutes for deeper connections to the city and "citizenship becomes conflated with the entrepreneurial act of investing in, and profiting from" homeownership.[12]

This kind of critique, however, is far from applicable to all co-ownership. It is based on a specific reading of the meaning and experience of just one kind of condo living: in this case, single women in brand-new city-center buildings. Their example may suggest that condominiums are "narrow communities that police their boundaries and limit contact with surrounding communities" and that the "shorter-term nature of condominium ownership decreases a sense of connectedness to the home and the neighborhood, and it limits the development of affective attachments and a sense of belonging." Such conditions, however, surely have as much to do with the specific demographics, class aspects, and geographies of this genre of neighborhood and building than with co-ownership per se.[13]

One potential fix, it has been suggested, is education of new residents: the method that Abraham Kazan and the Play Schools Association found success with in low-cost New York City co-ops in earlier eras. Silverman and Barton, however, are pessimistic. Boards "misunderstand their role," they write, "as solely concerning property management, when they ought to have been encouraging participation." Yet "getting people involved and making their involvement productive are not easy. The immediate incentives all run against involvement. It brings conflict . . . it is inefficient . . . it brings time-consuming, boring meetings."[14]

A variant of this suggestion has been to encourage use of the co-op plan of ownership rather than more liberal forms, such as the condo and common-interest townhouse. This argument was foreshadowed in Kazan's hostility to the condo. It maintains that co-ops are superior to condos because they do less to disguise the collective obligations, especially vis-à-vis the custom of screening new buyers. As political scientist Evan McKenzie, an expert in community associations, has argued, co-ops "routinely interview and screen prospective owners to ensure that they understand and accept the premises of shared ownership."[15] McKenzie is not alone in looking back toward the co-op; this form, and in particular the limited-equity co-op, continues to be admired, worldwide, as a way to lower the cost of housing.[16]

In these discussions, however, failure of the limited-equity co-op to catch on tends to be erroneously attributed to "feeble" state support for it, rather than to conflict between the need to generate sufficient interest in governance in order to ensure longevity, on the one hand, and the need to restrict private rights in ownership through paternalistic by-laws, on the other. Proposals to replace the condo with the co-op also overlook the fact that screening is neither inherent to the co-op nor prohibited in the condo.

More troubling is that co-op romantics fail to acknowledge how the format also trades on misinformed ideas that conflate co-ownership with individual ownership, but in a potentially far more damaging way than in the condo. In the case of the co-op, homeowners are encouraged to believe that they may exclude whomever they like from the entire building, as if the building—and not just their unit—were their home. An apartment house is private in certain respects, but in others it is no more so than a movie theater or restaurant. To suggest otherwise is to court a dangerous, retrograde world of arbitrary exclusion.

There is, additionally, the more practical issue that, with the exception of New York, Washington, and perhaps a few other places it remains difficult to get mortgages for co-ops in the U.S. Even seemingly well-qualified candidates (such as tenured college professors) buying into limited-equity projects in places like Boston in the twenty-first century find they must put down thirty percent or more in cash to qualify for financing.

The co-op, in the form of limited-equities, remains a valuable tool for maintaining affordable housing. And since UHF collapsed in the 1970s, others have worked to support this model, most recently in mobile-home parks and in community land trusts. The co-op, however, is unlikely to solve problems of agency and governance in co-owned housing.[17]

A more productive solution might be to find new ways to educate buyers. States could, for example, encourage or require highly circumscribed board interviews in all co-owned housing. Or states could introduce mandatory preoccupancy training at closing, perhaps in the form of a simple statement to be read and signed—or a video to be screened—explaining that there are mutual obligations in condos and townhouses and that one is required by contract, and by law, to pay maintenance and follow by-laws. As Silverman and Barton suggest, a yet better solution might be to make education part of boards' duties. But boards are composed of volunteers, busy with their daily lives and not necessarily skilled in the art of training. Furthermore, even the most basic strategy—knocking on new residents' doors— could be awkward, especially where new owners are hostile to the idea of community governance. A simple document or video, presented in a neutral setting like the office of the closing attorney, might help.

The Condominium Promise

Collective homeownership in the U.S. is far from perfect. Piecemeal evidence from the field suggests that litigation among co-owners is rising, along with the number of co-ownership associations. A leading Sunday afternoon radio show in Broward County, Florida, is *Condo Craze and HOA's*, hosted by a local real-estate attorney.

Several states, including Florida, Nevada, New York, and Connecticut, have created, or are considering, offices dedicated to resolving disputes among co-owners, along with new statewide requirements for internal dispute-resolution procedures within co-op, condo, and townhouse associations.[18]

In other respects, however, the American system of co-ownership is exemplary. In China, Israel, Australia, New Zealand, and beyond, problems run far deeper. In Hong Kong, for example, co-ownership is organized, in effect, on the model of the makeshift San Francisco TIC, and while a governing homeowners' association is encouraged, none is required by the state. In mainland China, associations are more common. But because their goals are at odds with developers' imperative to minimize interference from homeowners during sales, these bodies are extremely weak. In New South Wales, lack of prohibitions against management contracts has led to a recent spate of abuses in Sydney that recalls Miami in the 1960s. In Israel, weak legislation has meant endemic lack of maintenance and early obsolescence in many moderate-income buildings.[19]

To the extent that physical or social deterioration is evident in U.S. co-ops, condos, and townhouses at all, it is very mild. And in many cases, gentle decline has, in the long tradition of "filtering," created housing opportunities for new clienteles. At Aventura, for example, age has opened the community to younger households and to middle-class families from Latin America, who keep Miami condos as pieds-à-terre. This is not to suggest that there has been physical neglect. To the contrary, the original Morris Lapidus buildings are well maintained. They are, however, quite dated and the apartments far more modest in size and appointment than those in more recent buildings. Original units were eight hundred to sixteen hundred square feet, typically with one or two balconies of sixty or eighty square feet. By the 1990s, the smallest new apartments at many neighboring buildings had thirty-three hundred square feet, with two bedrooms, three and a half baths, and a media room, plus an outdoor terrace with an additional three hundred square feet. These units sold for around $675,000 at the millennium. Older units which had initially cost $22,000 in 1971 ($116,000 in 2010 dollars) resold for $55,000 in 1982 ($124,000) but just $85,000 in 2001 ($101,000)—one-third the price per square foot of the newer, better-equipped apartments.

This sort of filtering is also evident in year-round cities and suburbs. In the Gulfton section of Houston, for example, garden-apartment complexes developed in the 1970s as rentals for young, white "swinging singles" are now inhabited by new immigrants of limited means. Several buildings tenanted by Vietnamese families—and, thanks to Houston's lack of zoning, shops—have been converted to condo under the direction of a local pastor. Called "village communities," they offer recent arrivals an affordable way to buy real estate outside of the mainstream market. More importantly, they furnish a degree of control over living conditions that most recent immigrants, in rented housing, lack. Although condo (and therefore not a rejection of the speculative market), these efforts parallel those of earlier generations of Finnish and Jewish immigrants to house themselves through the limited-equity co-op.[20]

In Sunbelt cities like Atlanta, co-ownership has also served the additional (and surely unintended) purpose of protecting lower-cost multifamily housing from redevelopment. Much of the city's multifamily housing is in older suburban sections near secondary business districts. As middle-class white consumers, for whom the apartments were originally intended, choose newer complexes, older ones become tenanted primarily with new-immigrant families. To purge these populations developers are encouraged to replace buildings with newer, higher-rent ones, in part with new zoning incentives permitting higher densities and mixed uses, including highly profitable retail space, all in the name of smart growth. The result has been myriad new Peachtree palazzos and gated "townhome" groups, except where the older buildings are in co-ownership. Ironically, many of the new buildings are also owner-occupied, which all but guarantees them a place in the city far beyond their initial run as middle class.[21]

Ownership Matters

That a building is co-op or condo remains central to its identity in the twenty-first century. As in the 1880s it transforms an ordinary apartment building into a "private residence" (fig. 125). The disruption caused by renters underscores this idea. In a recent Sunday *New York Times* real-estate profile, a twenty-eight-year-old magazine editor rejected an apartment in an Art Deco building designed by Emery Roth (converted to co-op in 1987) because of the number of subtenants. Not only would they make financing more difficult (lenders are wary of the problems caused by renters), but he looked elsewhere because he "wanted a sense of community." Conversely (and perhaps ironically), co-ops and condos tend to carry higher status for renters than conventional complexes, and often fetch premium rents.[22]

The importance of ownership is also evident in distinctions between formats. In New York especially, co-ops and condos not only are treated differently under the law, but they confer different levels of status and command different sales prices. For many years, condos were rare in New York. New York had much experience with co-ops by the time condos were introduced, and banks were wary. Things began to change with Olympic Tower, a fifty-story condominium on Fifth Avenue designed by Skidmore, Owings & Merrill, developed by Aristotle Onassis and Arlen

Fig. 125: "Midtown's Premier Private Residence," Mayfair Tower, 199 Fourteenth Street NE, Atlanta, ca. 1989. Laing Properties, developer; Smallwood, Reynolds, Stewart, Stewart & Associates, architect.

Properties (Don Soffer's partner at Aventura), which opened in 1975. Five years later, Donald Trump began work on his first condominium tower. By the mid-1980s the condo began to overtake the co-op among new buildings. By the twenty-first century, more then ninety percent of new for-sale buildings in New York City were condo. As everywhere else in the U.S., most people in New York preferred fewer restrictions, especially on resales.[23]

To this end, a distinct price gap emerged beginning in the 1980s, with condos commanding premiums of between eight and thirteen percent over comparable co-ops (sales agents claimed gaps of up to twenty percent). A similar trend was observed in Washington, D.C. The comparison was imprecise. Condos, especially in New York, are overwhelmingly new construction, while co-ops are generally older. Even so, the condo premium holds. As if to concede the point, most new co-ops by the millennium advertised that they had "condo" resale rules.[24] The one exception to this rule is the very top of the market, where the condo bonus not only disappears but becomes a liability of twenty-five percent. A good part of the reason for this seems to be that co-ops continue to enjoy legal and financial privileges, including arbitrary exclusion. With time, one hopes, this ill-gotten premium will disappear—and by the early twenty-first century extremely expensive new condominiums like 15 Central Park West began to destabilize the old order. Sixty years after the city's anti-bias bill, however, many in New York still see the co-op as high-class and the condo as nouveau riche.[25]

Especially worrisome in this regard is that as condos become more expensive some are adopting co-op rules. FHA has long prohibited even the right of first refusal in the condos it insures. But in expensive neighborhoods, where FHA is of little concern, some associations have started screening buyers. In 2005 a state court upheld an amendment to an East Side condominium's by-laws prohibiting unapproved sales and rentals except to people who already own in the building. Active engagement on the part of boards is to be commended. This legal creep toward arbitrary exclusion, however, ought to be prohibited.[26]

Condominium Prospects

In the early 1960s, when the condo idea first circulated, many described co-ownership as offering a solution to the nation's urban problems, especially the low rates of low-income and city-center homeownership, and untrammeled suburbanization. As the trade journal *California Builder* reported in 1963, "Enthusiasm . . . had led to sweeping claims that this form of ownership will solve many if not most of the current housing problems."[27] Similarly optimistic expectations were evident in the early 2010s in discussions about the overproduction of suburban single-family houses, and in hopes that the nation could climb out of the Great Recession by stimulating production of "walkable" New Urbanism: compact neighborhoods with a high share of row houses and apartments.[28]

While an unlikely panacea, co-owned housing may well dominate new construction when the housing market lifts. Baby boomers brought condomania to metropolitan America between the 1960s and 1980s, and as seniors they are poised to unleash a new wave between the 2010s and 2030s. At the same time, there are ever more households of all kinds who can afford to own a home but who neither want nor need whole houses. As in the 1970s they include single women, smaller families, and dual-income families. Indeed, since condomania, household size has continued to fall. Meanwhile, in spite of growing income inequality, purchasing power in housing has grown, in part as a result of risky mortgage financing, but mainly due to innovations in prefabrication and other construction technologies that have lowered the cost of housing relative to that of other goods and services.

Also pointing to a bright condominium future for metropolitan America is the substantial long-term growth in the cosmopolitan middle class of creative types and of white-collar workers. This promises an expansion of "bourgeois bohemia" to new areas of cities and, in turn, more co-ownership. The politics of rent control and conversion will also continue to mediate change, as suggested by recent support for conversion of yet another Met Life project (Stuyvesant Town, in Manhattan), and new debate in San Francisco about TIC and restrictions on condo conversion. In the suburbs, meanwhile, townhouses remain more popular than ever, especially with the growth of New Urbanism.

Regardless of the specific conditions—new construction or conversion, co-op or condo, city or suburb, townhouse or high-rise, newlywed or nearly dead, single mom or *Sex and the City*—ownership will continue to matter to Americans, ensuring that the condo will remain a common fact of the American built environment in the twenty-first century.

For at least two generations, co-owned housing has been regarded by many critics as aberrant—a mysterious, temporary violation of U.S. suburban exceptionalism. But what if the mass suburbanization of the 1950s and the inner-city disinvestment of the 1960s were the historical exceptions, fueled by a brief period of highly progressive income taxes or temporary restrictions against foreign immigration? What if these changes were part of a one-time historical shift of the working-class from center to periphery? What if middle-class living at both center and periphery is the norm? What if homeownership matters more than physical form? The history of the condo cannot answer these questions, but it does suggest new ambiguities, new gaps in our knowledge, and new continuities between city and suburb, between house and apartment, and between the imagined golden age of American urbanism before World War II, when people lived in apartment houses and shopped downtown, and the degraded and polarized now of shrinking cities, starchitecture, and sprawl.

According to the most recent published national housing data, the U.S. has nearly ten million co-ops and condos, and perhaps an additional seven million townhouses. In metro New York and Miami, including suburban districts, nearly one in three owner-occupied homes is multifamily. In Washington and Chicago, one in four; in greater Boston one in five, and in both Northern and Southern California, one in six. Even in thinly settled cities like Houston, Phoenix, and Atlanta, between one in fifteen and one in twenty owner-occupied homes is an apartment or townhouse. A driving tour of any of these cities today, including their newest, most peripheral suburban sections, reveals a varied and complex residential landscape. Now more than ever we are living in the age of the condo. Many problems with co-ownership persist. But history all but assures it will continue to adapt, and improve.[29]

Notes

The following abbreviations appear in the notes.

ChT   Chicago Tribune
CB   California Builder
EM   El Mundo (San Juan, Puerto Rico)
FB   Florida Builder
FT   Florida Trend
GPO   Government Printing Office
HH   House & Home
LAT   Los Angeles Times
MH   Miami Herald
NYT   New York Times
VF   Vertical Files, Loeb Design Library, Harvard University
WP   Washington Post

INTRODUCTION

1. "Filosophical Phoolishness," Bell Park News XX, no. 7 (Oct. 1970): 3.
2. Charles H. Lavigne, "Why Did These Co-ops Fail?" Bell Park News XIX, no. 1 (Feb. 1969): 2.
3. Ibid.
4. "Joseph King Appointed Chief Security Guard," Bell Park News XIX, no. 3 (Apr. 1969): 1; Bell Park News XX, no. 1 (Jan. 1970).
5. Lavigne, "Why Did These Co-ops Fail?"
6. Bell Park News XIX, no. 1 (Feb. 1969): 3; XIX, no. 3 (Apr. 1969): 1; XIX, no. 4 (May 1969): 1.
7. "17 Teenagers Block Council Offices, Hold Bell Park News Editor Captive, Present 7 'Non-Negotiable' Demands," Bell Park News XIX, no. 8 (Dec. 1969): 1.
8. "Status of Apartment Lists," Bell Park News XX, no. 7 (Oct. 1970): 3.
9. William Hollingsworth Whyte, The Organization Man (New York: Simon and Schuster, 1956); Betty Friedan, The Feminine Mystique (New York: Norton, 1963); "co-op-er-a-tive," Bell Park News XX, no. 7 (Oct. 1970): 1.
10. On "suburban century," see, for example, Robert Beuka, SuburbiaNation: Reading Suburban Landscape in Twentieth-century American Fiction and Film (New York: Palgrave Macmillan, 2004), 230; Mark Clapson, The Suburban Century: Social Change and Urban Growth in England and the USA (Oxford: Berg, 2003).
11. U.S., Department of Housing and Urban Development, Office of Policy Development and Research and Department of Commerce, Economics and Statistics Administration, U.S. Census Bureau, American Housing Survey for the United States: 2009, Current Housing Reports (Washington, D.C.: GPO, 2011), 1; U.S. Department of Commerce, Bureau of the Census, 1960 Census of Housing, vol. 1, part 1 (Washington, D.C.: GPO, 1961), 1–1.
12. Since the 1950s it has been a trope in writing about cities that the American system has restricted variety in housing. For a critique, see David Steigerwald, "All Hail the Republic of Choice: Consumer History as Contemporary Thought," Journal of American History 93, no. 2 (Sept. 2006).
13. Maryann Haggerty, "A Hand Up, Together," WP 13 Feb. 2010; Jeff Vandam, "Making History in a Brooklyn Neighborhood," NYT 14 Jan. 2010: RE2; Eugénie L. Birch,

"Downtown in the 'New American City,'" The Annals of the American Academy of Political Science 626, no. 11 (Nov. 2009).

14. Michael Gross, "15 CPW," New York Observer 17 July 2007; Mireya Navarro, "Downsizing in Los Angeles: From Mansion to $47 Million Condo," NYT 21 Aug. 2008: A1.
15. See, for example, Loretta Lees, Tom Slater, and Elvin Wyly, Gentrification (New York: Routledge, 2008), 89–121. For work that does specifically consider the housing, see Joe Moran, "Early Cultures of Gentrification in London, 1955–1980," Journal of Urban History 34, no. 1 (Nov. 2007); Sharon Zukin, Loft Living: Culture and Capital in Urban Change (New Brunswick: Rutgers University Press, 1989); Paul Groth, Living Downtown: The History of Residential Hotels in the United States (Berkeley: University of California Press, 1994); A. K. Sandoval-Strausz, Hotel: An American History (New Haven: Yale University Press, 2007); Elizabeth Collins Cromley, Alone Together: A History of New York's Early Apartments (Ithaca, N.Y.: Cornell University Press, 1990).
16. On gentrification debate, see Lees et al., Gentrification, chaps. 2 and 3.
17. Mason C. Doan, American Housing Production, 1880–2000: A Concise History (Lanham, Md.: University Press of America, 1997), 3; Dowell Myers and John Pitkin, "Demographic Forces and Turning Points in the American City, 1950–2040," Annals of the American Academy of Political Science 626, no. 11 (Nov. 2009); Arthur C. Nelson, "The New Urbanity: The Rise of a New America," Annals of the American Academy of Political Science 626, no. 11 (Nov. 2009); Sabrina Tavernise, "Married Couples Are No Longer a Majority, Census Finds," NYT 26 May 2011: A22.
18. Michelle Bina and Kara M. Kockelman, "Location Choice vis-à-vis Transportation: The Case of Recent Homebuyers," International Association of Travel Behavior Research Conference, Kyoto, Japan, 16–20 Aug. 2006, http://www.ce.utexas.edu/prof/kockelman/public_html/TRB06HomeChoice.pdf [1 Mar. 2010]: 8; Gwendolyn Wright, Building the Dream: A Social History of Housing in America (New York: Pantheon, 1981), 274.
19. Neil Smith, "Of Yuppies and Housing: Gentrification, Social Restructuring, and the Urban Dream," Environment and Planning Society and Space 5, no. 2 (1987): 164.
20. See, for example, Suleiman Osman, The Invention of Brownstone Brooklyn: Gentrification and the Search for Authenticity in Postwar New York (Oxford: Oxford University Press, 2011).
21. On inequality, see Douglas S. Massey et al., "The Changing Bases of Segregation in the United States," Annals of the American Academy of Political Science 626, no. 11 (Nov. 2009): 81–82. On distaste for renting, see Roger Starr, "An End to Rental Housing?" National Affairs 57 (Fall 1979). On historical rates of homeownership by income, see Irving Welfeld, Where We Live: A Social History of American Housing (New York: Simon and Schuster, 1988), 58.
22. On women and the condo market, see Lisa Iannucci, "Women Homeowners on the Rise," New Jersey Cooperator, Feb. 2007.

23. Osman, *Invention of Brownstone Brooklyn,* 8–10; Moran, "Early Cultures of Gentrification in London."

24. Daniel Rodgers, *Atlantic Crossings: Social Politics in a Progressive Age* (Cambridge: Belknap, 1998), 162; Louis Winnick, *Rental Housing: Opportunities for Private Investment* (New York: McGraw-Hill, 1958), 241; Welfeld, *Where We Live,* 64–69; U.S., Department of Housing and Urban Development, *The Conversion of Rental Housing to Condominiums and Cooperatives: National Study of Scope, Causes and Impacts* (Washington, D.C.: GPO, 1980), VI-19.

25. On the link between government suburbanization, see, for example, Kenneth T. Jackson, "A Nation of Cities: The Federal Government and the Shape of the American Metropolis," *Annals of the American Academy of Political Science* 626, no. 11 (Nov. 2009): 15. For an opposing view, see Doan, *American Housing Production 1880–2000,* 61–62.

26. bell hooks, "City Living: Love's Meeting Place," in *The Unknown City: Contesting Architecture and Social Space,* ed. Iain Borden, Joe Kerr, and Jane Rendell (Cambridge: MIT Press, 2001), 440–41.

27. Richard H. Thaler, "Economic View: Underwater, But Will They Leave the Pool?" *NYT* 23 Jan. 2010: BU3; Constance Perin, *Everything in Its Place: Social Order and Land Use in America* (Princeton: Princeton University Press, 1977); Matthew D. Lassiter, *The Silent Majority: Suburban Politics in the Suburban South* (Princeton: Princeton University Press, 2007), 9.

28. For a skeptical account, see Evan McKenzie, *Privatopia: Homeowner Associations and the Rise of Residential Private Government* (New Haven: Yale University Press, 1994), 108. For a rebuttal, see Julia Lave Johnston and Kimberly Johnston-Dodds, *Common Interest Development: Housing at Risk?* (Sacramento: California Research Bureau, 2002), 12.

29. Pearl Janet Davies, *Real Estate in American History* (Washington, D.C.: Public Affairs, 1958), 1. For a survey of the field of property rights advocacy, see Harvey M. Jacobs, "Introduction: Is All That Is Solid Melting into Air?" in *Private Property in the 21st Century,* ed. Harvey M. Jacobs and Lincoln Institute of Land Policy (Cheltenham, U.K.: Edward Elgar, 2004).

30. Richard Louv, *America II* (Los Angles: Jeremy P. Tarcher, 1983), 123; Jack Ziegler, cartoon, *New Yorker* 3 Sept. 1984: 47.

31. On the evolution and malleability of rights in property in the twentieth-century U.S., see, for example, Jerold S. Kayden, "Charting the Constitutional Course of Private Property: Learning from the 20th Century Ideal," in *Private Property in the 21st Century,* ed. Harvey M. Jacobs.

32. David T. Beito, Peter Gordon, and Alexander Tabarrok, *The Voluntary City: Choice, Community, and Civil Society* (Ann Arbor: The Independent Institute; Ann Arbor: University of Michigan Press, 2002); Witold Rybczynski, *Last Harvest: How a Cornfield Became New Daleville—Real Estate Development in America from George Washington to the Builders of the Twenty-first Century, and Why We Live in Houses Anyway* (New York: Scribner, 2007), 133, 137; McKenzie, *Privatopia,* chap. 6.

33. Nelson N. Foote et al., *Housing Choices and Housing Constraints* (New York: McGraw Hill, 1960), 430; Myers and Pitkin, "Demographic Forces and Turning Points in the American City, 1950–2040," 95; Bina and Kockelman, "Location Choice vis-à-vis Transportation"; Brian Roe, Elena G. Irwin, and Hazel A. Morrow-Jones, "Changes in Homeowner Preferences for Housing Density Following 11 September 2001," *Applied Economics Letters* 12 (2005): 73–78; Misun Hur and Hazel Morrow-Jones, "Factors That Influence Residents' Satisfaction with Neighborhoods," *Environment and Behavior* 40, no. 5 (Sept. 2008); Hazel A. Morrow-Jones, "The Thinning Metropolis: The Role of Repeat Home Buyer Purchases in Decreasing Density," Thinning Metropolis Conference, Cornell University, Ithaca, N.Y., 8–9 Sept. 2000, http://facweb.knowlton.ohio-state.edu/hmorrow-jones/crpinfo/research/thinning.pdf [1 Mar. 2010]; Rybczynski, *Last Harvest,* 227.

34. Marjorie Garber, *Sex and Real Estate: Why We Love Houses* (New York: Pantheon, 2000), 24.

35. Existing studies include Peter Eisenstadt, *Rochdale Village: Robert Moses, 6,000 Families, and New York City's Great Experiment in Integrated Housing* (Ithaca, N.Y.: Cornell University Press, 2010); Leslie Kern, *Sex and the Revitalized City: Gender, Condominium Development, and Urban Citizenship* (Vancouver: UBC, 2010); Sarah Blandy, Ann Dupuis, and Jennifer Dixon, eds., *Multi-owned Housing: Law, Power and Practice* (Farnham, Surrey, U.K.: Ashgate, 2010); McKenzie, *Privatopia;* Stephen E. Barton and Carol J. Silverman, eds., *Common Interest Communities: Private Governments and the Public Interest* (Berkeley: Institute of Governmental Studies Press, University of California, Berkeley, 1994).

36. David Parry, "First Three Quarters 2009 San Francisco Market Survey," www.classicsfproperties.com [3 June 2010]; Scott James, "A Path to Homeownership Is Becoming a Burden," *NYT,* San Francisco Bay Area Edition, 4 Feb 2011: A19A.

37. For an overview of the legal history of the co-op in New York, see Rosemarie Maldonado and Robert D. Rose, "The Application of Civil Rights Laws to Housing Cooperatives: Are Co-ops Bastions of Discriminatory Exclusion or Self-selecting Models of Community-based Living?" *Fordham Urban Law Journal* 23 (Summer 1996).

38. Explanation of these indices, as well as a value calculator that converts historic prices to current (and earlier) equivalents, may be found on the "Measuring Worth" pages (www.measuringworth.com) of the Economic History Services Internet site (www.eh.net), co-sponsored by Miami University in Ohio and Wake Forest University.

39. A few histories have at least mentioned the condo. See, for example, Robert Bruegmann, *Sprawl: A Compact History* (Chicago: University of Chicago Press, 2005); Wright, *Building the Dream,* 258–61; Dolores Hayden, *Redesigning the American Dream: The Future of Housing, Work, and Family Life,* rev. ed. (New York: W. W. Norton, 2002), 184; John Hancock, "The Apartment House in Urban America," in *Buildings and Society: Essays on the Social Development*

of the Built Environment, ed. Anthony D. King (London: Routledge and Kegan Paul, 1980).

40. Dell Upton, "Architectural History of Landscape History?" *Journal of Architectural Education* 44, no. 4 (Aug. 1991); Robert Venturi, Denise Scott Brown, and Steven Izenour, *Learning from Las Vegas*, rev. ed. (Cambridge: MIT Press, 1972); Katharine G. Bristol, "The Pruitt-Igoe Myth," *Journal of Architectural Education* 44, no. 3 (May 1991); Peirce F. Lewis, "Axioms for Reading the Landscape: Some Guides to the American Scene," in *The Interpretation of Ordinary Landscapes*, ed. D. W. Meinig (New York: Oxford University Press, 1979); Edward Relph, *The Modern Urban Landscape, 1880 to the Present* (Baltimore: Johns Hopkins University Press, 1987).

41. Larry R. Ford, "Multiunit Housing in the American City," *Geographical Review* 76, no. 4 (Oct. 1986); Larry R. Ford, *Cities and Buildings: Skyscrapers, Skid Rows, and Suburbs* (Baltimore: Johns Hopkins University Press, 1994), chap. 5.

42. Lizabeth Cohen, *A Consumer's Republic: The Politics of Mass Consumption in Postwar America* (New York: Knopf, 2003); John Archer, *Architecture and Suburbia: From English Villa to American Dream House, 1690–2000* (Minneapolis: University of Minnesota Press, 2005); Dolores Hayden, *Building Suburbia: Green Fields and Urban Growth, 1820–2000* (New York: Pantheon Books, 2003); Kenneth T. Jackson, *Crabgrass Frontier: The Suburbanization of the United States* (1985; New York: Oxford University Press, 1987); Robert Fishman, *Bourgeois Utopias: The Rise and Fall of Suburbia* (New York: Basic Books, 1987); Wright, *Building the Dream*. For critiques, see Mary Corbin Sies, "North American Suburbs, 1880–1950: Cultural and Social Considerations," *Journal of Urban History* 27, no. 3 (Mar. 2001); Bruegmann, *Sprawl*.

43. Early references equating co-ownership with modernity are too many to list. See, for example, Frank Parker, "Cooperative Apartments Good Home Investment," *WP* 23 Aug. 1925: E2; display advertisement, *ChT* 13 July 1926: 5.

44. In Scotland "house" still refers to a suite of rooms in a multifamily building, regardless of tenure. In France *maison* may refer to both a single-family house and a multifamily building. In other former English colonies the situation is much the same as in the U.S. In most of Canada the term "condominium" is used as in the U.S., although in British Columbia, as in Australia, the system is referred to as "strata title." In Australia, homes under strata ownership are typically called "units."

On Scotland, see Frank Worsdall, *The Tenement: A Way of Life; A Social, Historical and Architectural Study of Housing in Glasgow* (Edinburgh: Chambers, 1979). On France, see Sharon Marcus, *Apartment Stories: City and Home in Nineteenth-century Paris and London* (Berkeley: University of California Press, 1999). On Australia, Caroline Butler-Bowdon and Charles Pickett, *Homes in the Sky: Apartment Living in Australia* (Carlton, Australia: Miegunyah, 2007).

45. Henri Lefebvre, "Right to the City," in *Writings on Cities*, trans. and ed. Eleonore Kofman and Elizabeth Lebas (Malden, Mass.: Blackwell, 1996), 78; John Brinckerhoff Jackson, "Other-directed Houses" (1956–57), in *Landscape in Sight: Looking at America*, ed. Helen Lefkowitz Horowitz

(New Haven: Yale University Press, 2000); Herbert J. Gans, *The Levittowners: Ways of Life and Politics in a New Suburban Community* (New York: Pantheon, 1967); Venturi, Brown, and Izenour, *Learning from Las Vegas*.

46. Margaret Crawford, "Introduction," in *Everyday Urbanism*, expanded ed., ed. John Leighton Chase, Margaret Crawford, and John Kaliski (New York: Monacelli, 2008), 8.

47. Michel de Certeau, *The Practice of Everyday Life*, trans. Steven Rendall (Berkeley: University of California Press, 1984); Ben Highmore, "Introduction: Questioning Everyday Life," in *The Everyday Life Reader*, ed. Ben Highmore (London: Routledge, 2002), 5, 12–13.

48. Lewis, "Axioms for Reading the Landscape," 15; Relph, *Modern Urban Landscape*, 2; Upton, "Architectural History of Landscape History?" 197.

49. On postwar homebuilding, see D. J. Waldie, *Holy Land: A Suburban Memoir* (New York: W. W. Norton, 1996); Barbara M. Kelly, *Expanding the American Dream: Building and Rebuilding Levittown* (Albany, 1993); Gregory C. Randall, *America's Original GI Town: Park Forest, Illinois* (Baltimore: Johns Hopkins University Press, 2000); Rob Keil, *Little Boxes: The Architecture of a Classic Midcentury Suburb* (Daly City, Calif.: Advection, 2006); James Thomas Keane, *Fritz B. Burns and the Development of Los Angeles: The Biography of a Community Developer and Philanthropist* (Los Angeles: Thomas and Dorothy Leavey Center for the Study of Los Angeles, Loyola Marymount University; Historical Society of Southern California, 2001); Edward P. Eichler and Marshall Kaplan, *The Community Builders*, 2d ed. (Berkeley: University of California Press, 1970).

50. Setha Low, *Behind the Gates: Life, Security, and the Pursuit of Happiness in Fortress America* (New York: Routledge, 2003); McKenzie, *Privatopia*; Edward J. Blakely and Mary Gail Snyder, *Fortress America: Gated Communities in the United States* (Washington D.C.: Brookings Institution, and Cambridge: Lincoln Institute of Land Policy, 1999); Robert Fogelson, *Bourgeois Nightmares: Suburbia, 1870–1930* (New Haven: Yale University Press, 2005).

51. Hayden, *Building Suburbia*, 213.

52. Charles Abrams, *The Future of Housing* (New York: Harper, 1946), 75.

53. Exemplary is the recent Eisenstadt, *Rochdale Village*.

CHAPTER 1. THE BROWNE DECADES

1. Elizabeth Collins Cromley, *Alone Together: A History of New York's Early Apartments* (Ithaca, N.Y.: Cornell University Press, 1990), 11–20; A. K. Sandoval-Strausz, "Home for a World of Strangers: Hospitality and the Origins of Multiple Dwellings in Urban America," *Journal of Urban History* 33, no. 6 (Sept. 2007): 937–44; Richard Plunz, *A History of Housing in New York City* (New York: Columbia University Press, 1990), 22.

2. Junius Henri Browne, *The Great Metropolis; a Mirror of New York: A Complete History of Metropolitan Life and Society, with Sketches of Prominent Places, Persons and Things in the City, as they Actually Exist* (Hartford: American, 1869), 205, 398.

3. Junius Henri Browne, "The Problem of Living in New York," *Harper's New Monthly Magazine* 65 (Nov. 1882): 920.

4. Elizabeth Cromley, "The Development of American Apartment Houses from the Civil War to the Depression; I. Introduction, Boston, Chicago, New York, and Washington, D.C.: Housing Context for the First Apartment House Development," *Architectura* 21 no. 1 (1991): 50; A. K. Sandoval-Strausz, *Hotel: An American History* (New Haven: Yale University Press, 2007), chap. 9; Cromley, *Alone Together*, chaps. 1–3; Wendy Gamber, *The Boardinghouse in Nineteenth-century America* (Baltimore: Johns Hopkins University Press, 2007).

5. "Junius Henri Browne," *NYT* 3 Apr. 1902: 9.

6. Daniel Rodgers, *Atlantic Crossings: Social Politics in a Progressive Age* (Cambridge: Belknap, 1998), 8.

7. Dell Upton, *Another City: Urban Life and Urban Spaces in the New American Republic* (New Haven: Yale University Press, 2008), 323–24. See also Elizabeth Blackmar, *Manhattan for Rent, 1785–1850* (Ithaca, N.Y.: Cornell University Press, 1989), chap. 6.

8. John R. Stilgoe, *Borderland: Origins of the American Suburb, 1820–1939* (New Haven: Yale University Press, 1988), 98. See also John Archer, *Architecture and Suburbia: From English Villa to American Dream House, 1690–2000* (Minneapolis: University of Minnesota Press, 2005), chap. 4; Robert Fishman, *Bourgeois Utopias: The Rise and Fall of Suburbia* (New York: Basic, 1987); Kenneth T. Jackson, *Crabgrass Frontier: The Suburbanization of the United States* (New York: Columbia University Press, 1985), Introduction, chaps. 3 and 5.

9. Gary Cross, "The Suburban Weekend: Perspectives on a Vanishing Twentieth-Century Dream," in *Visions of Suburbia*, ed. Roger Silverstone (London: Routledge, 1997); Sandoval-Strausz, "Home for a World of Strangers," 943.

10. "Apartment Houses," *NYT* 14 Jan. 1872: 4; "French Flats," *NYT* 26 Dec. 1876: 2; Robert A. M. Stern, Thomas Mellins, and David Fishman, *New York 1880: Architecture and Urbanism in the Gilded Age* (New York: Monacelli, 1999), 553.

11. Central Home Association, *Palace Home*, prospectus (1860), Classics Collection, Avery Architectural and Fine Arts Library, Columbia University.

12. Ibid. On Johnson, see Turpin C. Bannister, "Bogardus Revisited: Part I, The Iron Fronts," *Journal of the Society of Architectural Historians* 15, no. 4 (Dec. 1956): 17; Bannister, "Bogardus Revisited: Part II, The Iron Towers," *Journal of the Society of Architectural Historians* 16, no. 1 (Mar. 1957): 14.

13. "Where and How to Live in New-York," *NYT* 26 Apr. 1870: 4; "Looking for a House," *NYT* 9 Apr. 1871: 5.

14. "Homes at Small Expense," *NYT* 30 Jan. 1881: 10.

15. "Apartment Houses," 14 Jan. 1872: 4; "Why Don't They Marry?" *NYT* 24 Oct. 1874: 6; "A Revolution in Living," *NYT* 3 June 1878: 4; "Where and How to Live in New-York," *NYT* 26 Apr. 1870: 4; "Looking for a House," *NYT* 9 Apr. 1871: 5.

16. Jared N. Day, *Urban Castles: Tenement Housing and Landlord Activism in New York City, 1890–1943* (New York: Columbia University Press, 1999), 19–21.

17. "Apartment-Houses," *NYT* 7 Sept. 1870: 4; Roger Starr, "An End to Rental Housing?" *National Affairs* 57 (Fall 1979): 25–38.

18. Stern et al., *New York 1880*, 538; Cromley, *Alone Together*, chap. 4.

19. On Hubert's life, see "Philip Gengembre Hubert," *A History of California and an Extended History of Los Angeles and Environs*, vol. 3 (Los Angeles: Historic Record Company, 1915); "New York Apartments Little Changed in 30 Years," *NYT* 12 July 1914: SM8; Emilie McCreery, "The French Architect of the Allegheny City Hall," *Western Pennsylvania Historical Magazine* 14, no. 3 (July 1931); C. Matlack Price, "A Pioneer in Apartment House Architecture," *Architectural Record* 26, no. 1 (July 1914); City of New York, Landmarks Preservation Commission, *146 East 89th Street House, Borough of Manhattan* (New York: City of New York, 1979); Christopher Gray, "Philip Gengembre Hubert: The 19th-century Innovator Who Invented the Co-op," *NYT* 15 Aug. 2004: RE8.

20. Hubert's writings include Hubert, Pirsson & Hoddick, "New York Flats and French Flats," *Architectural Record* 2, no. 1 (1892): 55–64; Hubert, Pirsson & Company, *The Central Park Apartments*, prospectus (ca. 1881), Classics Collection, Avery Architectural and Fine Arts Library, Columbia University; Hubert, Pirsson & Hoddick, *Where and How to Build with Plans and Sketches of Cottages and City Houses, Schools, Churches, Theatres, and Apartment Houses*, prospectus (ca. 1892), Classics Collection, Avery Architectural and Fine Arts Library, Columbia University.

21. Hubert, Pirsson & Hoddick, "New York Flats and French Flats," 56–57.

22. Ibid., 58–59.

23. Hubert, Pirsson & Company, *Central Park Apartments*, 17–18.

24. City of New York, Landmarks Preservation Commission, *146 East 89th Street House;* "New Apartment-Houses," *Scribner's Monthly* 21, no. 6 (Apr. 1881): 964–65; "Co-operative Buildings," *Real Estate Record and Builder's Guide* 19 Feb. 1881: 156.

25. On Flagg, see Mardges Bacon, *Ernest Flagg: Beaux-Arts Architect and Urban Reformer* (New York: Architectural History Foundation, and Cambridge: MIT Press, 1986), 6–11; Ernest Flagg, "A Fish Story: An Autobiographical Sketch of the Education of an Architect," *Journal of the American Institute of Architects* 3 (1945): 185–86.

26. Betsy Blackmar and Elizabeth Cromley, "On the Verandah: Resorts of the Catskills," in *Victorian Resorts and Hotels: Essays from a Victorian Society Autumn Symposium*, ed. Richard Guy Wilson (Philadelphia: Victorian Society in America, 1982), 54.

27. On the Rembrandt, see Browne, "Problem of Living in New York," 921.

28. Ibid.

29. Daniel Bluestone, *Constructing Chicago* (New Haven: Yale University Press, 1991), 150.

30. Robert H. Wiebe, *The Segmented Society: An Introduction to the Meaning of America* (New York: Oxford University Press, 1975), 21; *Barrington Apartment Association v. Watson*, DE Sup Ct. (38 Hun.) 545 (1886). See, for example, Frances W. H. Kuchler, *Landlord, Tenant and Co-op Housing* (New York: Oceana 1960), 85–86.

31. Browne, "Problem of Living in New York," 922, 923; "Junius Henri Browne," *NYT* 2 Feb. 1935: 30.

32. Ibid., 921; Untitled article, *NYT* 16 Feb. 1881: 4; "Typical Examples of Modern Apartments," *NYT* 1 Sept. 1912: AHD1.

33. Browne, "Problem of Living in New York," 918–19.

34. Ibid., 921.

35. Ibid.

36. "John Elderkin Dies," *NYT* 25 Aug. 1926: 21. Quotations from "Old West Side House Being Razed; Last of Pioneer Group Facing Park," *NYT* 8 Mar. 1936: RE1.

37. Browne, *Great Metropolis*, 86.

38. Neil Harris, *Chicago Apartments: A Century of Lakefront Luxury* (New York: Acanthus, 2004), 24–25.

39. For typical proprietary leases from somewhat later, see Robert F. Thorley and William H. Stickney, *Real Estate Forms* (New York: Prentice-Hall, 1926), 150–51; Nathan William MacChesney, *The Principles of Real Estate Law: Real Property, Real Estate Documents and Transactions* (New York: Macmillan, 1927), 397.

40. "Homes at Small Expense," *NYT* 30 Jan. 1881: 10; Dolores Hayden, *The Grand Domestic Revolution: A History of Feminist Designs for American Homes, Neighborhoods, and Cities* (Cambridge: MIT Press, 1981), especially chaps. 4 and 5; Cromley, *Alone Together*, 229n36.

41. "Co-operative Building Societies," *NYT* 26 Aug. 1867: 2; Edward Everett Hale, *Workingmen's Homes: Essays and Stories* (Boston: J. R. Osgood, 1874); David L. Mason, *From Buildings and Loans to Bail-outs: A History of the American Savings and Loan Industry 1831–1995* (Cambridge, U.K.: Cambridge University Press, 2004), chap. 1; Lendol Glen Calder, *Financing the American Dream: A Cultural History of Consumer Credit* (Princeton: Princeton University Press, 1999), chap. 4.

42. Robert G. Natelson, "Comments on the Historiography of Condominium: The Myth of Roman Origin," *Oklahoma City University Law Review* 12, no. 1 (1987); Charles-Louis Julliot, *Traité Formulaire de la Division des Maisons Par Étages et Par Appartements*, 2d ed. (Paris: L'Administration du Journal des Notaires et des Avocats, 1927); Frank Worsdall, *The Tenement, A Way of Life: A Social, Historical and Architectural Study of Housing in Glasgow* (Edinburgh: Chambers, 1979); Richard Rodger, *The Transformation of Edinburgh: Land Property and Trust in the Nineteenth Century* (Cambridge, U.K.: Cambridge University Press, 2001).

43. Fédération Internationale des Géomètres, Office International du Cadastre et du Régime Foncier, *Apartment Property and Cadastre* (The Hague: Fédération Internationale des Géomètres, 1965), 10.

44. Natelson, "Comments on the Historiography of Condominium," 29–30; Worsdall, *Tenement*, 30, 30n58.

45. On Albany, see Harry Furniss, *Paradise in Piccadilly: The Story of Albany* (London: John Lane, 1925); Sheila Birkenhead, *Peace in Piccadilly: The Story of Albany* (New York: Reynal, 1958). Prospectus quoted in Birkenhead, *Peace in Piccadilly*, 44.

46. Samuel Swift, "Llewellyn's Park West Orange, Essex Co., New Jersey, The First American Suburban Community," *House & Garden* 3, no. 6 (June 1903); Kenneth Jackson, *Crabgrass Frontier*, 78; James M. Mayo, *The American Country Club: Its Origins and Development* (New Brunswick: Rutgers University Press, 1998), 68, 163; Richard J. Moss, *Golf and the American Country Club* (Urbana: University of Illinois Press, 2001), 12, 29.

47. Alexia Yates, "Owning Walls and Floors: The Emergence of Apartment Co-ownership in Twentieth-century Paris," 5th Biennial Conference, Urban History Association, Las Vegas, 20–23 Oct. 2010; Sharon Marcus, *Apartment Stories: City and Home in Nineteenth-Century Paris and London* (Berkeley: University of California Press, 1999), 161; Marc H. Choko, "Investment of Family Home? Housing Ownership in Paris at the Turn of the Twentieth Century," *Journal of Urban History* 23, no. 5 (July 1997): 532.

48. "Homes at Small Expense," *NYT*.

49. On Hubert's imagined utopian leanings, see Hayden, *Grand Domestic Revolution*, 108; Carl J. Guarneri, *The Utopian Alternative: Fourierism in Nineteenth-Century America* (Ithaca, N.Y.: Cornell University Press, 1991), 398–99, 502n49; Elizabeth Hawes, *New York, New York: How the Apartment House Transformed the Life of the City (1869–1930)* (New York: Knopf, 1993), 56–57. For opposing views, see Bacon, *Ernest Flagg*, 11; Stern et al., *New York 1880*, 546–48; Andrew Alpern, *Luxury Apartment Houses of Manhattan: An Illustrated History* (New York: Dover, 1992), 17; "Philip Gengembre Hubert," *A History of California*, 623.

50. "Another First-Class Apartment Improvement," *Record and Guide* 29 Mar. 1884: 315; "Out Among the Builders," *Record and Guide* 4 Apr. 1884: 343; Hubert, Pirsson & Hoddick, "New York Flats and French Flats," 61.

51. Hubert, Pirsson & Hoddick, "New York Flats and French Flats," 57. Emphasis original.

52. Hubert, Pirsson & Company, *The Central Park Apartments*, 17–18n.

53. Quotations from ibid., 18.

54. Stern et al., *New York 1880*, 559.

55. "The Prospect for Apartment Houses," *Record and Guide* 27 Oct. 1883: 830. See also Flagg, "A Fish Story," 185–86.

56. On the *Social Register*, see "Society Moving to Country, Figures Say," *NYT* 1 Jan. 1905: 7. Hubert's other known buildings were the Hubert, the Hubert Annex, the Hawthorne, the Mount Morris, a building at Fifth Avenue and 54th Street, and a building at Lexington Avenue and East 80th Street. He may also have built the Milano (see Hayden, *Grand Domestic Revolution*, 108 and 323n43.) Other co-ops included the Berkshire, the Randolph, and the Barrington.

57. "Asking for a Receiver: Trouble over a Mortgage on Big Apartment House," *NYT* 24 July 1886: 8; "In and About the City: Cost of the Navarro Flats, An Interesting Statement by an Expert Accountant," *NYT* 3 June 1887: 8; *American Architect and Building News* 24, no. 676 (8 Dec. 1888): 261–62; Christopher Gray, "The Navarro Flats," *NYT* 17 June 2007: RE6.

58. "Real Estate and Building," *NYT* 11 Feb. 1884: 4. On the U.K., see Johnston Birchall, "Co-partnership and the Garden City Movement," *Planning Perspectives* 10, no. 4 (1995): 332–33.

59. "Co-operative Buildings," *Real Estate Record and Builder's Guide*, 156.

60. "Homes of the Rich," *Building: An Architectural Weekly* 9, no. 20 (17 Nov. 1888): 177–78.

61. "The Navarro Flats, *NYT* 11 Nov. 1888: 4.

62. Christopher Gray, "The 1880 Sherwood Studios, Once at 57th and Sixth," *NYT* 9 Aug. 1998: RE5.

63. "A New Hive of Artists," *NYT* 27 May 1903: 8; A. C. David, "A Co-operative Studio Building," *Architectural Record* 14, no. 4 (Oct. 1903).

64. W. H. Russell, "The Methods of Financing Building Operations," *Proceedings of the Thirty-eighth Annual Convention of the American Institute of Architects* (Washington, D.C.: Gibson, 1905), 95.

65. "A Cooperative Apartment House in New York," *Architectural Record* 24, no. 1 (July 1908); Allan L. Benson, "The Spread of the 'Own-Your-Own-Apartment' Idea," *NYT* 25 July 1909: SM9; Christopher Gray, "An Artists' Co-op, Put Up for Art's Sake," *NYT* 10 Sept. 1995: RNJ7.

66. On this genre of apartment house, see, for example, Robert A. M. Stern, Gregory Gilmartin, and John Massengale, *New York 1900: Metropolitan Architecture and Urbanism 1890–1915* (New York: Rizzoli, 1983), 294–99.

67. Quotations from Benson, "Spread of the 'Own-Your-Own-Apartment' Idea."

68. City of New York, Tenement House Department, *Sixth Report*, 1910–11: 35.

69. Dorothy Que, "Choosing a Home," *Everywhere* 21 no. 4 (Dec. 1907): 158.

70. Display advertisements, *NYT* 21 Apr. 1907: C4; 12 May 1907: C6; 26 May 1907: C5.

71. On resales, see Benson, "Spread of the 'Own-Your-Own-Apartment' Idea"; "Latest Realty Deals," *NYT* 13 Feb. 1910: X11.

72. "The Duplex Apartment House: A Comparison of the Newest Buildings of This Type," *Architectural Record* (Apr. 1911): 326.

73. Robert M. Fogelson, *Bourgeois Nightmares: Suburbia, 1870–1930* (New Haven: Yale University Press, 2005), 4, 13–15, 66.

74. Que, "Choosing a Home," 157.

75. "Society Moving to Country, Figures Say," *NYT* 1 Jan. 1905: 7.

76. Browne, "Problem of Living in New York," 919, 924. On suburban anxieties, see, for example, Clifford Clark, T*he American Family Home, 1800–1960* (Chapel Hill: University of North Carolina Press, 1986), chap. 1, especially 23–24.

77. City of New York, Tenement House Department, *Sixth Report*, 1910–11: 34.

CHAPTER 2. TOWN & COUNTRY

1. U.S., Congress, Senate, Committee on the District of Columbia, 67th Congress, 1st Session, *Extension of Ball Rent Act: Hearing Relative to Rent Situation in the District of Columbia*, 25, 31 May and 1–3 June 1921 (Washington, D.C.: GPO, 1921), 31, 92; James M. Goode, *Best Addresses: A Century of Washington's Distinguished Apartment Houses*, 2d ed. (Washington, D.C.: Smithsonian, 2002), 256.

2. Display advertisements, *WP* 13 June 1920: 37; 28 Mar. 1920: 39.

3. U.S., *Extension of Ball Rent Act*, 103.

4. Ibid., 103, 144; "Apartment Brings $310,000," *WP* 29 Apr. 1920: 37.

5. U.S., *Extension of Ball Rent Act*, 92, 101, 145.

6. Ibid., 103–4, 168.

7. Sinclair Lewis, *Babbitt* (New York: Harcourt, Brace, 1922). On suburban development, see, for example, Carolyn Loeb, *Entrepreneurial Vernacular: Developers' Subdivisions in the 1920s* (Baltimore: Johns Hopkins University Press, 2001); Kenneth T. Jackson, *Crabgrass Frontier: The*

Suburbanization of the United States (New York: Oxford University Press, 1985), chap. 10.

8. Mason C. Doan, *American Housing Production 1880–2000: A Concise History* (Lanham, Md.: University Press of America, 1997), 5, 11–12, 19–24; Coleman Woodbury, *Apartment House Increases and Attitudes Toward Homeownership*, Studies in Land Economics Research Monograph 4, ed. Richard T. Ely (Chicago: Institute for Economic Research, 1931), table 3.9; George A. Lundberg et al., *Leisure: A Suburban Study* (New York: Columbia University Press, 1934), 35.

9. Woodbury, *Apartment House Increases and Attitudes Toward Homeownership*, vii.

10. Quoted in Lundberg, *Leisure*, 43–44.

11. Doan, *American Housing Production, 1880–2000*, 31; John M. Gries and James Ford, eds., *The President's Conference on Home Building and Home Ownership Called by President Hoover, Final Reports of Committees IV: Home Ownership, Income and Types of Dwellings* (Washington, D.C.: President's Conference on Home Building and Home Ownership, 1932), 200; Henry Wright, "The Place of the Apartment in the Modern Community," *Architectural Record* 67, no. 3 (Mar. 1930): 207–9.

12. Metro housing markets known or reported to have had at least one owner-occupied apartment housing in the 1920s are Akron, Asheville (N.C.), Atlanta, Atlantic City, Baltimore, Birmingham, Boston, Champaign (Ill.), Cincinnati, Cleveland, Davenport (Iowa), Des Moines, Detroit, Flint (Mich.), Kansas City, Lincoln, Madison (Wis.), Miami, Milwaukee, Minneapolis, New Orleans, Norfolk, Philadelphia, Pittsburgh, St. Louis, St. Paul, St. Petersburg, and Seattle.

13. Merryle Stanley Rukeyser, *Financial Advice to a Young Man: A Program for Getting Along in the World* (New York: Simon and Schuster, 1927), 331–32.

14. Doan, *American Housing Production 1880–2000*, 28; Joseph A. Spencer, "New York City Tenant Organizations and the Post-World War I Housing Crisis," in *The Tenant Movement in New York City, 1904–1984*, ed. Ronald Lawson (New Brunswick: Rutgers University Press, 1986), 53–57; "Board of Alderman May Investigate the Recent Advances in Rental of New York City Apartments," *NYT* 2 June 1918: RE14.

15. Display advertisement, *NYT* 1 Feb. 1920: S9.

16. "Latest Dealings in the Realty Field," *NYT* 9 June 1918: 92; "Latest Dealings in the Realty Field," *NYT* 15 Dec. 1918: 92; Christopher Gray, "The Prasada, at 65th Street and Central Park West," *NYT* 20 Aug. 2000: RE5.

17. Wendell P. Bradley, "Flynn Plans Low-Cost Housing to Cap Career," *WP* 20 Oct. 1957: C10 ; "On the Co-operative Plan," *WP* 10 May 1891: 10; display advertisement, *WP* 16 Oct. 1894: 11; "New Downtown Development," *WP* 24 Apr. 1965: F4; "Plan $300,000 House," *WP* 28 Mar. 1909: N2; Goode, *Best Addresses*, 112–13; Wendell P. Bradley, "Flynn Plans Low-Cost Housing to Cap Career," *WP* 20 Oct. 1957: C10.

18. On rent strikes, see "60 Organize in Rogers Park to Fight Rent Raise," *ChT* 6 Mar. 1920: 17; "City-wide Union to Fight Unjust Rents Demanded," *ChT* 1 Mar. 1920: 17; Spencer, "New York City Tenant Organizations."

19. Chase, "Gold Coasters Rent Own Flats for 99 Years," *ChT* 28 July 1920: 20; Frank Parker Stockbridge, "Own Your

Own Flat," *Saturday Evening Post* 198, no. 16 (17 Oct. 1925):
58; display advertisements, *WP* 28 Mar. 1920: 39; *WP* 1 Apr.
1920: 4; 16 May 1920: 39; 13 June 1920: 37.

20. "Tenants Buy Fine Apartment House to Avoid Gouging,"
Brooklyn Eagle 21 Mar. 1920; "Buying by Tenants Found
Practical," *NYT* 4 Apr. 1920: RE2. Quotation from "Realty
Brokers Defend the Co-operative Plan of Ownership
Attacked by Alderman Quinn," *NYT* 4 Jul. 1920: W1.

21. Display advertisement, *WP* 28 Mar. 1920: 39.

22. "Tenants Take over Apartment Houses," *NYT* 11 Mar. 1920:
26; "5th Av. Tenants Buy $2,500,000 Home," *NYT* 4 Apr.
1920: E1; "Tenants Buy Drive Apartment House," *NYT* 7
Apr. 1920: 24; "Tenants Buy West Side Apartments," *NYT*
21 Apr. 1920: 26.

23. "Realty Brokers Defend the Co-operative Plan of Ownership
Attacked by Alderman Quinn," *NYT*; "Co-operative Plan
Upheld by Court," *NYT* 1 Dec. 1920: 35.

24. Stockbridge, "Own Your Own Flat," 58.

25. "Board of Alderman May Investigate the Recent Advances
in Rental of New York City Apartments," *NYT* 2 June
1918: RE14; "Co-operative Home Buyers are Warned,"
NYT 27 June 1920: W14; "Fears Co-operative Housing
Projects," *NYT* 30 June 1920: 12; "Realty Brokers Defend
the Co-operative Plan of Ownership Attacked by Alderman
Quinn," *NYT* 4 Jul. 1920: W1; "Gives Safeguards for Tenant
Owners," *NYT* 18 July 1920: 8.1; "Houses Sold on the 'Cooperative Plan' Are Often Owned by Agents of Realty
Sharks," *Bronx Home News* 18 July 1920; C. R. White, "Co-
operative Housing," *NYT* 10 Oct. 1920: XX10.

26. "Gives Safeguards for Tenant Owners," *NYT* 18 July 1920: 8.1

27. Will Irwin, *Highlights of Manhattan* (New York: Century,
1927), 223.

28. On design, see, for example, Robert A. M. Stern,
Gregory Gilmartin, and Thomas Mellins, *New York 1930:
Architecture and Urbanism Between the Two World
Wars* (New York: Rizzoli, 1987); Neil Harris, *Chicago
Apartments: A Century of Lakefront Luxury* (New York:
Acanthus, 2004).

29. Woodbury, *Apartment House Increases and Attitudes
Toward Homeownership*, 194; "East Side Survey of
Cooperatives," *NYT* 28 Nov. 1926: E9; Douglas L. Elliman,
*Cooperative Ownership: A Brief Presentation of Facts
Viewed from the Standpoint of Owner and Occupant* (New
York: Douglas L. Elliman, 1927); Irwin, *Highlights of
Manhattan*, 221.

30. James R. McGonagle, *Apartment House Rental,
Investment, and Management* (New York: Prentice-Hall,
1937), 374.

31. On prices, see "Last Word," *New Yorker* 15 Sept. 1928:
18–19; "Cooperative Suit Won by Havemeyer," *NYT* 30
Mar. 1930: W15; Walter H. Waggoner, "Brewster Ives Is
Dead at 81," *NYT* 7 May 1985: B10; Edward F. Rogers,
"Co-ops in New York City," *Cooperative Apartments: Their
Organization and Profitable Operation*, 2d ed. (Chicago:
Institute of Real Estate Management of the National
Association of Realtors, 1961), 51.

32. "Construction Progress Is Made on Apartment," *WP* 9
May 1926: R1; display advertisement, *WP* 27 June 1926: R9;
"Warrens Pioneers in Cooperatively Owned Apartments,"
WP 20 Feb. 1927: R3; "$35,000 Apartment Included in

Home Beautiful Exhibit," *WP* 16 Apr. 1928: 20; Goode, *Best
Addresses*, 177, 242.

33. Quotation from Stockbridge, "Own Your Own Flat," 58.

34. John Taylor Boyd, Jr., "Garden Apartments in Cities," part
II, *Architectural Record* 48 (Aug. 1920): 121–35: 122, 124;
Richard Plunz, *A History of Housing in New York City*
(New York: Columbia University Press, 1990), 138.
     On the history of Jackson Heights generally, see, for
example, Daniel Karatzas, *Jackson Heights: A Garden in
the City*, 2d ed. (Jackson Heights, N.Y.: Jackson Heights
Beautification Group, 1998); Plunz, *History of Housing*,
138–47.

35. Louis Pink, *The New Day in Housing* (New York: John Day,
1928), 154; on Thomas's life, see 156; "Architect Lauds Smith
Housing Plan," *NYT* 27 Feb. 1926: 2; "Andrew Thomas, a
City Architect," *NYT* 27 July 1965: 33. On Thomas and his
work generally, see Stern et. al., *New York 1930*, 478–86.

36. Quotation from display advertisement, *NYT* 14 June 1919: 20.

37. Queensboro Corporation, *Jackson Heights News: The
New Garden Apartments, Co-operative Ownership
Plan*, prospectus, VF; John Taylor Boyd, Jr., "Garden
Apartments in Cities," part I, *Architectural Record* 48
(July 1920): 52–74.

38. "Million Dollar Apartment House Development for Queens,"
NYT 25 May 1919: RE20.

39. Display advertisements, *NYT* 27 Aug. 1919: 23; 24 Oct. 1920:
RE9; 9 Nov. 1919: S7; 30 Aug. 1919 14.

40. On real-estate marketing generally, see the volume on this
topic in Richard T. Ely's "Land Economics Series": Ward C.
Gifford, *Real Estate Advertising* (New York: Macmillan,
1925).

41. Lloyd Morris, *Not So Long Ago* (New York: Random House,
1949), 436–47; display advertisement, *NYT* 15 Jan. 1921: 10.

42. "Co-operative Apartment Buying on the Increase," *NYT*
18 June 1922: RE1; "Architects Visit Model Apartments,"
NYT 3 May 1925: RE2; "Groups of Co-operatively Owned
Apartments Being Erected in Paris Closely Following
American Methods—'French in Style and American in
Comfort' the Slogan," *NYT* 25 Mar. 1925: RE1; Plunz,
History of Housing, 147.

43. Andrew Scott Dolkart, "Hudson View Gardens: A Home in
the City," *SITES* 20 (1988); "Hudson View Gardens," *NYT* 18
May 1924: RE2.

44. "Walton Hall, a Cooperative, Planned for East 72d St.," *NYT*
12 Jan. 1926; "City Apartments with Rear Gardens," *NYT* 10
Apr. 1927: RE1; Christopher Gray, "Junior League, Garden
Co-op and Pumpkin House," *NYT* 5 Dec. 1999: RE7; *Garden
Plan Apartments*, prospectus, VF.

45. Lundberg, *Leisure*, 173.

46. "Wants to Buy a 'Co-op,' and Maybe 6 Dogs," *ChT* 20 Jan.
1929: B1.

47. "Country Life Lures Cooperative Buyers," *NYT* 20 Mar.
1927: RE16; "Suburban Cooperative," *NYT* 15 May 1927:
E19; display advertisement, *NYT* 10 Jan. 1926: RE12;
display advertisement, *WP* 27 Sept. 1925: R7; "Bungalow
Type Co-op for 5421 Cornell Avenue," *ChT* 15 Jan. 1928: B3.

48. *Alden Park Manor Philadelphia*, prospectus, VF; and *The
Kenilworth at Alden Park Philadelphia*, prospectus, VF.

49. E. McNerney, cartoon, *New Yorker* 16 Oct. 1926: 31; Alan
Dunn, cartoon, *New Yorker* 23 Nov. 1929: 28.

50. "Country Life Lures Cooperative Buyers," *NYT* 20 Mar. 1927: RE16.

51. On professional efforts to improve the co-op in the 1920s generally, see NAREB's *Annals of Real Estate Practice.* See also "Realtors to Talk on Sales of Flats," *WP* 10 June 1923: 45; "Cooperative Purchase of Apartments Urged," *WP* 4 June 1924: 4; "Real Estate Men to Discuss Tenant Ownership Plans," *WP* 3 May 1925: R2; Robert Bates Warren, "New York Session on Cooperatives Attended by 100," *WP* 12 Dec. 1926: R1; "Apartment Division Gets Higher Status," *WP* 20 Feb. 1927: R1; "First Certificate by Realtors' Board Will Go to Chicago," *WP* 15 July 1928: R1.

52. Emily Post, *The Personality of a House: The Blue Book of Home Design and Decoration* (New York: Funk and Wagnall, 1930), 138–39. See also: "Women Will Erect Apartment De Luxe," *NYT* 14 May 1925: 10.

53. "Favors 80% 'Co-ops,'" *NYT* 28 Sept 1924: RE2.

54. Robert Bates Warren, "Selecting the Proper Purchaser for the Coöperative Apartment," *Annals of Real Estate Practice, 1927* (Chicago: National Association of Real Estate Boards, 1927), 2: 59–62.

55. "Growth of Cooperative Movement Shown by Demand and Building," *NYT* 14 Sept., 1924: RE1; "20,000 People Live in Chicago's 100% Co-ops, Survey Says," *ChT* 27 July 1930: A12.

56. "Million Dollar Apartment House Development for Queens," *NYT* 25 May 1919: RE20; "Cooperative Home Methods Explained," *NYT* 22 Mar. 1925: RE2; McGonagle, *Apartment House Rental*, 366; Lee E. Cooper, "New Lease Gives Gradual Rent Reduction To Encourage Long Apartment Tenancies," *NYT* 7 Mar. 1939: 43.

57. "Realtors to Talk on Sales of Flats," *WP* 10 June 1923: 45; Douglas L. Elliman, *Cooperative Ownership;* McGonagle, *Apartment House Rental;* U.S., Federal Housing Administration, *A Survey of Apartment Dwelling Operating Experience in Large American Cities* (Washington, D.C.: GPO, 1940).

58. Stockbridge, "Own Your Own Flat," 54.

59. Ibid.

60. "First Tenants of Shore Co-op to O.K. Others," *ChT* 21 Sept. 1924: A12.

61. On industry support of restrictions, see, for example, Robert Fogelson, *Bourgeois Nightmares: Suburbia, 1870–1930* (New Haven: Yale University Press, 2005); Laura Bobeczko and Richard Longstreth, "Housing Reform Meets the Marketplace: Washington and the Federal Housing Administration's Contribution to Apartment Building Design, 1935–40," in *Housing Washington: Two Centuries of Residential Development and Planning in the National Capital Area*, ed. Richard Longstreth (Chicago: Center for American Places at Columbia College Chicago, 2010), 163.

62. Robert Bates Warren, "Selecting the Proper Purchaser for the Coöperative Apartment."

63. Stockbridge, "Own Your Own Flat," 18.

64. "Bar Jews From Co-operative N. Y. Apartments," *ChT* 28 July 1923: 6.

65. Display advertisements, *NYT* 30 Aug. 1919: 14; 30 Oct. 1923: 33; 25 Oct. 1921: 35.

66. Quoted in Plunz, *History of Housing*, 131.

67. Andrew Scott Dolkart, "Homes for People: Non-Profit Cooperatives in New York City 1916–1929," *SITES* 21–22 (1989): 37–38; Dolkart, "Hudson View Gardens," 37–38.

68. Gwendolyn Wright, *Building the Dream: A Social History of Housing in America* (New York: Pantheon, 1981), 212.

69. Silas Bent, "Mr. Ochs's 'Times,'" *Menorah Journal* 14 no. 5 (May 1928): 439–40.

70. Deborah Dash Moore, *At Home in America: Second Generation Jews in New York* (New York: Columbia University Press, 1981), 36.

71. "High-income Men Are Tenants Here," *NYT* 20 June 1926: RE21; Irwin, *Highlights of Manhattan*, 224; Doan, *American Housing Production 1880–2000*, 11, 30.

72. U.S., *Extension of Ball Rent Act*, 103.

73. Lendol Glen Calder, *Financing the American Dream: A Cultural History of Consumer Credit* (Princeton: Princeton University Press, 1999), chap. 4; "$500,000 Building Loan," *NYT* 22 June 1919: RE18.

74. "Million Dollar Apartment House Development for Queens," *NYT* 25 May 1919: RE20; "$500,000 Building Loan," *NYT* 22 June 1919: RE18; "First Loan in Queens," *NYT* 29 June 1919: RE18; Edward A. MacDougall, "Cooperative Housing," *Housing Problems in America: Proceedings of the Eighth National Conference on Housing, Bridgeport December 9, 10, and 11, 1920* (New York: National Housing Association, 1920), 51–55.

75. Queensboro Corporation, *Investment Features of Cooperative Apartment Ownership at Jackson Heights*, sales prospectus, 1925: 26; "Fourteen New Apartments for Jackson Heights," *NYT* 17 Sept. 1922: RE1; "Jackson Heights Sales," *NYT* 20 May 1923: RE1; "Garden Suites in Demand," *NYT* 22 July 1923: RE2; "Cooperative Apartments Sales Show Their Increasing Popularity," *NYT* 27 July 1924: RE2.

76. Stockbridge, "Own Your Own Flat," 56; "Company to Finance 'Co-ops' Is Organized," *NYT* 21 Dec. 1924: W1; Henry G. Montgomery, "New Method of Financing by Acceptance Corporation," *NYT* 11 Jan. 1925: RE2; "Form Company to Make Loans on Co-op Flats," *ChT* 10 June 1928: B1.

77. Grace Hegger Lewis, *With Love from Gracie: Sinclair Lewis, 1912–1925* (New York: Harcourt, Brace, 1955), 37.

78. "Fourteen New Apartments for Jackson Heights," *NYT*; "Jackson Heights Sales," *NYT* 20 May 1923: RE1; "Garden Suites in Demand," *NYT* 22 July 1923: RE2; "Cooperative Apartments Sales Show Their Increasing Popularity," *NYT* 27 July 1924: RE2; "Apartment Brings $310,000," *WP* 29 Apr. 1920: 37; "Tenants Acquire The Netherlands," *WP* 15 Aug. 1920: 41; "Apartment House Trading," *NYT* 21 Sept. 1920: 30.

79. Carl Abbot, *Political Terrain: Washington, D.C., from Tidewater Town to Global Metropolis* (Chapel Hill: University of North Carolina Press, 1999), 95, 101; U.S., *Extension of Ball Rent Act*, 95; "Allan E. Walker & Co. Report $350,000 Sales," *WP* 15 Jan. 1922: 47; "Warrens Pioneers in Cooperatively Owned Apartments," *WP* 20 Feb. 1927: R3; display advertisement, *WP* 3 Oct. 1926: M2; "Hilltop Manor List of Buyers Rapidly Closes Out Units," *WP* 16 Jan. 1927: R5.

80. A Business Woman, "Unfinished Jobs," *Atlantic Monthly* 138, no. 5 (Nov. 1926): 639–45.

81. Wanda Fraiken Neff, *We Sing Diana* (Boston: Houghton Mifflin, 1928), 14–46.

82. Rukeyser, *Financial Advice to a Young Man*, 307.

83. Robert L. Davison, "Apartment Design to Meet Family Needs," *Architectural Record* 67 no. 3 (Mar. 1930): 268, 279.

84. Gries and Ford, *Home Onwership, Income and Types of Dwellings*, 201.

85. "Business Methods in Apartment Sales," *NYT* 7 June 1925: RE2.

86. "What Tenants Seek in New Apartments," *NYT* 19 May 1929: RE14.

87. Display advertisements, *NYT* 21 Aug. 1924: 5; 8 Sept. 1924: 7.

88. Wood, Dolson Company, *Hudson View Gardens*, prospectus, VF; display advertisement, *NYT* 1 Sept. 1924: 4.

89. Andrew Dolkart, *The Row House Reborn: Architecture and Neighborhoods in New York City, 1908–1929* (Baltimore: Johns Hopkins University Press, 2009), 68, 85, 123; Caroline F. Ware, *Greenwich Village, 1920–1930: A Comment on American Civilization in the Post-war Years* (Boston: Houghton Mifflin, 1935); Christine Stansell, *American Moderns: Bohemian New York and the Creation of a New Century* (New York: Metropolitan, 2000).

90. "Resale Facilities of Tenant Owners," *NYT* 24 May 1925: RE1; John B. Willmann, "Happening in Real Estate," *WP* 22 Sept. 1979: E1; Goode, *Best Addresses*, 177–78, 260–61; "Cooperative Payments," *NYT* 6 Apr. 1930: RE1; "Calls Tax Change Aid to Cooperatives," *NYT* 19 Apr. 1931: 50.

91. "20,000 People Live in Chicago's 100% Co-ops, Survey Says," *ChT* 27 July 1930: A12; "Cooperative Opening at 834 Fifth Avenue," *NYT* 20 Sept. 1931: RE1; "Cooperative Suit Won by Havemeyer," *NYT* 30 Mar. 1930: W15.

92. "Park Av. Suites Rented," *NYT* 26 Jul. 1933: 32; "Rentals Maintain Brisk Fall Pace," *NYT* 28 Sept. 1934: 43; "Park Avenue Houses Draw More Tenants," *NYT* 3 Oct. 1936: 31; "Look for Interest in Cooperatives," *NYT* 7 Feb. 1937: RE1; "Large Suites Cut Up into Smaller Units," *NYT* 8 Oct. 1939: RE1.

93. John P. Marquand, *Point of No Return* (Boston: Little, Brown, 1949), 87.

CHAPTER 3. COOPERATIVE COMMONWEALTH

1. "Co-operative Housing De Luxe," *Co-operation* XII, no. 12 (Dec. 1926): 221–23, 222; Richard Plunz, *A History of Housing in New York City* (New York: Columbia University Press, 1990), 152, 165.

2. On advertising costs, see Foster Ware, "Profiles: Make of Castles," *New Yorker* 2 July 1927: 19–20.

3. Louis Pink, *The New Day in Housing* (New York: John Day, 1928), 165; Plunz, *History of Housing*, 152; "Co-operative Housing De Luxe," 223; David Tucker, "What Is the United Workers' Co-operative Association and What Are Its Aims?" *Co-operation* IX, no. 7 (July 1923): 115–16; "A Co-operative Camp," *Co-operation* XII, no. 9 (Sept. 1926): 173.

4. Plunz, *History of Housing*, 152, 156; "Co-operative Housing De Luxe," 223; "Progress of United Workers' Co-operative Association," *Co-operation* XIII, no. 8 (Aug. 1927): 152; "United Workers' Co-operative Association," *Co-operation* XIV, no. 4 (Apr. 1928): 74; Pink, *New Day in Housing*, 166.

5. On homeownership as conservative, see, for example, Thomas J. Sugrue, *The Origins of the Urban Crisis: Race and Inequality in Postwar Detroit* (Princeton: Princeton University Press, 1996); Matthew D. Lassiter, *The Silent Majority: Suburban Politics in the Suburban South* (Princeton: Princeton University Press, 2007).

6. Frank Parker Stockbridge, "Own Your Own Flat," *Saturday Evening Post* 198, no. 16 (17 Oct. 1925): 18–19, 54–58: 18.

7. On philanthropic housing, see Eugenie Ladner Birch and Deborah S. Gardner, "The Seven-Percent Solution: A Review of Philanthropic Housing, 1870–1910," *Journal of Urban History* 7, no. 4 (Aug. 1981); Cynthia Zaitzevsky, "Housing Boston's Poor: The First Philanthropic Experiments," *Journal of the Society of Architectural Historians* 42, no. 2 (May 1983); Elizabeth Hannold, "'The Influence of Sanitary Houses Cannot Be Over Estimated': Philanthropic Housing in Washington, D.C.," *Housing Washington: Two Centuries of Residential Development and Planning in the National Capital Area*, ed. Richard Longstreth (Chicago: Center for American Places at Columbia College Chicago, 2010).

8. Alexander von Hoffman, "The End of the Dream: The Political Struggle of America's Public Housers," *Journal of Planning History* 4, no. 3 (Aug. 2005): 225.

9. Johnston Birchall, "Co-partnerhip and the Garden City Movement," *Planning Perspectives* 10, no. 4 (1995); Robert Fishman, *Urban Utopias in the Twentieth Century: Ebenezer Howard, Frank Lloyd Wright, Le Corbusier* (New York: Basic Books, 1977), part 1; Kristin M. Szylvian, "Industrial Housing Reform and the Emergency Fleet Corporation," *Journal of Urban History* 25, no. 5 (July 1999): 648; von Hoffman, "End of the Dream," 225.

10. On Rochdale co-ops in Europe, see, for example, Daniel Rodgers, *Atlantic Crossings: Social Politics in a Progressive Age* (Cambridge: Belknap, 1998), 188–201, 455–77; Eve Blau, *The Architecture of Red Vienna, 1919–1934* (Cambridge: MIT Press, 1999), chaps. 3 and 4; Fishman, *Urban Utopias in the Twentieth Century*, chap. 3; F. C. Howe, "Dusseldorf, Industrial Center," *Wall Street Journal* 3 Dec. 1910: 6; U.S., Department of Labor, Bureau of Labor Statistics, *Organization and Management of Cooperative Housing Associations* (Washington, D.C.: GPO, 1934); Pink, *New Day in Housing*, 158–59; Agnes Dyer Warbasse, "Coöperative Homes for Europe's Homeless," *American Review of Reviews: An International Magazine* LXV (Jan.–June 1922).

11. On limited-equity housing, see Gerald W. Sazama, "Lessons from the History of Affordable Housing Cooperatives in the United States: A Case Study in American Affordable Housing Policy," *American Journal of Economics and Sociology* 59, no. 4 (Oct. 2000): 575. On Milwaukee, see Wayne Attoe and Mark Latus, "The First Public Housing: Sewer Socialism's Garden City for Milwaukee," *Journal of Popular Culture* X no. 1 (Summer 1976); Gail Radford, *Modern Housing for America: Policy Struggles in the New Deal Era* (Chicago: University of Chicago Press, 1996), 50–51.

12. On short leases, see "Tenants Renew Dunbar Leases," *NYT* 9 Aug. 1931: RE1.

13. See, for example, Bureau of Social Hygiene, Inc., *Housing Conditions of Employed Women in the Borough of*

Manhattan (New York: Bureau of Social Hygiene, 1922), 71; Pink, *New Day in Housing*, 160–61.

14. Edith Elmer Wood, *Recent Trends in American Housing* (New York: Macmillan, 1931), 171, 172. Emphasis original.

15. Anja Hellikki Olin-Fahle, "Finnhill: Persistence of Ethnicity in Urban America," diss., New York University, 1983 (Ann Arbor: UMI, 1984), esp. 28–29, 122–38; Daniel W. Hoan, "Co-operative Housing," *Co-operation* IX, no. 4 (Apr. 1923): 61; "Seven Strides Onward Toward the Co-operative Commonwealth," *Co-operation* XI, no. 4 (Apr. 1925); Wood, *Recent Trends in American Housing*, 174–75; Stockbridge, "Own Your Own Flat," 56; Andrew Scott Dolkart, "Homes for People: Non-Profit Cooperatives in New York City, 1916–1929," *SITES* 21–22 (1989): 37–38.

16. State of New York, Reconstruction Commission, Housing Committee, "Housing Conditions," 26 Mar. 1920, State of New York, *Message from the Governor Transmitting the Report of the Reconstruction Commission on the Housing Situation* (Albany: State of New York, 1920), 51–52, 65. See also "Offers Plan to Aid Housing Situation," *NYT* 26 May 1919: 10.

17. Quotations C. R. White, "Co-operative Housing," *NYT* 10 Oct. 1920: XX10. See also Olin-Fahle, "Finnhill," 123, 135; "Co-operative Apartments," *NYT* 13 June 1920: XX10; "Explains Housing Co-operative Plan," *NYT* 19 Sept. 1920: E1.

18. "Another Housing Society," *Co-operation* VII, no. 8 (Aug. 1921): 134; Bureau of Social Hygiene, *Housing Conditions of Employed Women*, 71–72; Mary Kingsbury Simkhovitch, *Neighborhood: My Story of Greenwich House* (New York: W. W. Norton, 1938), 180.

19. "Co-operative Housing in New York," *Co-operation* X, no. 7 (July 1924): 113; "'Co-ops' Cut Costs," *NYT* 9 Nov. 1924: RE2; "Speakers at the Fourth Congress," *Co-operation* X, no. 11 (Nov. 1924): 183; "Monthly Bill of Small 'Co-op,'" *NYT* 11 Jan. 1925: RE2; Clarke A. Chambers, "The Cooperative League of the United State of America, 1916–61: A Study of Social Theory and Social Action," *Agricultural History* 36, no. 2 (Apr. 1962): 60–62.

20. "Wage-earners Succeed in Cooperative Housing," *NYT* 24 Feb. 1924: XX8; for details on the financing, see Stockbridge, "Own Your Own Flat," 58.

21. See, for example, Wood, *Recent Trends in American Housing*, 211.

22. Quotation from "Co-operative Plan Builds Many Homes," *NYT* 10 Feb. 1924: RE1. See also "Wage-earners Succeed in Cooperative Housing," *NYT* 24 Feb. 1924: XX8; "Co-operative Housing Exhibit," *Co-operation* X, no. 4 (Apr. 1924): 68–69; von Hoffman, "End of the Dream," 226.

23. On tax-related savings, see "Amalgamated Cooperative Apartments," *Co-operation* XIV, no. 1 (Jan. 1928): 24.

24. "Radicals in the Bronx," Museum of the City of New York, 9 Nov. 2004–30 Mar. 2005; *At Home in Utopia*, DVD, directed by Michal Goldman (San Francisco: Filmmakers Collaborative, 2008); Richard Plunz, "Reading Bronx Housing, 1890–1940," in *Building a Borough: Architecture and Planning in the Bronx, 1890–1940*, ed. Evelyn Gonzales, Richard Plunz, and Timothy Rub (Bronx: Bronx Museum of the Arts, 1986); Plunz, *History of Housing*, 151–68; Dolkart, "Homes for People"; Radford, *Modern Housing for America*, 115–19.

25. Plunz, *History of Housing*, 132. See also Jenna Weissman Joselit, "'A Set Table': Jewish Domestic Culture in the

New World, 1880–1950," in *Getting Comfortable in New York: The American Jewish Home, 1880–1950*, ed. Susan L. Braunstein and Jenna Weissman Joselit (New York: Jewish Museum, 1990), 45–47; Deborah Dash Moore, *At Home in America: Second Generation New York Jews* (New York: Columbia University Press, 1981), 53–54.

26. Moore, *At Home in America*, 23, 55.

27. Abraham Kazan, *The Reminiscences of Abraham Kazan*, interview by Lloyd Kaplan, 1970, Oral History Research Office, Columbia University, 26–39; Peter Eisenstadt, *Rochdale Village: Robert Moses, 6,000 Families, and New York City's Great Experiment in Integrated Housing* (Ithaca, N.Y.: Cornell University Press, 2010), 26.

28. Kazan, *Reminiscences of Abraham Kazan*, 69–70; Kenneth W. Rose, "Partners in Housing Reform: The Apartment Developments of John D. Rockefeller, Jr., Charles O. Heydt, and Andrew J. Thomas," The Conference on New York State History, New York State Historical Association, Cooperstown, N.Y., 8 June 2007.

29. Rose, "Partners in Housing Reform."

30. Bureau of Social Hygiene, *Housing Conditions of Employed Women*, 71; Rose, "Partners in Housing Reform"; Kazan, *Reminiscences of Abraham Kazan*, 70; Plunz, *History of Housing*, 141–68; Andrew J. Thomas, *Industrial Housing* (Bayonne, N.J.: Bayonne Housing Corporation); "Employers Unite to House Workers," *NYT* 5 Feb. 1924: 40; "$1,000,000 Housing Project for Bayonne, N.J.," *NYT* 10 Feb. 1924: RE2; "Yorkville May See Many Model Homes," *NYT* 22 Jan. 1925: 32; quoted in "Unions to Spend $1,000,000 on Homes," *NYT* 25 Dec. 1924: 16.

31. Rose, "Partners in Housing Reform"; Constance Rosenblum, *Boulevard of Dreams: Heady Times, Heartbreak, and Hope Along the Grand Concourse in the Bronx* (New York: New York University Press, 2009), 52–54; "Needle Trades Unions Buy Bronx Site for Big Cooperative Apartment House," *NYT* 5 Mar. 1925: 33; "Unions Plan Start on Housing Project," *NYT* 22 Apr. 1925: 9; "Rockefeller Buys Labor Homes Site," *NYT* 19 Sept. 1925: 17; "The Rockefeller Wage Earners' Apartments Scheduled for Completion This Fall," *NYT* 1 Aug. 1926: RE1; "Architects Give Medals to Encourage Better Building," *NYT* 3 Mar. 1929: RE9.

32. Charles O. Heydt quoted in Rose, "Partners in Housing Reform." On the Brooklyn and Sleepy Hollow projects, see Rose, "Partners in Housing Reform"; Pink, *New Day in Housing*, 112; "Rockefeller to Back New Housing Project," *NYT* 22 May 1928: 46; "Rockefeller Apartments at North Tarrytown To Be Opened This Week," *NYT* 19 Jan. 1930: RE2.

33. William Henry Jones, *The Housing of Negroes in Washington, D.C.: A Study in Human Ecology, an Investigation Made Under the Auspices of the Interracial Committee of the Washington Federation of Churches* (Washington, D.C.: Howard University Press, 1929), 143; John M. Gries and James Ford, eds., *The President's Conference on Home Building and Home Ownership Called by President Hoover, Final Reports of Committees, VI: Negro Housing* (Washington, D.C.: President's Conference on Home Building and Home Ownership, 1932), 82; "Apartment House Sales," *NYT* 24 Aug. 1920: 27; L. Bayard Whitney, "Plan 10 Co-operative Apartments," *New York*

Amsterdam News 7 Mar. 1928: 3; "$2 Per Room Boost Hits
Co-operatives on Seventh Avenue," *New York Amsterdam
News* 16 July 1930, 1.

34. Quotation from Paul Laurence Dunbar Apartments, *Paul
    Laurence Dunbar Apartments*, prospectus, VF. See also
    Pink, *New Day in Housing*, 151–56; "Big Families Shun
    Rockefeller House," *NYT* 5 July 1930: 20; Plunz, *History of
    Housing*, 159–60; Gries and Ford, *Negro Housing*.
35. Gries and Ford, *Negro Housing*, 107.
36. Will Irwin, *Highlights of Manhattan* (New York: Century,
    1927), 223.
37. At Jackson Heights, for example, where use of golf and
    tennis facilities required extra dues, these amenities began
    to contract; in the late 1930s and 1940s most were built over.
    Daniel Karatzas, *Jackson Heights: A Garden in the City*, 2d
    ed. (Jackson Heights, N.Y.: Jackson Heights Beautification
    Group, 1998), 100, 120, 155.
38. Irwin, *Highlights of Manhattan*, 223.
39. Kazan, *Reminiscences of Abraham Kazan*, 125–26.
40. On design, see "The Coöperative Plan—One Answer to the
    Low Cost Housing Problem," *Architectural Forum* (Feb.
    1931): 242. On lack of right to transfer ownership to heirs, see
    "Rockefeller Opens Cooperative Flats," *NYT* 10 Feb. 1927: 4.
41. Helen Kooiman Hosier, "Little Is Much with God," *Profiles:
    People Who Are Helping to Change the World* (New York:
    Hawthorn, 1977), 128.
42. "Three New Cooperatives Planned," *FB* July 1959:
    5; Matthew Gordon Lasner, "No Lawn to Mow: Co-
    ops, Condominiums, and the Revolution in Collective
    Homeownership in Metropolitan America, 1881–1973," diss.,
    Harvard University, 2007 (Ann Arbor: UMI, 2007), 333–39;
    "New Scenario," *LAT* 21 Sept. 1925: A7.
43. On business corporations laws affecting co-ops, see Herbert
    Emmerich, "The Problem of Low-priced Cooperative
    Apartments: An Experiment at Sunnyside Gardens,"
    Journal of Land and Public Utility Economics 4 no. 3 (Aug.
    1928): 227.
44. Rose, "Partners in Housing Reform," 13–14.
45. Quotation from display advertisement, *NYT* 21 Jan. 1923:
    RE6. See also "Big Apartment House to be Erected
    Under Joint Ownership Plan at Flushing, L.I.," *NYT*
    12 Dec. 1920: RE5; "Portional Purchase Apartments,"
    NYT 2 Oct. 1921: RE1; "Apartment Houses Planned and
    Nearing Completion," *NYT* 1 Apr. 1923: RE2; "Apartment
    and Commercial Building," *NYT* 8 Mar. 1925: RE1; "Plan
    First 'Co-op' for Jersey City," *NYT* 5 Apr. 1925: 30; "Rapid
    Growth and Development of Cooperative Ownership Plan,"
    NYT 19 Apr. 1925: RE1.
46. Display advertisements, *NYT* 28 May 1922: RE7; 4 June
    1922: RE4.
47. Walter Russell, Inc., *Russell Rent Mutualization Plan for
    National Rent Relief*, prospectus, VF; "Offers a Scheme
    to Reduce Rents," *NYT* 16 Aug. 1923: 25; "Mutual Rent
    Plan Interests Coolidge," *NYT* 21 Aug. 1923: 18; display
    advertisement, *NYT* 5 Sept. 1923: 18.
48. Versailles, Inc., *New Versailles*, prospectus (New York,
    1916); "Plan an American Versailles on Long Island," *NYT*
    14 May 1916: SM15; Frederic J. Haskin, "Whole Town Will
    Be Housed Inside One Big Dwelling," Lima, Ohio, *Times-
    Democrat*, evening ed., 25 Aug. 1916: 3; "Grassy Sprayn

Manor, A Proposed Apartment Group at Bronxville, N.Y.,"
    Architectural Record 12, no. 1. (old series vol. 28) (Jan. 1921).
49. "Rent Mutual Plan," *NYT* 16 Sept. 1923: RE1; display
    advertisement, *NYT* 21 Oct. 1923: RE8.
50. "Monthly Bill of Small 'Co-op,'" *NYT*; Pink, *New Day in
    Housing*, 152–53; "Rockefeller Opens Cooperative Flats,"
    NYT 10 Feb. 1927: 48; "New Homes Appear," *NYT* 11 Feb.
    1927: 20.
51. C. Long, "Consumers Cooperative Services," *Co-operation*
    XVI, no. 3 (Mar. 1930): 42–44; "A High Grade Cooperative
    Investment," *Co-operation* XVI, no. 4 (Apr. 1930): 66–67;
    "C.C.S. Annual," *Co-operation* XVII, no. 8 (Aug. 1931): 147;
    Wood, *Recent Trends in American Housing*, 184.
52. "Co-operative Housing in New York," *Co-operation* X, 115;
    Kermit C. Parsons, "Collaborative Genius: The Regional
    Planning Association of America," *Journal of the American
    Planning Association* 60, no. 4 (Autumn 1994): 464–65, 470.
53. Emmerich, "Problem of Low-priced Cooperative
    Apartments," 225. See also Richard T. Ely, "The City
    Housing Corporation and 'Sunnyside,'" *Journal of Land
    and Public Utility Economics* 2, no. 2 (Apr. 1926): 173.
54. Emmerich, "Problem of Low-priced Cooperative
    Apartments," 227–30; City of New York, Landmarks
    Preservation Commission, "Sunnyside Gardens Historic
    District Designation Report," 26 June 2007: 46.
55. Emmerich, "Problem of Low-priced Cooperative
    Apartments," 225–26.
56. City of New York, "Sunnyside Gardens Historic District
    Designation Report," 34, 74; Emmerich, "Problem of Low-
    priced Cooperative Apartments," 233.
57. Emmerich, "Problem of Low-priced Cooperative
    Apartments," 230–33.
58. Quoted in Roy Lubove, *Community Planning in the 1920s:
    The Contribution of the Regional Planning Association of
    America* (Pittsburgh: University of Pittsburgh Press, 1963),
    38. See also Lewis Mumford, *Green Memories: The Story of
    Geddes Mumford* (New York: Harcourt, Brace, 1947), 27.
59. Quotation form Emmerich, "Problem of Low-priced
    Cooperative Apartments," 233; Edith Elmer Wood, *Recent
    Trends in American Housing*, 176.
60. Housing data from Mason C. Doan, *American Housing
    Production, 1880–2000: A Concise History* (Lanham, Md.:
    University Press of America, 1997), 32–34.
61. "Small Co-operative Apartments," *ChT* 13 May 1926: 8.
62. "Own Your Own Home," *ChT* 17 May 1926: 8.
63. Quoted in James M. Goode, *Best Addresses: A Century of
    Washington's Distinguished Apartment Houses*, 2d ed.
    (Washington, D.C.: Smithsonian, 2002), 102.
64. "Table Talk," *Century* 117, no. 5 (Mar. 1929): 610; Sidney
    Howard, "The Homesick Ladies," *O. Henry Memorial
    Award Prize Stories of 1929*, ed. Blanche Colton Williams
    (Garden City, N.Y.: Doubleday, Doran, 1930), 35.
65. Salomon Toledano, letter, *NYT* 5 Apr. 1916: 12.
66. "Community Property Buyers Subjects of Pity," *Apartment
    House Journal* (San Francisco) June 1925: 6.
67. George S. Wehrwein and Coleman Woodbury, "Tenancy
    Versus Ownership as a Problem in Urban Land Utilization,"
    *Annals of the American Academy of Political and Social
    Science* 148, part 1: Real Estate Problems (Mar. 1930).
68. Merryle Stanley Rukeyser, *Financial Advice to Young

Man: A Program for Getting Along in the World (New York: Simon and Schuster, 1927), 330, 331.

69. *Guide to the Lathrop C. and Mabel H. Urban Harper Photograph Collection, ca. 1872–1954, n.d. (Bulk 1891–1934)*, New-York Historical Society, http://dlib.nyu.edu:8083/nyhsead/servlet/SaxonServlet?source=/harper.xml&style=/saxon01n2002.xsl&part=body [28 Sept. 2005].

70. Mabel Helen Urner, "The Married Life of Helen and Warren," *WP* 24 Oct. 1920: 63.

71. Mabel Helen Urner, "The Married Life of Helen and Warren," *WP* 11 June 1922: 70.

72. James Peter Warbasse, "Hoover's Committee Sheds Wisdom on Cooperative Housing," *Cooperation* XVII, no. 7 (July 1932): 138; John M. Gries and James Ford, eds., *The President's Conference on Home Building and Home Ownership Called by President Hoover, Final Reports of Committees, IV: Home Ownership, Income and Types of Dwellings* (Washington, D.C.: President's Conference on Home Building and Home Ownership, 1932), vii, 2.

73. Radford, *Modern Housing for America*, 92–99; von Hoffman, "End of the Dream," 229–31.

74. Laura Bobeczko and Richard Longstreth, "Housing Reform Meets the Marketplace: Washington and the Federal Housing Administration's Contribution to Apartment Building Design, 1935–40," *Housing Washington: Two Centuries of Residential Development and Planning in the National Capital Area*, ed. Richard Longstreth (Chicago: Center for American Places at Columbia College Chicago, 2010).

75. Bradford D. Hunt, "Was the 1937 Housing Act a Pyrrhic Victory?" *Journal of Planning History* 4, no. 3 (Aug. 2005): 202, 206; von Hoffman, "End of the Dream," 225.

76. Quoted in Lubove, *Community Planning in the 1920s*, 38.

77. Radford, *Modern Housing for America*, 188.

78. von Hoffman, "End of the Dream," 236.

79. Radford, *Modern Housing for America*, 59–64, 69–71, 76–78, 180–81, 185–87; Helen Alfred, letter to the editor, *NYT* 11 Dec. 1936: 26; "Co-operative Housing in New York," *Cooperation* X, 14; Hunt, "Was the 1937 Housing Act a Pyrrhic Victory?" 198.

80. Abraham E. Kazan, "Coöperative Housing in the United States," *Annals of the American Academy of Political and Social Science* 191 (May 1937): 137.

81. Kazan, "Coöperative Housing in the United States," 138, 140.

82. Arthur E. Albrecht, "A Student Venture in Coöperative Living," *Journal of Educational Sociology* 10, no. 5 (Jan. 1937); Chambers, "Cooperative League of the United States of America, 1916–61," 68–76; John H. Wuorinen, review of *Sweden: The Middle Way* by Marquis W. Childs (New Haven: Yale University Press, 1936), *Political Science Quarterly* 52, no. 2 (Jun 1937); Ralph Thompson, "Books of the Times," *NYT* 29 Sept. 1936: 25.

83. Hunt, "Was the 1937 Housing Act a Pyrrhic Victory?" 204–6.

84. Bobeczko and Longstreth, "Housing Reform Meets the Marketplace," 178; U.S., Federal Housing Administration, *Annual Report of the Federal Housing Administration, 1947* (Washington, D.C.: GPO, 1948), 44.

85. Bobeczko and Longstreth, "Housing Reform Meets the Marketplace," 167–69.

86. Ibid., 166–67, 169.

87. "Operative Builders Call Hoover's Plan Ruinous to Owners,"

WP 11 Aug. 1926: 2; Edmund J. Flynn, "Expert Elucidates Cooperative Plan Apartment Sales," *WP* 5 Sept. 1926: R3; "$15,000,000 to Build Hoover Home Idea," *WP* 12 May 1929: R4; Wendell P. Bradley, "Flynn Plans Low-Cost Housing to Cap Career," *WP* 20 Oct. 1957: C10; display advertisement, *WP* 25 Aug. 1929: R4; James M. Goode, *Best Addresses*, 290.

88. Edward A. MacDougall, "Cooperative Housing," *Housing Problems in America: Proceedings of the Eighth National Conference on Housing, Bridgeport, December 9, 10, and 11, 1920* (New York: National Housing Association, 1920), 52.

89. Quotation from U.S., Congress, House of Representatives, Committee on Ways and Means, Interim 69th-70th Congress, *Hearings Before the Committee on Way and Means, Revenue Revision 1927–1928*, 31 Oct. to 10 Nov. 1927 (Washington, DC: GPO, 1927), 215. See also "Tax Relief Sought for Cooperative Apartment Owners," *WP* 19 Dec. 1926: R2; "Change in Tax Law Urged on House by Realty Interests," *WP* 6 Nov. 1927: R1; "Land Development Aided by Revisions in 1928 Revenue Act," *WP* 10 June 1928: R1; "Income Tax Change Urged at Albany," *NYT* 29 Jan. 1931: 4; "Calls Tax Change Aid to Cooperatives," *NYT* 19 Apr. 1931: 50; "Allows Deductions on Cooperatives," *NYT* 1 Nov. 1942: RE2.

90. Herbert Undeen Nelson and Marion Lawrence Nelson, *New Homes in Old Countries* (Chicago: National Association of Real Estate Boards, 1937); Herbert U. Nelson, "Realty Notes," *WP* 1 Nov. 1936: R7; Herbert U. Nelson, "Realty Notes," *WP* 13 Dec. 1936: R12; Helen C. Monchow, review of Herbert Undeen Nelson and Marion Lawrence Nelson, *New Homes in Old Countries* (Chicago: National Association of Real Estate Boards, 1937), *Journal of Land and Public Utility Economics* 14, no. 1 (Feb. 1933): 107–8.

91. Herbert U. Nelson, "Urban Housing and Land Use," *Law and Contemporary Problems* (Duke University School of Law) 1, no. 2 (Mar. 1934): 165; "Cooperative Home Called Beneficial," *NYT* 15 June 1937: 42.

92. "Cooperative Home Called Beneficial," *NYT* 15 June 1937: 42. See also Hunt, "Was the 1937 Housing Act a Pyrrhic Victory?" 206; "New FHA Ruling Asked," *NYT* 22 May 1938: RE10.

93. "Parisian Likes Skyscrapers for Housing," *WP* 20 Aug. 1939: R2. See also "Discusses Housing for Workers," *NYT* 8 Aug. 1937: RE10; "Munich Provides Low-cost Homes," *NYT* 22 Aug. 1937: RE1; "Housing Stressed in German Exhibit," *NYT* 29 Aug. 1937: RE1; "England Building Homes for 300,000," *NYT* 5 Sept. 1937: RE1; "Italy Is Building Many New Homes," *NYT* 19 Sept. 1937: RE1; "Ancient Towns in Europe Have Building Boom," *WP* 23 Jan. 1938: R7.

94. Herbert U. Nelson, "USHA Urged to Aid Mutual Home Societies," *WP* 21 Jan. 1940: R3.

95. "College Teachers Plan Cooperative," *NYT* 15 May 1936: 23; "Civil Service Men Plan Joint Housing," *NYT* 28 Nov. 1936: 19; "Boss, Phelps Add New Department," *WP* 26 Sept. 1937: R10; "South Shore Flats Will Be Sold as 'Co-op,'" *ChT* 5 Mar. 1939: C18; " 'Cooperative' Proposed," *NYT* 15 May 1938: RE1; John P. Marquand, *Point of No Return* (Boston: Little, Brown, 1949), 87.

CHAPTER 4. VERTICAL SUBDIVISIONS

1. Andrea A. Krest, "The Postwar Garden Apartment: Housing for the Middle Class in Bell Park Gardens,

Queens," M.S. thesis, Columbia University, 1984, 28; display advertisement, *NYT* 13 June 1948: R2. On the suburban character of Bell Park and Bayside, see Sylvie Murray, *The Progressive Housewife: Community Activism in Suburban Queens, 1945–1965* (Philadelphia: University of Pennsylvania Press, 2003), 30.

2. Quoted in Krest, "Postwar Garden Apartment," 29–30.
3. New York State, Division of Housing, *Annual Report of the Commissioner of Housing to the Governor and the Legislature* (1949), 6.
4. Krest, "Postwar Garden Apartment," 57, 58.
5. Ibid., 51–52, 56; Martha Biondi, *To Stand and Fight: The Struggle for Civil Rights in Postwar New York City* (Cambridge: Harvard University Press, 2003), 227. On political activity among women at Bell Park and suburban Queens generally, see Murray, *Progressive Housewife* (on Bell Park specifically, 79–82).
6. Krest, "Postwar Garden Apartment," iv, 58–59, 62; Barbara A. Smith, *Still Giving Kisses: A Guide to Helping and Enjoying the Alzheimer's Victim You Love* (Raleigh: Lulu, 2008), 38.
7. Herbert Mitgang, "From the Suburbs Back to the City," *NYT* 15 May 1955: SM17.
8. Mason C. Doan, *American Housing Production 1880–2000: A Concise History* (Lanham, Md.: University Press of America, 1997), 43–44, 51, 60, 67, 74; Laura Bobeczko and Richard Longstreth, "Housing Reform Meets the Marketplace: Washington and the Federal Housing Administration's Contribution to Apartment Building Design, 1935–40," in *Housing Washington: Two Centuries of Residential Development and Planning in the National Capital Area*, ed. Richard Longstreth (Chicago: Center for American Places at Columbia College Chicago, 2010), 178.
9. On rent control, see, for example, Joel Schwartz, "Tenant Power in the Liberal City, 1943–1971," in *The Tenant Movement in New York City, 1904–1984*, ed. Ronald Lawson (New Brunswick: Rutgers University Press, 1986).
10. Quotation from "Rent Rule Changes for Cooperatives," *NYT* 17 Feb. 1945: 26. See also "OPA Sifts Offers on 'Co-op' Housing," *NYT* 20 Dec. 1944: 33; Charles Grutzner, "Officials Battle Widening Racket in 'Co-op' Home Sales," *NYT* 16 May 1946: 1; "See 'Cooperative' Racket," *NYT* 18 May 1946: 19; "Cooperatives for Whom?" *WP* 16 Oct. 1948: 6; Better Business Bureau of New York City, *The Conversion of Apartment Buildings into Cooperatives* (New York, 1946).
11. "Tenants Reviving Old Cooperatives," *NYT* 16 Dec. 1944: 17; Grutzner, "Officials Battle Widening Racket in 'Co-op' Home Sales," 1, 37; "Tenants Advised on 'Co-op' Racket," *NYT* 29 May 1946: 25; "Court Upholds Tenant Evictions in Cooperative Apartment Sales," *NYT* 12 July 1947: 1; Douglas L. Elliman, "State the Case for the Landlord," *NYT* 20 July 1947: R1.
12. Kristin Szylvian Bailey, "The Federal Government and the Cooperative Housing Movement, 1917–1955," diss., Carnegie Mellon University, 1988 (Ann Arbor: UMI, 1989), abstract, 34–39, 51–59, 72–74; Kristin M. Szylvian, "The Federal Housing Program During World War II," in *From Tenements to the Taylor Homes: In Search of an Urban Housing Policy in Twentieth Century America*, ed. John F. Bauman, Robert Biles, and Kristin M. Szylvian (University

Park: Pennsylvania State University Press, 2000), 133.
13. Elsie Danenberg, *Get Your Own Home the Co-operative Way* (New York: Greenberg, 1949); U.S., National Housing Agency, *Mutual Housing, a Veterans Guide: Organizing, Financing, Constructing, and Operating Several Selected Types of Cooperative Housing Associations, with Special Reference to Available Federal Aids* (Washington, D.C.: GPO, 1946); Florence E. Parker, *Nonprofit Housing Projects in the United States*, Bulletin of the United States Bureau of Labor Statistics No. 896 (Washington, D.C.: GPO, 1947); Jean Robert Karin, "Cooperative Housing in the United States," M.S. thesis, University of Chicago, 1947 (Ann Arbor: UMI, 1947); Herman T. Stichman, "Cooperation in the Field of Housing Can Break the Log Jam: An Address by Herman T. Stichman, Commission of Housing, State of New York at the Annual Meeting of New York State Conference of Mayors and Other Municipal Officials, Buffalo, June 19, 1947," pamphlet, VF.
14. Joel Schwartz, *The New York Approach: Robert Moses, Urban Liberals, and Redevelopment of the Inner City* (Columbus: Ohio State University Press, 1993), 134–35.
15. "Veterans' Housing in Queens Speeded," *NYT* 3 Sept. 1948: 38; Krest, "Postwar Garden Apartment," 44; Joseph Lapal, "H. T. Stichman and B. P. G.," *Bell Park News* XXIII, no. 6 (Oct. 1973): 3; Stichman, "Cooperation in the Field of Housing Can Break the Log Jam"; Herman T. Stichman, "Labor's Role in Shaping Home Building Policy and the Future of Cooperative Housing in America: An Address by Herman T. Stichman, Commissioner of Housing, State of New York, at the Meeting of the Executive Council of the American Federation of Labor, Miami Beach, January 31, 1950," VF.
16. Display advertisement, *NYT* 31 May 1949: 42.
17. Hilary Botein, "Visions of Community: Post-war Housing Projects of Local 3, International Brotherhood of Electrical Workers, and Local 1199, Hospital Workers Union," *Planning Perspectives* 24, no. 2 (Apr. 2009); Schwartz, *New York Approach*, 126–28, 137; Lee E. Cooper, "$8,000,000 Private Project to Offer Non-Profit Homes," *NYT* 19 Sept. 1948: 1.
18. "Veterans Buy East Side House; Separate Loan on Each 'Co-op,'" *NYT* 22 Dec. 1946: R1; "Veterans Get Apartment Deeds Outright As 'Co-ops' Are Sold Out Under New Plan," *NYT* 30 Mar. 1947: R1; "Ex-GI's Get 'Co-op' Deeds," *NYT* 3 Aug. 1947: R1; Stanley W. Penn, "Novelty in Realty," *Wall Street Journal* 8 Mar. 1962: 1.
19. "Closets Feature Plan for Housing," *NYT* 17 Apr. 1949: R4; "O'Dwyer Program on Housing Hailed," *NYT* 9 Sept. 1949: 27.
20. Richard Siegler and Herbert J. Levy, "Brief History of Cooperative Housing," *Cooperative Housing Journal* (1986): 16.
21. "Realtors to Ask U. S. Aid for Cooperatives," *WP* 19 Dec. 1948: V1.
22. U.S., Congress, Senate, Committee on Banking and Currency Subcommittee Investigating and Studying European Housing Programs, *Cooperative Housing in Europe* (Washington, D.C.: GPO, 1950), 10–11, 22–25, 36–38; Harald Dickson, "Sweden Plans Its Housing Policy," *Journal of Land and Public Utility Economics* 23, no. 4 (Nov. 1947).
23. "Realtors to Ask U. S. Aid for Cooperatives," *WP* 19 Dec. 1948: V1.

24. "Realty Group 'Cool' Toward Co-op Program," *WP* 16 Jan. 1949: R1.

25. "Congress Now Has 6 Housing Bills," *WP* 28 Jan. 1949: 18; Mary Spargo, "Sparkman Offers New Housing Bill," *WP* 13 July 1949: 2; editorial, "Cooperative Housing," *WP* 14 Aug. 1949: B4; Bailey, *Federal Government and the Cooperative Housing Movement*, 90; U.S., Congress, House of Representatives, Committee on Banking and Currency, 81st Congress, 2d Session, *Cooperative Housing: Hearings on H.R. 6618 and H.R. 6742*, 30, 31 Jan., 1–3, 6–10, 14 Feb. 1950 (Washington, D.C.: GPO, 1950), 13; Murray, *Progressive Housewife*, 43–45; Cooperative League of the U.S.A., *Help for Housing's Forgotten 40 Million* (Chicago: Cooperative League of the U.S.A., 1949); American Federation of Labor, *Homes for Union Members* (Washington, D.C.: American Federation of Labor, 1949); Jack Carter, letter to the editor, "Middle Income Housing," *WP* 30 May 1949: 6.

26. Editorial, "Cooperative Housing," *WP* 14 Aug. 1949: B4; John O'Grady, "Flaws in the Middle Income Housing Bill," *WP* 1 Sept. 1949: 9.

27. U.S., Congress, Senate, Committee on Banking and Currency, 81st Congress, 2d Session, *Middle-income Housing: Hearings on Amendments to S. 2246, to Amend the National Housing Act, as Amended, and for Other Purposes*, 12, 13, 16–18 Jan. 1950 (Washington, D.C.: GPO, 1950), 138.

28. Charles M. Haar, "Middle Income Housing: The Cooperative Snare?" *Land Economics* 29, no. 4 (Nov. 1953): 293.

29. U.S., Senate, *Cooperative Housing in Europe*, 5.

30. U.S., *Cooperative Housing*, 13.

31. "Builders Warned About Housing Aid," *NYT* 21 Feb. 1950: 40; Clayton Knowles, "'Co-op' Housing Defeat May Be Campaign Issue," *NYT* 26 Mar. 1950: E10.

32. "Veterans Forming Co-ops on Housing," *NYT* 6 Mar. 1946: 29; "Veterans Buy East Side House; Separate Loan on Each 'Co-op'"; "Apartment Boom," *Architectural Forum* 92 (Jan. 1950): 106; display advertisements, *NYT* 21 Nov. 1946: 6; 19 Jan. 1947: R5, 20 Jan. 1947: 17.

33. Roger Willcox, "Consumer Sponsored, Presold, New Construction Housing Cooperatives," TS, National Association of Housing Cooperatives, http://www.coophousing.org/DisplayPage.aspx?id=716&bMenu=76&bItem=76 [14 Sept. 2010], 2.

34. Doan, *American Housing Production, 1880–2000*, 62; Louis Winnick, *Rental Housing: Opportunities for Private Investment* (New York: McGraw-Hill, 1958), 242; Irving Welfeld, *Where We Live: A Social History of American Housing* (New York: Simon and Schuster, 1988), 64–66; U.S., Federal Housing Administration, *Annual Report,* 1950 (Washington, D.C.: GPO, 1951); Joseph B. Mason, *History of Housing in the U.S., 1930–1980* (Houston: Gulf, 1982), 67–69; "Apartment Boom," *Architectural Forum;* "Co-op Housing Urged on Nonprofit Groups," *NYT* 2 Apr. 1953: 48.

35. U.S., Federal Housing Administration, *Brochure of Information and Forms on Cooperative Housing Under Section 213 of the National Housing Act,* FHA No. 3251 (Washington, D.C.: Federal Housing Administration, 1958).

36. Roger Willcox, "Cooperative Techniques and Effective Reduction in Housing Costs," *Land Economics* 29, no. 4 (Nov. 1953): 295; U.S., Congress, House of Representatives, Committee on Banking and Currency, Subcommittee on Housing, 84th Congress, 1st Session, *Investigation of Housing, 1955: Hearings on H. Res. 203,* Los Angeles, 16–18 Nov. 1955 (Washington, D.C.: GPO, 1955), Part 2.

37. "New Set of Garden Apartments Offered at 'Co-op' in Bayside," *NYT* 15 Apr. 1956: 283; "Norman K. Winston, Housing Developer," *NYT* 17 Oct. 1977: 34.

38. Display advertisements, *NYT* 13 Apr. 1947: R7; 11 May 1947: R6; 30 May 1947: 32; 15 June 1947: R3; 2 Nov. 1947: R2; 21 Mar. 1948: R5; 1 Apr. 1951: R3; 30 Mar. 1952: R5; 4 May 1952: R2; and 15 June 1952: R11.

39. "Families Buying 'Garden' Suites," *NYT* 11 July 1964: R1.

40. Schwartz, *New York Approach*, 135–36, 176; Hilary Ballon and Kenneth T. Jackson, eds., *Robert Moses and Modern City: The Transformation of New York* (New York: W. W. Norton, 2007), 251–54.

41. Joshua B. Freeman, *Working-class New York: Life and Labor Since World War II* (New York: New Press, 2000), 116–19; Ballon and Jackson, *Robert Moses and Modern City*, 267–69, 274–75, 289–94, 303–7; Peter Eisenstadt, *Rochdale Village: Robert Moses, 6,000 Families, and New York City's Great Experiment in Integrated Housing* (Ithaca, N.Y.: Cornell University Press, 2010), 109.

42. Ira S. Robbins, "Conversion of Public Housing into Cooperatives," *Proceedings of the Third National Conference on Cooperative Housing*, 15–16 Feb. 1960, Washington, D.C. (Washington, D.C.: National Association of Housing Cooperatives, 1960), 17; "City Housing Eyes Cooperative Plan," *NYT* 22 Sept. 1955: 28; Charles Grutzner, "Co-ops Proposed in Public Housing," *NYT* 13 Mar. 1959: 14; "City Board Acts to Convert East Side Project to Co-op," *NYT* 15 Feb. 1965: 20; Peter Kihss, "Forest Hills Co-op Plan Poses Complex Problems," *NYT* 17 Dec. 1972: BQLI99.

43. Steven R. Weisman, "Mitchell-Lama Housing Periled," *NYT* 27 Dec. 1970: 48; Cynthia Ann Curran, "Administration of Subsidized Housing in New York State Co-op City: A Case Study of the Largest Subsidized Cooperative Housing Development in the Nation," diss., New York University, 1978 (Ann Arbor: UMI, 1978), 5; Michael T. Kaufman, "Labor Sponsoring New City Housing," *NYT* 11 Mar. 1962: R1.

44. Carol King, "Village Creek Founder Honored For Life's Work," *Hour* (Norwalk, Conn.), 7 Sept. 2010, http://www.thehour.com/story/491196 [14 Sept. 2010]; Betty Friedan, "We Built a Community for Our Children," *Redbook* Mar. 1955,http://www.vchoa.com/vc_history.html [14 Sept. 2010]; Tom Andersen and Gina Federico, "Village Creek, Norwalk: Connecticut's First Historic District of Modern Houses," modern, http://modernhousenotes.blogspot.com/2010/01/village-creek-norwalk-connecticuts.html [14 Sept. 2010]; Gordon Cavanaugh, "Globalization of an Affordable Housing Nonprofit," *Journal of Affordable Housing and Community Development* 11 (2001–2): 121–27; Andrew Scott Dolkart, *Row House Reborn: Architecture and Neighborhoods in New York City, 1908–1929* (Baltimore: Johns Hopkins University Press, 2009), 151; "Village Landmark May Be Replaced," *NYT* 26 June 1932: RE1; Willcox, "Consumer Sponsored, Presold, New Construction Housing Cooperatives," 1.

45. Willcox, "Consumer Sponsored, Presold, New Construction Housing Cooperatives," 1–5; Charles Nutting, "Conversion of Rental Housing to Cooperative," *Proceedings of the*

Fourth National Conference on Cooperative Housing, 13–14 Feb. 1961, Washington, D.C. (Washington, D.C.: National Association of Housing Cooperatives, 1961), 6–7.

46. Leandro Benmergui, "The Alliance for Progress and Housing Policy in Rio de Janeiro and Buenos Aires in the 1960s," *Urban History* 36, no. 2 (2009): 303–26: 317; Francisco Rafael Jordán Garcia, "El Cooperativismo de Vivienda en Puerto Rico," TS, 1996, special collections, Biblioteca Lázaro, Universidad de Puerto Rico, Recinto Rio Piedras; Willcox, "Consumer Sponsored, Presold, New Construction Housing Cooperatives," 7, appendix.

47. Herbert J. Gans, "Urbanism and Suburbanism as Ways of Life," in *People, Plans, and Policies: Essays on Poverty, Racism, and Other National Urban Problems* (New York: Columbia University Press, 1991), 63.

48. Mitgang, "From the Suburbs Back to the City."

49. Clara Fox, *Community Living in Cooperative Housing: A Report on a Two-year Pilot Project* (New York: Play Schools Association, 1958).

50. Schick Grossman and Susan K. Kinoy, *Learning to Live in a Middle Income Cooperative,* Play Schools Association Cooperative Housing Report, 1961 no. 2 (New York: Play Schools Association, 1961), 1, 7–8, 20; Clara Fox, *Volunteer Leadership in Cooperative Housing* (New York: Play Schools Association, 1960), 49.

51. Thomas W. Ennis, "2 Co-ops Set Here Under State Act," *NYT* 25 Aug. 1957: R1; Edmond J. Barnett, "Architects Use Difficult Sites," *NYT* 15 Jan. 1961: R1; Grossman and Kinoy, *Learning to Live in a Middle Income Cooperative,* 10–11.

52. D. J. Waldie, *Holy Land: A Suburban Memoir* (New York: W. W. Norton, 1996); Corinne Demas, *Eleven Stories High: Growing Up in Stuyvesant Town, 1948–1968* (Albany: State University of New York Press, 2000).

53. Krest, "Postwar Garden Apartment," 48; Olga Pierce Lytle, "Queens Private Line," *New York Amsterdam News* 19 July 1958: 20; U.S., National Commission on Urban Problems, *Hearings,* vol. 5, Oct. 1967, Detroit, St. Louis, East St. Louis, Washington, D.C. (Washington, D.C.: GPO, 1968), 70–71; Grossman and Kinoy, *Learning to Live in a Middle Income Cooperative,* 1, 15–16.

54. Fox, *Community Living in Cooperative Housing,* 20, 44; Grossman and Kinoy, *Learning to Live in a Middle Income Cooperative,* 17.

55. Schwartz, *New York Approach,* 111; Biondi, *To Stand and Fight,* 223; Grossman and Kinoy, *Learning to Live in a Middle Income Cooperative,* 20. On Queensview, see Charles Abrams, *Forbidden Neighbors: A Study of Prejudice in Housing* (New York: Harper, 1955), 274, 318.

56. Fox, *Community Living in Cooperative Housing,* 53.

57. Kurt Lang and Gladys Engel Lang, "Resistance to School Desegregation: A Case Study of Backlash Among Jews" (1965), in *Problems and Prospects of the Negro Movement,* ed. Raymond John Murphy and Howard Elinson (Belmont, Calif.: Wadsworth, 1966), 146–50, 155–56.

58. Fox, *Community Living in Cooperative Housing,* 12, 25.

59. Willcox, "Consumer Sponsored, Presold, New Construction Housing Cooperatives," 2; Kaufman, "Labor Sponsoring New City Housing."

60. Nelson N. Foote et al., *Housing Choices and Housing Constraints* (New York: McGraw Hill, 1960), 387–443.

61. Ibid., 388, 392, 395–97, 408, 430–35, 438.

62. Schwartz, *New York Approach,* 244; Ballon and Jackson, *Robert Moses and Modern City,* 267–69, 274–75; "Our Housing Needs," editorial, *New York Amsterdam News* 30 June 1951: 8; "Slice Payments on L.I. Houses," *New York Amsterdam News* 30 June 1951: 10; "Making Steps Forward," editorial, *New York Amsterdam News* 13 Oct. 1951: 8; "Merrick Park Gardens," *Journal of Housing* 10 (Oct. 1953): 338–39, 353.

63. "Merrick Park Gardens," *Journal of Housing;* State of New York, Division of Housing and Community Renewal, *The ABC of Ownership in State-aided Cooperative Housing* (1960), 5–12.

64. David Clurman and Edna L. Hebard, *Condominiums and Cooperatives* (New York: Wiley-Interscience, 1970), 209.

65. William S. Everett, "Condominium and Co-operative Apartments—the New Frontier in Housing," *Journal of Property Management* 27, no. 1 (Fall 1961): 15.

66. Thomas W. Ennis, "Profits from Co-ops," *NYT* 8 Jan. 1961: R1; Edmond J. Barnett, "Self-government Reigns in Co-ops," *NYT* 22 May 1960: R1; Clurman and Hebard, *Condominiums and Cooperatives,* 209.

67. Charles H. Lavigne, editorial, "Why Did These Co-ops Fail?" *Bell Park News* XIX, no. 1 (Feb. 1969): 2.

68. Riverbay Corporation, *United Housing Foundation Invites Your Participation in Co-op City: A Cooperative Housing Community* (New York: United Housing Foundation, 1965).

69. Freeman, *Working-class New York,* 111–19.

70. Whyte quoted in Roger Schafer, letter to the editor, "New York's Housing Cooperatives," *NYT* 3 July 1968: 24; Ada Louis Huxtable, "A Singularly New York Product," *NYT* 25 Nov. 1968: 43.

71. Eisenstadt, *Rochdale Village,* 247; Freeman, *Working-class New York,* 120–23; Ballon and Jackson, *Robert Moses and Modern City,* 275, 306; Curran, "Administration of Subsidized Housing in New York State Co-op City"; David K. Shipler, "City Takes Action Against 14 Co-ops," *NYT* 20 Nov. 1968: 51.

72. U.S., *Investigation of Housing,* 1955, Part 1, 386.

73. U.S., Federal Housing Administration, *Annual Report,* 1955 (Washington, D.C.: GPO, 1956), 6; U.S., Federal Housing Administration, *Annual Report,* 1956 (Washington, D.C.: GPO, 1957), 3.

74. U.S., National Commission on Urban Problems, *Hearings,* vol. 5, 85.

75. U.S., *Investigation of Housing, 1955,* Part 1, 197.

76. Ibid., Part 1, 209; U.S., Federal Housing Administration, *Annual Report,* 1956 (Washington, D.C.: GPO, 1957), 3; U.S., Comptroller General, *Report to the Congress: Limited Success of Investor-sponsor Cooperative Housing Program* (Washington, D.C.: General Accounting Office, 1968).

77. U.S., National Commission on Urban Problems, *Hearings,* 89–90. See also U.S., *Investigation of Housing, 1955,* Part 2, 143–47, and Part 3, 236–38.

78. Alexander Garvin, *The American City: What Works, What Doesn't,* 2d ed. (New York: McGraw-Hill Professional, 2002), 226, 262; Jack T. Conway, "Cooperative Housing Has Flourished," *Proceedings of the Fifth National Conference on Cooperative Housing,* 12–13 Feb. 1962, Washington, D.C. (Washington, D.C.: National Association of Housing

Cooperatives, 1962), 21–24; U.S., Federal Housing Administration, *Annual Report*, 1962 (Washington, D.C.: GPO, 1963), 6–7.

79. Henri Lefebvre, "Right to the City," in *Writings on Cities*, trans. and ed. Eleonore Kofman and Elizabeth Lebas (Malden, Mass.: Blackwell, 1996), 77–81 (quotation 79).

80. Quoted in Gurney Breckenfeld, "Misleading Myths of Middle-income Housing," *HH* 25, no. 3 (Mar. 1964): 137.

81. Quoted in ibid., 137.

82. Ibid., 147.

83. Thomas W. Ennis, "Low-Income Co-ops Are Planned Here," *NYT* 20 Apr. 1969: R1; "Co-ops for Poor Gaining," *NYT* 27 Aug. 1972: R7; Robert E. Tomasson, "Slow Gains Made in Ownership Drive," *NYT* 31 Dec. 1972: R1; "Why Rush to Condominiums Is Picking Up Speed," *U.S. News and World Report* 6 Aug. 1973: 48–49.

84. Gerald W. Sazama, "Lessons from the History of Affordable Housing Cooperatives in the United States: A Case Study in American Affordable Housing Policy," *American Journal of Economics and Sociology* 59, no. 4 (Oct. 2000): 586; U.S., National Commission on Urban Problems, *Hearings*, vol. 5, iii, 56; Willcox, "Consumer Sponsored, Presold, New Construction Housing Cooperatives," 7–8.

85. Freeman, *Working-class New York*, 123; Sazama, "Lessons from the History of Affordable Housing Cooperatives in the United States," 587–88; Curran, "Administration of Subsidized Housing in New York State Co-op City"; Steven R. Weisman, "Mitchell-Lama Housing Periled," *NYT* 27 Dec. 1970: 48.

86. See, for example, Sukumar Ganapati, "Enabling Housing Cooperatives: Policy Lessons from Sweden, India and the United States," *International Journal of Urban and Regional Research* 34, no. 2 (June 2010).

87. Willcox, "Consumer Sponsored, Presold, New Construction Housing Cooperatives," 10; Bailey, *Federal Government and the Cooperative Housing Movement*, 112–23; Ballon and Jackson, *Robert Moses and Modern City*, 291, 295.

CHAPTER 5. LEISURE WORLDS

1. Joseph B. Mason, *History of Housing in the U.S., 1930–1980* (Houston: Gulf, 1982), 91, 114; Judith Ann Trolander, *From Sun Cities to the Villages: A History of Adult, Age-restricted Communities* (Gainesville: University Press of Florida, 2011).

2. Norman D. Ford, *Norman Ford's Florida: A Complete Guide to Finding What You Seek in Florida* (Greenlawn, N.Y.: Harian, 1955), 44, 52.

3. Mason, *History of Housing in the U.S., 1930–1980*, 42–49, 53, 69–73; "Florida's First Retirement City Near Miami," *MH* 18 Nov. 1951: 6-G; "'Retirement Village' Is Started by N. Y. Developers in Florida," *NYT* 23 Sept. 1951: R1; "Leisure City," *Florida Building Journal* Feb. 1954: 28; Trolander, *From Sun Cities to the Villages*, 39–46.

4. Ford, *Norman Ford's Florida*, 47, 52; display advertisement, *MH* 20 July 1958: 21-G.

5. Quotation from Polly Redford, *Billion-dollar Sandbar: A Biography of Miami Beach* (New York: Dutton, 1970), 206; Deborah Dash Moore, *To the Golden Cities: Pursuing the American Jewish Dream in Miami and L.A.* (New York: Free Press, 1994), 19–20.

6. Mrs. Leon Weiner quoted in Kay Murphy, "Living's So Much Clubbier," *MH* 29 Jan. 1961: 1-G.

7. Alice T. Friedman, "Merchandising Miami Beach: Morris Lapidus and the Architecture of Abundance," *Journal of Decorative and Propaganda Arts* 25 (2005); Redford, *Billion-dollar Sandbar*, 204–5, 216, 237; "Florida I: Miami," *Fortune* 8, no. 1 (Jan. 1936): 40; "Miami and Miami Beach," *Life*, 4 Mar. 1940: 60; "Motel Row," *MH* 28 Oct. 1951: 1-H; "Comment: Miami Adds 1000 Residents Weekly," *FB* Feb. 1955: 72; City of Miami, *Outwitting Winter in the Cities of the Sun: Miami, Coral Gables, Miami Beach* (Miami: Graydon E. Bevis, 1935), Historical Museum of South Florida, pamphlets collection, folder "Dade County, Description and Travel, 1930–1939, Pamphlets."

8. Ford, *Norman Ford's Florida*, 44.

9. Display advertisement, *NYT* 20 July 1924: RE7; "Miami Beach to Have 22-Story Co-op Palace," *ChT* 25 Oct. 1925: B4; C. W. Barron, "Tells Great Plans for Coral Gables," *NYT* 13 Mar. 1926: 36; "Coral Gables Apartment," *NYT* 16 May 1926: RE2; Micah Mayell (Lionel V. Mayell's grandson), personal interview, 25 Apr. 2006; Dick Meyers, "High-rise Buildings Boost County Growth," *MH* 29 Jan. 1967: 20-G; Arva Moore Parks, "Where the River Found the Bay: A Historical Study of the Granada Site," MS, Historical Museum of South Florida, manuscripts collection, MS box 11.

10. Charles Abrams, *Forbidden Neighbors: A Study of Prejudice in Housing* (New York: Harper, 1955), 198–203.

11. "Florida I: Miami," *Fortune*, 35; Budd Schulberg, "Florida's Gold Coast," *Holiday* Jan. 1952: 26; John Kobler, "Roughing It at Miami Beach," *Saturday Evening Post*, 23 Feb. 1957: 19; Charles Darragh, "Grater Miami: Big, Overgrown Youngster," *FT* Jan. 1961: 17; Redford, *Billion-dollar Sandbar*; Stephen Birmingham, "Fort Lauderdale: 'How Big Is Your Boat?'" *The Right Places (for the Right People)* (Boston: Little, Brown, 1973).

12. Carl L. Biemiller, "Fort Lauderdale," *Holiday* Nov. 1954: 61.

13. Dick Meyers, "High-rise Buildings Boost County Growth," *MH* 29 Jan. 1967: 20-G; Marilyn Unmacht, "Local Group Has Its Own Florida Home," *ChT* 10 Jan. 1956: B4; Judith Cass, "'Under Heavenly Protection'—in Florida," *ChT* 19 Feb. 1957: A5; and photo standalone, *MH* 26 Jan. 1958: 2-F.

14. Eric P. Nash and Randall C. Robinson, Jr., *MiMO: Miami Modern Revealed* (San Francisco: Chronicle, 2004), 104–7, 179–81; "Funeral Notice: McKirahan," *New Orleans Times-Picayune* 29 June 2005: Metro 5; display advertisement, *ChT* 20 Feb. 1955: A9; "Warren Folding Doors Extensively Used in Sea Club Apartments," *Florida Building Journal* July 1955: 46; Thomas W. Ennis, "Co-ops Play Part in Florida Boom," *NYT* 30 June 1957: R1; and display advertisements, *MH* 20 Mar. 1955: 4-G; 1 May 1955: 12-F; 3 Feb. 1957: 13-F.

15. On Continental Square, see "Miami Apartments to Cost $16,000,000," *FB* May 1947: 9. On Gold Coast Apartments, see photo standalone, *MH* 6 Mar. 1949: 1-G; "Two Cooperative Projects Proposed Here," *MH* 13 Mar. 1949: 6-G; "First Cooperative Apartment Set for Miami Beach," *WP* 3 Apr. 1949: R1; "Plans to Build a Cooperative on Miami Beach," *ChT* 24 Apr. 1949: H4.

16. "New Co-op Apartment," *MH* 7 Aug. 1955: 3-G; "New Luxury Apartment Buildings," *MH* 18 Dec. 1955: 7-F;

"New Co-op Apartments" *MH* 15 Jan. 1956: 6-F; "Another Co-op on Bay Harbor," *MH* 21 Oct. 1956: 1-G; "The Living Is Carefree," *MH* 18 Nov. 1956: 1-F; letter and brochure packets for Harbour Club Cooperative Apartments, 26 Aug. 1959 and 26 Jan. 1960, Historical Museum of South Florida, folder "Miami Beach, Pamphlets."

17. "New Co-op Apartment on Bay Harbor Island," *MH* 10 Feb. 1957: 2-F; display advertisement, *MH* 24 Feb. 1957: 17-F; "Coral Sea Towers Nears Completion," *FB* May 1957: 5.

18. "Cold Coast's New Aspect," *NYT* 7 Apr. 1957: XX13.

19. Kay Murphy, "For Moneyed Visitors: The Co-operative! A New Model of Luxurious Living," *MH* 22 May 1955: 9-F.

20. "Warren Folding Doors Extensively Used in Sea Club Apartments," *Florida Building Journal* July 1955: 46.

21. John Senning, "Co-operative Apartments! A New Mode for Florida Living Arrives in Miami," *MH* 12 Feb. 1956: 1-F.

22. Murphy, "For Moneyed Visitors"; display advertisement, *MH* 24 Feb. 1957: 17-F.

23. Jeff Donelly, independent scholar, personal interview, 4 Apr. 2005; and Mitch S. Novack, Sherbrooke owner, personal interview, 4 Apr. 2005.

24. "Senior Citizens Project Sets New Sales Record," *LAT* 31 Dec. 1961: C4; "Co-op Units Readied at Elderly Project," *LAT* 4 Feb. 1962: M10; "Buyers from 38 States Attracted to Senior Citizens' Community," *LAT* 16 Sept. 1962: M23; "Record Sales Pace at Project Reported," *LAT* 22 Oct. 1962: I2; "Sales Department Shows Its Thanks," *LAT* 7 July 1963: O3. For a more detailed history of Leisure World, see Trolander, *From Sun Cities to the Villages*, chap. 3.

25. "Features of New Homes Winning Owner Approval," *LAT* 11 July 1954: E8; "Builder Reports Near Sellout of New Tract," *LAT* 6 Nov. 1955: F21; "Extensive Community Program Announced," *LAT* 9 Sept. 1956: E19; "Wall Encircles New Long Beach Project," *LAT* 1 June 1958: F4; Trolander, *From Sun Cities to the Villages*, 83–84.

26. Mason, *History of Housing in the U.S., 1930–1980*, 53; Trolander, *From Sun Cities to the Villages*, 23–25, 39–42, 56.

27. Mason, *History of Housing in the U.S., 1930–1980*, 117. On Sun City, see also John M. Findlay, *Magic Lands: Western Cityscapes and American Culture After 1940* (Berkeley: University of California Press, 1992), chap. 4; Trolander, *From Sun Cities to the Villages*, chap. 2; Paul O'Neil, "For the Retired, a World All Their Own," *Life* 68, no. 18 (15 May 1970): 45–50.

28. Tom Cameron, "$150 Million Retirement City Set," *LAT* 30 July 1961: I2; "Huge Globe Will Mark Entranceway of Project," *LAT* 6 Aug. 1961: I13; Frank Mulcahy, "Unique City Opening Today," *LAT* 29 Oct. 1961: I1. Quotation from display advertisement, *LAT* 12 Nov. 1961: N9.

29. "Widening World of Retirement Towns," *Life* 55, no. 19 (8 Nov. 1963): 102.

30. Tom Cameron, "Nailing It Down," *LAT* 4 Aug. 1963: O1. On design of Leisure World: Tom Barratt, director of Golden Rain Foundation, personal interview, 25 Oct. 2007.

31. Quoted in Tom Cameron, "Retirement Housing Projects Rising Throughout Southland," *LAT* 27 Aug. 1961: I1.

32. "Widening World of Retirement Towns," *Life*, 94–95; Mason, *History of Housing in the U.S., 1930–1980*, 123.

33. Cameron, "Nailing It Down," *LAT* 4 Aug. 1963.

34. Mason, *History of Housing in the U.S., 1930–1980*, 117.

35. For prices, see display advertisements, *LAT* 22 Nov. 1959: L39; 6 Nov. 1960: M9.

36. "Size up Florida as a Place to Retire," *Kiplinger Magazine* Mar. 1961: 25–32.

37. Frederic Sherman, "A Co-op Gets in a Tight," *MH* 25 Nov. 1962: 1-F; Frederic Sherman, "Safety Valve for FHA Co-ops," *MH* 20 Jan. 1963: 2-F; Fred E. Fogarty, "Point View Makes Try as Co-op," *MH* 3 Oct. 1965: 1-H; Fred E. Fogarty, "A Bargain Price on High-rise?" *MH* 12 Dec. 1965: 1-L.

38. On Whatley, see Brown L. Whatley, "Today's Home Mortgage Outlook," *FB* Mar. 1953: 13; Brown L. Whatley, "Today's Home Mortgage Outlook," *FB* Apr. 1953: 12; display advertisement, *FB* Oct. 1958: 18; "Bal Harbour FHA Project Is Sewed Up," *MH* 15 Jan. 1961: 3-G; Brown L. Whatley, "Condominium in Florida: Will it Cause a Real Estate Revolution?" *FT* Sept. 1962: 20; Fred Sherman, "Florida Decrees Full Disclosure and Three-year Warranty on Condominiums," *HH* July 1972: 40; and "Condomania— The Craze Intensifies," *FT* Oct. 1972: 35. On lending in Puerto Rico, see David Clurman and Edna L. Hebard, *Condominiums and Cooperatives* (New York: Wiley-Interscience, 1970), 4.

39. Fédération Internationale des Géomètres, Office International du Cadastre et du Régime Foncier, *Apartment Property and Cadastre* (The Hague: Fédération Internationale des Géomètres, 1965); Alexia Yates, "Owning Walls and Floors: The Emergence of Apartment Co-ownership in Twentieth-century Paris," 5th Biennial Conference, Urban History Association, Las Vegas, 20–23 Oct. 2010; Emmanuel B. Marmaras, "Speculative Upper and Middle Class Apartment Building in Interwar Athens: Institutional Context, Spatial Location, and Production Process," Ph.D. Thesis Summary TS, 1985, National Technical University of Athens.

40. Fédération Internationale des Géomètres, *Apartment Property and Cadastre*, 7–8; Comentarios y Notas, Legislación, "En Torno A La Nueva Ley de la Propiedad Horizontal," *Revista Juridica de la Universidad de Puerto Rico* 28, no. 3 (Mar.–Apr. 1959): 301–12.

41. Fédération Internationale des Géomètres, *Apartment Property and Cadastre*, 10; Robert G. Natelson, "Comments on the Historiography of Condominium: The Myth of Roman Origin," *Oklahoma City University Law Review* 12, no. 1 (1987): 29–30; Frank Worsdall, *The Tenement: A Way of Life. A Social, Historical, and Architectural Study of Housing in Glasgow* (Edinburgh: Chambers, 1979), 14–15.

42. Rachelle Alterman, "The Maintenance of Residential Towers in Condominium Tenure: A Comparative Analysis of Two Extremes—Israel and Florida," and Ngai Ming Yip, "Management Rights in Multi-owned Properties in Hong Kong," in *Multi-owned Housing: Law, Power and Practice*, ed. Sarah Blandy, Ann Dupuis, and Jennifer Dixon (Farnham, Surrey, U.K.: Ashgate, 2010).

43. Uriel Manheim, *Puerto Rico Builds: Recent and Future Housing Trends* (San Juan: Housing Investment Company, and New York: Housing Securities Inc., 1963); José A. Fernández, *Architecture in Puerto Rico* (New York: Architectural Book Publishing, 1965); Henry Wells, *The Modernization of Puerto Rico: A Political Study of Changing Values and Institutions* (Cambridge: Harvard

University Press, 1969); George Edward Stetson, "San Juan, Puerto Rico: A Case Study of the Evolution and Functional Role of a Primate City," diss., University of North Carolina, 1976 (Ann Arbor: UMI, 1977); José Emilio Bonilla Rivera, "Casa Agrupada," thesis, Universidad de Puerto Rico, 1979; Enrique Vivoni Farage, *San Juan Siempre Nuevo: Arquitectura y Modernización en el Siglo XX* (San Juan: Universidad de Puerto Rico, AACUPR, 2000); Enrique Vivoni Farage, personal interview, 8 Nov. 2004.

44. Jose M. Urfet, "Condominios Podrían Resolver la Escasez de Viviendas," *EM* 6 July 1957: 13; "Los Condominios en Puerto Rico," *EM* 21 June 1958: 14; Rafael Picó, "Dan Un Nuevo Uso a Vieja Ley Romana," *EM* 12 Sept. 1959: 21; Miguel Salas Herrero, "Explica Cómo Introdujo Idea del Condominio Aquí," *EM* 12 Sept. 1959: 21; "Señalan Obstáculos Halló Primer Proyecto en Isla," *EM* 18 Nov. 1959: 4; and Malén Rojas Daporta, "Enmiendas Reglamento JP Facilitan su Construcción," *EM* 19 Nov. 1959: 5.

45. "Ancient Towns in Europe Have Building Boom," *WP* 23 Jan. 1938: R7; Herbert U. Nelson, "Parisian Likes Skyscrapers for Housing," *WP* 20 Aug. 1939: R2; "Cooperatives Popular in France; Each Tenant Has Own Mortgage," *NYT* 20 Dec. 1959: R1.

46. Carl D. Schlitt, "History of Condominiums," *Appraisal Journal* 30, no. 4 (Oct. 1962): 453–57 (quotations 455). See also Robert W. Murray, Jr., "con'do•min'i•um," *HH* Dec. 1961: 148D.

47. Stockton, Whatley, Davin, *The Condominium Act and What It Means to Investors, Developers, and Purchasers of Florida Real Estate* (Jacksonville: Stockton, Whatley, Davin, 1964), VF, 11.

48. Miguel Salas Herrero, "Picó Asiste a Reunión Sobre Vivienda en EU," *EM* 20 Nov. 1959: 13; Luis M. Escribano, "Gestionan Hacer Más Condominios en Isla," *EM* 15 Jan. 1960: 5; "Tratan Conseguir Seguros FHA Para Condominios PR," *EM* 26 Mar. 1960: 1; Sam Brady, "Old Roman Law Eyed in Housing," *NYT* 3 Apr. 1960: R1; "Fernós Presenta Hoy Bill Sobre Los Condominios," *EM* 20 Apr. 1960: 1; Sam Brady, "Medida Permitirá la FHA Preste para Condominios," *EM* 18 June 1960: 20; "Bill de Fernós Autorizaría Hipotecas Sobre Condominios," *EM* 5 Jan. 1961: 18.

49. Hubert, Pirsson & Company, *The Central Park Apartments*, prospectus (ca. 1881), Classics Collection, Avery Architectural and Fine Arts Library, Columbia University, 19–20.

50. Matthew D. Lassiter, *The Silent Majority: Suburban Politics in the Sunbelt South* (Princeton: Princeton University Press, 2006), 11–12; Redford, *Billion-dollar Sandbar*, 207–13.

51. "Modern Living," *Time* 17 Apr. 1964: 76.

52. William S. Everett, "Condominium and Co-operative Apartments—the New Frontier in Housing," *Journal of Property Management* 27, no. 1 (Fall 1961); Carl D. Schlitt, "History of Condominiums," and William J. Lippman, "Legal Problems of Condominiums," *Appraisal Journal* 30, no. 4 (Oct. 1962); Jay Romano, "Court Backs Condos on Sale Restrictions," *NYT* 19 June 2005: J15.

53. "Suit to Bar Apartment to Negroes Dismissed," *LAT* 23 June 1965: A3; "Racial Bias Charges Filed," *LAT* 23

June 1967: 26; Jack Jones, "Inner-city Integration Hope Survives Setbacks," *LAT* 15 July 1968: A1; and John Pastier, "Stuyvesant Town Replicas Repeat Mistakes of Past," *LAT* 1 Nov. 1970: J2. "Co-op Board Hell," *New York* 28, no. 44 (6 Nov. 1995): 26.

54. J. P. Taravella of Fort Lauderdale's Coral Ridge Properties quoted in "What's Happening in Florida Real Estate?" *FT* June 1964: 22.

55. Fernós and Whatley quoted in U.S., Congress, Senate, Committee on Banking and Currency, 86th Congress, 2d Session, *Housing Legislation of 1960: Hearings on Various Bills to Amend the Federal Housing Laws*, 9–12, 16–20, 23–25, and 27 May 1960 (Washington, D.C.: GPO, 1960), 585 (Fernós), 592 (Whatley). Picó quoted in U.S., Congress, House of Representatives, Committee on Banking and Currency, Subcommittee on Housing, 86th Congress, 2d Session, *Housing General Housing Legislation: Hearings*, 16–20, 23–25, 27 May 1960 (Washington, D.C.: GPO, 1960), 257.

56. "Dramatic Changes in Florida Housing," *FT* Apr. 1970: 67.

57. Quoted in "Condominium Concept Takes Hold," *FB* May 1965: 10.

58. Institute of Real Estate Management of the National Association of Real Estate Boards, "Forward . . . ," *Cooperative Apartments: The Organization and Profitable Operation, All Types Including Condominiums Conventional FHA Insured* (Chicago: NAREB, 1961), 3.

59. Clurman and Hebard, *Condominiums and Cooperatives*, 43; Juliána Goldbert, ed., *Managing a Successful Community Association* (Washington, D.C.: Urban Land Institute and Community Associations Institute, 1974), 77–78; *Transcript of the Text Prepared for Delivery at the Symposium on the Practical Problems of Condominium, Sponsored by the Committee on Real Property Law, the Association of the Bar of the City of New York* (New York: Home Title Division, Chicago Title Insurance Company, 1964).

60. Testimony of David Krooth in U.S., National Commission on Urban Problems, *Hearings*, vol. 5, Oct. 1967, Detroit, St. Louis, East St. Louis, Washington, D.C. (Washington, D.C.: GPO, 1968), 63.

61. Tom Cameron, "Nailing It Down," *LAT* 10 Dec. 1961: I1.

62. Stanley W. Penn, "Novelty in Realty," *Wall Street Journal* 8 Mar. 1962: 1.

63. "2 Co-op Builders Hit Condominiums," *NYT* 29 Mar. 1964: R1.

64. Penn, "Novelty in Realty."

65. U.S., Senate, Committee on Banking, Housing and Urban Affairs, Subcommittee on Housing and Urban Affairs, 93rd Congress, 2d Session, *Condominiums: Hearings on S. 3658 and S. 4047*, 9–10 Oct. 1974 (Washington, D.C.: GPO, 1974).

66. "Reynolds Backs Urban Projects," *NYT* 2 Apr. 1961: R1; "Mitchell Offers Eased Co-op Law," *NYT* 29 Jan. 1962; Natalie Jaffe, "State May Widen Home Ownership," *NYT* 1 Nov. 1963: 33; "2 Co-op Builders Hit Condominiums," *NYT*.

67. On Cole, see Everett, "Condominium and Co-operative Apartments," 6. On Colean, see Miles L. Colean, "What Condominium May Mean to You," *House Beautiful* Oct. 1963. On Kerr, see Murray, "con'do•min'i•um," 149; Thomas W. Ennis, "Advantages Seen in Condominiums," *NYT* 15 Mar. 1964: R1. On Raymond O'Keefe, see Dennis Duggan, "F.H.A. Will Insure New Kind of Co-op," *NYT* 29 Apr.

1962: R1; Raymond T. O'Keefe, "Financial Aspects of Condominiums," *Appraisal Journal* 30, no. 4 (Oct. 1962).

68. Harold N. Vogel, "A New Break for Apartment Owners," *Architectural Forum* Sept. 1961: 132–33; Murray, "con'do•min'i•um," 148–49, 148A-D; Harold N. Vogel and Jonathan V. Pollack, "Con'do•min'i •um Enterprise: The 3rd Dimension in Apartment House Ownership" (Jackson Heights, N.Y.: Cities, U.S.A. Research, 1962); "New Condominium Is F.H.A.-insured," *NYT* 1 Dec. 1963: R1.

69. On changes in real estate generally, see Clurman and Hebard, *Condominiums and Cooperatives*, 43–46; Mason, *History of Housing in the U.S., 1930–1980*, 98–106. On corporations, see Evan McKenzie, *Privatopia: Homeowner Associations and the Rise of Residential Private Government* (New Haven: Yale University Press, 1994), 99–100.

70. On trade media coverage, see Brown L. Whatley, "Condominium in Florida: Will It Cause a Real Estate Revolution?" *FT* Sept. 1962: 20; Murray, "con'do• min'i•um"; "'California Builder' Pioneers Condominium," *CB* Apr. 1963: 7; Robert L. Siegel, "Condominium's Many Faces Reflect Its Surprising Versatility," *HH* June 1964; "Analysis-in-depth of Retirees' Needs Leads to New Concept of Apartment Living," *FB* May 1964: 20.

71. "Paradise Harbour Project Launched in Golden Isles," *MH* 5 June 1966: 9-G.

72. Kenneth Reich, "Elderly Flee N.Y. for Florida's Peace," *LAT* 26 Nov. 1971: A7.

73. Quotation in ibid.; Dorothea M. Brooks, "The Key in Retiree Housing?" *MH* 31 Jan. 1965: 1-G; Redford, *Billion-dollar Sandbar*, 255; U.S. Department of Housing and Urban Development, *Condominium/Cooperative Study* (Washington, D.C.: GPO, 1975), 1: A-11, A-13. On social conditions and physical decay in South Beach generally see M. Barron Stofik, *Saving South Beach* (Gainesville, Fla.: University Press of Florida, 2005).

74. U.S, *Condominium/Cooperative Study*, 1: table A-6.

75. Reich, "Elderly Flee N.Y. for Florida's Peace," A7; Redford, *Billion-dollar Sandbar*, 225–26; "For the Retired, a World All Their Own," 48.

76. "Condominiums—A New Life-style," *FT* Oct. 1970: 24. See also "The Gold Coast Booms Again," *Business Week* 12 July 1969: 144; U.S., *Condominium/Cooperative Study*, 2: A-1–8.

77. Quoted in Gaeton Fonzi, "Architect Morris Lapidus," *Miami Magazine* Sept. 1973: 26.

78. Alice T. Friedman, *American Glamour and the Evolution of Modern Architecture* (New Haven: Yale University Press, 2010), chap. 4; "Miami Beach Changes Image," *FT* Dec. 1973: 74; "Meetings and Conventions: Limping But Still Growing," *FT* Aug. 1977: 34.

79. Ted Reed, "Aventura Growing, Up and Out," *MH* 14 Nov. 1988: Business 7; "Power Developers of South Florida," *Miami Sun Post* 27 Nov. 2003: 1; George Berlin, Turnberry Associates, successor to Oxford Development, personal interviews, 5 Apr. 2005; 20 Apr. 2005.

80. "Aventura Project Opened," *MH* 11 Oct. 1970: 5-F; "Aventura Plans Golf Complex," *MH* 1 Nov. 1970: 5-L; Eli Adams, "Condominiums Seen Emerging from Slump," *MH* 17 Jan. 1971: 18-K; Eli Adams, "Aventura Project Is Taking Shape," *MH* 15 Aug. 1971: 11-G; "Aventura to Open Nov. 15," *MH* 7 Nov. 1971: 20-K; "Aventura 'Tees Off,'" *MH* 7 Nov.

1971: 21-M; Eli Adams, "The Good Life for the Golf Fan," *MH* 27 Feb. 1972: 1-G; George Volsky, "Floridians Buying Condominiums," *NYT* 22 Oct. 1972: R14; "Condominiums Capture the Florida Market," *Business Week* 4 Nov. 1972: 82; Robert M. Swedroe, successor to Lapidus, Miami Beach, personal interviews, 26 Mar. 2003; 4 Apr. 2005.

81. Quoted in Charles Darragh, "Danger in Florida Land Developments," *FT* Sept. 1959: 12.

82. Display advertisements, *MH* 15 Nov. 1970: 4L; 13 Dec. 1970: 18L.

83. George Berlin, Turnberry Associates, personal interview, 20 Apr. 2005.

84. Fonzi, "Architect Morris Lapidus," 26.

85. Display advertisements, *MH* 8 Nov. 1970: 4L; 13 Dec. 1970: 8K.

86. "Ivy League Housing for Retirement," *MH* 19 Feb. 1961: 25-G; display advertisement, *NYT* 14 Apr. 1963: R3; Mason, *History of Housing in the U.S., 1930–1980*, 110, 117–20.

87. U.S., *Condominium/Cooperative Study*, 1: IV-18.

88. U.S., *Condominium/Cooperative Study*, "Lake Tahoe Basin," 2: A-1.

89. Ibid., 2: A-2.

90. Jack Kelley, "Condominiums," *MH* 15 Dec. 1968: 1-L. On condos and leasing generally, see also "Condominiums—A New Life-style," *FT* Oct. 1970: 24.

91. Jenness Keene, "Developer Tries a New Way of Selling Vacation Condominiums: By the Month," *HH* Dec. 1972: 20; Lou Desser, "Time-sharing Ownership Widens Allure of Resort Condominiums," *LAT* 14 Jan. 1973: L1.

92. U.S, *Condominium/Cooperative Study*, 2: A-1–8.

93. Mary Ruiz, "Direct Democracy and Urban Governance: The Experience of Condominium Associations," B.A. thesis, New College, Sarasota, Fla., 1978, 39–43.

94. John D. MacDonald, *Condominium* (Philadelphia: Lippincott, 1977). See also Leonard Downie, Jr., "Condominiums: New Ripoffs," *Nation* 9 Mar. 1974; Fred Sherman, "Florida Decrees Full Disclosure and Three-year Warranty on Condominiums," *HH* July 1972: 40; U.S, *Condominium/Cooperative Study*, 1: I-12; 2: A-1–8.

95. U.S., *Condominiums: Hearings on S. 3658 and S. 4047*, 107, 227.

96. "Garden Co-op Models Open," *MH* 25 Feb. 1962: 18-F; Don Bohning, "Low Cost Cooperatives Boom in South Broward," *MH* 27 Jan. 1963: 35-G; display advertisements, *MH* 23 Feb. 1964: 7-H; 9 Jan. 1966: 11-G.

97. U.S., *Condominiums: Hearings on S. 3658 and S. 4047*, 211.

98. Ibid., 210–12.

99. George A. Volsky, "Buyers of Florida Condominiums Seek Reforms," *NYT* 13 Sept. 1970: R1; "Condomania—The Craze Intensifies," *FT* Oct. 1972: 35; Volsky, "Floridians Buying Condominiums"; "Needed: A Cure for a Sick Condo Industry," *FT* Oct. 1974: 36; "Condomania: Corruption Seeks a Cure," *FT* Oct. 1974: 41.

100. James L. Winokur, "Choice, Consent, and Citizenship in Common Interest Communities," in *Common Interest Communities: Private Governments and the Public Interest*, ed. Stephen E. Barton and Carol J. Silverman (Berkeley: Institute of Governmental Studies Press, University of California, 1994), 99.

101. Marc Weiss and John W. Watts, "Community Builders and Community Associations: The Role of Real Estate

Developers in Private Residential Government," MIT Center for Real Estate Development, working paper 22 (July 1989): 23–24; McKenzie, *Privatopia*, 110–21.

102. U.S, *Condominium/Cooperative Study*, 2: A-1-8.

103. Display advertisement, *MH* 18 Mar. 1973, punctuation removed.

104. Quoted in Volsky, "Buyers of Florida Condominiums Seek Reforms."

105. U.S. *Condominium/Cooperative Study*, 2: A-1-8; "Condominiums—A New Life-style," *FT* Oct. 1970: 24.

CHAPTER 6. CALIFORNIA TOWNHOUSES

1. Santa Clara County (Calif.) Planning Department, *Condominium: Summary Proceeding on the Briefing Presented to the Santa Clara County Planning Commission* (San Jose, Calif.: Santa Clara County Planning Department, 1962), 2–3. See also "'California Builder' Pioneers Condominium," *CB* 9, no. 4 (Apr. 1963): 7.

2. "'California Builder' Pioneers Condominium," 6.

3. Ibid., 7.

4. David Clurman and Edna L. Hebard, *Condominiums and Cooperatives* (New York: Wiley-Interscience, 1970), 4, 22. On the co-op in Puerto Rico, see, for example, Francisco Rafael Jordán Garcia, "El Cooperativismo de Vivienda en Puerto Rico," TS, 1996, special collections, Biblioteca Lázaro, Universidad de Puerto Rico, Recinto Rio Piedras.

5. Robert E. Tomasson, "David Clurman," *Condominium World* 1, no. 1 (Autumn 1974): 76.

6. Mrs. Carl Mattos, letter to Joseph Eichler, 6 Mar. 1970, Oakland and Imada Collection, Pomeroy Green, v. 30 folder, Environmental Design Archives, University of California, Berkeley.

7. "The Apartment Boom," *Architectural Forum* Apr. 1963: 82–99; Kim V. L. England, "Changing Suburbs, Changing Women: Geographic Perspectives on Suburban Women and Suburbanization," *Frontiers: A Journal of Women Studies* 14, no. 1 (1993): 24–43; U.S. Department of Commerce, Bureau of the Census, "Historical Census of Housing Tables: Living Alone," http://www.census.gov/hhes/www/housing/census/historic/livalone.html [15 Dec. 2007]; U.S. Department of Commerce, Bureau of the Census, "Living Arrangements of Children Under 18 Years Old: 1960 to Present," 7 Jan. 1999, http://www.census.gov/population/socdemo/ms-la/tabch-1.txt [15 Dec. 2007].

8. See, for example, Evan McKenzie, *Privatopia: Homeowner Associations and the Rise of Residential Private Government* (New Haven: Yale University Press, 1994).

9. Suzanne Keller, "Creating Community: The Role of Land, Space, and Place," Land Policy Roundtable Case Studies, Series Number 306, Lincoln Institute of Land Policy, 5.

10. On efforts to limit density, see, for example, Jeremiah B. C. Axelrod, "'Keep the "L" out of Los Angeles': Race, Discourse, and Urban Modernity in 1920s Southern California," *Journal of Urban History* 34, no. 1 (Nov. 2007). On urban form generally, see Scott L. Bottles, *Los Angeles and the Automobile: The Making of the Modern City* (Berkeley: University of California Press, 1987); Todd Douglas Gish, "Building Los Angeles: Urban Housing in the Suburban Metropolis, 1900–1936," diss., University of Southern California, 2007 (Ann Arbor, Mich.: UMI,

2007); Richard Longstreth, *City Center to Regional Mall: Architecture, the Automobile, and Retailing in Los Angeles* (Cambridge: MIT Press, 1997); Robert Fogelson, *The Fragmented Metropolis: Los Angeles, 1850–1930* (Cambridge: Harvard University Press, 1967).

11. Greg Hise, *Magnetic Los Angeles: Planning the Twentieth-century Metropolis* (Baltimore: Johns Hopkins University Press, 1997); Becky M. Nicolaides, *My Blue Heaven: Life and Politics in the Working-class Suburbs of Los Angeles, 1920–1965* (Chicago: University of Chicago Press, 2002); D. J. Waldie, *Holy Land: A Suburban Memoir* (New York: W. W. Norton, 1996); Marc A. Weiss, *The Rise of the Community Builders: The American Real Estate Industry and Urban Land Planning* (New York: Columbia University Press, 1987).

12. U.S., Department of Commerce, Bureau of the Census and Department of Housing and Development, *Annual Housing Survey: 1974, Los Angeles–Long Beach, Calif.* (Washington, D.C.: GPO, 1976); *Annual Housing Survey: 1974, Anaheim–Santa Ana–Garden Grove, Calif.* (Washington, D.C.: GPO, 1976); *Annual Housing Survey: 1975, San Diego, Calif.* (Washington, D.C.: GPO, 1977); *Annual Housing Survey: 1975, San Bernardino–Riverside–Ontario, Calif.* (Washington, D.C.: GPO, 1977); Robert Bruegmann, *Sprawl: A Compact History* (Chicago: University of Chicago Press, 2005), 62–63, fig. 9.

13. Reyner Banham, *Los Angeles: The Architecture of Four Ecologies* (1971; repr., Berkeley: University of California Press, 2001), 167.

14. Tom Cameron, "Multiple-unit Building Leads in Dwelling Race," *LAT*, 29 July 1962: L1. On Lakewood, see Waldie, *Holy Land*; Allison Leslie Baker, "The Lakewood Story: Defending the Recreational Good Life in Postwar Southern California Suburbia, 1950–1999," diss., University of Pennsylvania, 1999 (Ann Arbor, Mich.: UMI, 1999).

15. Jane Dixon, "'Own Your Own' Best Reply to Rent Hogs," *LAT* 10 Sept. 1920: II2.

16. On the history of apartments in L.A. generally, see Gish, "Building Los Angeles"; Stefanos Polyzoides, Roger Sherwood, and James Tice, *Courtyard Housing in Los Angeles* (Berkeley: University of California Press, 1982).

17. Display advertisements, *LAT* 14 Mar. 1920: V3; 31 Oct. 1920: V6; 7 Nov. 1920: V7; and 21 Nov. 1920: V8; "Warrant for Promoter Bars Strange Tangle," *LAT* 18 Feb. 1921: II1; "To Finish Promoter's Apartment," *LAT* 23 Feb. 1921: II1 and "Improvement for Southwest Section," *LAT* 1 Oct. 1922: V4; Steve Harvey, "Around the Southland," *LAT* 19 Feb. 1980: C1.

18. "Hotel to Cost Three Millions," *LAT* 25 Mar. 1921: II1; "Propose to Build Great Apartment House Here," *LAT* 3 Apr. 1921: V1; "To Open Sale of Barcelona Apartments," *LAT* 10 Apr. 1921: V2; "To Start Sale of Apartments in Barcelona," *LAT* 17 Apr. 1921: V5; "Model Apartment Is Being Built on Barcelona Site," *LAT* 1 May 1921: V7; and display advertisements, *LAT* 17 Apr. 1921: V4; 1 May 1921: V4; 4 May 1921: I3.

19. On Avenel, see Anthony Denzer, *Gregory Ain: The Modern Home as Social Commentary* (New York: Rizzoli, 2008), 128–38.

20. On Pasadena, see Ann Scheid Lund, *Historic Pasadena: An Illustrated History* (San Antonio: Historical Pub. Network,

1999); Manuel Pineda and E. Caswell, *Pasadena Area History* (Pasadena: J. W. Anderson, 1972); Joyce Y. Pinney, *A Pasadena Chronology, 1769–1977* (Pasadena: Pasadena Public Library, 1978); and Dorothy Townsend, "Pasadena's Crown City Image Tarnished," *LAT* 27 Apr. 1969: B1.

21. Banham, *Los Angeles*, 178.

22. On clientele, see Gish, "Building Los Angeles"; Polyzoides, Sherwood, and Tice, *Courtyard Housing in Los Angeles*.

23. "Three New Cooperatives Planned," *FB* July 1959: 5; Environmental Planning Associates (prepared for City of Pasadena, Department of Planning and Development), *Ambassador West Project: Final Environmental Impact Report*, 2006.

24. "Carpenters' Hammers Ringing Knell for Once-Famed 'Millionaire Row,'" *LAT* 11 July 1949: A3.

25. Joan Burnham, "Pasadena Folk Switch Abodes," *LAT* 21 Oct. 1954: B3.

26. Villa San Pasqual, prospectus, private collection of Amanda Elioff, resident; Candice Hemming, resident, e-mail to the author, 25 Sept. 2007 and 19 Oct. 2007.

27. Villa San Pasqual, sales prospectus; display advertisements, *LAT* 12 Feb. 1955: 8; 29 Apr. 1959: 25.

28. Display advertisements, *LAT* 27 Jan. 1954: 6; 11 Feb. 1954: 24; 12 Feb. 1955: 8; 29 Apr. 1959: 25; Samuel Grafton, "Florida or California: Which?" *McCall's* May 1959: 74.

29. "$10,000,000 Apartments Set for Wilshire," *LAT* 29 Aug. 1956: B3; "$10,000,000 Beverly Hills Project Set," *LAT* 2 Sept. 1956: B8; Charles C. Cohan, "Huge Investment Set for Program," *LAT* 26 May 1957: F1; Barbara Lenox, "Apartment Living," *LAT* 7 June 1959: J12; "Co-operative Apartments Reflect New Living Trend," *LAT* 27 Dec. 1959: G3; and display advertisements, *LAT* 27 Oct. 1957: D4; 31 July 1958: B2; 6 Jan. 1959: A3; 18 Jan. 1959: D10.

30. On Braemar Towers, see Jean Stewart, "At the Home Show," *LAT* 12 June 1955: I15; classified advertisement, *LAT* 22 Jan. 1956: I1; display advertisement, *LAT* 22 Jan. 1956: C8; "Co-operative Apartment Set to Rise in Hollywood," *LAT* 25 Nov. 1956: G17.

31. On the failure of Braemar Towers and the emergence of Ardmore, see John Senning, "Close-up: Profits in Nonprofit Co-ops," *HH* June 1961: 51–54; Robert Charles Lesser, Ardmore partner, personal interview, 26 Apr. 2005.

32. John Chase and John Beach, "The Stucco Box" (1983), John Chase, *Glitter Stucco and Dumpster Diving: Reflections on Building Production in the Vernacular City* (New York: Verso, 2000); Banham, *Los Angeles*, 157–59.

33. Display advertisement, *LAT*, 27 Oct. 1957: F13; Senning, "Close-up."

34. "Co-op Apartment Boom Gains Momentum Here," *LAT* 11 Sept. 1960: I1; "$4 Million in Apartments Being Built at Four Sites," *LAT* 20 Nov. 1960: 117; "Co-op Apartments Popular," *LAT* 27 Aug. 1961: J2; "Valley Co-op Completed," *LAT* 31 Dec. 1961: C4; Bob Boich, "He Sensed a Market for Co-op Apartments," *LAT* 2 Sept. 1962: I1; Senning, "Close-up."

35. On war- and public-housing projects, see Don Parson, *Making a Better World: Public Housing, the Red Scare, and the Direction of Modern Los Angeles* (Minneapolis, 2005); David Gebhard, *Schindler (*1971; repr. San Francisco, 1997); Thomas S. Hines, *Richard Neutra and the Search for Modern Architecture* (New York: Rizzoli, 2005).

36. Robert Charles Lesser, personal interview; Senning, "Close-up."

37. Senning, "Close-up." Most of Ardmore's suburban sites had long been zoned for multifamily housing because they fronted major roads, yet they remained surrounded almost entirely by single-family subdivisions. On zoning, see Gish, "Building Los Angeles," chap. 6.

38. Display advertisements, *LAT* 24 Jan. 1960: WS6; 24 Jan. 1960: SF_A9; 6 Mar. 1960: WS4; 22 May 1960: M19; 29 May 1960: GB4; 5 Mar. 1961: SF2.

39. "Work Starts on Valley Co-operative Apartment," *LAT* 4 Sept. 1960: D13.

40. On use of "condominium style," see, for example, "Condominium Homes Started in Costa Mesa," *LAT* 23 June 1963: N12. On use of "California Townhouse," see "Aventura Introduces New Condominiums," *MH* 12 Sept. 1971: 6-K.

41. See, for example, Angelique Bamberg, *Chatham Village: Pittsburgh's Garden City* (Pittsburgh: University of Pittsburgh Press, 2011); Clarence S. Stein, *Toward New Towns for America*, rev. ed. (New York: Reinhold, 1957); Caroline Mesrobian Hickman and Sally Lichtenstein Berk, "Harry Wardman's Row House Development in Early Twentieth-Century Washington," in *Housing Washington: Two Centuries of Residential Development and Planning in the National Capital Area*, ed. Richard Longstreth (Chicago: Center for American Places at Columbia College Chicago, 2010); Michael H. Lang, "The Design of Yorkship Garden Village: Product of the Progressive Planning, Architecture, and Housing Reform Movements," in *Planning the Twentieth-century American City*, ed. Mary Corbin Sies and Christopher Silver (Baltimore: Johns Hopkins University Press, 1996); "The Communal Court, or 'Close,'" and "The Suburban, or Village, Apartment," *Architectural Record*, apartment house number, Mar. 1928.

42. U.S., Federal Housing Administration, *Planning Cooperative Housing Projects* (Washington, D.C.: GPO, 1952); "Row Housing: Can It Help Solve the Builders' No. 1 Problem?" *HH* July 1955: 102–17; "Families Buying 'Garden' Suites," *NYT* 11 July 1954: R1; Carl Norcross and Sanford Goodkin, *Open Space Communities in the Market Place . . . a Survey of Public Acceptance*, ULI Technical Bulletin 57 (Washington, D.C.: Urban Land Institute, 1966), 11; U.S., Federal Housing Administration, *Annual Report*, 1947 (Washington, D.C.: GPO, 1948), 66; U.S., Federal Housing Administration, *Annual Report*, 1949 (Washington, D.C.: GPO, 1950), 87; U.S., Federal Housing Administration, *Annual Report*, 1951 (Washington, D.C.: GPO, 1952), 91.

43. "Design Your Apartments to Look Like a House," *HH* Oct. 1959: 142–57; "Merchandising Has a Different Look This Year," *HH* May 1960: 137.

44. "Is This New Idea for Subdivision Layout a Good Answer to 'Big-lot' Zoning?" *HH* Sept. 1959: 116–17; "Houses in Clusters Suggested in Plan for Whitney Estate," *NYT* 23 Mar. 1960: 39; "This Cluster Plan Puts Only 283 Houses on 530 Acres," *HH* May 1960: 279; "Cluster Concept for L.I. Praised," *NYT* 25 June 1960: 12; "Builder Ends Plans for Whitney Tract," *NYT* 9 Aug. 1960: 54; William H. Whyte, *Cluster Development* (New York: American Conservation Association, 1964).

45. "Town house" appears to describe row houses at Southwest in Washington in Mary Mix Foley, "What Is Urban Redevelopment," *Architectural Forum* 97, no. 2 (Aug. 1952): 124–31. On use of the term, see also Wolf Von Eckardt, "Cityscape," "The Row Houses Revival Is Going to Town—Not to Mention Country," *WP* 24 July 1966: G7; Joseph B. Mason, *History of Housing in the U.S., 1930–1980* (Houston: Gulf, 1982), 78.

46. Display advertisements, *LAT* 4 Sept. 1960: WS10; 2 Oct. 1960: WS13.

47. On Spahn, see John R. Spahn, "Condominium's Advantages: Specialist Explains Concept; Tells of Southern California Experience," *CB* 9, no. 4 (Apr. 1963): 29, 34, 48.

48. "New Plan in Apartment Ownership Considered," *LAT* 29 July 1962: GB1; "Condominium Under Way in Burbank," *LAT* 12 Aug. 1962: M11; "Own-Your-Own Suites Available," *LAT* 6 Jan. 1963: I10; "Condominium Turned Over to Owners Unit," LAT 17 Nov. 1963: P13; display advertisements, *LAT* 25 Nov. 1962: O12, and 2 Dec. 1962: SF12. On enforcement of age restrictions, see "Dispute on Apartment," *LAT* 10 Aug. 1965: SF9.

49. "Engineering Firm for Huge Project Named," *LAT* 24 Feb. 1963: N6; "600 Town Houses Will Open Today," *LAT* 13 Oct. 1963: O22; "Family Purchases Again, Town House This Time," *LAT* 15 Dec. 1963: O2; "Murdock Named Activities Chief," *LAT* 9 Feb. 1964: L25; "Condominium City Begun," *LAT* 2 Aug. 1964: M1.

50. Display advertisements, *LAT* 9 Sept. 1962: O18; 22 Sept. 1963: O14; 9 June 1963: OC6.

51. Display advertisement, *LAT* 3 Mar. 1963: OC10.

52. Display advertisement, *LAT* 22 Sept. 1963: O14.

53. Display advertisement, *LAT* 9 Aug. 1964: OC15.

54. Display advertisement, *LAT* 16 Aug. 1964: OC16.

55. For an L.A. examples, see Polyzoides, Sherwood, and Tice, *Courtyard Housing in Los Angeles*, 172–79.

56. John Chase, *Exterior Decoration: Hollywood's Inside-out Houses* (Los Angeles: Hennessey and Ingalls, 1982); Charles Jencks, *Daydream Houses of Los Angeles* (New York: Rizzoli, 1978).

57. "These New Town Houses Are Selling Fast in Louisville for $63 to $77 a Month," *HH* Mar. 1961: 116–23; Mason, *History of Housing in the U.S., 1930–1980*, 78–79; Whyte, *Cluster Development*, 51–53, 70.

58. Dick Turpin, "U.S. Builders Export Know-How," *LAT* 4 Oct. 1970, J1; Dick Turpin, "Closed Kitchens a Must in France," *LAT* 6 Dec. 1970, L1; "Kaufman, Broad Sells 65 Homes in French Project," *LAT*, 18 Mar. 1973: K2.

59. Tom Cameron, "Nailing It Down," *LAT* 3 Nov. 1963: O1; "Commitment Obtained for New Co-op," *LAT* 9 Aug. 1964: M31; display advertisements, *LAT* 22 Sept. 1963: SF-A6, 12 Sept. 1965: SF-B16; "Major Integrated Community Scheduled in Southeast Area," *Los Angeles Sentinel*, 18 July 1963: A10, D1; Tom Cameron, "Builder with Know-How Will Undertake Low-Cost Housing," *LAT* 19 Apr. 1964: I1; Robert Charles Lesser, e-mail to the author, 15 Oct. 2009.

60. Quoted in Dan MacMasters, "Condominiums," *LAT* 17 Apr. 1966: Home Magazine 26–31.

61. Tom Cameron, "Condominium in Newport Bay Area Good Example of Proper Land Use," *LAT* 4 Oct. 1964: H1; Norcross and Goodkin, *Open Space Communities in the*

Market Place, 1, 10, 13, 45, 64, appendix; Mason, *History of Housing in the U.S., 1930–1980*, 123; MacMasters, "Condominiums."

62. MacMasters, "Condominiums"; Mason, *History of Housing in the U.S., 1930–1980*, 60; U.S., Federal Housing Administration, *Planned-unit Development with a Homes Association*, Land Planning Bulletin No. 6 (Washington, D.C.: Federal Housing Administration, 1963).

63. Tom Cameron, "600-unit Condominium Tract Rising Near Beach," *LAT* 1 Aug. 1965: O1; Tom Cameron, "Buena Park Project Combines Two Concepts," *LAT* 19 Jun 1966: M1; Henry Sutherland, "'Leisuretown' for All Ages," *LAT* 28 May 1967: F1; Dick Turpin, "Bren Company Opens 8th Housing Complex," *LAT* 31 Jan. 1971: I1; Terrence M. Green, "Planned Unit Developments on Rise Here," *LAT* 19 Dec. 1971: F12.

64. Terence M. Green, "Builder Races Clock in Construction Stunt," *LAT* 9 May 1971: J18.

65. Thomas C. Hubka and Judith T. Kenny, "Examining the American Dream: Housing Standards and the Emergence of a National Housing Culture, 1900–1930," *Perspectives in Vernacular Architecture* 13, no. 1 (2006).

66. Green, "Builder Races Clock in Construction Stunt"; "Four on the Floor," *Newsweek* 20 Nov. 1972: 106; "McKeon Starts Third Development in Florida," *LAT* 5 Aug. 1973: E10; U.S., Department of Housing and Urban Development, *HUD Condominium / Cooperative Study* (Washington, D.C.: GPO, 1975), table III-28.

67. "Housing Comes Cheaper by the Fourplex," *Business Week* 28 Oct. 1972: 54, 59.

68. See n. 12.

69. Frances D. Gollogly, "Housing Decisions in Selecting a Residence in a Planned Townhouse Development," *Home Economics Research Journal* 2, no. 4 (June 1974); David A. Andelman, "'Condos' Get Foothold on Long Island . . . and Toehold in Midtown Manhattan," *NYT* 18 Mar. 1973: R1.

70. Ada Louise Huxtable, "'Clusters' Instead of 'Slurbs,'" *NYT* 9 Feb. 1964: Sunday Magazine 36; Norcross and Goodkin, *Open Space Communities in the Market Place*, 5.

71. Norcross and Goodkin, *Open Space Communities in the Market Place*, 6, quotation 67.

72. Herbert J. Gans, review of *Cluster Development*, by William H. Whyte, *Progressive Architecture* 45, no. 3 (1964); Norcross and Goodkin, *Open Space Communities in the Market Place*, 10–11.

73. Carol J. Silverman and Stephen E. Barton, "Private Property and Private Government: Tension Between Individualism and Community in Condominiums," Institute of Urban and Regional Development, University of California, Berkeley, working paper 451 (Dec. 1986): 10.

74. Quotation from display advertisement, *LAT* 17 Mar. 1963: I6. See also "Hunt Breakfast to Mark Opening of Townhouses," *LAT* 6 Sept. 1964: D20; "Kaufman, Broad Plan Three Area Projects," *LAT* 28 Mar. 1965: M9; and "Decision Due on Controversial Housing Plan," *LAT* 27 Mar. 1966: SF_B1.

75. Byron R. Hanke, "The Historical Perspective," Community Associations Institute, *Summary of Proceedings, First National Conference on Community Associations*, 7–10 Dec. 1975 (Washington, D.C.: CAI, 1976), 10. On Hanke, see McKenzie, *Privatopia*, 91–93.

76. Kinney, Paul T; Orange County (Calif.) Planning Department, *Planned Unit Development in Orange County* (Fullerton, Calif.: School of Business Administration and Economics, California State College at Fullerton, 1968); Carol J. Silverman and Stephen E. Barton, "Condominiums: Individualism and Community in a Mixed Property Form," Institute of Urban and Regional Development, University of California, Berkeley, working paper 434 (Nov. 1984): 6–10.

77. Marilyn R. Lowney, "The Dissolution of an HOA," in *Sharing Association Success in Condominium and Homeowners Association Communities*, Summary of Proceedings, the Fourth National Conference on Community Associations, 2–5 Oct. 1977 (Washington, D.C.: Community Associations Institute, 1978), 114. On renters, see Silverman and Barton, "Private Property and Private Government," 9.

78. On Woodland Hills, see "Residents Protest Rezoning of Land," *LAT* 31 July 1963: A8; "Property Owners Await Next Move in Fight to Halt Apartment Zoning," *LAT* 27 Mar. 1964: F8; and "County OKs Long Disputed Development," *LAT* 11 June 1964: H1. On Orange, see "Council Vetoes Townhouse Plan," *LAT* 25 Aug. 1963: Q33. On Northridge, see "$20 Million Project Awaits City Decision," *LAT* 25 Aug. 1963: Q27; "Residents Oppose Apartment Plans," *LAT* 9 Sept. 1963: F8. On West Covina, see "Homeowner Group Hails Council Reversal," *LAT* 12 Dec. 1963: J1.

79. On this process, see Mike Davis, *City of Quartz: Excavating the Future in Los Angeles* (London: Verso, 1990), chap. 3.

80. Quotation (paraphrased from interview with opponent) from "Arguments Heard on Condominium Proposal," *LAT* 30 Sept. 1964: G9. On nostalgia and the built environment, see Margaret Crawford, "The Ghosts in City Hall: Urban Planning and the Emotions," *Harvard Design Magazine* 22 (Spring–Summer 2005): 33–35.

81. W. B. Brod, "Homeowner Groups: They Govern Mini-cities," *LAT* 22 Aug. 1971: OC1.

82. Ibid.

83. On tensions, see Davis, *City of Quartz*, 179–80. On associations as governments, see McKenzie, *Privatopia*, chap. 6.

84. Quoted in John F. Lawrence, "Pools, Politics," *LAT* 1 Oct. 1971: A1.

85. Lawrence, "Pools, Politics."

86. Urban Land Institute, *Homes Association Handbook*, rev. ed. (Washington, D.C.: ULI, 1966), 4.

87. Suzanne Keller, "Twin Rivers, Study of a Planned Community," TS, School of Architecture and Urban Planning, Princeton University, 1976: 22–31; Keller, "Creating Community," 4–5.

88. Keller, "Creating Community," 1, 3, 5, 6.

89. Richard Louv, *America II* (Los Angles: Jeremy P. Tarcher, 1983), xi, 123.

90. Keller, "Creating Community," 6; Robert D. Putnam, *Bowling Alone: The Collapse and Revival of American Community* (New York: Simon and Schuster, 2000), 209–10; Dolores Hayden, *Redesigning the American Dream: The Future of Housing, Work, and Family Life*, rev. ed. (New York: W. W. Norton, 2002), 184.

91. Keller, "Creating Community," 5, 6, 11–12.

92. Gwendolyn Wright, *Building the Dream: A Social History of Housing in America* (New York: Pantheon, 1981), 261.

93. Keller, "Creating Community," 7–8.

94. Bernstein quoted in Chris Baud, "1967: A New Way of Suburban Living," *Trentonian*, http://capitalcentury.com/1967.html [19 Mar. 2011].

CHAPTER 7. BACK TO THE CITY

1. Linda Grover, *The House Keepers: A True and Funny Story About a New York Apartment House and Its People* (New York: Harper and Row, 1970), 6, 14.

2. Ibid., 6, 15, 42–43; "Apartment Plot in East Side Deal," *NYT* 28 Feb. 1958: 38.

3. Grover, *House Keepers*, 8–9.

4. Ibid., 10, 14, 16, 31.

5. "Look for Interest in Cooperatives," *NYT* 7 Feb. 1937: RE1; "Explains Status of Cooperatives," *NYT* 15 Oct. 1939: RE6; "Costly Fittings Left in 1070 Fifth Avenue by Former Tenant-Owners of Apartments," *NYT* 17 Dec. 1939: RE1; "Tenants Reviving Old Cooperatives," *NYT* 16 Dec. 1944: 17; Edward F. Rogers, "Co-ops in New York City," in *Cooperative Apartments: Their Organization and Profitable Operation*, Institute of Real Estate Management, 2d ed. (Chicago: National Association of Realtors, 1961).

6. On the co-op plan, see Robert H. McCormick, Jr., "Glass Towers for Co-ops," in *Cooperative Apartments: Their Organization and Profitable Operation*.

7. "Sylvan Bien, 66, Noted Architect," *NYT* 13 May 1959: 37; Lee E. Cooper, "New Houses on a Cooperative Basis Will Provide 520 East Side Suites," *NYT* 8 May 1947: 44.

8. "Large Suites Cut Up into Smaller Suites," *NYT* 8 Oct. 1939: RE1; "Owners, Expecting Decontrol, to Convert Luxury Apartments into Smaller Suites," *NYT* 10 Apr. 1949: R1; "Tenants Acquire Fifth Ave. Suites," *NYT* 26 Aug. 1948: 35; "Builders Get Loan on Fifth Ave. House," *NYT* 22 Sept. 1948: 53.

9. "Work Begun on 162-family House at Fifth Avenue and 69th Street," *NYT* 20 Apr. 1947: R1; "All Suites Sold in 5th Ave. 'Co-op,'" *NYT* 7 May 1950: R1.

10. "Stability Is Noted in Co-op Purchasing," *NYT* 27 Feb. 1955: R8; "Tax Ruling Aids Buying of Homes," *NYT* 27 Feb. 1955: R5.

11. Louis Winnick, *Rental Housing: Opportunities for Private Investment* (New York: McGraw-Hill, 1958), 237–41; Nelson N. Foote et al., *Housing Choices and Housing Constraints* (New York: McGraw-Hill, 1960), 16, 201–3, 391–92. On suburbia, see D. J. Waldie, *Holy Land: A Suburban Memoir* (New York: W. W. Norton, 1996), 112; Diane Harris, "Introduction: A Second Suburb," in *Second Suburb: Levittown, Pennsylvania*, ed. Diane Harris (Pittsburgh: University of Pittsburgh Press, 2010).

12. "East Side House Will Be a 'Co-op,'" *NYT* 12 Jan. 1947: R1; display advertisements, *NYT* 5 Nov. 1947: 48; 24 Oct. 1948: R2; McCormick, "Glass Towers for Co-ops."

13. Thomas W. Ennis, "Co-op Prices High, But So Is Demand," *NYT* 30 Nov. 1958: R1; "Luxury Tenants Warm to Co-ops," *NYT* 19 Apr. 1959: R1; "More Co-ops Due on the West Side," *NYT* 9 Apr. 1961: R1; Thomas W. Ennis, "Conversions to Co-ops Growing Here," *NYT* 28 July 1968: R1.

14. Joel Schwartz, "Tenant Power in the Liberal City, 1943–1971," in *The Tenant Movement in New York City*,

1904–1984, ed. Ronald Lawson (New Brunswick: Rutgers University Press, 1986); Alan S. Oser, "Shift to Co-ops Grows in City," *NYT* 23 Nov. 1969: R1.

15. On landlords, see Douglas L. Elliman, "State the Case for the Landlord," *NYT* 20 July 1947: R1. On Washington, see James M. Goode, *Best Addresses: A Century of Washington's Distinguished Apartment Houses*, 2d ed. (Washington, D.C.: Smithsonian, 2002), 305–6; Thomas W. Ennis, "Experts Outline 'Co-op' Methods," *NYT* 13 May 1956: R1.

16. "Sales Show Gain in 'Co-op' Demand," *NYT* 3 Apr. 1955: R4; David Clurman, "'Point of View' Law on Converting to Co-ops Faulty," *NYT* 24 May 1970: R1; U.S., Department of Housing and Urban Development, *The Conversion of Rental Housing to Condominiums and Cooperatives: National Study of Scope, Causes and Impacts* (Washington, D.C.: GPO, 1980), III-5.

17. Robert C. Doty, "Population Upset in Housing Seen, with Manhattan Middle Class Out," *NYT* 2 Oct. 1950: 1; "Decontrol Urged of Luxury Housing," *NYT* 15 Mar. 1953: R1; Arthur T. Kaplan, letter to the editor, "To Decontrol Higher Rents," *NYT* 27 May 1955: 22; John A. Bradley, "Change Is Cited on Park Avenue," *NYT* 16 Oct. 1955: R1.

18. Leo Egan, "Biennial Rent-control Tussle On," *NYT* 3 Mar. 1957: E9; Thomas W. Ennis, "Some Rents Here May Be Pushed Up," *NYT* 14 Apr. 1957: R1; Thomas W. Ennis, "Rent Law Poses 'Luxury' Puzzle," *NYT* 21 Apr. 1957: R1; "Rent Curb to End on Luxury Homes," *NYT* 15 June 1957: 19; Charles Grutzner, "Rent Chief Frees 600 Luxury Units," *NYT* 17 Sept. 1957: 37; "State Co-op Rules Upheld by Court," *NYT* 22 Feb. 1958: 27; "Co-op Established Before First Sale," *NYT* 22 Apr. 1958: 57; John P. Callahan, "Switch to Co-ops Fought by Some," *NYT* 15 June 1958: R1; Alan S. Oser, "Owners Press Drive to Convert Rental Buildings into Co-ops," *NYT* 22 Nov. 1970: R1.

19. Martha Biondi, *To Stand and Fight: The Struggle for Civil Rights in Postwar New York City* (Cambridge: Harvard University Press, 2003), 112–13, 223–27.

20. Charles Abrams, *Forbidden Neighbors: A Study of Prejudice in Housing* (New York: Harper, 1955), 318.

21. Charles Abrams, *The Future of Housing* (New York: Harper, 1946), 182–83.

22. Francis Steegmuller, "A Few Little Words," *Common Ground* (Autumn 1948): 27–30. Emphasis original.

23. "Bias in Private Housing," editorial, *NYT* 15 June 1957: 16.

24. "City May Ban Bias in Private Rental," *NYT* 21 May 1957: 1; Paul Crowell, "Rental Bias Fought at Council Hearing," *NYT* 8 June 1957: 1; "Real Estate Men Combat Bias Bill," *NYT* 15 June 1957: 19; "Realtors Scored on Anti-bias Law," *NYT* 17 June 1957: 25.

25. Display advertisement, *NYT* 14 June 1957: 14. Emphasis original.

26. On Butterfield House, see display advertisements, *NYT* 13 June 1962: 35; 4 July 1962: 14; William Grimes, "James Rossant, Architect and Planner, Dies at 81," *NYT* 19 Dec. 2009: A21.

27. Robbins, "Rebuilding of Co-op Provides a Lesson in Cooperation"; Grover, *House Keepers*, 105–6.

28. U.S., National Commission on Urban Problems, *Hearings*, vol. 5, Oct. 1967, Detroit, St. Louis, East St. Louis, Washington, D.C. (Washington, D.C.: GPO, 1968), 73.

29. Thomas W. Ennis, "Co-ops Keep Right to Choose Buyers," *NYT* 2 Aug. 1959: R1;

30. John Wicklein, "City Charges Bias to Park Ave. Co-op," *NYT* 4 Oct. 1962: 1.

31. Wicklein, "City Charges Bias to Park Ave. Co-op"; see also Nicholas Pileggi, "Restricted Co-ops: The Gentlemen's Agreement," *New York* 17 Mar. 1969: 24–27.

32. "Co-op in Bronxville Agrees to Respect Discrimination Ban," *NYT* 14 Nov. 1962: 41. See also Thomas W. Ennis, "Major Gain Made in Drives Against Bias," *NYT* 18 Nov. 1962: R1.

33. See, for example, Thomas W. Ennis, "East Side Co-ops Still Show Bias," *NYT* 19 June 1961: 29; Murray Illson, "Park Ave. Co-ops Said to Bar Jews," *NYT* 5 Apr. 1963: 17; "Jewish Group Accuses Co-ops on East Side of Discrimination," *NYT* 22 May 1969: 30; David K. Shipler, "Co-op on East Side Fined in Bias Case," *NYT* 24 Sept. 1969: 1; "Co-op Study Finds Number of Biases," *NYT* 10 Apr. 1970: 46.

34. "Legal Characterization of the Individual's Interest in a Cooperative Apartment: Realty or Personality?" *Columbia Law Review* 73, no. 2 (Feb. 1973): 259–62 (quotation 259–60).

35. John B. Willmann, "Happening in Real Estate," *WP* 22 Sept. 1979: E1; Bob Tedeschi, "Mortgages: Reaching Out to Condo Buyers," *NYT* 20 Nov. 2009: RE6.

36. "Peter Lawford Barred from East Side Co-op," *NYT* 7 Apr. 1964: 41. On the social atmosphere of East Side co-ops, see Thomas W. Ennis, "The Co-op Way of Life," *NYT* 19 May 1963: R1; "'Acceptable,'" *LAT* 8 July 1964: 28; "Co-op Board Hell," *New York* 28, no. 44 (6 Nov. 1995): 26.

37. Quoted in Jane Edmunds, "Breaking the Gentleman's Agreement," *New York* 13 Apr. 1970: 43. See also Ernest Dickinson, "Clouds Speckle the Condominium Horizon," *NYT* 23 Sept. 1973: R1.

38. Rita Berger, "Getting by the Board: The Mysteries of Co-op Discrimination," *New York* 3, no. 15 (13 Apr. 1970): 36–43. See also Edmunds, "Breaking the Gentleman's Agreement."

39. Foote, *Housing Choices and Housing Constraints*, 395; "House Trade-ins for Co-ops Eased," *NYT* 15 Nov. 1959: R12.

40. Thomas W. Ennis, "Waterfront Site for Apartments," *NYT* 5 Feb. 1956: R1; Faith Corrigan, "New Apartments Ignore Traditional Urban Look," *NYT* 31 Oct. 1956: 38; "Apartments with Levitt Touch Rise on Waterfront in Queens," *NYT* 24 Feb. 1957: R1; Richard Longstreth, "The Levitts Mass-produced Houses, and Community Planning in the Mid-twentieth Century," in Harris, *Second Suburb*, 170–71.

41. "Largest Conventional Loan Made on N. J. Co-op House," *NYT* 24 Sept. 1963: 80. On the surge in high-rise development in just one suburban center, the New Jersey Palisades, see "Hackensack Becoming the New 'Ft. Lee,'" *NYT* 4 Feb. 1973: NJ66.

42. U.S., Department of Housing and Urban Development, *Condominium/Cooperative Study* (Washington, D.C.: GPO, 1975), 2: C-2–4; Oser, "Shift to Co-ops Grows in City"; U.S., *Conversion of Rental Housing to Condominiums and Cooperatives*, IV-6; Shlaes and Company, *Condominium Conversions in Chicago: Facts and Issues* (Chicago: Shlaes and Company, 1979).

43. Murray Illson, "Tenants Object to TV Monitors as Substitutes for Elevator Men," *NYT* 10 Oct. 1959: 23;

Lawrence O'Kane, "TV Eye to Guard Elevators Here," *NYT* 21 Nov. 1959: 25. See also Bernard Taper, "A Reporter at Large: The Landlord, the Tenant, and Mrs. Dotts," *New Yorker* 2 June 1956: 94–129.

44. "More Co-ops Due on the West Side," *NYT* 9 Apr. 1961: R1; "More Co-ops Seen on West End Ave.," *NYT* 30 June 1962: 32; "West Side Suites Becoming Co-ops," *NYT* 18 Mar. 1962: R1.

45. Jane Jacobs, *The Death and Life of Great American Cities* (New York: Vintage, 1961), 195, 382.

46. Grover, *House Keepers*, 17, 23–25; Theodore Jones, "Doomed Building Wins a Reprieve," *NYT* 13 July 1963: 19; William Robbins, "Rebuilding of Co-op Provides a Lesson in Cooperation," *NYT* 22 May 1966: R1.

47. Grover, *House Keepers*, 69; Robbins, "Rebuilding of Co-op Provides a Lesson in Cooperation."

48. Grover, *House Keepers*, 68–69, 176–77.

49. For an analysis of these longstanding debates and an introduction to the ideas of critical participants, including Neil Smith, David Ley, Damaris Rose, Chris Hamnett, Dennis Gale, Saskia Sassen, and Richard Florida, see Loretta Lees, Tom Slater, and Elvin Wyly, *Gentrification* (New York: Routledge, 2008), chaps. 2 and 3.

50. On the concept of "taste publics" and "taste cultures," see Herbert Gans, *Popular Culture and High Culture: An Analysis and Evaluation of Taste*, rev. ed. (New York: Basic Books, 1999), 6–8, 15, 41, 99, 121, 195. On Gans and housing preferences in the context of gentrification debate, see Smith, "Toward a Theory of Gentrification," 540. On bourgeois bohemia, see Suleiman Osman, *The Invention of Brownstone Brooklyn: Gentrification and the Search for Authenticity in Postwar New York* (Oxford: Oxford University Press, 2011), 12; Neil Smith, *The New Urban Frontier: Gentrification and the Revanchist City* (London: Routledge, 1996), 25; Ada Louise Huxtable, "In New York, a Losing Battle," *NYT* 30 Dec. 1969: 18. On the 1920s, see Andrew Scott Dolkart, *The Row House Reborn: Architecture and Neighborhoods in New York City, 1908–1929*, chap. 4. On the 1950s in New York, see Osman, *Invention of Brownstone Brooklyn*, 8, chap. 3.

51. "Middle Class Dominating Co-op Picture," *NYT* 9 Feb. 1969: R1; U.S., *Conversion of Rental Housing to Condominiums and Cooperatives*, VI-5, VI-19.

52. U.S., *Conversion of Rental Housing to Condominiums and Cooperatives*, VIII-31, VIII-35–36; Lance Freeman, "Displacement of Succession? Residential Mobility in Gentrifying Neighborhoods," *Urban Affairs Review* 40, no. 4 (Mar. 2005).

53. Roger Starr, "An End to Rental Housing?" *National Affairs* 57 (Fall 1979): 31. See also Arthur Unger, letter to the editor, "The Joy of Co-oping," *NYT* 21 Oct. 1973: R10; Shlaes and Company, *Condominium Conversions in Chicago*, 37.

54. Quoted in "Why Rush to Condominiums Is Picking Up Speed," *U.S. News and World Report* 6 Aug. 1973: 48–49.

55. Joel Mandelbaum, "A 'Money Machine' Attracts Investors," *NYT* 3 June 1973: R1.

56. David K. Shipler, "Thousands Phone on Lack of Heat," *NYT* 3 Jan. 1970: 1; Alan S. Oser, "Housing Supply in City Eroding Amid Construction Standstill," *NYT* 8 Feb. 1970: R1; Maurice A. Reichman, "Point of View: Controls on Rent

Not Basic Cause of Abandonment," *NYT* 1 Mar. 1970: R1; "Rise in Abandonment in 1970s Feared by State Aide," *NYT* 5 Mar. 1970: 34; Lindsey Helfman, "Burning Down the House: Devil's Night and the Politics of Abandoned Space in Postwar Detroit," 5th Biennial Conference, Urban History Association, Las Vegas, Oct. 20–23, 2010; U.S., *Conversion of Rental Housing to Condominiums and Cooperatives*, V-31.

57. Setha Low, "A Multi-disciplinary Framework for the Study of Private Housing Schemes: Integrating Anthropological, Psychological, and Political Levels of Theory and Analysis," *GeoJournal*, 10 Jan. 2010, http://www.springerlink.com/content/p7517530v3412171/ [6 June 2010], 11.

58. James P. Premgen, "'Flynn's Folly' Endures After 53 Years," *WP* 5 June 1982: F1.

59. Charles Grutzner, "Speed-up Is Urged for Co-op Housing," *NYT* 12 Mar. 1959: 16; Thomas W. Ennis, "Low-income Co-ops Are Planned Here," *NYT* 20 Apr. 1969: R1; Alvin L. Arnold and Carol M. Launer, *Developing a Condominium: Feasibility, Financing, Marketability* (Boston: Warren, Gorham and Lang, 1973); U.S., *Conversion of Rental Housing to Condominiums and Cooperatives*, III-3.

60. Robert E. Tomasson, "David Clurman," *Condominium World* 1, no. 1 (Autumn 1974): 74; Lawrence O'Kane, "Co-ops Groups Fight State Rules Called Needless for Investors," *NYT* 23 Dec. 1961: 42.

61. "New Co-op Rules Drawn by State," *NYT* 20 Nov. 1961: 33; "New Rules Set Up for Sale of Co-ops," *NYT* 26 Nov. 1961: R1.

62. "Co-op Established Before First Sale," *NYT*, 57; Alan S. Oser, "Shift to Co-ops Grows in City"; David Clurman, "Point of View: Law on Converting to Co-ops Faulty," *NYT* 24 May 1970: R1; William G. Connolly, "Helmsley Makes Parkchester a Testing Ground," *NYT* 24 Dec. 1972: R1.

63. Quoted in Thomas W. Ennis, "State Bars Plan to Set Up Co-ops," *NYT* 14 May 1969: 4.

64. Carter B. Horsley, "'Condos' Get Foothold on Long Island . . . and Toehold in Midtown Manhattan," *NYT* 18 Mar. 1973: R1; Glenn Fowler, "New Rules Urged on Cooperatives," *NYT* 17 Feb. 1970: 67.

65. "Concern Finances Co-op Purchases," *NYT* 20 Mar. 1960: R1; Glenn Fowler, "Conversion to Co-ops Called Strain for Many," *NYT* 8 Mar. 1970: R1; Alan S. Oser, "Stock Slump Cuts Resales of Co-ops," *NYT* 17 May 1970: R1.

66. "Rockefeller Asks Aid in Co-op Sales," *NYT* 1 Mar. 1970: 6; William E. Farrell, "Governor Signs Measure to Decontrol Empty Flats," *NYT* 3 June 1971: 3; Daniel Wise, "Co-op Tyranny: How the Boards of Directors Rule the Roost," *New York* 18, no. 16 (22 Apr. 1985): 36; display advertisement, *NYT* 6 Nov. 1972: 46.

67. Thomas W. Ennis, "Condominium Up; First in City," *NYT* 24 Jan. 1965: R1; "Suites on View at Condominium," *NYT* 21 Feb. 1965: R8; Glenn Fowler, "News of Realty: St. Tropez Sold," *NYT* 3 Aug. 1966: 55; "Condominium Completed in 'Village,'" *NYT* 31 Mar. 1968: R6.

68. Franklin Whitehouse, "Condominiums Received Coolly by Manhattan," *NYT* 1 Feb. 1970: R1.

69. Tomasson, "David Clurman," 77–78; Whitehouse, "Condominiums Received Coolly by Manhattan."

70. Setha Low, Gregory Donovan, and Jennifer Gieseking, "Shoestring Democracy: Private Governance in Co-ops

and Gated Community in New York City," International Conference, Private Urban Governance and Gated Communities, Private Urban Governance International Research Network, Paris, 5–8 June 2007.

71. Leslie Kern, *Sex and the Revitalized City: Gender, Condominium Development, and Urban Citizenship* (Vancouver: UBC, 2010), 3, 115.

72. U.S., *Conversion of Rental Housing to Condominiums and Cooperatives*, III-5; Oser, "Owners Press Drive to Convert Rental Buildings into Co-ops."

73. Thomas W. Ennis, "Hotels Convert to Plush Co-ops," *NYT* 15 July 1956: R1; Thomas W. Ennis, "Pierre Will be Sold to Tenants, But Will Remain a Luxury Hotel," *NYT* 12 Feb. 1958: 31; Thomas W. Ennis, "East Side Tenants Fight Owner's Plan to Co-op Building, Protesting Prices," *NYT* 4 May 1969: R1; David A. Andelman, "In the Excelsior, Bitterness Replaces Tenant Unity," *NYT* 2 Aug. 1970: R1; Alan S. Oser, "Helmsley Trying a Condominium Conversion," *NYT* 21 Nov. 1971: R1; William G. Connolly, "Parkchester Condominium Authorized," *NYT* 15 Dec. 1972: 49; Joseph P. Fried, "Condominiums Sought at Tudor City," *NYT* 23 Dec. 1973: 25; Terence M. Green, "Sales Start at Converted Condominium Complex," *LAT* 28 Apr. 1974: G1.

74. Robert J. Cole, "Personal Finance: Buyers of Co-op Apartments Finding Loans are Easier to Get These Days," *NYT* 13 Jan. 1972: 59; Josh Barbanel, "Still a Beacon, Parkchester Climbs Back," *NYT* 14 Mar. 2004: RE1.

75. Israel Shenker, "A Party for Co-op Building Rated a Collective Success," *NYT* 11 Feb. 1972: 39; Joan Cook, "Even on the East Side, Tenants' Cause Can Inspire Camaraderie," *NYT* 9 June 1970: 44; Andelman, "In the Excelsior, Bitterness Replaces Tenant Unity."

76. Asa Barber, "The Condominium Conspiracy," *Playboy* Nov. 1979: 141, 255.

77. Ada Louise Huxtable, "In New York, a Losing Battle," *NYT* 30 Dec. 1969: 18.

78. Kathleen Nesi, "Condominium Conversion—Balancing Tenants' Rights and Property Owners' Interests," *Wayne Law Review* 27 (1980–81): 353.

79. Quoted in U.S., Senate, Committee on Banking, Housing, and Urban Affairs, Subcommittee on Housing and Urban Affairs, 96th Congress, 1st session, *Condominium Housing Issues*, Hearing on Condominium Conversions and S. 612, 28 June 1979 (Washington, D.C.: GPO, 1979), 316.

80. Peter Dreier, "Condo Conversion Catches On, for Some, a Moving Experience," *Dollars and Sense* 55 (Mar. 1980).

81. U.S., Senate, *Condominium Housing Issues*, 314–15.

82. John D. Benjamin et al., "Clientele Effects and Condo Conversions," *Real Estate Economics* 36 (2008): 611–12.

83. U.S., *Conversion of Rental Housing to Condominiums and Cooperatives*, IX-32, V-31.

84. Barber, "Condominium Conspiracy," 172, 252, 254; "Finance: Like Owning a House," *Business Week* 29 Aug. 1964: 108, 110.

85. U.S., *Conversion of Rental Housing to Condominiums and Cooperatives*, VI-20; John A. Jones, "Condominium Living: Home Can Be Heaven or Headache," *LAT* 23 Dec. 1973: B12; Jonathan D. Ross-Harrington, "Property Forms in Tension: Preference Inefficiency, Rent-seeking, and the Problem of Notice in the Modern Condominium," *Yale Law and Policy Review* 28 (2009–10): 188, 201–8.

86. U.S. Code Title 15, Commerce and Trade, Chapter 62, Condominium and Cooperative Conversion Protection and Abuse Relief, 1 Feb. 2010.

87. Kathryn B. Richards, "The Illinois Condominium Property Act: An Analysis of Legislative Efforts to Improve Tenants' Rights in the Condominium Conversion Process," *DePaul Law Review* 57 (2007–8): 836–37, 842–45.

88. U.S., *Conversion of Rental Housing to Condominiums and Cooperatives*, XII-4, XII-5; Starr, "An End to Rental Housing?" 32–33; Richards, "Illinois Condominium Property Act," 851–55.

89. U.S., *Conversion of Rental Housing to Condominiums and Cooperatives*, XII-1, XII-6, XII-17; San Francisco Planning and Urban Research Organization, "Promoting Homeownership Through Condominium Conversion," 2004, http://www.spur.org/publications/library/report/promotinghomeownershipthroughcondominiumconversion_090704 [22 Nov. 2010].

90. U.S., *Conversion of Rental Housing to Condominiums and Cooperatives*, VI-5.

91. U.S., *Condominium Housing Issues*, 320–21, 357–58; Goode, *Best Addresses*, 432–41.

92. Quoted in U.S., *Condominium Housing Issues*, 381, 383.

93. Ibid., 321–22, 355–56,

94. Grover, *House Keepers*, 104–8, 111–12.

95. Ibid., 103, 106.

96. Ibid., 237, 243; Linda Grover, "Topics: Central Park West Side Story," *NYT* 25 July 1970: 16.

97. Grover, *House Keepers*, 243–44; Robbins, "Rebuilding of Co-op Provides a Lesson in Cooperation"; Grover, "Topics: Central Park West Side Story."

EPILOGUE

1. U.S., Department of Housing and Urban Development, *The Conversion of Rental Housing to Condominiums and Cooperatives: National Study of Scope, Causes, and Impacts* (Washington, D.C.: GPO, 1980), IV-6–IV-8.

2. U.S., Department of Housing and Urban Development, Office of Policy Development and Research, *U.S. Housing Market Conditions: Preview of Data for U.S. Housing Market Conditions 3rd Quarter 2010* (Washington, D.C.: U.S. HUD, 2010), 30; William G. Blair, "After a Lull, Construction of Co-ops Picks Up in Manhattan," *NYT* 22 June 1980: R1.

3. Christopher B. Leinberger, "The Next Slum?" *Atlantic* Mar. 2008.

4. U.S., House of Representatives, Committee on Banking, Currency, and Housing, Subcommittee on General Oversight and Renegotiation, 94th Congress, 2d Session, *Condominium Development and Sales Practices*, 18–19 Feb. and 19 and 22 May 1976 (Washington, D.C.: GPO, 1976), 166–67.

5. Carol J. Silverman and Stephen E. Barton, "Condominiums: Individualism and Community in a Mixed Property Form," working paper, Institute of Urban and Regional Development, University of California, Berkeley (1984), 2.

6. Display advertisements for Jackson Heights, *New York Times* 17 Aug. 1921: 27; Salisbury Manor, 21 Sept. 1958: R6; Bowling Greens, 5 Dec. 1965: R5.

7. Carol J. Silverman and Stephen E. Barton, working papers, Institute of Urban and Regional Development,

University of California, Berkeley: "Private Property and Private Government: Tension Between Individualism and Community in Condominiums" (1986), 10; "Common Interest Communities and the American Dream" (1987), 13–14; "Management and Governance in Common-interest Community Associations" (1987), 1; "Public Life in Private Governments: Neighborhoods with Shared Property" (1987), 14; display advertisements, *NYT* 21 Sept. 1958: R6; 5 Dec. 1965: R5.

8. Silverman and Barton, "Condominiums," 1–3.

9. James L. Winokur, "Choice, Consent, and Citizenship in Common Interest Communities," in *Common Interest Communities: Private Governments and the Public Interest*, ed. Stephen E. Barton and Carol J. Silverman (Berkeley: Institute of Governmental Studies Press, University of California, Berkeley, 1994), 109, 114; Evan McKenzie, "Emerging Regulatory Trends, Power, and Competing Interests in U.S. Common Interest Housing Developments," in *Multi-owned Housing: Law, Power, and Practice*, ed. Sarah Blandy, Ann Dupuis, and Jennifer Dixon (Farnham, Surrey, U.K.: Ashgate, 2010), 63–64, 70.

10. McKenzie, "Emerging Regulatory Trends," 53; Evan McKenzie, *Privatopia: Homeowner Associations and the Rise of Residential Private Government* (New Haven: Yale University Press, 1994), 130–32; Silverman and Barton, "Condominiums," 6–10; Lisa Prevost, "New Law Calls Condo Boards to Account," *NYT* 6 Aug. 2010: RE10.

11. Silverman and Barton, "Public Life in Private Governments," 16.

12. Leslie Kern, *Sex and the Revitalized City: Gender, Condominium Development, and Urban Citizenship* (Vancouver: UBC, 2010), 202.

13. Ibid.

14. Silverman and Barton, "Public Life in Private Governments," 16; Silverman and Barton, "Management and Governance," 11.

15. McKenzie, "Emerging Regulatory Trends," 55.

16. See, for example, Sukumar Ganapati, "Enabling Housing Cooperatives: Policy Lessons from Sweden, India, and the United States," *International Journal of Urban and Regional Research* 34, no. 2 (June 2010): 375; Gerald W. Sazama, "Lessons from the History of Affordable Housing Cooperatives in the United States: A Case Study in American Affordable Housing Policy," *American Journal of Economics and Sociology* 59, no. 4 (Oct. 2000); Jennifer Cohoon McStotts, "Dwelling Together: Using Cooperative Housing to Abate the Affordable Housing Shortage in Canada and the United States," *Georgia Journal of International and Comparative Law* 32 (2004); David S. Wilson, "First-aid for Housing the Low- and Fixed-income Elderly: The Case for Resuscitating Cooperative Housing," *Elder Law Journal* 15 (2007).

17. Lorin Berlin, "At More Mobile-home Parks, a Greater Sense of Security," *New York Times* 17 Mar. 2011: D8.

18. "Condo Craze and HOA's Becomes Arbitron Rated #1 Listened to Show in Its Timeslot," http://www.condocrazeandhoas.com/press_releases.php [13 June 2011]; Lisa Prevost, "New Push for a Condo Ombudsman," *New York Times* 3 Apr. 2011: RE10.

19. Ngai Ming Yip, "Management Rights in Multi-owned Properties in Hong Kong"; Feng Wang, "Regulations and the Imbalance of Power Relationships in Newly Developed Residential Neighbourhoods in Urban China"; Cathy Sherry, "Long-term Management Contracts and Developer Abuses in New South Wales"; Rachelle Alterman, "The Maintenance of Residential Towers in Condominium Tenure: A Comparative Analysis of Two Extremes—Israel and Florida," in Blandy et al., *Multi-owned Housing*.

20. Roy Vu, "Retaining the Home not the Homeland: The Significance of Vietnamese Ethnic Identity in Houston's Village Communities," 4th Biennial Conference, Urban History Association, Houston, 5–8 Nov. 2008. On Gulfton generally, see Susan Rogers, "Superneighborhood 27: A Brief History of Change," *Places* 17, no. 2 (2005).

21. Michael Wall, "Big, Bad Boxes," *Creative Loafing Atlanta* 29 July 2004.

22. Quoted in Joyce Cohen, "The Hunt: Location Important; Ditto Condition," *NYT* 13 Aug. 2010: RE4; Eve M. Kahn, "182 Studios, 182 Slices of New York Reality," *NYT* 9 Nov. 1989: C1.

23. Thomas W. Ennis, "Onassis Invests in 5th Ave. Property," *NYT* 8 Mar. 1970: R1; Edward Ranzal, "50-story Building to Rise by St. Patrick's Cathedral," *NYT* 1 Sept. 1971: 74; William G. Blair, "After a Lull, Construction of Co-ops Picks Up in Manhattan," *NYT* 22 June 1980: R1.

24. Michael H. Schill, Ioan Voicu, Jonathan Miller, "The Condominium v. Cooperative Puzzle: An Empirical Analysis of Housing in New York City," working paper, Furman Center for Real Estate and Urban Policy, New York University, 2006, 12–13, 30–31.

25. Ibid.

26. Jay Romano, "Court Backs Condos on Sale Restrictions," *NYT* 19 June 2005: J15. See also Christopher Bonanos, "The Enforcers: Downtown Condo Boards Discover They Have Muscle—and Start to Use It," *New York* 37, no. (6 Sept. 2004): 142; and "Q&A: Restrictions on Sales in a Condo," *NYT* 31 July 2005: RE11.

27. Philip J. Gregory, "Condominium Legislation," *CB* 9, no. 4 (Apr. 1963): 6.

28. Christopher B. Leinberger, "Here Comes the Neighborhood," *Atlantic* June 2010.

29. U.S., Department of Housing and Urban Development, Office of Policy Development and Research and Department of Commerce, Economics and Statistics Administration, U.S. Census Bureau, *American Housing Survey for the United States: 2009, Current Housing Reports* (Washington, D.C.: GPO, 2011).

Index

Page numbers in **boldface** type indicate illustrations.

Illustration Credits